With so much attention being monopolized by Jihadism, *'Tomorrow Belongs to Us'* is a timely and sobering reminder that in the last fifty years Britain's extreme right subculture, far from withering away, has continued to adapt to domestic and international events, and still retains a disturbing capacity for fomenting local ethnic hatreds, poisoning democracy, and inspiring political murders, despite its impotence as a party-political force.

Roger Griffin, author of *Fascism: An Introduction to Comparative Fascist Studies* (2018)

This edited volume brings the historian's concern with a richly temporal and contextual understanding of events and processes to the study of a range of key issues in contemporary studies of the far and populist radical right. Its cross-disciplinary approach does much more than fill in the gaps in our knowledge. It provides new insight into the shifting ideologies and mobilisational successes and failures of political movements on the far right of the political spectrum but also, and innovatively, into their subcultural, symbolic, gendered and emotional worlds.

Hilary Pilkington, Professor of Sociology, University of Manchester, UK

'TOMORROW BELONGS TO US'

This book traces the varied development of the far right in Britain from the formation of the National Front in 1967 to the present day. Experts draw on a range of disciplinary and methodological perspectives to provide a rich and detailed account of the evolution of the various strands of the contemporary far right over the course of the last fifty years. The book examines a broad range of subjects, including Holocaust denial, neo-Nazi groupuscularity, transnational activities, ideology, cultural engagement, homosexuality, gender and activist mobilisation. It also includes a detailed literature review. This book is essential reading for students of fascism, racism and contemporary British cultural and political history.

Nigel Copsey is Professor in Modern History in the School of Social Sciences, Humanities and Law, Teesside University, UK.

Matthew Worley is Professor of Modern History in the Department of History at the University of Reading, UK.

ROUTLEDGE STUDIES IN FASCISM AND THE FAR RIGHT

Series editors
Nigel Copsey, *Teesside University*, and Graham Macklin,
Oslo University, Norway

This new book series focuses upon fascist, far-right and right-wing politics primarily within a historical context but also drawing on insights from other disciplinary perspectives. Its scope also includes radical-right populism, cultural manifestations of the far right and points of convergence and exchange with the mainstream and traditional right.

Titles include:

Fascist in the Family
The Tragedy of John Beckett MP
Francis Beckett

Farming, Fascism and Ecology
A Life of Jorian Jenks
Philip M. Coupland

Searching for Lord Haw-Haw
The Political Lives of William Joyce
Colin Holmes

France and Fascism
February 1934 and the Dynamics of Political Crisis
Brian Jenkins and Chris Millington

Cultures of Post-War British Fascism
Edited by Nigel Copsey and John E. Richardson

'Tomorrow Belongs to Us'
The British Far Right since 1967
Edited by Nigel Copsey and Matthew Worley

'TOMORROW BELONGS TO US'

The British Far Right since 1967

Edited by Nigel Copsey and Matthew Worley

Routledge
Taylor & Francis Group

LONDON AND NEW YORK

First published 2018
by Routledge
2 Park Square, Milton Park, Abingdon, Oxon OX14 4RN

and by Routledge
711 Third Avenue, New York, NY 10017

Routledge is an imprint of the Taylor & Francis Group, an informa business

British Library Cataloguing-in-Publication Data
A catalogue record for this book is available from the British Library

Library of Congress Cataloging-in-Publication Data
A catalog record has been requested for this book

ISBN: 978-1-138-67516-2 (hbk)
ISBN: 978-1-138-67517-9 (pbk)
ISBN: 978-1-315-56382-4 (ebk)

Typeset in Bembo
by Out of House Publishing

CONTENTS

List of contributors   *ix*

Introduction   1
Nigel Copsey and Matthew Worley

1 'The men who rewrite History': Holocaust denial and the
   British far right from 1967   9
   Mark Hobbs

2 The National Socialist Group: a case study in the
   groupuscular right   27
   Daniel Jones and Paul Jackson

3 The National Front: the search for a 'nationalist'
   economic policy   48
   John E. Richardson

4 Exporting fascism across the Commonwealth: the case of
   the National Front of Australia   69
   Evan Smith

5 The dog that didn't bark? Assessing the development of
   'cumulative extremism' between fascists and anti-fascists
   in the 1970s   90
   Alex Carter

 6 White Youth: the far right, punk and British youth culture,
   1977–87   113
   Matthew Worley and Nigel Copsey

 7 New visual identities for British neo-fascist rock (1982–1987):
   White Noise, 'Vikings' and the cult of Skrewdriver   132
   Ana Raposo and Roger Sabin

 8 The 'obnoxious mobilised minority': homophobia and
   homohysteria in the British National Party, 1982–1999   150
   George J. Severs

 9 Closing the gender gap: women and the far right in
   contemporary Britain   169
   Hannah Bows

10 'There's a vital lesson here. Let's make sure we learn it':
   transnational mobilisation and the impact of Greece's
   Golden Dawn upon extreme right-wing activism in Britain   185
   Graham Macklin

11 Love will tear us apart: emotions, patriotism and the
   English Defence League   208
   C. M. Quinn

12 Britain's far right since 1967: a bibliographic survey   224
   Craig Fowlie

 Index   *268*

LIST OF CONTRIBUTORS

Hannah Bows is a Senior Lecturer in criminology and sociology at Teesside University. Her research interests centre on violence and gender, in particular violence against women and sexual offending. Her current projects include a national study examining homicide offences involving older people and a piece of research examining the characteristics of stranger stalking in the UK.

Alex Carter is a PhD student at Teesside University and is an associate of the Centre for Fascist, Anti-Fascist and Post-Fascist Studies. He is currently completing his thesis on cumulative extremism from a comparative-historical perspective. He has published on cumulative extremism and the escalation of movement–countermovement dynamics in Northern Ireland between 1967 and 1972 in *Behavioral Sciences of Terrorism and Political Aggression*.

Nigel Copsey is Professor of Modern History and Co-Director of Teesside University's Centre for Fascist, Anti-Fascist and Post-Fascist Studies. He recently completed a revised second edition of *Anti-Fascism in Britain* (2017). In 2015 he co-edited *Cultures of Post-War British Fascism* with John Richardson (also in the Routledge Studies in Fascism and the Far Right series) and forthcoming projects include a co-edited volume on Nordic anti-fascism (also in the Routledge Studies in Fascism and the Far Right series).

Craig Fowlie is Global Editorial Director for Social Science books at Routledge. He is the founding publisher of the Extremism & Democracy series and the Fascism and the Far Right series.

Mark Hobbs is Lecturer in the Humanities in the Interdisciplinary Institute for the Humanities at the University of East Anglia (UEA). Mark has also worked as an

Associate Tutor in the School of History at UEA and was a part-time Lecturer in History at the University of Winchester. Mark obtained his PhD from the University of Winchester in 2014 (Using Lies: Holocaust Denial and the British Far Right 1942–2001). His research interests are Holocaust and genocide studies, representations of genocide, the study of far-right politics and public memory and memorialisation.

Paul Jackson is a Senior Lecturer in History at the University of Northampton and specialises in the history of fascism and the extreme right. He is editor of Bloomsbury's book series A Modern History of Politics and Violence, and his most recent book is *Colin Jordan and Britain's Neo-Nazi Movement: Hitler's Echo* (2017).

Daniel Jones is Associate Lecturer in History, *Searchlight* Collections Officer and PhD candidate in History at the University of Northampton. His PhD is on the construction and use of identity within *Spearhead* and *Searchlight* magazines from 1964 to 1982, and is under the supervision of Dr Paul Jackson. His research interests include fascist and anti-fascist movements and thought.

Graham Macklin is Assistant Professor/Postdoctoral Fellow at the Centre for Research on Extremism (C-REX), Faculty of Social Sciences, at the University of Oslo, Norway. He has published extensively on extreme right-wing and anti-minority politics in Britain in both the inter-war and post-war periods including *Very Deeply Dyed in the Black: Sir Oswald Mosley and the Resurrection of British Fascism after 1945* (2007) and, with Nigel Copsey, *British National Party: Contemporary Perspectives* (2011). His forthcoming monograph on the history of white racial nationalism in Britain will be published by Routledge in 2018. He co-edits the Routledge Studies in Fascism and the Far Right book series.

C. M. Quinn is a peace and social justice activist, feminist, and community development worker from the north of Ireland. She has lectured in sociology and youth and community development practice for over 25 years but has always maintained her own professional practice outside academia. C. M. Quinn was the first person to conduct overt research within the EDL nationally from 2011–2013. She has conducted research on behalf of a broad range of strategic organisations and grass-roots community groups and is currently Head of Operations of a national charity working to tackle sexual violence.

Ana Raposo is a graphic designer, educator and design researcher. Her PhD, entitled '30 years of agitprop: the representation of "extreme" politics in punk and post-punk music graphics in the United Kingdom from 1978 to 2008' was concluded in 2012 at the University of the Arts London. She is a member of the Editorial Board for the journal *Punk and Post-Punk* (Intellect).

John E. Richardson is a Reader in Critical Discourse Studies, Department of Social Sciences, Loughborough University. His research interests include structured social inequalities, British fascism, argumentation and multimodal commemoration. His most recent books are *British Fascism: A Discourse-Historic Analysis* (2017), *Cultures of Post-War British Fascism* (2015, co-editor Nigel Copsey) and *The Routledge Handbook of Critical Discourse Studies* (forthcoming, co-editor John Flowerdew). He is editor of the international journal *Critical Discourse Studies*. From February 2017 to January 2018 he was a Leverhulme Trust Research Fellow, researching the ways that Holocaust Memorial Day in the UK has changed since 2002.

Roger Sabin is Professor of Popular Culture at the University of the Arts London. His books and essays have ranged over the cultural politics of comics, TV, sub-cultures and countercultures, and in 1999 he edited the collection *Punk Rock: So What?* (Routledge).

George J. Severs is a PhD student at Selwyn College, Cambridge where he is researching the history of HIV/AIDS activism in the UK in the 1980s and 1990s. He holds an MPhil in Modern British History from Pembroke College, Cambridge and a First Class Honours degree from Royal Holloway, University of London, where this chapter was first researched and written. George also sits on the Oral History Society's LGBTQ special interest group.

Evan Smith is a Visiting Adjunct Fellow in the School of History and International Relations at Flinders University, South Australia. He has written widely on the far left and the far right in Britain, Australia and southern Africa. His monograph, *British Communism and the Politics of Race*, was published by Brill as part of its Historical Materialism series in 2017.

Matthew Worley is Professor of Modern History at the University of Reading. He has written extensively on British politics in the interwar period, and more recently on the relationship between youth culture and politics in the 1970s and 1980s. His articles have been published in *History Workshop Journal*, *Twentieth Century British History* and *Contemporary British History*. His books include *Oswald Mosley and the New Party* (2010), *Labour Inside the Gate: A History of the British Labour Party between the Wars* (2005) and *Class against Class: The Communist Party in Britain between the Wars* (2002). As a co-founder of the Subcultures Network, he has contributed to books such as *Fight Back: Punk, Politics and Resistance* (2015) and *Youth Culture, Popular Music and the End of 'Consensus'* (2015). His latest monograph – *No Future: Punk, Politics and British Youth Culture, 1976–1984* – was published by Cambridge University Press in 2017.

INTRODUCTION

Nigel Copsey and Matthew Worley

Let us begin with some words regarding the title of this volume, *'Tomorrow Belongs to Us'*. During the 1970s the anthem *'Il domani appartiene a noi'* ('Tomorrow belongs to us') was sung by the youth wing of the neo-fascist *Movimento Sociale Italiano*. It was, or so it was said, a traditional ballad popular with Italian Alpine soldiers during the First World War. The reality, however, was that it was derivative of 'Tomorrow Belongs to Me', the song which featured in *Cabaret*, the 1972 musical drama film. Sung in a beer garden by a young, blonde-haired, blue-eyed Nazi, the supreme irony is that 'Tomorrow Belongs to Me' was written by two American Jews: the composer John Kander and the lyricist Fred Ebb. The recipient of numerous Oscars, *Cabaret* was a much-acclaimed *anti-Nazi* film.

So why, in view of its 'cosmopolitan' provenance, did this song strike such an emotional chord with Britain's far right? British National Party (BNP) activist Joe Owens recalls watching a videotape of the film's scene in 1984, and 'With this we all stood to our feet right arm raised and sung along with the song. It was a great feeling of camaraderie and brought back to all those present, what Adolf Hitler and National Socialism meant to us' (Owens 2007: 78). That same year, Ian Stuart Donaldson, lead singer for the white nationalist band Skrewdriver, plagiarised the lyrics and reworked them into an abrasive rock anthem for the white power movement. Skrewdriver's rendition of 'Tomorrow Belongs to Me' was the eighth track on the band's 1984 album, *Hail the New Dawn* (see Forbes and Stampton 2015).[1]

The battle cry 'Tomorrow Belongs to Us!' would feature on BNP posters of that era too. And what this specific slogan symbolised for Britain's white racial nationalists was the 'special quality of steel' that National Front and BNP leader John Tyndall waxed lyrically about, a single-minded faith in their destiny, a credo capable of sustaining white racial nationalists in their 'long march through the cold night – which must precede the glorious dawn' (Tyndall 1998: 536). Tyndall (who died in 2005) would not live long enough to see the sun rise on the glorious day of white revolution (and neither, for that matter, would Ian Stuart). Unhappily for Britain's fascists, they would suffer an endless succession of freezing nights with temperatures raised only momentarily by the occasional *false* dawn.

The chronological starting point for our volume is 1967. Fifty years have now passed since the National Front (NF) was officially launched on 7 February 1967 (although the 50th anniversary of the release of the Beatles' *Sgt. Pepper's Lonely Hearts Club Band* was properly accorded more cultural significance). Nonetheless, historian Richard Thurlow (1998: 245) was right to refer to the formation of the NF in this year as 'the most significant event on the radical right and the fascist fringe of British politics since internment'. For the first time since Mosley's British Union of Fascists, most of Britain's far right had come together in one distinct entity, unified under one single banner. The Front's subsequent electoral growth – it captured nearly a quarter of a million of votes in local elections in 1977, beating the Liberals in the Greater London Council elections in 33 seats – led many to view the NF as Britain's fourth political party, poised even to displace the Liberals as Britain's third political party.

A merger of a number of different far-right groups which included A.K. Chesterton's League of Empire Loyalists; John Bean's British National Party; Robin Beauclair and the majority of the Racial Preservation Society; and from June 1967 onwards, individual members of John Tyndall's Greater Britain Movement (Tyndall would become involved with the NF from late 1967), the National Front was a household name in 1970s Britain.[2] Within the urban landscape, in the form of a menacing 'typographical ligature', the letters 'NF' would be spray-painted on many an inner-city wall.[3] For years, the Front owned the far-right brand. It would be the twenty-first century before Nick Griffin's 'rebranded' BNP would take ownership of it.

A.K. Chesterton, Oswald Mosley's former political secretary, was the NF's first leader. However, the figure most synonymous with the NF is not Chesterton (he died in mid-August 1973 and had spent most of his final years wintering in South Africa) but John Tyndall. In 1972, John Tyndall took over the NF's leadership, and despite a brief period when he was deposed, it was Tyndall that led the NF through-out its 1970s heyday – a period in which the NF developed sufficient strength to contest over 300 seats in the 1979 general election. As it turned out, although the 1970s promised much for the fascist right, it all came to nothing. 'So per-ishes the myth of Britain's fastest growing party' the anti-fascist magazine *Searchlight* declared following the NF's catastrophic 1979 general election (*Searchlight*, no. 48, 1979). Tyndall would have to wait until the early 1990s before next tasting anything approaching electoral 'success' (a solitary local council by-election victory for his BNP, a splinter party from the NF). Nearly two decades later, and the most recent false dawn for Britain's far right came in the 2010 general election when the BNP, this time under the leadership of Nick Griffin, stood a record 338 parliamentary candidates and captured half a million votes. Contrast this with five years later. In the 2015 general election, the BNP could only muster eight parliamentary candi-dates (330 fewer than 2010).

On an international stage dominated by the election of Donald Trump, the rise of radical-right, neo-nationalist or nativist populism has become increasingly difficult to ignore. In France, Marine Le Pen captured a record 34 per cent of the vote for the French far right in the second round of the 2017 presidential elections. Domestically, UKIP stole the BNP's voters, captured 12.6 per cent of the vote in the 2015 general election and claimed victory in the 2016 Brexit referendum (in a vitriolic campaign that saw the murder of Labour MP Jo Cox by a neo-Nazi sympathiser). But with its job apparently done, UKIP saw its vote collapse in the 2017 general election (UKIP's share of the vote contracted to less than 4 per cent). As for the traditional far right, the BNP's demise was further confirmed when new party leader Adam Walker could only garner a derisory 2.3 per cent of the vote in the parliamentary constituency of Bishop Auckland, in north-east England. Britain's far right (even if we include UKIP) has once again become an electoral irrelevancy. So why is this topic worthy of our attention now?

In the first place, as Nigel Copsey pointed out in 2015:

> the far right is part of Britain's national story. It will continue to be part of that national story even when voters abandon it, as they have recently done in their droves – almost 764,000 voters in the 2014 European elections when compared to 2009. Of course election results count, but there is a much bigger picture, and yet it is one which we struggle to see […] there is much more to be said about Britain's far right 'fringe' than its interminable inability to make a serious challenge for representation in Westminster.
>
> *(Copsey 2015: 12)*

This far right, as we reveal in this volume, has a multi-dimensional character. And make no mistake, we fail to see its many sides if we do not look outside the ballot box.

If we are still tempted to dismiss the far-right fringe altogether as 'cranks', unworthy of serious study, then Daniel Trilling's words are surely worth heeding:

> Societies that promise equality, freedom and democracy, yet preside over massive inequalities of wealth, are breeding grounds for racism and other vicious resentments. And wherever these resentments exist, the far right will try to exploit them. The fascism of the 20s and 30s succeeded because it played on wider fears, winning the support of those who would never have thought of themselves as extremists […] We do not need to wait for a successor to the BNP to emerge before addressing these much deeper problems.
>
> *(The Guardian, 12 September 2012)*

How many NF voters in the 1970s, or indeed BNP voters in the 2000s, would have defined themselves as 'extremists'? How many of those who took to the streets in support of the English Defence League (EDL) would have considered themselves 'right-wing extremists'? Consider for a moment *that* EDL news conference in October 2009 in the disused factory in Luton when a group of EDL supporters wearing balaclavas unfurled a swastika flag, doused it in petrol, and set it alight.[4]

This volume was never conceived with the ballot box in mind. Its focus is not on the many (usually inglorious) electoral interventions of Britain's far right since 1967; these have been covered sufficiently elsewhere in the literature (see, for example, on the NF, Taylor 1982; Husbands 1983; and on the BNP, Copsey 2008; Goodwin 2011). Rather, the editors of this volume solicited contributions that enhance our understanding of Britain's contemporary far right as a *broader* political and cultural phenomenon. We have tried, in this volume, to set out new ways of seeing our subject, of approaching it from a variety of different disciplinary perspectives. The aim has been to fill some long-standing gaps in existing knowledge, and take analyses of the far right in directions that have been hitherto ignored or as yet under-explored.

The chapters presented in this volume examine the last fifty years of the British far right from the perspectives of holocaust denial and conspiracy; *groupuscularity*; political economy; transnational mobilisation; youth culture and visual identities; through to attitudes towards homosexuality, gender and women; emotions and patriotism, and processes of 'cumulative extremism'. Instead of drawing from the narrowly based statistical analysis that typifies much of the field of hard political science, these contributions take their methodological cues from elsewhere, namely from history, as well as from cultural studies and social movement/behavioural studies.

The volume begins with a contribution from Mark Hobbs on Holocaust denial. Chapter 1 explores how the presentation of Holocaust denial has changed in various far-right parties and movements since 1967. Hobbs argues that Holocaust denial, and the belief in a clandestine Jewish conspiracy, remained an integral part of the epistemology which underpinned the policy and rhetoric of Britain's far right since 1967. This chapter explores the paradox of such thinking: the claim that the genocide of European Jewry did not take place was based on the same redemptive anti-Semitism and tropes of conspiracy which contributed to the Holocaust during the Second World War.

Then in Chapter 2, Daniel Jones and Paul Jackson take us back to the late 1960s and explore the history of a short-lived British neo-Nazi *groupuscule*, the National Socialist Group (NSG). Letters, membership data, internal briefings, publications and other material produced by the group during its lifetime are used to develop a picture of the clandestine organisation's inner dynamics, and ultimate failings. The chapter also explores how the NSG's leading activists sought to carve out a unique position for the organisation in the changing arena of the far right in the late 1960s. The chapter concludes that, although in itself tiny and largely inconsequential, the NSG needs to be located in a much longer history of neo-Nazi groups promoting revolution and violence in Britain.

John E. Richardson, in Chapter 3, then turns our attention back to the National Front, the leading player on Britain's far right during the 1970s and 1980s. Surprisingly little attention has been paid to the Front's thoughts on political economy. Richardson discusses some important historic precursors that lay the groundwork for understanding fascist political economies in general. Following this he examines two political economies advocated by the NF: the party drew implicitly on the example of Nazi Germany, and argued for autarky during the 1970s; then during the 1980s, the party advocated distributism as a native rather than imported economic ideology. Richardson argues that, even at its most radical, the NF could not transcend a capitalist political economy. For Richardson, attempts to develop 'third way' solutions simply recalibrated and rehabilitated capitalism in the service of 'the nation'.

Chapter 4, Evan Smith's chapter, is the first of two chapters in this volume devoted to transnationalism. In the late 1970s and early 1980s, the National Front sought to expand its influence across the Anglophone world, and established the Commonwealth National Front (CNF). The object of the CNF was to establish solidarity between white supremacist organisations worldwide and foster a trans-national fascist movement to 'protect' white 'civilisation'. The National Front of Australia (NFA) was one of the few local NFs that was actually formed. Despite ambitions to replicate the populism of the British NF, the NFA was hindered by the notoriety of its sister organisation, by a hostile media, and by an anti-fascist move-ment mobilised quickly after the NFA's formation. As Smith's chapter reveals, with the NFA seemingly defunct by the early 1980s (and similar NFs in South Africa and New Zealand also collapsing), the attempt to build the CNF can be viewed as part of a wider history of a failed venture to export British-styled fascism across the white Dominions of the British Empire/Commonwealth.

Since the term was first coined by Roger Eatwell in 2006, 'cumulative extrem-ism' has become the focus of an increasing amount of work conducted by scholars, policymakers and journalists. This concept refers to the ways in which one form of extremism can incite another into a process of 'tit-for-tat' radicalisation. While our understanding of the concept has undoubtedly increased, it has been widely acknowledged that more work is necessary to develop this concept into a robust tool for understanding the interactive dynamics between groups which can cause the escalation, non-escalation or de-escalation of movement–countermovement contests. To that end, Chapter 5, Alex Carter's chapter, conducts a sustained analysis of the interactions that occurred between fascists and anti-fascists in 1970s Britain, paying close attention to the specific factors which led to the development of more or less radical protest repertoires amongst these opposing groups.

The co-editors of this volume then examine another relationship: the one between far-right organisations and British youth culture in the period between 1977 and 1987. Chapter 6 concentrates on the cultural spaces opened up by punk and the attempts made by both the NF and British Movement to claim them as conduits for racist and/or ultranationalist politics. Mapping shifting cultural and political influences across the far right, it assesses the extent to which extremist organisations proved able to adopt or utilise youth cultural practice as a means of recruitment and communication. The visual codes associated with neo-fascist rock would enter a new phase in the 1980s. With skinhead culture becoming more influential, previously favoured punk tropes were merged with hyper-masculine and violent images, encompassing openly Nazi associations, to produce a newly aggressive subcultural language – a language that would have a profound international impact. Chapter 7, the chapter by Ana Raposo and Roger Sabin, examines this visual culture. It traces the changing politics behind it, paying special attention to the aesthetic of record sleeves, magazines and other graphics.

In Chapter 8, George J. Severs examines the BNP's opposition to gay men during the 1980s and 1990s. Drawing on the sociological concept of 'homohysteria', it examines written material from BNP publications during those decades, looking specifically at the AIDS crisis, the party's belief in a 'queer conspiracy', and the role which homosexuality played in the decline of the NF and the birth of the BNP. The first study dedicated to British fascism's anti-gay prejudice, this chapter argues that the existing scholarship fails to understand the degree and nature of anti-gay sentiment in the BNP, concluding that the party was 'homohysteric' from its inception.

Across Europe, a plethora of studies has examined membership of far-right groups and has drawn theoretical links between socio-economic status and activism. However, some significant areas remain under-researched and there is a notable gap in relation to women's involvement in far-right political and activist groups. The chapter by Hannah Bows, Chapter 9, provides an overview of the small pool of existing empirical and theoretical literature in relation to women and the contemporary far right in Britain and Europe, highlighting the gaps in knowledge and suggesting future directions for research.

Like Evan Smith, in Chapter 10 Graham Macklin also engages with our subject from a transnational perspective and explores the impact that Golden Dawn's meteoric rise in Greece has had upon on Britain's far right. Macklin examines the waves of mobilisation by sympathetic extreme right-wing *groupuscules* in response to the 'persecution' of Golden Dawn during the crackdown upon its leadership by the Greek government and the murder of two of its activists. This chapter offers a detailed examination of the interactive diffusion of ideas and strategies that took place between the BNP and its Greek counterpart. It underscores the shift towards (and subsequent retreat from) a form of ideological militancy in the BNP's rhetoric which was quite clearly influenced by Golden Dawn.

Since the emergence of the English Defence League (EDL) in 2009, the EDL has been consistently situated by British media, opponents and academics as a far-right, nationalist, proto-fascist organisation motivated by hatred and racism. Drawing on rich ethnographic data from interviews with EDL activists from across England, the penultimate chapter in our volume, Chapter 11, challenges much of this representation and situates the EDL as an English patriot and loyalist social movement. Its author, C. M. Quinn, explores the intricacies of activist motivations and the pivotal role of *patriotism* in motivating and transforming individuals into activists.

We end this volume with a bibliographic essay penned by Craig Fowlie. Chapter 12 surveys the primary and secondary literature on the far right in Britain since 1967. It examines the social science and historical scholarship on Britain's main extreme-right and radical-right parties and social movements including the

National Front, the British National Party, UKIP and the English Defence League. Autobiographies and memoirs by far-right and anti-fascist activists, as well as investigations by journalists, are also reviewed and contextualised. The chapter explores extreme-right subcultures such as Holocaust denial, white power music, the 'metapolitical' New Right, digital activism and terrorism as well as various forms of transnational organising and the 'cultural' turn in fascism studies.

Many a right-wing extremist heralded the mergers on Britain's far right that took place during the winter of 1966/7, and which resulted in the launch of the National Front, as a 'new beginning'. For sure, this was an important milestone when a new coalition for a revitalised far right emerged, one that seemed capable of occupying legitimate political space to the right of the Conservatives and yet distanced from historical British fascism. At various moments, this appeared tantalisingly close – when NF candidate Martin Webster netted 16.2 per cent of the vote in a parliamentary by-election in West Bromwich in 1973; or when the BNP's Nick Griffin and Andrew Brons were elected to the European Parliament in 2009. But from our vantage point some five decades on, it is all too clear that tomorrow never did belong to *them*. Of course we do not know what fate will hold in store for Britain's far right over the course of the next fifty years. Even in our society's darkest moments, let us hope that the refrain 'Tomorrow belongs to us' will forever remain a Tantalus torment,[5] a tomorrow that will always remain stubbornly out of their reach.

Notes

1   Ian Stuart Donaldson recorded a number of versions of this song as did Saga, a Swedish white supremacist. For an interesting discussion of this song's 'recontextualisation', that is, the way in which the original meaning was subverted and undermined, see Richardson 2017: 68.

2   The name of this new organisation, the 'National Front', had been used by Chesterton before. It had been the name given to a short-lived group which had been formed by Chesterton and Collin Brooks towards the end of 1944 (at that time Brooks and Chesterton were Editor and Deputy Editor respectively of the political magazine *Truth*). In the early 1950s, Andrew Fountaine also established a 'National Front Movement'.

3   According to one recent poster on the Stormfront website,

> Regarding The 'N.F.' Symbol I remember that writing the letters N then F separately were reportedly quite cumbersome & time consuming, the upward line of The 'F' being the problem, along with the 2 apostrophes (sic). Mischievous scribblers & scrawlers of the time somehow developed through a kind of unspoken mass consciousness the simultaneous 'idea' of amalgamating the F into The N in one lightening move, by drawing an N then adding a quick couple of F horizontal lines! Into a sort of Loch Ness Monster Looking Symbol. Dont ask me how this came about, there was never any directive, it just came naturally for those in a hurry! It didnt detract from conveying its meaning & was well understood. A genius on par with A Corporate Logo!

See www.stormfront.org/forum/t1205164/, post by 'Thomas Harwick' (03-26-2017, 12:45 PM). The reality was that this logo had already appeared on official Front literature from the late 1960s.

4   See www.telegraph.co.uk/news/6284184/The-English-Defence-League-will-the-flames-of-hatred-spread.html. Footage appeared as part of a *BBC Newsnight* investigation, 'Under the skin of English Defence League'.

5   From Greek mythology: Tantalus stood in a pool of water underneath a fruit tree. When he tried to reach for the fruit, the branches would raise out of his reach; when he tried to drink the water from the pool, the water level would recede.

References

Copsey, N. (2008) *Contemporary British Fascism: The British National Party and the Quest for Legitimacy*, 2nd edn, Basingstoke: Palgrave.

Copsey, N. (2015) 'Britain's Far Right and the 2015 General Election: A View from History', in Kahn, O. and Sveinsson, K. (eds) *Race and Elections*. London: Runnymede Trust, pp. 11–13.

Forbes, R. and Stampton, E. (2015) *The White Nationalist Skinhead Movement, UK & USA 1979–1993*, Port Townsend, WA: Feral House.

Goodwin, M. J. (2011) *New British Fascism: Rise of the British National Party*, Abingdon: Routledge.

Husbands, C. T. (1983) *Racial Exclusionism and the City: The Urban Support of the National Front*, London: George Allen & Unwin.

Owens, J. (2007) *Action! Race War to Door Wars*, Lulu.com.

Richardson, J. E. (2017) *British Fascism: A Discourse-Historical Analysis*, Stuttgart: ibidem-Verlag.

Taylor, S. (1982) *The National Front in English Politics*, London: Macmillan.

Thurlow, R. (1998) *Fascism in Britain: From Oswald Mosley's Blackshirts to the National Front*, London: I.B. Tauris.

Tyndall, J. (1998) *The Eleventh Hour: A Call for British Rebirth*, 3rd edn, Welling: Albion Press.

1

'THE MEN WHO REWRITE HISTORY'

Holocaust denial and the British far right from 1967[1]

Mark Hobbs

> When an intelligent man expresses a view which seems to us obviously absurd, we should not attempt to prove that it is somehow true, but we should try to understand how it ever came to *seem* to be true. This exercise of historical and psychological imagination [...] enlarges the scope of our thinking.
>
> *(Russell 2008: 39)*

Introduction

Bertrand Russell's words may seem like an unusual place to begin a chapter on British far-right Holocaust denial, yet his discussion of how to approach different systems of historic and political thought are of great use to the academic study of Holocaust or genocide denial. All too often there has been an assumption that those who write and publish Holocaust denial are mad or stupid. While their beliefs about the history of the Holocaust have no foundation in historical fact or reality and are the product of closed minds locked into viewing the world through the lens of anti-Semitic conspiracy, these views are based on falsehood, manipulation and the exclusion of facts. Yet, we cannot ignore the reality that those who deny the Holocaust do often possess academic qualifications, and propagate a far-right, fascist or neo-Nazi way of thinking, abhorrent to the liberal imagination. To cast these individuals and their followers as mad or stupid is to ignore the serious danger that these ideologies pose and the violence that they produce. If we fail to understand why Holocaust denial and anti-Semitic conspiracy thinking underpins these movements then an important part of the history of the development of the British far right since 1945 is missing from the explanation of why these ideologies continue to exist.

The way in which denial and far-right policies were presented to the public reveals a great deal about the political direction of the various movements and parties on the far right but also the changing political and social character of Britain since 1945. This chapter will explore how Holocaust denial was both part of a political campaign to rehabilitate Nazism and how denial provided the epistemological platform for a 'history' that allowed far-right thinkers and followers to make sense of the world in which they lived and fought for power. It will argue, however, that these two positions were mutually exclusive.

The presence of Holocaust denial in the British far right was far from being a rehabilitative tool: it was a barrier to the political legitimacy of such movements in the minds of the public. Yet it was a trope that could not be jettisoned because it contained the key to the legitimacy of far-right political philosophy and ideology: it explained the failure of the movement to achieve power because a conspiracy led by Jews was working against it. Indeed the presence of the Holocaust in British collective memory and national commemoration was viewed as 'evidence' by the far right of the success of a clandestine Jewish world conspiracy. In short, the growing presence of the Holocaust in national narratives about the past confirmed their view that not only was a Jewish conspiracy at work but also that it was succeeding in its goals.

Denial and the ballot box

The defeat of Nazism by the Allied Powers in 1945 is of the utmost significance when examining Holocaust denial and far-right ideology. The military defeat of Hitler and the Third Reich meant that rather than seeing Nazism as a failed ideology or political system, supporters of Nazism and Fascism began to interpret this historical episode as a conspiracy: a re-run of the 'stabbed in the back' myth promulgated by right-wing circles in Weimar Germany. In far-right thinking, the Third Reich had not been toppled by popular uprisings as was the case with the February Revolution in Russia or later in the collapse of communism in Eastern Europe in 1989. The Nazi regime and its ideas were rightfully branded as 'evil' and terrorist by the Allies but the epistemology that created it and its role as a counterweight to the failures of capitalism and liberal democracy in the minds of the electorate were largely ignored. As Jean-François Lyotard noted, Nazism 'has not been refuted' because 'it has been beaten down like a mad dog, by a police action, and not in conformity with the rules accepted by its adversary's genres of discourse (argumentation for liberalism, contradiction for Marxism)' (1989: 106). It is clear that Nazism has been refuted morally and publicly as a result of the genocidal nature of the regime signified by the murder of six million European Jews.

However, for far-right thinkers and politicians, the popular attraction of Nazism to voters in the early 1930s in Germany and of fascism to Italians in Italy and later Spain meant that the ideology still has a resonance and role to play in shaping human culture, society and politics. Holocaust denial provides the answer to political legitimacy by removing the genocidal crimes of the regime. Yet it also has another role: in seeing the military defeat not as the result of the supremacy of Allied power and Hitler's military bungling, a new *false* history is created. This 'history' employs Jewish conspiracy theory to deny the Holocaust, but also explain why the war was fought and won by the allies: the war was a Jewish war created and brought about by the Jews themselves with the Allied powers playing the role of puppets of Jewish control. Hitler himself created the trajectory of this history and thinking, demonstrated in his political testament:

> It is untrue that I or anyone else in Germany wanted the war in 1939. It was desired and instigated exclusively by those international statesmen who were either of Jewish descent or worked for Jewish interests [...] Centuries will pass away, but out of the ruins of our towns and monuments the hatred against those finally responsible, whom we have to thank for everything, international Jewry and its helpers, will grow.

Hitler's words help us to understand the way in which the British far right began to interpret the defeat of Nazism and how, as a history, it could reformulate its own fortunes and understandings in a post-Third Reich world. The pre-war leader of the British Union of Fascists Oswald Mosley proved influential in helping formulate the counter 'cultural hegemonic' far-right narratives which would provide the framework for Holocaust denial. Yet despite Mosley's and his wife Diana's involvement with the dissemination of denial, their role in shaping the policies of the National Front (NF) towards denial was negligible (Hillman 2001: 13).

Hitler's words are especially significant in the trajectory of the British far-right Holocaust denial because Arnold Leese, a fanatical Nazi and anti-Semite sowed the post-war seeds of British fascism and National Socialism. Leese's disciples would dominate the NF and British National Party (BNP) and its ideological philosophy, a fact acknowledged by BNP leader Nick Griffin in 2003 when he sought to move the party away from the ideology of the 'sub-Mosleyite wackiness of Arnold Leese's Imperial Fascist League' (Copsey 2008: 15). The domination of a band of neo-Nazi followers in the British far right would shape policies towards Holocaust denial.

The overt nature was not necessarily always on display to the public and was often hidden with a rhetoric which had to appeal to the public for votes and who were implacably opposed to Nazism. A respectable face needed to be presented or as Nigel Copsey explains, the iron fist needed to be covered with a velvet glove (2008: 15). The first example of this was seen in the speech given by A.K. Chesterton at the inaugural meeting of the NF in 1967:

> The man who thinks this is a war that can be won by mouthing slogans about 'dirty Jews and filthy niggers' is a maniac whose place should not be in the National Front but in a mental hospital ... A nation once noble and very great cannot be rescued from the mire by jackasses who play straight into the enemy's hands by giving the public that image of us that the enemy most clearly wants to be given.

(Candour, October, 1967)

Chesterton's speech was a call to supporters to find a more acceptable face for post-war British far-right ideology that would move the public to place a cross in the box of fascism at the election booth. While the direct correlation between the neo-Nazi, Leesite ideology and of the various incarnations of British far-right groups since 1967 is overt, it is not to say that this ideology was set in stone and impervious to change. As Paxton has stated, definitions are inherently limiting and we must look not just to what movements said but also what they did (2005: 14). Like all political parties the British far right had to respond to events, public opinion and the internal tensions within the membership. Holocaust denial provides a means by which to measure the differing ways in which policy and ideology were presented to the public. An overt and rabid expression of denial indicated an extremist policy, which proclaimed revolution and paramilitary activity, but a more measured tone relying on a pseudo-scholarly framework indicated a movement more drawn to achieving power by elections and the pursuit of populism.

The history of the Holocaust, and its place in British collective memory, was inevitably tied up with the way in which Holocaust deniers presented their arguments. It is clear that knowledge of the Final Solution and the fate of European Jewry was well known by the British public in various media outlets during the war and after (Holmila 2011: 30–35). The liberation of Belsen by British and Canadian armed forces in April 1945 became the central focus in the popular British imagination of Nazi atrocities. Yet a perennial anti-Semitism remained within Britain after the war and this coloured the view that the public held about the murder of Europe's Jews by the Nazis (Orwell 2000: chapter 22). Indeed as Louise London opines, the British Government during and in the immediate aftermath played down the particularism of Jewish suffering in favour of stressing universal suffering in order to avoid a public wave of anti-Semitism (London et al. 2002: 511–515). Unlike the British-centric readings of the Second World War in the late 1960s and early 1970s, contemporary society has read the history of the war through the events of the Holocaust. Popular understanding of the Holocaust, fostered through education and national memorial days, has become infused with understandings of the Second World War and Nazism. This increasing development of 'Holocaust consciousness' clearly had an impact on the way in which the British far right presented their arguments about denial and will be the subject of discussion in what follows.

With the establishment of the NF in 1967, a competing array of different parties with varying views about the future of far-right policies merged. It was clear, as outlined in Chesterton's speech above, that anti-Semitism and outright Nazism had no place in the new united front. However, influential members of the far right harboured different views, particularly the future leader of the party from 1972, John Tyndall. Tyndall had been committed to a National Socialist vision for Britain, joining forces with Colin Jordan – a follower of Arnold Leese and beneficiary of Leese's property and political legacy (Walker 1977: 27–28). Jordan and Tyndall had formed various groups based on National Socialist principles and ideology in the

1950s and into the 1960s. They parted company in 1963 after conflicts over the future course of British National Socialism and romantic rivalry over Françoise Dior (Thurlow 1998: 238). Both Jordan and Tyndall had been excluded from the movement because of their commitment to National Socialism, yet while Jordan refused to water down or popularise his message Tyndall began to orchestrate a charm offensive to get himself and his Greater Britain Movement into the NF. It seems that on the part of Tyndall and Chesterton there was a good deal of negotiation through back channels (Copsey 2008: 15–16). When Tyndall dropped his commitment to National Socialism in his magazine *Spearhead* in 1966 and published a pamphlet entitled *Six Principles of British Nationalism* in 1966 which called for a united far-right front, and was devoid of Jewish conspiracy and calls for National Socialist solutions, Tyndall was admitted to the NF in exchange for the dissolution of the Greater Britain Movement.

While Tyndall remained loyal to Chesterton up to his retirement in 1970 his eyes had always been on the leadership of the movement. Tyndall would acquire the leadership in 1972, and remain leader until 1980, except for a two-year gap in which he was ousted from the position of chairman of the party by 'moderate populists' in October 1974 only to return as chairman in 1976 (Thurlow 1998: 251–254). These political machinations and PR exercises reveal a great deal about the tone and course of Holocaust denial in the NF. Tyndall was willing to publicly compromise his beliefs and views in order to secure power and influence while still privately retaining his commitment to National Socialist ideology.

The key to exercising this was his control of propaganda and public rhetoric and the support of Richard Verrall. Verrall was an intellectual figure, with a first class degree from the University of London; he also had a mind full of conspiracy and was appointed an editor of Tyndall's *Spearhead* magazine in 1976. He was to provide the rational arguments for conspiracy and racism. Under Verrall's tenure as editor, *Spearhead* began to directly push the question of conspiracy out into the open. An article in *Spearhead* in March 1976, 'The Jewish Question: Out in the Open or Under the Carpet?', sought to revisit the propaganda and issues sidelined under Chesterton's vision of the NF in 1967 (*Spearhead*, No. 96, 1976, p. 7). Verrall's *Did Six Million Really Die?* published in 1974, began to be referenced in *Spearhead*. The work is a canon of Holocaust denial literature, published under the pseudonym Richard Harwood, who was described as a specialist of the Second World War at the University of London. The use of a pseudonym underscores the NF's leadership and propaganda strategy with regard to Holocaust denial. By giving the text an author in an academic institution Verrall intended to imbue the book with academic merit. Furthermore, the presence of footnotes, bibliography and scholastic framework was all designed to present the idea that Holocaust denial was a viable form of legitimate historical revisionism. This technique was intended to give scholastic credence to the views that had been prevalent in the extreme right since the mid-to-late 1940s regarding the murder of Jews and further legitimate the presence of a Jewish conspiracy at work in the world.

In essence, the book was emblematic of an attempt by the NF, and other deniers who used the work, to give an academic cloak of respectability to Holocaust denial, sympathy for National Socialist ideologies and forward the thesis of a Jewish conspiracy. Denial and the 'Jewish question' was therefore both out in the open (with the veneer of pseudo-academic authority) while the more National Socialist genocidal mentalities remained hidden under the carpet. The ploy was unsuccessful; anti-fascist groups were successful in demonstrating the neo-Nazi credentials of the NF. The Front's attempt to win power by fielding over 300 candidates in the 1979 general election ended in failure when the party failed to gain one per cent of the votes cast. The presence of Holocaust denial alone was, of course, not the sole factor in the resulting humiliation and defeat. The defeat is largely attributed to the election campaign of the Conservative party. Margaret Thatcher repositioned the party's stance on immigration policy and as a result drained the NF's key election platform, a fact the NF leadership acknowledged in its publication *National Front News* (Durham 1996: 95). However, the popular rejection of the NF also reflected the extent to which British society had become increasingly aware of the Nazi genocide of the Jews. This awareness-raising has been attributed to the success of the Granada *World at War* episode 'Genocide' and the American mini-series *Holocaust*, first broadcast in 1978 (Pearce 2014: 30–31, 170–173).

Verrall's *Did Six Million Really die?* proved to be hugely influential and remains a staple in the catalogue of Holocaust denial literature. The work itself also directly impacted on the trajectory of denial. When published by Ernst Zündel in Canada, Zündel was put on trial in 1985 (and again in 1988). His defence was supported by testimony from Robert Faurisson, Bradley Smith and David Irving, all of whom were well known for their Holocaust denial, admiration and exoneration of Hitler. The trial also resulted in the publication of a further work that captured international significance, the *Leuchter Report*. Zündel hired Fred Leuchter for his defence case; his brief was to conduct experiments on the remains of the sites of extermination in Poland, focusing on the gassing facilities at Auschwitz-Birkenau and Majdanek camps. The report concluded that the gassing of human beings was not possible at these sites and that this meant that the Holocaust had not happened. The report was flawed in its scientific methodology and the conclusions reached untenable. Nonetheless, this slew of publications from members of the British far-right and international Holocaust deniers played well to the image that the NF leadership wanted to present. Instead of rabid anti-Semitism and crude denunciations of the Holocaust, NF propaganda could allude to 'scientific' studies and 'historical' texts that supported their claims despite the clearly bogus foundations that underpinned them.

The air of legitimacy the text bestowed was further demonstrated in Tyndall's 1988 book *Eleventh Hour: A Call for British Rebirth*. In the book Tyndall outlined how the Jewish conspiracy worked. Like Nick Griffin, Tyndall sought to distance himself, and his views, from the radical foundations of post-war British far-right movements. He attacked the machinations of Arnold Leese, writing 'the works of

Arnold Leese tends to overstate the Jewish role to a point, at times, of absurdity'
(p. 112). Tyndall wanted to show that the Holocaust was a barrier to the issue of
race, which Tyndall was keen to discuss:

> There is a growing school of historians today that in fact challenges the
> accuracy of the allegation that the German Nazis ever had any intended
> extermination programme, and puts forward the counter-claim that the high
> death rate in the concentration camps was caused mainly by sickness, famine
> and a breakdown of food and medical supplies that was general in Germany
> at the time, and to which Allied bombing largely contributed … [W]hether
> this revised view of that phase of history is correct or incorrect should not
> concern us here. Even if it could be proved beyond any possible doubt that
> the original and established view of what happened in Germany was factually
> correct, it would not have the slightest bearing on the validity or invalidity
> of 'racism'.
>
> *(p. 334)*

Tyndall's words contain many of the key facets that help us understand the way in
which the NF and later BNP had approached Holocaust denial under his leadership. The 'growing school of historians' was clearly the Holocaust deniers adopting
an increasing pseudo-scholastic writing style, appearing in the conspiratorial *Journal
of Historical Review* and notable figures like David Irving and Richard Verrall. The
notion that these men could be a legitimate school of historians was implicit in
his words, and could be seen simply as a throwaway comment. Yet the pedagogical
tone of the book, designed to inform his readers of his views and the direction for a
British 'rebirth', demonstrates the way in which the use of the word 'historians' was
invoked to give credibility to his views. The findings of Tyndall's 'historians' – that
the death rates in concentration camps were due to sickness, famine and poor food
and medical provision which was largely the fault of Allied bombing – was a standard argument of Holocaust deniers. Another significant point in Tyndall's phrasing
is that the issue of the Holocaust 'should not concern us here'. This is a standard way
in which far-right figures, who seek power by the ballot box, ignore the issue of the
Holocaust once they have questioned its historical legitimacy. This form of denial
seeks to remove the Holocaust from contemporary debates about racism and race.
The effect is to suggest that racist views or adherents to those views do not contain a potential for genocide, ethnic cleansing or the degradation of human rights.
This, therefore, removes the racist and anti-Semitic dimension of the Holocaust,
essentially reaching the untenable conclusion that a prime factor in driving the
Holocaust was not racism. What Tyndall was offering his readers was a two-pronged
approach to the Holocaust, first laying out the basis of the arguments of Holocaust
denial; and second, if the reader does not accept the denial of the Holocaust as a
legitimate argument, then the historical significance of the Holocaust is dismissed
so as not to impact on calls for a racist reorganisation of British culture and politics.
Both actions are historical negationism, the first a direct attack on the history of the

Holocaust, the second a call to ignore a genocide brought about by a racist Nazi worldview.

Tyndall furthered his message of a conspiracy working against him in the book, attacking the 'anti-Nazi industry'. In the book he explained how the Jewish conspiracy worked under the chapter title 'is there a conspiracy?'Tyndall likened discussions of the Holocaust and Nazism to self-censorship in the Soviet Union in which historians and authors were afraid to write anything which questioned the genocide of the Holocaust (1988: 92–116). Later in the book Tyndall also explained how Jews controlled the media, and claimed that David Irving had been 'blackball[ed]' and put on an international 'Zionist hit list' for 'questioning some of the "holocaust" propaganda surrounding World War II' (1988: 388). The timing of the book is significant in the historiography of the Holocaust, it was written during the *historikerstreit*, a time when the nature of the Nazi regime was being hotly debated in Germany and amongst historians of the Holocaust and Nazi Germany. While the ideas of Irving and Tyndall can never be described as a genuine historical debate over the Holocaust it is clear that they were keen to seize upon the debates taking place in Holocaust historiography and public debates on the place of the Holocaust in both German and British public life.

The development of Holocaust 'consciousness' in Britain is of particular importance to the trajectory of Holocaust denial in Britain since 1967. In the summer of 1979 eminent historian Yehuda Bauer, speaking in Switzerland at the Claims Conference of Jewish victims of the Holocaust, noted 'nothing at all has been done in Britain' in regard to Holocaust commemoration (Pearce 2014: 90–91). It is clear that the Holocaust, and its commemoration, had not yet permeated into British memory and narratives of the Second World War. As Andy Pearce has noted the word, Holocaust, in the 1970s and 1980s was unfamiliar to some of the population in the context of the genocide of the Jews during the Second World War (2014: 30–31, 166–167). However, despite the lack of active commemoration on the part of the Government and non-governmental organisations, the genocide of the Jews and Nazi anti-Semitism was well known and understood as a result of the above-mentioned television programmes and mini-series in the early and mid-1970s. Yet it is clear that as the 1970s drew to a close, the Holocaust was not as ubiquitous in the national psyche and its incorporation into national narratives about the Second World War as it is today. This would change as Britain entered into the new millennium.

Two points should be made in regard to the developing Holocaust 'consciousness' in Britain and Holocaust denial. First is the direct and continuous attack on the Jews and the historical reality of the Final Solution by the far right when juxtaposed with the apparent public apathy to the Holocaust in national narratives and the absence of any detailed or nationally orchestrated commemoration. While the crimes of the Nazis were apparent to the public, the far right's persistence in developing ever more complex and pseudo-academic denials of the Holocaust and Jewish conspiracy theory demonstrated the inherent adherence to the Neo-Nazi past of Tyndall and his acolytes in the NF. It also demonstrates the continuation of a long history of anti-Semitism and denial of Nazi atrocities against Jews dating back to the Second World War (Hobbs 2016). While a silence on the part of the far right in regard to the Holocaust, or refusal to outline a position on the historical significance of the Holocaust (characteristic of later far-right leaders), would have rightly been construed as denial, it would have seemed more politically prudent to adopt this stance. While parties like the NF were often careful to put distance between the party and the physical publication of denial material, they were only too happy to accept the conclusions made and promote those conclusions to support their own underlying ideological epistemology. Second, the increasing turn to public commemoration of, and education about, the Holocaust would change the way in which far-right parties who sought public endorsement at the ballot box discussed and presented their denials.

The place and presence of Holocaust denial in the NF was soon to become an increasingly subsidiary concern of the leaders and members as the party began to tear itself apart over the future direction of the movement as a product of changes in British society and politics. While the far right had always failed to capture the political space it needed for victory, after the failure of the 1979 election, the NF began to unravel (Durham 1996: 84–98). Tyndall formed the New National Front that became the British National Party two years later. The NF was led by Andrew Brons with Richard Verrall appointed his deputy. The split was riven with complex divisions in far-right politics with old and new parties creating new alliances. The inclusion of members of the British Movement in the NF, orchestrated by Tyndall and Ray Hill (ironically a mole for the anti-fascist movement *Searchlight*), saw the former members of the Greater British Movement reunite with their roots. The British Movement and its former leader Colin Jordan, and current leader Michael McLaughlin, were advocates of National Socialism.[2]

In this atmosphere a unified public position on denial became more erratic. For example, in 1988 Richard Edmonds, a staunch ally of Tyndall, published the denial pamphlet *Holocaust News*. Edmunds published and distributed 100,000 copies of *Holocaust News* from the BNP's own publishing outlet the 'Centre for Historical Review' (Copsey 2008: 44). Despite the obvious connection of the publication to the party in an article reporting on its origins in *The Times*, Tyndall claimed that although he was not involved in the production of *Holocaust News*, it had 'his full support'. This again serves as further evidence of Tyndall's commitment to the publication, dissemination and approval of denial from parties headed by him, but still maintained a position of public distance from such material when questioned. As Copsey has noted, the party often promoted denial to appeal to the views of hardliners in the party (mirroring Tyndall's own position vis-à-vis Holocaust denial) but was conscious of the implications of such material when it came to electioneering and the fodder it provided anti-fascist groups (2008: 91–92). The place of conspiracy and denial in the party was also enthusiastically advocated by the new generation of far-right politicians gathering to replace the old guard.

Nick Griffin, who would take the leadership of the BNP from Tyndall in 1999, was an avid advocate of Holocaust denial and anti-Semitic conspiracy theories, publishing widely under Tyndall's leadership on the subject. Griffin's *Who are the Mind Benders?* and an updated edition of Verrall's *Did Six Million Really Die?,* both written in 1997, as well as his post as editor of *The Rune* from 1995, all established his credentials as a Holocaust denier and anti-Semitic conspiracy theorist. Griffin was also willing to publicly and legally associate himself with Holocaust denial. During his trial for inciting racial hatred in 1998, Griffin stated: 'I am well aware that the orthodox opinion is that six million Jews were gassed and cremated and turned into lampshades. Orthodox opinion also once held that the world is flat' (Atkins 2009: 125). By the turn of the century the policy of Holocaust denial and anti-Semitism still remained an integral part of far-right policies, despite the perceived cost to the movement at the ballot box, thus demonstrating the ideological commitment and integral part it played in such views of the world and politics.

However, in 1999 a shift in the presentation of denial became apparent as Nick Griffin became the leader of the BNP, and donned the persona of a 'moderate' and 'moderniser'. Like Chesterton in 1967, he sought to give the BNP a more respectable face. In an article for *The Patriot* in 1999, Griffin stated that the party must present itself to the public with 'an image of moderate reasonableness' but stated that he 'did not intend this movement to lose its way' but that 'when it comes to influencing the public, forget about racial differences, genetics, Zionism and historical revisionism and so on – all ordinary people want to know is that we can do for them what other parties can't or won't'. These words were tempered with the phrase 'of course we must teach the truth to the hardcore'. The explicit reference to historical revisionism and Zionism demonstrated that under Griffin only the outward appearance of the party was to be changed: the ideological core of the party and movement was to remain intact. In other words, the ideological basis of the party, or the 'sub-Mosleyite wackiness of Arnold Leese's Imperial Fascist League' as Griffin dubbed it, remained unchanged and hidden behind the new public propaganda image of a BNP as supporting 'idealistic, unobjectionable, motherhood and apple pie concepts' (*Patriot*, No. 4, 1999).

The shift in public presentation of Holocaust denial can, in part, be explained by the changes that were taking place in relation to the Holocaust in British collective memory. The increasing Holocaust education, television programming, commemoration and Holocaust films, particularly Steven Spielberg's *Schindler's List* released in 1993, had heightened knowledge of the tragedy of the Holocaust in the minds of the public. The narratives of the Holocaust presented in such media and educational programmes, however, tended to be linear, in which the genocide was presented as a smooth and industrial process, in which prejudice and persecution led to the gas chambers of Auschwitz: what historians dubbed the 'straight path' thesis and a staple preoccupation of the now well-worn functionalist versus intentionalist debates of early Holocaust scholarship. This is of particular importance when understanding how far-right deniers have attacked the Holocaust. The more sophisticated and pseudo-academic denials of the Holocaust of the 1970s to the present day have tended to remain locked into dismantling this view of the Holocaust, first as a means by which to engage with the early scholarship of historians and present themselves as 'the other side of the argument' and second because it remains the narrative with which the public are most familiar. The main focus of attack has been Auschwitz itself because, as historian Peter Hayes acknowledges, Auschwitz is 'the capital' of the Holocaust and is 'indelibly linked with all of the multiple dimensions' of the genocide (2003: 331).

The prominent British Holocaust denier and military historian David Irving outlined the attack on Auschwitz as the most important mission for deniers.[3] Speaking at the Institute for Historical Review, and later transcribed in the *Journal for Historical Review* in 1990, Irving stated: 'since 1945 there has been the great battleship Auschwitz! And we have now, at last, the historical profession – above all, the Revisionist historical profession – have found as our own task, the major task: "Sink the Auschwitz!"'. The equation of the professional historians with the 'revisionist historical profession' further serves to underscore the way in which Holocaust deniers seek to align their propaganda and mendacious accounts of the past with legitimate academics and a scholastic framework. David Irving has become the international figure, the media poster child, most associated with Holocaust denial. This was the result of the 2000 *Irving v. Lipstadt and Penguin Books* libel trial, arrests and imprisonment for denial in European courts. Irving attracted considerable attention and support from the British far right in the 2000 libel trial. Irving's view of the Holocaust changed over the years with him first acknowledging that Jews had been exterminated but claiming that Hitler knew nothing of the genocide, while in the late 1980s he changed his position to full denial of the Holocaust after the publication of the *Leuchter Report*.

Nick Griffin was always dismissive of Irving's work and claimed that Irving was 'soft' and that he, rather than Irving, was the 'expert' on Holocaust denial (Trilling 2013: 66). During the 2000 trial, a *Searchlight* correspondent witnessed that a man was putting a note on the press benches that read: 'Irving is a paid agent of political Zionism. This trial is staged. Don't be deceived' (Evans 2002: 204). While not clear who the individual was or what connection, if any, he had to the BNP, the episode demonstrated the absurdity and unbounded elasticity which such a conspiracy could encompass.

The attitudes of Griffin towards his role in denial are significant and are representative of his attempt to ride two horses. On the one hand, he believed that the Holocaust was a 'Holo-Hoax' and was fully committed to the 'hardcore' underpinnings of the movement, however, on the other, he was aware that such views would hold no political traction at the ballot box (Trilling 2013: 67). Simplistic populism was easy: a call to reclaim a historic past that never was; blame of immigrants for job losses or dilution of the amorphous concept of British culture; and the promise of quick fix solutions, whatever the human rights cost. However, the BNP could not occupy the political landscape as a populist right-wing movement because of its residual ideological attachment to Holocaust denial and anti-Semitic conspiracy, the most notable example of which was in 2009 on the BBC *Question Time* programme. While on the show Griffin claimed he did not have a conviction for

Holocaust denial. While it was true in the strictest legal sense that he did not have a conviction for 'Holocaust denial' but for 'publishing or distributing racially inflammatory written material' for his Holocaust denial in *The Rune*, his use of wordplay, however, was not good enough. He claimed he had changed his views but claimed European Law would not allow him to divulge his new views and thus clearly demonstrated that they had not changed, as the laws to which he alluded are confined to outright denial of the Holocaust. His credentials as a denier were beyond doubt. The programme achieved record viewing figures, the highest in the show's history, and despite allegations that Griffin had been 'picked on', demonstrated the far right and neo-Nazi history of the leader and the movement (*The Guardian*, 23 October 2009).

Here was an example of a continued problem that has beset the far right since 1967 and Chesterton's opening NF address: how to keep the ideology of the movement pure and true to its neo-Nazi roots while attracting votes from the public. The bluff of a 'modernising' movement, which is in step with the changing views of society, while secretly remaining true to an immutable ideological trajectory, was easily confounded when the movements were examined under the glare of public scrutiny. Perhaps more politically dangerous are popular right-wing movements that have no rigid dogma and can claim to have learned the lessons of the past and will 'never forget', while still maintaining clandestine backroom allies who promulgate far-right ideologies and Holocaust denial.[4] It is clear that the electoral prospects for a party like the NF, or BNP, were always going to be negligible, and a prospect of such parties forming a government remote when still disseminating and producing Holocaust denial. The fact that such ideas were not jettisoned in hope of improving electoral prospects (even if such ideas were more hidden at times of elections) demonstrates the axiomatic importance of such ideas in holding the movement together. In essence, far-right parties seeking election could not dance to the tune of changed economic, political and social circumstance in Britain without constantly tripping over their jackboots, even when they thought their laces were properly tied.

Denial, revolution and terrorism

There were other individuals and groups on the far right which did not court public opinion and advocated revolution and underground paramilitary action. Holocaust denial in these factions did not require a pseudo-academic framework. Denial was unequivocal as was their worship of Hitler and National Socialist ideology. Holocaust denial in these circles remained unchanged from the initial refutation by men like Alexander Ratcliffe and Arnold Leese (Hobbs 2015: 198). This was primarily due to the unfaltering belief in a Jewish conspiracy, which always stood in for a detailed analysis of the events of the Holocaust. From the late 1950s into the early 1970s these movements tended to crystallise around Colin Jordan. Jordan advocated adherence to the principles of National Socialism and saw this as the means to save Britain from the perceived decline resulting from the loss of empire.

He believed that 'Hitler was right' and that the Second World War had resulted in the victory of world Jewry. Jordan's attitude to the Holocaust should come as no surprise; his staunch defence of a National Socialist reading of the past was at the centre of his worldview. Yet some of his rhetoric is curious when examining his comments on the Holocaust. Convinced the Second World War had been brought about by world Jewry and had resulted in 'the insane fratricidal inter-Aryan war' which had brought down Nazi Germany, Jordan believed that the war had indeed been one of a clash of races but that the reality was that Nordic Aryan races had fought against each other when they should have been united in a fight against Jews and Bolshevism. He stated that such a clash between Aryan peoples 'Never must happen again!'. The echo of Holocaust remembrance ('Never Again' or 'Never Forget') in such a statement illustrates another form of attack on the memory and history of the Holocaust, attempting to appropriate key elements of public memorial of the Holocaust and suffuse them with far-right rhetoric and a mendacious rewriting of the past.

The apex of Jordan's attack on Holocaust memory came in 1993 with the publication of *Merrie England: 2000*, a fictional novel in which Jordan depicts Britain after the millennium. The book is an imagining of a 'White Genocide' in Britain policed by the Ministry of Harmony (see Jackson 2015b: 214). Chapter six of the book, 'the staging of the Holocaust', depicts Holocaust memory reaching ridiculous (and offensive) levels in which a daily memorial service is held, carrier bags and carpets are emblazoned with the words 'Remember Auschwitz' and the death toll of the Holocaust had risen to ten million. While it is clear that Holocaust memorialisation and its significance in British historical memory of the Second World War was increasing, Jordan's notions demonstrate the extremity of his far-right views and denial (Jordan 1993: 34–39). This was not an attempt at pseudo-scholastic denial aimed at providing a cloak of respectably to his views, it was simple propaganda aimed at the lowest common denominator of racist, far-right traveller. The book was designed to be a warning about the impending 'white genocide' in Britain, but the core theme of chapter six reflected the increase in Holocaust memorialisation taking place in Britain, albeit through a rabidly anti-Semitic and distorted lens.

The increasing significance of the Holocaust in public and historical narratives was in part due to its compulsory inclusion on the new national curriculum in England in 1991; and the introduction of the War Crimes Act of the same year (Pearce 2014: 61–65, 181–183). In the book, Jordan explains that it was Jews that had created the society depicted in *Merrie England*; rather than being a covert conspiracy, as Jordan believed was operating in the real world, Jews wore a yellow Star of David to denote their privileged position in society, which gave them priority car parking, access to seats on fully occupied trains and buses, theatres and other public spaces at the expense of non-Jews (Jordan 1993: 37). Jordan furthered his standard trope of Jewish conspiracy in chapter eight of *Merrie England* when he described the Ministry of Harmony in Britain as being a subsidiary of the 'World Council of Harmony in Tel Aviv' that he described as 'Straddling the world in the mantle of Democracy.' The image evoked was the standard equation of Jews and world control with democracy as a vehicle by which power is achieved.

On the face of it, *Merrie England* seems to be a plagiarised parody of George Orwell's 1984 drenched in far-right ideological rhetoric, however on a more practical level the work reflects the way in which Jordan viewed the world in which he lived. The insidious danger contained within the work was not only the attack on Holocaust memory and memorial but also the way in which the work capitalised on a growing feeling of 'political correctness gone mad'. This idea became embodied in a series of high-profile stories in the British tabloids in the mid-to-late 1980s, most notably in the autumn of 1986 when the tabloids carried the headline falsely claiming the nursery rhyme 'Baa Baa Black Sheep' was to be banned in nursery groups by Haringey council. The claim was proved to be false but has since entered into the myriad of urban myths about political correct concepts taken as read (Turner 2013: 417). Jordan was both responding to this news and capitalising on it in the book to gain a grounding and traction with the public and his readers. When the British government banned the publication of *Merrie England* the ban only served to give the piece more legitimacy, a fact noted by Jordan in the dedication about his fight against ZOG (Zionist Occupation Government) (Jordan 1993, dedication). The theme and intent of the book was to frame Jordan's ideology, his supporters and like-minded individuals, as the victims of a world conspiracy that explained why their ideas had no political resonance in mainstream politics. In trying to suffuse their perceived victimhood into the real victimhood of the survivors and victims of the Holocaust, Jordan expressed his frustration at the preserved crisis that neo-Nazis believed was unfolding in Britain (Jackson 2015b: 97). Jordan's views and redemptive anti-Semitism were being suffocated by the history and commemoration of the Holocaust created by increased tolerance and liberal values in society, for which he believed world Jewry was responsible.

Unlike men like Tyndall and Griffin, Jordan was not restricted by the court of public opinion, he made no concession in his view and did not believe that the public could be persuaded of his views. Jordan explained the conspiracy was too deeply embedded in the minds of 'sheepish citizenry' and that only a revolution with the breakdown of 'the society of the old order' could see his ideas and ideology come to fruition (Jordan 2011: 95). Essentially, *Merrie England* may have been a far-right farce and comedy designed to have appeal to the racist minority who feared 'White Genocide' but took little other affirmative action but to vote for far-right parties in elections. The wider purpose was, however, to attract those who would perform acts of murder and terrorism to ensure that power was achieved and the perceived conspiracy by Jews dismantled with murder, genocide and ethnic cleansing being the chosen weapons. How this revolution would take place was the main theme of Jordan's next fictional work, *The Uprising* (2004), which tells the story of the British Freedom Force (BFF) which seeks far-right 'poetic justice' on a range of Jordan's enemies and individuals who have committed crimes against racial purity with the BFF finally creating a 'national reawakening' of the British peoples' 'true' national consciousness (see Jackson 2015b: 97–104). Jordan's Holocaust denial and appropriation of a 'victim' status for his views were not designed to convince the public of the need to vote for change or win people over with 'motherhood and apple pie' concepts, it was a call to arms. As such Jordan's Holocaust denial did not need the cloak of pseudo-academic respectability, rather, it was exposed for all to see: raw, intolerant, racist and mocking of both victims and survivors. This was the rhetoric by which he would attract like-minded individuals who would have no qualms with violent revolution and terrorism.

Conclusion

The presence of Holocaust denial in the far right did not begin in 1967 with the formation of the NF. The roots of the denial of the genocide of European Jewry were asserted while the Nazis were still killing the innocent in 1942 and emerged from the conspiracy that international Jewry had clandestine control of the world (Hobbs 2016). The enshrined metanarrative of a Jewish conspiracy in far-right ideology remained, and continues to remain, the epistemological filter through which all information and explanation of the world were filtered. Holocaust denial is one part of the conspiracy. While Holocaust denial provides a means to whitewash the history of the Third Reich and genocide to appeal to the public for votes, this function is only minimal. In fact, as the above chapter has shown, the presence of denial acts as a political repellent to the public, constantly serving to remind voters of the underlying neo-Nazi principles at the core of far-right parties and movements. That denial was never jettisoned from such parties or movements demonstrates its underlying value to far-right thought. As stated at the start of this chapter, those who deny the Holocaust are not mad or stupid, rather they have developed an effective epistemological position which explains their own failures and refusal to understand a changing world: it is not that they are wrong or their political ideology unpopular (Hitler's success is frequently invoked to prove this), it is that all their actions and all-embracing philosophy are constantly subverted by an effective and ruthless enemy bent on keeping them out of power – International Jewry.

As the opening quote by Russell indicates, to understand this line of thinking we must also look to how this came to *seem* to be true. As explained above, there can be no denying that an increased historical awareness of the Holocaust has become part of British culture and school education. The increasing memorialisation of the Holocaust, from a far-right perspective, is evidence of the Jewish conspiracy at work. Holocaust denial became increasingly necessary in British far-right movements to demonstrate the way in which 'alien' elements had entered national collective memory that benefited liberal values; underpinned democratic ideals of equality and tolerance; and ensured that such an event never happened again and was never forgotten. Increased Holocaust memorialisation, education and remembrance do not create more deniers and the institutions, which support such events, do much to educate the public about the atrocities and genocide committed by the Nazis. However, at times, the narratives that they present tend to crystallise the linear history attacked by deniers and use the Holocaust for pedagogical means which are often at odds which the true motivations and forces which drove the Holocaust.[5] The increased presence of the Holocaust in British national historical narratives and commemoration served to convince the far right of their belief in an all-encompassing conspiracy, but it also increased an internalised and institution-alised sense of victimhood within the movement, most clearly evidenced in Jordan's *Merrie England* and Tyndall's *The Eleventh Hour*; both works absorbed a sense of vic-timhood and oppression which were being expressed in the commemorative nar-ratives of the Holocaust. This was not just denial but also an attempt to hijack the label of 'victim' to foster sympathy because their views and ideologies were being repressed and vilified. It was a curious result of the dominant liberal narratives in Britain. Invoking the narrative of 'victim' or a potential 'white Genocide' in order to appeal to new supporters' far-right ideologies and solutions meant that the real victims of genocide and their suffering became marginalised.

Holocaust denial in Britain since 1967 remained an integral part of the appa-ratus that underpinned the epistemological grand narrative of a Jewish conspiracy that prevented far-right victory and their vision of British 'national renewal' and 'awakening'. Contained within this thinking was the redemptive and genocidal anti-Semitism that contributed to the Holocaust itself. While the core notion of a conspiracy being at work and the claim that the Holocaust had not taken place never changed, the presentation and dissemination of that message evolved in line with shifting social and cultural imperatives in British society; increased academic research on the Holocaust; and amplified institutionalised commemoration and education of the Holocaust. Rather than retire Holocaust denial and conspiracy from far-right ideology in order to achieve power, the pervasive power of a nar-rative of conspiracy became more important and entrenched. For British far-right movements, Holocaust denial and conspiracy was the way to unify like-minded individuals; its continued presence remained an important totem to signify its radical agenda and opposition to an imagined Jewish conspiracy. This obviously absurd view came to seem to be true because without it the realities of what such an ideological view resulted in during the first half of the twentieth century is all too apparent: failure, defeat, and genocide are not easy to explain or justify; anti-intellectualism, playing the victim, blaming imaginary enemies and denial are an ideologically expedient safeguard. Such trajectories remain impervious to reason and bestow in the believer a sense of purpose and conviction that only they know '*the* truth'. It is this belief that has remained at the core of British far-right ideology and Holocaust denial; it is the perfect maelstrom of hate, intolerance and genocidal intent that is both self-sustaining and resilient to the truth.

Notes

1   The title of this chapter is adapted from Ray Hill's (and A. Bell's) chapter of the same name in *The Other Face of Terror* (1988).
2   Along with Richard Harwood (Richard Verrall) McLaughlin contributed to the 'Historical Fact' series. McLaughlin wrote issue number three, *For Those Who Cannot*

Speak. The pamphlet sought to claim that Allied war crimes were worse than German war crimes. Issue number one was a republication of Verrall's 1974 *Did Six Million Really Die?* Issue number two was another Verrall authored publication entitled *Nuremberg and Other War Crimes Trials* which erroneously claimed that the Nuremberg trial was controlled and run by Jews.

3   Irving was judged to be a military historian at the 2000 *Irving v. Lipstadt and Penguin Books* trial in the verdict given by Mr Justice Grey. See www.hdot.org/en/trial/judgement/13–4.html.

4   Here I am referring to movements like the United Kingdom Independence Party in which Nigel Farage could publicly commemorate Holocaust Memorial day while keeping his alliance in the European Parliament with known exponents and sympathisers of denial. See https://twitter.com/nigel_farage/status/560007021316276224 and www.telegraph.co.uk/news/politics/ukip/11177724/Will-anyone-in-Ukip-condemn-Farages-despicable-new-EU-alliance.html.

5   Concerns about Holocaust commemoration and education have become a trend in the recent historiography of Britain and the representations of the Holocaust and genocide constructed in society. (For discussion see Stone 2013: 212–231; Cesarani 2015: xxv–xxxi.)

References

Atkins, S. E. (2009) *Holocaust denial as an international movement*. Santa Barbara, CA: Greenwood Publishing Group.

Cesarani, D. (2015) *Final solution: The fate of the Jews 1933–1949*. Basingstoke: Macmillan.

Copsey, N. (2008) *Contemporary British fascism: The British National Party and the quest for legitimacy*. 2nd edn. Basingstoke: Palgrave Macmillan.

Durham, M. (1996) 'The British Extreme Right and the problem of political space 1967–1983', in Cronin, M. (ed.) *The failure of British fascism: The far right and the fight for political recognition*. London: St. Martin's Press.

Evans, R. J. (2002) *Telling lies about Hitler: The Holocaust, history and the David Irving trial*. London: Verso Books.

Hayes, P. (2003) 'Auschwitz, capital of the Holocaust', *Holocaust and Genocide Studies*, 17, 330–350.

Hill, R. and Bell, A. (1988) *The other face of terror*. London: Grafton.

Hillman, N. (2001) 'Tell me chum, in case I got it wrong. What was it we were fighting during the War? The re-emergence of British Fascism, 1945–58', *Contemporary British History*, 15 (4), 1–34.

Hobbs, M. (2015) 'Writing "history" for Hitler: Holocaust denial since 1945', in Carmichael, C. and Maguire, R. C. (eds.) *The Routledge history of genocide*. London: Routledge, pp. 196–206.

Hobbs, M. (2016) 'Alexander Ratcliffe: British Holocaust denial in embryo', in Behrens, P., Jensen, O. and Terry, N. (eds.) *Holocaust and genocide denial: A Contextual perspective*. Devon: Routledge, pp. 9–27.

Holmila, A. (2011) *Framing genocide: The holocaust in the British, Swedish and Finnish press, 1945–50*. Houndmills, Basingstoke: Palgrave Macmillan.

Jackson, P. (2015a) '"White Genocide": Postwar Fascism and the ideological value of evoking existential conflicts', in Carmichael, C. and Maguire, R. C. (eds.) *The Routledge history of genocide*. London: Routledge, pp. 196–206.

Jackson, P. (2015b) 'British Neo-Nazi fiction: Colin Jordan's Merrie England – 2000 and The Uprising', in Copsey, N. and Richardson, J. E. (eds.) *Cultures of post-war British fascism*. Abingdon: Routledge, pp. 86–107.

Jordan, C. (1993) *Merrie England*. Harrogate: Gothic Ripples.

Jordan, C. (2004) *The uprising*. Milwaukee, WI: NS Publications.

Jordan, C. (2011) *National socialism vanguard of the future – selected writings of Colin Jordan*. Gresham Publishing.

Lyotard, J.-F. (1989) *The differend: Phrases in dispute*. Manchester: Manchester University Press.

Orwell, G. (2000) *George Orwell* (Penguin modern classics). London: Penguin Classics.

Paxton, R. O. (2005) *The anatomy of fascism*. London: Penguin Books.

Pearce, A. (2014) *Holocaust consciousness in contemporary Britain*. London: Routledge.

Russell, B. (2008) *History of Western philosophy*. New York: Touchstone Books.

Stone, D. (2013) 'From Stockholm to Stockton: The Holocaust and/as heritage in Britain', in Sharples, C. and Jensen, O. (eds.) *Britain and the Holocaust: Remembering and representing war and genocide*. New York: Palgrave Macmillan, pp. 212–229.

Thurlow, R. C. (1998) *Fascism in Britain: From Oswald Mosley's blackshirts to the national front*. London: I.B. Tauris.

Trilling, D. (2013) *Bloody nasty people: The rise of Britain's far right*. 2nd edn. London: Verso Books.

Turner, A. W. (2013) *Rejoice! Rejoice! Britain in the 1980s*. London: Aurum Press.

Tyndall, J. (1988) *The eleventh hour: A call for British rebirth*. London: Albion Press.

Walker, M. (1977) *The national front*. 2nd edn. London: HarperCollins Publishers.

Far-right periodicals

Candour
Spearhead
Journal of Historical Review
Patriot

2

THE NATIONAL SOCIALIST GROUP

A case study in the *groupuscular* right

Daniel Jones and Paul Jackson

Introduction

The history of the extreme right in Britain is littered with hundreds of tiny organisations, or *groupuscules*, that never grow beyond a small band of enthusiastic members setting out their aims and aspirations, before wider forces, or their own internecine disputes, stymie their chances of 'making it'. Among academics interested in the history of Britain's extreme right, there has been relatively little effort to date to study these tiny organisations, which usually operate on the smallest of scales. Aside from articles in magazines from anti-fascist groups such as *Searchlight*, many of these *groupuscules* have been forgotten. Nevertheless, despite their activity usually having little-to-no practical impact, they ought not to be simply excised from the historical record. Though easy to miss, they operate as a sort of 'dark matter' within extreme-right activism, taking up the energies of the devoted, as well as contributing to collective efforts that sustain the clandestine culture of the extreme right's cultic milieu. When these difficult to study *groupuscules* are better understood, the overarching structure of the British extreme right becomes clearer and more defined. This chapter will focus on one such ostensibly insignificant, clandestine, short-lived *groupuscule*, the National Socialist Group (NSG), placing it in a wider context. It analyses the NSG's aims, aspirations, and (albeit very limited) activity. While focusing on only one group, large or small, is restrictive, this type of close scrutiny also allows for an understanding of the impact it has on other, related elements within the extreme right. As well as plotting the NSG's links to other organisations, what follows will also try to unpick the inner dynamics of the NSG, which aimed to operate as both a cultural movement, carrying the flame for Nazi ideology in a hostile environment, while also aspiring to become a paramilitary outfit fostering delusions that it could be capable of ushering in a revolution.

Some key terms for analysis

The National Socialist Group was obviously a Nazi-inspired entity, and clearly wanted to be known as such to people who encountered it. Its name alone exemplifies the ideology it promoted. Debates about what constitutes neo-Nazism remain complex. However, for the purposes of this chapter, neo-Nazism will be considered as a sub-variant of the wider phenomenon of fascism, as the term has been defined by historians such as Roger Griffin (1991), Roger Eatwell (1995) and George Mosse (1999), among others. This approach styles fascism as an ideology driven by a quest to regenerate a modern society though an anti-liberal and revolutionary agenda. Forms of fascism are often steeped in a mythic understanding of the higher nature of race and the nation. In particular, Griffin's term 'palingenesis', a synonym for rebirth, evokes the mythic as well as the quest for an elemental sense of regeneration found within fascist cultures. Neo-Nazism can be seen as a variant of fascism, specifically one that is rooted in recalibrating the ideals of the Nazi regime, and seeks to make them relevant to social and political contexts that have developed since the fall to the Third Reich in 1945 (Jackson 2017). Like other fascisms, neo-Nazism possesses a mythic quest, an essential driving energy, a quality that is crucial to explore when examining how small *groupuscules* such as the NSG were able to sustain themselves. This approach of seeing neo-Nazism as a type of fascism points to some interesting research questions, especially linked to how a culture espousing rebirth, through a reformulated National Socialism, was kindled within the NSG; the ways this ideological culture informed and influenced the activities of the group; and how it militated against a dominant liberal culture that it radically rejected.

While neo-Nazism can be seen as a type of fascism, it is important to note that unlike fascism's earlier forms, neo-Nazi groups only ever operate at the edges of a modern society – and in a country like Britain, neo-Nazi organisations are never likely to be more than fringe phenomena. Analysts such as Jeffrey Bale (2002), Bonnie Burstow (2003), and Fabian Virchow (2004) have drawn on the terms *groupuscule* (small group) and *groupuscular* (network of small groups) to help describe and explore such marginalised forms of neo-Nazism. Griffin (2003), too, highlights that the marginalised, and so *groupuscular*, nature of post-1945 extreme right is a situation forced upon such political extremists as a consequence of the robust liberal and democratic environments that phenomena such as neo-Nazism have to operate within after 1945. Meanwhile, Bale stresses that the *groupuscular* extreme right possesses an ever-changing dynamic, and should not be considered static, and so stresses the need to explore its changing dynamics. Debates over the *groupuscular* nature of the extreme right also emphasise that, while individual *groupuscules* (such as the NSG) may well lack a large-scale presence and have a limited impact, the overarching dynamic does lend them several advantages. For example, Virchow claims it allows a variegated political milieu to be developed by a competing set of organisations, thereby offering those attracted to a general agenda a range of choices, generated by several rival groups. These can cater for different audiences too. Moreover, Bale stresses that different *groupuscules* can develop distinct areas of specialism, some styling themselves more akin to think tanks, others as paramilitary outfits, and others still as political parties. In sum, focusing on the *groupuscular* nature of the extreme right leads to questions over how one group waxes and wanes while others grow, and how relationships between groups develop, to foster an ever-shifting dynamic.

The debates linked to *groupuscularity* of the extreme right also highlight that, while marginalised, such fascist groups tend to develop complex subcultures that sustain their alternative visions for the world. One term that has developed in recent years among analysts, especially those concerned with more marginalized forms of fascism is 'cultic milieu', drawing on the concept as defined by Colin Campbell (Kaplan and Lööw 2002). For Campbell, the cultic milieu is an environment radially opposed to mainstream perspectives, steeped in ideas and philosophies that offer an alternative way of seeing the world, and usually drawing out in its adherents a sense of 'seekership', or mission, and a belief in something 'higher'. While not all elements of the cultic milieu are neo-Nazi, the term is valuable for conceptualising the dynamics of many neo-Nazi cultures. As with others who engage with the cultic milieu, neo-Nazi perspectives are inherently at odds with the political and cultural mainstream, while their hardened activists at least do tend to believe in the superior ideas supposedly offered by Hitler's politics. Moreover, it leads to enquiry into the elements of faith, and the ritualistic, often found in neo-Nazi environments.

Finally, neo-Nazi cultures that foster a cultic, *groupuscular* dynamic have become quite transnational in their activity as well. This is another element of the study of the extreme right that is increasingly being recognised as significant, moving away from a viewpoint that only tended to consider the extreme right as operating on a national scale. Historians of fascism, including Martin Durham and Margret Power (2010), Andrea Mammone (2015), Graham Macklin (2012), and Matteo Albanese and Pablo del Hierro (2016), have all contributed to these debates in recent times. The basic drivers of transnational endeavours for neo-Nazi groups include: helping to foster a wider impact through engagement with partner organisations in other countries; the sharing of ideas, including publications, and a general sense of camaraderie; and ultimately sustaining helping the illusion of a magnified sense of importance. Since 1945, British neo-Nazis have often been at the centre of such transnational activism (Jackson and Shekhovtsov 2014).

Drawing on the language discussed in this opening section, the rest of the chapter will examine just one British neo-Nazi *groupuscule* that was founded in 1968 and wound up in 1969: the National Socialist Group. It will analyse how it emerged and developed a unique identity within the wider context of extreme-right organisations in late 1960s Britain. It will also highlight that the NSG itself was actually a collection of micro organisations, and so had its own internal *groupuscular* dynamic. It will draw out the NSG's efforts to foster a cultic milieu, a central element of how it offered adherents a sense of meaning and purpose to their activity. Its literature often identified the NSG as a National Socialist cultural group as well as a political one with the overall aim of fostering an alternative way of life. It will set the NSG in a wider, international context, highlighting that, though consisting of merely a handful of activists, it attempted to locate itself within a transnational neo-Nazi network that had developed by the end of the 1960s. Finally, it will briefly examine the activities of some of the group's leading figures after the NSG was wound up at the end of 1969.

Establishing the National Socialist Group

The National Socialist Group appears to have begun as an initiative led by David Courtney. He had already accrued a profile as a neo-Nazi activist in Britain via his activism for Colin Jordan's National Socialist Movement, itself formed in 1962 and wound up in 1968 after Jordan was released from a period in prison. To summarise, in the spring of 1968 Jordan reconfigured his political identity, and sought to publicly distance himself from open neo-Nazism, creating a space for a new, openly neo-Nazi group to form. As Jordan changed the name of his National Socialist Movement (NSM) to the British Movement (BM), he also detached it from the international network of neo-Nazis he had helped to found in 1962, the World Union of National Socialists (WUNS). Despite wanting to formally dissociate himself from neo-Nazism, Jordan did seek to maintain a degree of influence over Britain's neo-Nazi milieu. Therefore, while he was reformulating his own political organisation, he also encouraged an organiser of the Greenwich branch of the NSM, a bank worker called David Courtney, to develop a parallel clandestine Nazi group.

How do we date its formation? The first directive issued by the NSG from 1968 stated the group was founded on 26 May of 'Year of the Führer, 79'. This document explained the aim of the organisation was to provide unity for disparate National Socialists across the country, adding 'we exhort every one of the now disorganised, and often undisciplined, members of National Socialists in Great Britain today to join the Group', and added that it had 'laid down the foundations for the continuance of our struggle'. This document also boasted that the organisation had funds to acquire land to develop a new national headquarters, and would offer a variety of 'academic' cultural activities, such as lectures. Finally, a paragraph length quote from *Mein Kampf* made clear that the 'only one right that is sacrosanct' was the preservation of racial purity (National Socialist Group 1968). Another document issued around this time listed ten points that explained the methods and intentions of the NSG. This clarified that full membership would follow from a probationary period, while the group would develop a 'system of co-operates' to allow wider support from 'non-member sympathisers'. Membership would incur a financial commitment (elsewhere initially set as 2/6 per week), though this would be paid to a variety of accounts to support specific projects. All members were expected to show leadership potential, in preparation for the coming 'racial and cultural awakening' that the movement was trying to foster. 'The positive political, cultural and social aspects of National Socialist doctrine' were of course to be promoted, though members were also expected to display 'a certain degree of flexibility' and adapt to changing circumstances (National Socialist Group 1968a).

A second directive, signed by Simon Gifford (a pseudonym used by Courtney), expanded further on the NSG's idealisation of Hitler. It explained that the British population had been betrayed by the defeat of the Nazi regime in 1945, and that this was a victory for an old elite, who by the 1960s had been joined by a 'new "aristocracy" of pop singers, book-makers and the exploiters in our financial system', deemed responsible for 'alien immigration resulting in race mixing'. Good National Socialists primarily sought to direct their hate towards 'the evil influences that have caused the degenerate system' and support the regeneration of 'our Aryan population'. As the movement viewed the entire democratic system as degenerate, a truly revolutionary organisation such as the NSG needed to cultivate genuine 'men of action' who were 'prepared for sacrifice' (Gifford 1968). Around this time, the NSG also created a document headed 'Security Directive', which it often sent out to recruits. This complained of the ways security had been dealt with by previous groups. Moreover, this articulated the way the group believed it faced a stark threat from the state, explaining that when 'we are found to pose a threat to the existing system … our adversaries, will stop at nothing to destroy us'. However, apart from articulating such paranoia, this document contained no details on how security would be developed by the new group. From other documents, it is clear that this included giving members false or abbreviated names, code numbers, the burning of correspondence and the use of anonymised postal boxes with no overtly neo-Nazi names or branding on the outside of letters, amongst other procedures (National Socialist Group 1968b). Though its literature explained that all of this was to be taken very seriously, it is somewhat ironic that it is possible to understand such security operations from the constant failures of members to adhere to them, including reprimands sent to correct them. The openly stated defiance of some members also underscored the limited control its leadership had in this regard.

In its early months, the NSG claimed it sought co-operative relationships with other organisations. In particular, this can be seen with the emergent British Movement, led by Colin Jordan. Jordan founded the British Movement in 1968 as a replacement for his National Socialist Movement. The change of name indicated Jordan's own move away from overt Nazism, yet inwardly he still manifested sympathies for Nazi ideology – clearly demonstrated by his ongoing interest in Courtney's new venture. In a letter to Courtney on 9 June 1968, when the NSG was still quite embryonic, Jordan explained that there were two options open to him. First, he could simply join the British Movement and retain his old NSM organisational position; or second, he could develop a separate, cultural organisation to promote National Socialism overtly. At this point, Jordan was even unclear on keeping the latter group distinct, and so suggested Courtney could be both a member of the British Movement and promote a neo-Nazi cultural group. As he continued, 'if you prefer to remain outside British Movement in order to concentrate on this group, my attitude will be no less agreeable', adding

> it will … be a very good thing for some such overtly National Socialist body to come into existence, having its lines of contact in one way or another with British Movement, so that suitable people can be drawn together in an inner circle or core, on the higher levels of ideology.
>
> *(Jordan 1968)*

The relationship between the BM and the NSG was blurred from the outset.

Jordan remained in communication with Courtney as the NSG developed throughout 1968 too. In July he arranged a meeting with Courtney in London, one of many, even offering to phone him at work using the pseudonym 'Roger McDermott' to 'avoid any embarrassment to you' (Jordan 1968a). In August, another letter to Courtney highlights the way Jordan sought to pass on his role as the British leader within the World Union of National Socialists to Courtney, explaining that Matt Koehl of the WUNS would contact Courtney directly to develop a relationship where the NSG would become the British representative of the WUNS (Jordan 1968b). Jordan also passed over some of his other international contacts to make them aware of the NSG. In December, he wrote a letter to Otto Munkwitz, an associate of Einer Aberg who was based in Sweden, explaining that, as a consequence of the 'new Race Relations Law in this country', his own NSM has been replaced by the British Movement; and added that Munkwitz should contact the NSG in London and gave an address to establish this link. A letter from November 1968 documents that Jordan passed on old NSM 'Red Ali' leaflets, which basically attacked Tariq Ali, to Courtney. Another letter from December informed Courtney of an upcoming British Movement event in Birmingham, on 26 January. It asked Courtney to advertise the event to NSG members, and even asked if some would act as stewards (Jordan 1968c). While Jordan wanted to publicly distance himself from Courtney's activities, such letters show he clearly supported the development of the NSG.

Fostering the new movement

Ambitions for creating a new neo-Nazi centre seem to have been at the heart of the group by the summer of 1968. Some anti-fascist monitoring of the extreme right in this period included running moles in such extreme-right groups. One set of anonymous reports, now in the *Searchlight* Archive collection, sketch out a picture of these ambitions. These anonymous reports were written by activists who infiltrated the group and reported back, yet their identities are now unknown. One such report dated 1 September 1968 explains how the NSG aspired to develop a national network, described as a 'sort of Nazi mafia', which would be divided into nine units across the country along a paramilitary structure. It also explained how in September 1968 the group sought to acquire land in Kent, near to Charterhouse, where they hoped to build their centre for Nazi activism, which would be above ground and public. Here were planned 'barracks, lecture hall, drill grounds and offices', all of which were modelled on the headquarters of the American Nazi Party in Arlington, Virginia. The report explained that one of the NSG activists, Kieron Woods, had recently visited America and received the blessing of the Koehl in this venture. It also explained that, later in September 1968, the group was planning to run a Nazi camp in Scotland where they hoped to 'have lectures, hikes and combat training' (Unknown Infiltrator 1968). Following on from this, another anonymous report by an anti-fascist infiltrator, dated 24 October, explained that by this time the NSG had attracted the interest of Special Branch. Events, such as the camp in Scotland that had taken place in September 1968, had become a cause for concern. The scale of the group still seemed tiny, though it was noted that there was a growth in activity outside London, 'from the North and West Country', suggestive of it piquing the interest of other pockets of neo-Nazi activism around the country (Unknown Infiltrator 1968a).

The group also recruited new members in the autumn of 1968, and the *Searchlight* Archive contains 17 membership application forms dated from August 1968 to January 1969. While this does not include all members, these do at least offer a cross-section of supporters. These forms asked for basic data, such as contact details, age, height, nationality and occupation, and also had more detailed sections where applicants needed to explain their military experience, and the capacity in which they could contribute to the organisation. Ten of these applications were from those who described their nationality as English or British, one was of dual German and British nationality, and six more were not British. This included French, Swiss, South African and German nationals. Leading figure within the WUNS, Bruno Luedke, was among the German members. Fifteen of these applications were from men, and a further two from women. The age range was varied too: the oldest was born in 1916, the youngest in 1950. In terms of describing what types of contribution could be made, responses were varied. One simply read 'IN ANY WAY POSSIBLE', while others talked of the need to create a large, well-known organisation. One commented in French, and expressed the need to create a permanent centre, perhaps in France, and to eliminate 'LES PARASÍTES' from the movement, 'ENSUITE FORMER UNE MELICE DE SÉCURITÉ'. Within this collection is also material with a rudimentary sketch of explosives and a detonator. Such data does not capture all the members of the group, but certainly gives a picture of the variegated makeup of those interested in the NSG (Various 1968–1969).

More details on attitudes among those attracted to the NSG can be drawn from the letters interested parties sent at this time. One letter, dated 31 October 1968, came from a Mr S. Griffiths in Chichester. Griffiths explained how he had wanted to join Jordan's old National Socialist Movement, and had written to Jordan, who in turn sent him a letter explaining the nature of the new British Movement, and also gave an address for the NSG. Griffiths felt that the British Movement was less appealing because he wanted to join a group akin to old Jordan's defunct NSM that was overtly neo-Nazi (Griffiths 1968). A similar letter, dated 13 November, from J. H. Nickolls again explained that Jordan had passed on contact details. It added

> I am a member of both N.F. and B.M. and do a certain amount of work for them both … all movements of the "right" should refrain from attacking each other and on certain occasions act in unison against the Red, coloured and jewish oposition [sic].
>
> *(Nickolls 1968)*

Letters exchanged also highlight that the NSG had some language skills, as some were written in French, and were replied to in French as well. Other letters highlight the ways the NSG could be seen as something fresh by veteran figures within the extreme right. One, from K. L. Wood, explained that he was 64 and nearing retirement. Wood added he had been active in the British Fascists and the BUF before the Second World War, that he had been interned under Defence Regulation 18B, and after 1945 had supported both Oswald Mosley and Arnold Leese (Wood 1968).

Other letters from new recruits show efforts to acquire land were sustained. A letter dated 14 November 1968 from a member given the codename N.23-A (who it seems was actually called Lindsay Hodge based in Dundee, Scotland) suggested the movement should advertise in farming newspapers, as any previous effort at 'contacting the various county authorities seems to have drawn a blank' (Hodge 1968). Another letter shows that Hodge had been in contact with Perth County Council to inquire into gaining some unused heathland to set up a 'sports training camp'. A later letter informed Gifford that an advert for land had been placed, and added that Hodge intended to join the Territorial Army (Hodge 1968a). Another letter to Courtney, dated 2 January 1969, continued the story. Signed by a member designated A.10.2, it both commented on Directive 4 that had been issued by this time, and explained that both the author and Hodge, who it transpired were related somehow, were continuing to pursue land acquisition in Scotland, but with no further developments to report. 'Any land that has been offered', it added, 'has been a ridiculous price'. Curiously, this letter noted that Bruno Lüdke had come to stay with Courtney that 'Yuletide' (A.10.2, 1969).

Letters documenting the quest for the headquarters continued into 1969. On 20 January 1969, Hodge wrote to the County Council of Angus, to enquire into schools that could be used by the movement, and on 13 February was told none were available. Another, letter responding to Hodge's enquiry, this time from Aberdeen County Council, was more helpful though. It stated that one disused school building was available for hire in Towie, which was 35 miles from Aberdeen. The annual rent for the School alone was £18 and for the attached schoolhouse £33 (Aberdeen County Council n.d.; County Council of Angus 1969). However, these were prices that would likely be off-putting for the poorly resourced NSG, and there is no evidence that they took this any further.

These letters help to reveal the ways the group's obsession with security, including the use of pseudonyms, led to problems. One letter, from Karl Wallace dated 30

September 1968, explained why the group initially appealed. Wallace had attended a meeting run by Colin Jordan on 27 September, and he felt that the politics Jordan now promoted had become too close to that of the National Front, and also was disappointed by the lacklustre response from Jordan's followers to an attempt by anti-fascists to disrupt the event. Interestingly, the letter was addressed to 'Mr. Gifford', while Wallace mentioned that 'Mr. Courtney' had recommended the NSG. Clearly, Wallace was unaware Gifford was also Courtney (Wallace 1968). A later letter from Wallace, addressed to 'Dave', that is, David Courtney, dated 'Year of the Führer 80', so after March 1969, suggested Wallace had lost patience with the NSG. 'The most disturbing fact to me', it explained, 'is that you seem to just see a National Socialist "mini" state in an H.Q. in Kent or Scotland, this to me is a very negative attitude, if ever a country need the cleansing action of National Socialism its Britain today'. The letter also went on to criticise the leadership in the NSG by 1969, noting with bemusement that no-one in his network had ever actually met Simon Gifford, and concluded that the 'Führer or his closest supporters never hid from the supporters' (Wallace 1969). In other words, the NSG's obsession with pseudonyms and secrecy could foster distrust, and could become counterproductive.

Meanwhile, later Directive documents, such as that noted by member A.10.2 produced by the NSG, also help to paint a picture of the struggling group. Directive 4, undated but seemingly written in December 1968, commented on aims for the coming year. This again reiterated the ideal of developing the group as an internationally recognised headquarters for neo-Nazism in Britain. It also claimed the group had attracted a strong nucleus of members, and noted positively the interest from European activists. Again, a quote from Hitler formed part of the Directive, here in the form of a passage on developing propaganda (National Socialist Group 1968c). Contrasting with this positivity though, Directive 5 was far less complimentary on the types of people the NSG found itself recruiting. It noted that one major problem when creating a Nazi-inspired group was 'the alarming number of sadists, perverts, social misfits, bigoted racialists and chronic psychopaths with the "jackboot and whip complex"' they attracted, many of whom, apparently, were also secretly Jewish. Here, leading lights of American neo-Nazism, especially the late George Lincoln Rockwell and Koehl, were praised again, underscoring the central influence of the American Nazi Party, by this time renamed as the National Socialist White People's Party, on these British-based neo-Nazis (National Socialist Group 1969).

Finally, a subsequent Directive 6 once again commented critically on members of the NSG, especially those who did not seem to be fully committed to the cause and were becoming sympathetic to other groups. This undated directive also talked of a recent purge of 'revisionists', again suggesting a fragmented group. More positively, it proclaimed that a new magazine would be published soon, *Phoenix*, and even included a reproduction of its front cover. Unsurprisingly, it featured an idealised image of Adolf Hitler. To publish *Phoenix*, it stated, the group needed to find £90, and members were instructed to contact 'Unterleader D. Mudie' and 'lend' some money to contribute to this cost. A complete edition of *Phoenix* never appeared (National Socialist Group n.d.). The fate of this publication epitomises the sense of dashed hopes in reviving Hitler's legacy that drove its activism. This also raises the question, who was 'Unterleader D. Mudie'?

Groupuscules within groupuscules

So far, it is clear that the NSG was a tiny group, though with grand aspirations. Moreover, its directives certainly claimed it sought to bring unity to British neo-Nazis across the country. Though it remained small-scale, the NSG was able to foster a wider network. This can be seen from the activities developed by one of its supposed nine branches that left extensive documentation: a group based in Cleethorpes, which became Area 5 of the NSG in March 1969. This group was active beforehand as an unaffiliated, neo-Nazi *groupuscule*. Its animating figure was Donald Mudie, and in a clear nod to Norse mythology, his pre-existing group operated under the name the Noble Order Knights of the Volsung.

Before it affiliated with the NSG, Mudie's Noble Order Knights of the Volsung group had been engaged in a series of ritualistic activities that appear to have helped cement their Nazi-inspired beliefs. For example, some of the earliest documents in the *Searchlight* Archive linked to this grouping show that on the 4 March 1968, 'Volsung Officer' Donald Mudie married Pearl Barnes in the company of other Volsung officers. In a ritual steeped in a neo-Nazi cultic milieu, they signed documents that remain marked by a ritualised mixing of blood, wine and charcoal that occurred at this ceremony. This was not the only ritual of this type. On 9 April 1968, Pearl Mudie was promoted to a 'Lady Officer' of the group, and again the documents in the *Searchlight* Archive are stained with blood. Yet another blood-stained document promoted Donald Mudie to a new rank, which read:

> Bear Witness, ye all.
>
> Before a lawful Swastika and in front of lawful witnesses, night Captain Donald P. Mudie was this early hour of 13 June, 1968, elevated to the rank of Major Captain, Knight Headquarters England, Noble Order Knights of the Volsung. Due National Socialist Ceremonies were performed. A General Salute (vide Horst Wessel) was also celebrated afore a duly appointed Nordic Altar.
>
> *(Knights of the Volsung 1968)*

Notably, these ceremonies echoed the wedding of Colin Jordan to Françoise Dior in 1963, which also featured the mingling of blood and engagement with Norse mythic themes. Again reminiscent of Jordan, these documents were steeped in a language of preserving an England seen as part of a Northern European racial culture that required defending.

Subsequent letters linked to Mudie reveal some interesting ambitions. For example, in November he wrote about his desire to stand for his local borough council as a committed Nazi in local elections in May 1969 (Mudie 1968). Contact with

Courtney's NSG came in February 1969, when Mudie wrote to the NSG explaining he led a small group of committed National Socialists based in Cleethorpes. He boasted that he had made the locality aware of their political identities, and claimed they were even starting to convince some people in the area of the correctness of National Socialist principles. While making contact in this way, he reiterated their aspiration of putting an openly Nazi candidate for local elections in May 1969. Shortly after, someone from the London-based NSG telephoned Mudie and arranged to send a small NSG delegation to Cleethorpes, to inspect their activities (Mudie et al. 1969). Here Mudie also set out some of the core elements of his own *groupuscule*, the Noble Order Knights of the Volsung:

> On our private properties we wear the Brown uniform of the old S.A., jackboots etc. Under our standards, we hold a weekly Grosser Zapfenstreich – the age-old North European Lights Out, after which, under the flag pole in my garden, we hold a military style torchlight procession, our battle flag festooned under a black and gold Hakenkreuz and Hochadler.
>
> *(Mudie, n.d.)*

For those outside their neo-Nazi cultic milieu at least, the absurd juxtaposition of boasting, seriousness of intent and ritualised politics, set against its clearly microscopic scale – all this being carried out in a back garden in Cleethorpes suburbia – shine through in such statements. However, for the NSG, ever looking to add to its support base, dedicated pro-Nazi activists of this type were certainly people to be cultivated.

Another letter, sent before the start of March, explained the NSG's position on several key matters. It stated that Mudie's ambition to stand for election was described as 'foolhardy and untimely'. It also explained that Mudie's idealisation of bringing together all right-wing parties was also out of keeping with NSG policy, which saw itself as superior to larger groups of the period:

> We only accept National Socialism and the Swastika … We look on the National Front in the same way as our American comrades look on George Wallace, and in the same way our German comrades look on the N.D.P. – They are government sponsored, or at least government tolerated … not true revolutionaries.

It added more details on the NSG's international links with activists in France, Germany, Spain, Italy, South Africa, New Zealand and Mexico (Hansen 1969). If such contacts existed at all, it is likely they were references to the NSG's links to the now fragmenting WUNS network.

Despite some tensions though, Mudie's group did link up with the NSG at this time. He seems to have completed an application form on or just before the 28 February 1969. This too was marked with Mudie's own blood, and added 'if any one of you be not true, by Thor I'll kill you with my bare hands!' (Mudie 1969a).

Then, on 15 March 1969, Donald and Pearl Mudie, along with George Palmer, Mudie's number two, and Leslie Lynch signed a document agreeing that their 'independently-contrived group of National Socialists centred upon Cleethorpes ... recognise without reservation that the National Socialist Group is the only lawful National Socialist Group in Britain', and that they would become Area Five of the NSG. They agreed to make their uniform conform to those of the NSG, and that 'our Nordic Order of Knights Volsung shall be placed available to N.S.G. for development, if required, by World Union as a National Socialist Order of Chivalry in answer to the odious cult of Freemasonry'. The document was signed on behalf of the NSG by K. L. Wood (Mudie et al. 1969). On 30 March 1969, Mudie, Lynch and Palmer signed another blood-soaked document, stating 'Pledge we officers Volsung by our lives to the furtherance of National Socialism and the Fourth Reich through the medium of the National Socialist Group, which is the lawful English authority of the International Union' (Mudie et al. 1969a). The two *groupuscules* had merged.

Campaigns and conflicts in 1969

Mudie was active and became increasingly central to the NSG as it developed in 1969. 18 March saw Gifford and Peter Hansen, described elsewhere as the Under-Officer of the NSG, write to Mudie welcoming him to the NSG. Again they reiterated their ambition to gain some property to create an 'international National Socialist centre'. This also added that the NSG saw society composing of three categories of people: those already aware of their National Socialist consciousness; a wider population which was 'basically sound' but was not aware of the higher cause; and a third category of those who would never be able to be won round. The aim of the NSG was to target only the first category, a supposed elite, and offer them training and support to develop their activism. Once the elite was established, they would convert the second category who could then be used to eliminate the third category, those who were incompatible with National Socialist principles. The movement was again described as a revolutionary one, seeking to destroy an old order and usher in a new one (Hansen 1969a).

Despite such statements confirming the NSG's revolutionary ambitions, in reality activity remained small-scale. In March, Mudie was able to publish a letter in the *Grimsby Evening Telegraph*, claiming that Conservative MP Duncan Sandys has given him authority to help with his petition on capital punishment. Mudie did receive a short, standard letter of support, and Sandys presented this petition in December 1969, by which time he claimed to have gathered around one million signatures. In May, while the *Phoenix* remained unpublished, a local bulletin was developed for the Lincolnshire members. Its opening article lamented a rise in immigration destroying Britain. This bulletin also noted that, to mark the anniversary of Hitler's birth, on 20 April District Officer George Palmer took a four-foot wooden swastika to a 'prominent religious establishment in Grimsby' (i.e. a synagogue though this was not printed) set it alight and called the fire brigade. When the services turned up, he 'paraded up and down, in a raincoat and swastika armband until he was arrested' (NSG Area 5 1969). Mudie attempted to have George, who was ill with cancer, released on the grounds that he was simply following Mudie's orders, but to no avail. Such episodes highlight the small-scale publicity stunts developed by NSG members.

Moreover, interactions with other groups also come through in letters from 1969. For example, a letter from Martin Webster, himself formerly active in Colin Jordan's National Socialist Movement in the early 1960s, to 'Mr. Gifford', sent on 2 May 1969, explained that 'the National Front finds your organisation, its structure, tactics and eventual aims thoroughly abhorrent, dangerous and sinister'. It added the NF would expel any NSG activists. Most devastatingly though, its final lines explained that the NF had compiled a dossier of details on the NSG and had passed this to Special Branch, whose later investigations would prompt the shutting down of the NSG by Courtney and the London command (Webster 1969). Tensions with other groups were manifest in other ways by this time. May 1969 also saw Jordan write a short letter to Mudie, and explain that the NSG was separate from the British Movement, and stressed 'there shall not be any appearance of affiliation, which in fact does not exist' (Jordan 1969). Clearly other extreme-right groups saw the NSG as a threat to their own activity.

Mudie was also not impressed by the state of the NSG by May 1969 either. He wrote a lengthy report that was very critical of the London operation. 'Official correspondence and literature gave the overall impression of immaturity', he stated at one point, complaining about their lack of a business-like approach, adding 'the veneer of professionalism appearing to be the work of students at some arts college rather than that of seasoned campaigners'. The conclusion noted that Mudie was still to meet the elusive Gifford, and stated that until he did he would not work in co-operation with the NSG. Moreover, he would also try to establish a relationship with Americans linked to the WUNS directly (Mudie 1969b: 3). This outburst prompted some complaint from others, especially noting that Mudie had published his bulletin on an electric replicator belonging to NSG that he had been given use of, though Mudie was dismissive of these concerns. In July, despite earlier hostility, Mudie even wrote to Martin Webster of the National Front. It suggested that Webster contact a local businessman who had publicly backed Enoch Powell. As Mudie continued, 'this chap occurs to me to be a staunch patriot who could become influential N. F. material in this area' (Mudie 1969c). Clearly there remained ambiguities in the ways members of these rival groups interacted.

Mudie's efforts were also directed to attracting others from around the country. He often lamented the way a handful of activists were spread some distance from each other. One figure he was in touch with in 1968 and 1969 was Peter Ling, formerly part of Jordan's NSM in the early 1960s. With a reputation as a loner, and a figure later active in Column 88, it is interesting to see Ling develop a connection, albeit not formalised, with the NSG. In the spring of 1969, Mudie wrote to Ling to explain that he had awarded George Palmer what he called an 'Arnold Leese Hakenkreuz medal' for his stunt to mark Hitler's birthday (Mudie 1969d: 3). He also wrote to Ling and the pair discussed developing a method of communicating via exchanging taped recordings. Mudie described this 'tape service' as 'vital ... We have to communicate with the public' (Mudie 1969e). Ling himself was based in Hampshire, and Mudie was in contact with several others in the county. This included Frank Rogers in Southampton, who wrote several lengthy letters to Mudie expressing his sympathies with National Socialists ideas. One praised Mudie for recognising that 'the Führer was a god and not a man', and encouraged Mudie to create 'some form of military underground movement for real staunch supporters' (Rogers n.d.). Another, undated, explained 'down here an underground army has been formed and it is gaining a lot of members', and asked Mudie if he knew of anyone who might like to join (Rogers n.d.a).

Mudie was still hoping to draw Ling to the NSG in October 1969. Another figure based in Hampshire who Mudie communicated with was simply addressed as Ted. One letter shows he joined the NSG at the beginning of October 1969. Ted also wrote to Mudie about bringing Ling into the group:

> Now for a few ideas that may be of use to you, Peter is getting a air rifle and air pistol club going, would'nt [sic] it be a good idea if he was approached by one of your men in London to bring this idea, plus his tape magazine project into the overall N.S.G., organisation, as you know our Peter is a bit of an individualist who likes to run his own outfit, in this way the N.S.G. would gain his, undeniable talents and the Gun Club plus the idea of the tape magazine which would be a marvellous propaganda vehicle for the Group. He is a real worker and I feel sure would put his heart and soul into the project, what do you think of the idea Don?
>
> *(Ted 1969)*

Mudie replied a few days later expressing clear interest, and told Ted he would contact Ling about including the gun club later that month (Mudie 1969f). Similar tactics would emerge later, in Column 88.

Final months

The evolution of the NSG took a new turn in September 1969. Mudie wrote of a 'far-reaching series of conferences in London' in September where future National Socialism in Britain was discussed. This lamented that only around 120 activists across the country could be found. Moreover, Mudie was also clearly shocked by what he encountered in London, claiming large areas of the city were now 'for all practical purposes non-British', and called for a radical change in activity (Mudie 1969g). In another letter from September, Mudie explained that he had been made Joint-Deputy Leader of the NSG, which he hoped would help restore the NSG's reputation (Mudie 1969h). He was also in direct correspondence with William Pierce in America by this time, writing to him in October 1969, asking for Associate Membership of the WUNS, perhaps another indication that the NSG was failing in its efforts to become a substantive organisation. Nevertheless, Mudie was upbeat about its progress, claiming it 'has done sterling work … and, with recent re-organisation, bids fair to really make progress' (Mudie 1969i: 3). That Mudie's return to vocal support of the NSG coincided with his appointment into a position of power, and the transfer of an electric replicator to his Area 5, demonstrated importance placed upon the NSG's primarily fictional power structures.

Some of his final activism for the NSG was recorded in the local bulletin for the Grimsby area, the fifth edition, which gives further indication of some of their activities at this time. This included a report on how Mudie and Palmer leafleted the borough council members dressed in their S. A. style uniform. They carried out a blood pledge before the event, and afterwards the pair returned to Mudie's house and carried out 'a ceremonial Zapfenstreich … at which ALL anthems were sung and salutes to Nordic warriors of all ages and Nordic dead presented in front of the Führer' (NSG Area 5 1969a: 2–3). The bulletin showed an interest in Holocaust denial themes too. It claimed the Jewish population of New York was 6 million, around the same number as died in the Holocaust. 'I wondered where they all settled!', it added suggestively. The article also explained that the movement drew its core understanding of the history of the Second World War from WUNS bulletins, yet felt the need to add in a comment of its own:

> Just after Bergen-Belsen was captured by the Allies, the British newspaper Daily Mirror printed a ghoulish picture of a charred man in an extinguished oven. Harrowing stuff. The body was solidified ash and bone. Concentration camp garb was well and truly recognizable! Funny thing this fire – particularly when we hear stories of burned-out Panzer crews being suitably dressed and posed for such pictures.
>
> (NSG Area 5 1969a: 2)

Aside from developing quite overt Holocaust denial messages, the bulletin also offered readers a 'BARGIN OFFER', for anyone who needed help to perform a National Socialist function, the Grimsby-based neo-Nazis would be happy to help. All they asked for were petrol costs and a donation to the London NSG (NSG Area 5 1969a: 4). However, after October 1969, traces of evidence to the NSG seemed to dry up, and around this time the groupuscule ceased being operative. Nevertheless, its various members certainly did not cease all their activism. Courtney, Mudie and others displayed an interesting afterlife, following the collapse of the NSG at the end of 1968.

Activism after the NSG

After *Searchlight* magazine developed into a regular publication, the role of the NSG took on new life in various features commenting on the roots of British neo-Nazism in the 1970s and 1980s. Its account of the demise of the NSG stressed that it ended as the authorities became concerned with its efforts to develop paramilitary activities. Nevertheless, this had not stopped former activists continuing to pose a threat in various new groups (*Searchlight* 1983: 15). One of the main follow-on groups from the NSG was Column 88, another poorly understood neo-Nazi groupuscule, one which was also linked to other neo-Nazi groups of the period, such as the League of St George. Unlike the NSG, Column 88 was more success-ful in developing violent activism, which included carrying out letter bombs and other terrorist-style activity. Its leader was Leslie Vaughan, a former member of the 1960s British National Party as well as its paramilitary wing, Spearhead (Barberis et al. 2005: 181). Like the NSG, Column 88 saw itself as an elite National Socialist organization that would provide training for a coming revolution. Members of the NSG found their way into Column 88 by the mid-1970s included Mudie. In the autumn of 1976, *Searchlight* noted that Mudie was on the 'outer fringe' of Column 88, adding that he had been expelled from the British Movement at this time, and was also a contributor to a neo-Nazi magazine called *Phoenix* that was linked to both the National Socialist Irish Workers Party and the National Socialist Party UK (*Searchlight* 1976: 9; *Searchlight* 1976a: 13). A couple of months later, *Searchlight* also published a picture of Mudie from this time dressed in full Nazi-style uniform (*Searchlight* 1977: 15). *Searchlight* informer Ray Hill has also commented on Mudie's activities for Column 88, recalling his love for dressing in Nazi-style regalia and a monocle (Hill 1988: 224). Mudie helped organise Column 88 events too. For example a document from the group listed him as Director of Operations at a camp run by Column 88 in November 1975 (*Searchlight* 1977a: 4).

In 1978, *Searchlight* also published a transcript of an instructional tape record-ing produced by Column 88, echoing Ling's earlier idea for a tape service. The recording, made in the early 1970s, gave various details on how Column 88 would be able to rekindle British Nazism and that it would operate through a small cell-based structure. It explained that the group would overturn the cowardice shown by Colin Jordan's decision to turn away from overt National Socialist activism in 1968, and even claimed that the National Front's John Tyndall was a secret member of Column 88. *Searchlight*'s feature showed the group sought to kindle an 'elite' who would then infiltrate other far-right groups and turn them to a Nazi agenda, and explained that Ling was one of the leading figures in the group. In particular, Ling was helping to co-ordinate Column 88 activists based on the south coast (*Searchlight* 1978: 3–9).

Column 88 fell into decline by the early 1980s, especially following a *World in Action* report in 1981, which linked the group's leading activists, including Vaughan, to gunrunning into the UK. Yet in 1982 *Searchlight* reported on Mudie again, this time for being linked the previous year to an effort by former Column 88 figures to develop a British Free Corps group (*Searchlight* 1982: 5). With this ongoing activ-ity as a backdrop, *Searchlight* then reported with some surprise the following year that Mudie had been selected by his local Conservative Party to contest a council seat in Cleethorpes (*Searchlight* 1983a: 5). When the BBC's *Panorama* programme broadcast an exposé of racists within the Conservative Party in 1984, Mudie was an obvious target. He refused to talk to the programme ahead of its broadcast, though the BBC did screen an interview with him from 1976 where he praised Hitler.

Mudie also released a statement after the Panorama exposé to the *Grimsby Evening Telegraph*, explaining that he still admired Hitler, and saw him as 'the saviour not only of the white race but the human race'. Incredibly, the chairman of the constituency party defended Mudie, stating the BBC was left-wing, and that it was merely muck-raking and digging up old material that 'does nobody any good at all' (*Searchlight* 1984: 10–11). Aside from Mudie's turn to the Conservative Party, there were other documented cases of entryism by former NSG figures. *Searchlight* also tracked Bill Whitehead, another former NSG member who in the 1970s was active in a number of extreme-right groups, including the leader of the National Front-linked trade union Tru-Aim. In 1981, *Searchlight* reported Whitehead had joined the Haringey branch of the Social Democratic Party (*Searchlight* 1981: 6).

Finally, what of David Courtney? He briefly resurfaced in 1980 as editor of a new neo-Nazi magazine called *Loki*. This publication claimed it was a hard-line magazine for militants who admired fascism and National Socialism, and sought to 'propagate the political philosophy of Adolf Hitler as superior to the stagnant bungling of the present day Semite manipulated democracies'. As well as offering reports and revolutionary inspiration, *Loki* advised its readers who wanted to participate in action to 'join the "88 Organisation"'. Once more, Courtney was keen on using pseudonyms and edited this magazine under the pen name S. G. Holloway (*Searchlight* 1981a: 4–6).

Conclusion

Despite being ultimately ineffective, the NSG is certainly a curious neo-Nazi *groupuscule*, one that reflects the wider dynamics of a shifting extreme-right space in later 1960s Britain. Its activists, such as Courtney and Mudie, were certainly people dedicated to cultivating a British variant of the neo-Nazi cultic milieu, and clearly engaged in some very bizarre rituals to help sustain their beliefs. This culture was likely to have both sustained their conviction in the importance of their activism, and also probably helped blind them to their insignificance and failure to achieve an impact. When looking at the inner dynamics of the NSG, it is also possible to see the regionalism that defined its operations, with activity in both London and Cleethorpes, as well as less effectively co-ordinated activity on the south coast. Regional bases appear to have their own distinct identity, and this again could lead to tensions. Letters and other data on its membership show that a quite variegated collection of people was attracted to the movement, young and old, male and female, British and European. It is also clear that the *groupuscule* was able to develop paramilitary training events, discussed issues such as making bombs, and did try to find a headquarters for their organisation, but to no avail.

Nevertheless, if simply seen as a standalone group, then it is easy to conclude that the NSG was of little wider consequence, ultimately shut down following pressure from the state. However, by considering the NSG as one *groupuscule* among many similar neo-Nazi *groupuscules* of this era, it becomes possible to see its wider relevance to its development of a neo-Nazi culture, and conclude that it did play a wider role in sustaining the most extreme forms of far-right activity in Britain. It acted as a bridge between the neo-Nazi cultures generated through the energies of people such as Colin Jordan and John Tyndall in the 1960s and the activities of violent and extremist groups such as Column 88 of the 1970s. Moreover, by considering it within a wider extreme-right *groupuscular* dynamic, it is possible to see elements of both collegiality and collaboration between likeminded groups, as well as overt hostility. Jordan's efforts to support the fledgling group in 1968 underscore the collegial relationships the NSG achieved, while Martin Webster's letter to Special Branch in 1969 demonstrated hostility among competing groups. Jordan could support it as it sought a different identity to his own British Movement but was a cause he believed in; Webster opposed it as he saw the NSG as a threat to the aims of the National Front to develop a more respectable form of extreme-right activism. Moreover, the transnational linkages can be seen both through its efforts to become integrated within the World Union of National Socialists, and through its efforts to copy elements of the dynamics of the American Nazi Party.

Finally, exploration of the NSG points to the need to develop further research into the fringes of British extreme-right *groupuscules*. Their clandestine culture needs to be better understood for a number of reasons. These include being able to better assess what limited risks to wider society are posed by such organisations, which talk of violent revolution, and aspire to develop paramilitary activity. Moreover, they need to be better understood so that the ambiguous relationships they develop with larger extreme-right organisations can be better understood, leading to a richer, more nuanced history of extremist activism in Britain.

References

Secondary sources

Albanese, M. and del Hierro, P. (2016) *Transnational Fascism in the Twentieth Century: Spain, Italy and the Global Neo-Fascist Network*. London: Bloomsbury Academic.

Bale, J. (2002) '"National Revolutionary" Groupuscules and the Resurgence of "Left-Wing" Fascism: The Case of France's Nouvelle Résistance', *Patterns of Prejudice*, 36 (3): 24–49.

Barberis, P., McHugh, J. and Tyldesley, M. (eds) (2005) *Encyclopedia of British and Irish Political Organizations Parties, Groups and Movements of the 20th Century*. London: Continuum.

Burstow, B. (2003) 'Surviving and Thriving by Becoming More "Groupuscular": The Case of the Heritage Front', *Patterns of Prejudice*, 37 (4): 415–428.

Durham, M. and Power, M. (eds) (2010) *New Perspectives on the Transnational Right*. London: Palgrave Macmillan.

Eatwell, R. (1995) *Fascism: A History*. London: Chatto & Windus.

Griffin, R. (1991) *Nature of Fascism*. London: Pinter.

Griffin, R. (2003) 'From Slime Mould to Rhizome: An Introduction to the Groupuscular Right', *Patterns of Prejudice*, 37 (1): 27–50.

Hill, R. (1988) *The Other Face of Terror: Inside Europe's Neo-Nazi Network*. London: Grafton.

Jackson, P. (2017) *Colin Jordan and Britain's Neo-Nazi Movement: Hitler's Echo*. London: Bloomsbury Academic.

Jackson, P. and Shekhovtsov, A. (eds) (2014) *The Anglo-American Far Right: A Special Relationship of Hate*. London: Palgrave Pivot.

Kaplan, J. and Lööw, H. (eds) (2002) *The Cultic Milieu: Oppositional Subcultures in an Age of Globalization*. Lanham, MD: Rowman & Littlefield.

Macklin, G. (2012) 'Transatlantic Connections and Conspiracies: A.K. Chesterton and "The New Unhappy Lords"', *Journal of Contemporary History*, 47 (2): 270–290.

Mammone, A. (2015) *Transnational Neofascism in France and Italy*. Cambridge: Cambridge University Press.

Mosse, G. (1999) *The Fascist Revolution: Toward a General Theory of Fascism*. New York: H. Fertig.

Virchow, F. (2004) 'The Groupuscularization of Neo-Nazism in Germany: The Case of the Aktionsbüro Norddeutschland', *Patterns of Prejudice*, 38 (1): 56–70.

Primary sources

A.10.2 (1969) *Letter from A.10.2 to David Courtney – January 1969*. [ms.]. *Searchlight* Archive – SCH/01/Res/BRI/24/001, University of Northampton, Northampton.

Aberdeen County Council (n.d.) *Cairncoullie School and Schoolhouse*. [ts.]. *Searchlight* Archive – SCH/01/Res/BRI/24/002, University of Northampton, Northampton.

County Council of Angus (1969) *Letter from Angus Council to L. Hodge – February 1969*. [ts.]. *Searchlight* Archive – SCH/01/Res/BRI/24/002, University of Northampton, Northampton.

Gifford, S. (1968) *National Socialist Group Directive*. [ts.]. *Searchlight* Archive – SCH/01/Res/BRI/24/001. University of Northampton, Northampton.

Griffiths, S. (1968) *Letter from S. Griffiths to NSG – October 1968*. [ms.]. *Searchlight* Archive – SCH/01/Res/BRI/20/013, University of Northampton, Northampton.

Hansen, P. (1969) *Letter from Peter Hansen to Donald Mudie*. [ts.]. *Searchlight* Archive – SCH/01/Res/BRI/24/002, University of Northampton, Northampton.

Hansen, P. (1969a) *Letter from Peter Hansen to Donald Mudie – March 1969*. [ts.]. *Searchlight* Archive – SCH/01/Res/BRI/24/002, University of Northampton, Northampton.

Hodge, L. (1968) *Letter from N.23-A to NSG – November 1968*. [ms.]. *Searchlight* Archive – SCH/01/Res/BRI/23/002, University of Northampton, Northampton.

Hodge, L. (1968a) *Letter from N.23-A to NSG*. [ms.]. *Searchlight* Archive – SCH/01/Res/BRI/23/002, University of Northampton, Northampton.

Jordan, C. (1968) *Letter from Colin Jordan to David Courtney*. [ms.]. *Searchlight* Archive – SCH/01/Res/BRI/23/002. University of Northampton, Northampton.

Jordan, C. (1968a) *Letter from Colin Jordan to David Courtney – July 1968*. [ms.]. *Searchlight* Archive – SCH/01/Res/BRI/23/002. University of Northampton, Northampton.

Jordan, C. (1968b) *Letter from Colin Jordan to David Courtney – August 1968*. [ms.]. *Searchlight* Archive – SCH/01/Res/BRI/23/002. University of Northampton, Northampton.

Jordan, C. (1968c) *Letter from Colin Jordan to David Courtney – December 1968*. [ms.]. *Searchlight* Archive – SCH/01/Res/BRI/23/002, University of Northampton, Northampton.

Jordan, C. (1969) *Letter from Colin Jordan to Donald Mudie – May 1969*. [ts.]. *Searchlight* Archive – SCH/01/Res/BRI/24/002, University of Northampton, Northampton.

Knights of the Volsung (1968) *Promotion of Donald Mudie to Major Captain* [ms.]. *Searchlight* Archive – SCH/01/Res/BRI/24/002, University of Northampton, Northampton.

Mudie, D. (1968) *Letter from Donald Mudie to Ted and Peter – November 1968*. [ts.]. *Searchlight* Archive – SCH/01/Res/BRI/24/002, University of Northampton, Northampton.

Mudie, D. (1969) *Letter from Donald Mudie to NSG – February 1969*. [ts.]. *Searchlight* Archive – SCH/01/Res/BRI/24/002, University of Northampton, Northampton.

Mudie, D. (1969a) *Letter from Donald Mudie to NSG*. [ts.]. *Searchlight* Archive – SCH/01/Res/BRI/24/002, University of Northampton, Northampton.

Mudie, D. (1969b) *Interim Report on N.S.G, 21st May, 1969 (YOF 80).* [ts.]. *Searchlight* Archive – SCH/01/Res/BRI/24/002, University of Northampton, Northampton.

Mudie, D. (1969c) *Letter from Donald Mudie to Martin Webster – July 1969.* [ts.]. *Searchlight* Archive – SCH/01/Res/BRI/24/002, University of Northampton, Northampton.

Mudie, D. (1969d) *Letter from Donald Mudie to Peter.* [ts.]. *Searchlight* Archive – SCH/01/Res/BRI/24/002, University of Northampton, Northampton.

Mudie, D. (1969e) *Letter from Donald Mudie to Peter Ling.* [ts.]. *Searchlight* Archive – SCH/01/Res/BRI/24/002, University of Northampton, Northampton.

Mudie, D. (1969f) *Letter from Donald Mudie to 'Ted' – 4 October 1969.* [ts.]. *Searchlight* Archive – SCH/01/Res/BRI/24/002, University of Northampton, Northampton.

Mudie, D. (1969g) *Letter from Donald Mudie to Frank Rogers – 10 September 1969.* [ts.]. *Searchlight* Archive – SCH/01/Res/BRI/24/002, University of Northampton, Northampton.

Mudie, D. (1969h) *Letter from Donald Mudie to George Palmer – September 1969.* [ts.]. *Searchlight* Archive – SCH/01/Res/BRI/24/002, University of Northampton, Northampton.

Mudie, D. (1969i) *Letter from Donald Mudie to William Pierce – October 1969.* [ts.]. *Searchlight* Archive – SCH/01/Res/BRI/24/002, University of Northampton, Northampton.

Mudie, D. (n.d.) *Letter from Donald Mudie to Unknown – Partial Letter.* [ts.]. *Searchlight* Archive – SCH/01/Res/BRI/24/002, University of Northampton, Northampton.

Mudie, D. et al. (1969) *Order of the Day No. 2: Future of Vergeltungtruppen.* [ts.]. *Searchlight* Archive – SCH/01/Res/BRI/24/002, University of Northampton, Northampton.

Mudie, D. et al. (1969a) *Order of the Day No. 3: Document of Blood Warranty.* [ts.]. *Searchlight* Archive – SCH/01/Res/BRI/24/002, University of Northampton, Northampton.

National Socialist Group (1968) *Directive No. 1.* [ts.]. *Searchlight* Archive – SCH/01/Res/BRI/24/001. University of Northampton, Northampton.

National Socialist Group (1968a) *National Socialist Group Membership Advert.* [ts.]. *Searchlight* Archive – SCH/01/Res/BRI/24/001. University of Northampton, Northampton.

National Socialist Group (1968b) *NSG Security Directive.* [ts.]. *Searchlight* Archive – SCH/01/Res/BRI/24/001. University of Northampton, Northampton.

National Socialist Group (1968c) *Directive No. 4.* [ts.]. *Searchlight* Archive – SCH/01/Res/BRI/24/001, University of Northampton, Northampton.

National Socialist Group (1969) *Directive No. 5.* [ts.]. *Searchlight* Archive – SCH/01/Res/BRI/24/001, University of Northampton, Northampton.

National Socialist Group (n.d.) *Directive No. 6.* [ts.]. *Searchlight* Archive – SCH/01/Res/BRI/24/001, University of Northampton, Northampton.

Nickolls, J. (1968) *Letter from J. H. Nickolls to NSG – November 1968.* [ms.]. *Searchlight* Archive – SCH/01/Res/BRI/23/002, University of Northampton, Northampton.

NSG Area 5. (1969) *Bulletin No. 1.* [ts.]. *Searchlight* Archive – SCH/01/Res/BRI/24/002, University of Northampton, Northampton.

NSG Area 5. (1969a) *Bulletin No. 5.* [ts.]. *Searchlight* Archive – SCH/01/Res/BRI/24/002, University of Northampton, Northampton.

Rogers, F. (n.d.) *Letter from Frank Rogers to Donald Mudie.* [ms.]. *Searchlight* Archive – SCH/01/Res/BRI/24/002, University of Northampton, Northampton.

Rogers, F. (n.d.a) *Letter from Frank Rogers to Donald Mudie – Typed.* [ts.]. *Searchlight* Archive – SCH/01/Res/BRI/24/002, University of Northampton, Northampton.

Searchlight (1976) More Strange Ways at Strangeways *Searchlight*, November, p. 9.

Searchlight (1976a) Column 88 Fringe Man Joins Nazis *Searchlight*, November, p. 13.

Searchlight (1977) News in Brief *Searchlight*, January, p. 15.

Searchlight (1977a) Peter Marriner Labour's Fascist Infiltrator *Searchlight*, July, p. 4.

Searchlight (1978) Column 88: The Nazi Underground *Searchlight*, May, pp. 3–9.

Searchlight (1981) Odinist Joins SDP *Searchlight*, December, p. 6.

Searchlight (1981a) The Re-Birth of the National Socialist Group *Searchlight*, March, pp. 4–6.

Searchlight (1982) Still Within These Walls: Prison Officer's Column 88 Connections *Searchlight*, June, p. 5.

Searchlight (1983) RECAP No. 19: The Paramilitary Right *Searchlight*, October, p. 15.

Searchlight (1983a) Nazi Dirty Tricksters Spike Infiltrator *Searchlight*, July, p. 5.

Searchlight (1984) Maggie's Militant Tendency *Searchlight*, April, pp. 10–11.

Ted (1969) *Letter from 'Ted' to Donald Mudie – 1 October 1969.* [ts.]. *Searchlight* Archive – SCH/01/Res/BRI/24/002, University of Northampton, Northampton.

Unknown Infiltrator (1968) *Report from Anti-Fascist Infiltrator on NSG – September 1968.* [ts.]. *Searchlight* Archive – SCH/01/Res/BRI/23/002, University of Northampton, Northampton.

Unknown Infiltrator (1968a) *Report from Anti-Fascist Infiltrator on NSG – October 1968.* [ts.]. *Searchlight* Archive – SCH/01/Res/BRI/23/002, University of Northampton, Northampton.

Various (1968) *Completed Membership Application Forms for the NSF.* [ms.]. *Searchlight* Archive – SCH/01/Res/BRI/23/002, University of Northampton, Northampton

Wallace, K. (1968) *Letter from Karl Wallace to Simon Gifford.* [ms.]. *Searchlight* Archive – SCH/01/Res/BRI/20/013, University of Northampton, Northampton.

Wallace, K. (1969) *Letter from Karl Wallace to David Courtney.* [ms.]. *Searchlight* Archive – SCH/01/Res/BRI/23/002, University of Northampton, Northampton.

Webster, M. (1969) *Letter from Martin Webster to Simon Gifford.* [ts.]. *Searchlight* Archive – SCH/01/Res/BRI/24/002, University of Northampton, Northampton.

Wood, K. (1968) *Letter from K. L. Wood to NSG* [ms.]. *Searchlight* Archive – SCH/01/Res/BRI/23/002, University of Northampton, Northampton.

3

THE NATIONAL FRONT

The search for a 'nationalist' economic policy

John E. Richardson

Introduction

Summarising the economic policies of the National Front (NF) is a little problematic. Compared to their copious discussion of race and nation, of immigration, culture, history and even the environment, British fascists since WWII have had little to say, in detail, on their political-economic ideology. In one of the first content analytic studies of the NF's mouthpiece *Spearhead*, for example, Harris (1973) identified five themes which dominated the magazine's all pervasive conspiracy thinking: authoritarianism, ethnocentrism, racism, biological naturalism and anti-intellectualism. The economy was barely discussed, other than in the context of the imagined generosity of the welfare state. The topic is so underdeveloped that even Rees' (1979) encyclopaedic bibliography on British fascism, covering over 800 publications on and by fascists from 1923 to 1977, does not include a section on the political economy. Frequently, the closest fascists get to outlining their political-economic ideology is to identify 'the problem': the forces of 'cosmopolitan internationalism' (that is: the Jews) importing migrants, whose cheap labour threatens white livelihoods, and whose physical presence threatens the racial purity of the nation. 'The solution', on the other hand, is far less frequently spelled out. In essence, fascist parties, like the NF, are comparatively clear about what political economies they oppose – international capitalism and international communism – but are far less clear or consistent about the political economy they support.

This under-theorisation in fascist discourse is also reflected in an underrepresentation of economic policies in academic analysis of post-war British fascism, where the two principal political-economic theories – autarky and distributism – are discussed only rarely (although see Sykes 2005, chapter 4, for a detailed discussion of pre-war 'alternative economics'). Lunn (1980) does discuss the links between distributism (see p. 34 below) and fascism, pointing out that G.K. Chesterton's *Weekly Review* 'showed much sympathy towards fascism' and that 'Speakers from the BUF [British Union of Fascists] and the IFL [Imperial Fascist League] took part in Distributist meetings and used the correspondence columns of the *Review* to put over their fascist principles' (1980: 34). Lunn suggests the 'emphasis on the efficiency of the authoritarian corporatist state as well as their strong condemnation of liberalism and parliamentary government, disposed the Distributist circle to an acceptance of fascism' (quoting Corrin 1976: 296, in Lunn 1980: 34). Sykes (2005) discusses Mosley's post-war abandonment of the Corporate State and his proposed 'wage-price mechanism' which drew on Social Credit. Through 'definite, conscious and deliberate economic leadership' – which was fascist newspeak for 'dictatorship' – Mosley believed that he had come up with 'the most potent instrument for shaping the future development of industry which could be devised' (quoted in Sykes 2005: 96). Sykes (2005: 82) also acknowledges, but does not go on to detail, the fact that distributism shaped the economic and environmental thinking of the NF during the 1980s (see also Fielding 1981).

In an article written for the NF's esoteric magazine *New Nation*, Martin Webster provides a revealing and self-reflexive examination for the under-theorisation of fascist political economics. First, he acknowledges that the NF was rather late to discuss and settle upon its economic policies, preferring to emphasise its 'racial nationalist' ideology and the party's 'one paramount objective: *to save and enhance our race and nation*' (Webster 1980: 12). Such a commitment tended to reduce any discussion, where it actually appeared, to a base opposition to 'internationalism' and its twin conspiratorial forces of finance capitalism and international communism. However, the key question of how to organize a national economy in which the influence of 'the internationalists' is removed was not answered. Webster cites as an example the first leader of the NF, A.K. Chesterton, who 'waged relentless war on the British Empire destroying One World building activities of the "International Money Power". He did not, however, as far as I can recall, attempt to articulate a basis for a Nationalist economic and social policy' (1980: 12–13). But, Webster suggests, this absence of economic policy was not an oversight on the part of Chesterton, but a deliberate omission. At a leadership training event organised for the NF,

> A.K. was asked about the party's lack of clear policies on economic and social matters. He replied that to develop policies on such issues would be dangerous as the exercise might divide the party on 'class war' lines and/or might lose the party's capacity to attract voting support from all classes in society.
>
> *(1980: 13)*

Whilst fascists universally opposed communism, 'on account of its anti-national, anti-racial and anti-patriotic subversion' (Webster 1980: 12), capitalism is very rarely criticised *in toto* in fascist discourse since this would logically entail adopting class as an analytic concept. Pointing out the structural inequalities endemic to capitalism might deter the more conservative supporters of the NF; but, equally, praising capitalism is likely to repel their radical or working-class supporters. The answer lay in a 'third way' economy, but the party was not that forthcoming about what that would look like in practice. The objectives of the NF, agreed at the merger of the League of Empire Loyalists and the British National Party on 7 February 1967, seemed to pull in two political-economic directions. Their Objective 3 announced their autarkic principles, committing 'To achieve for the system adequate economic and agricultural self-sufficiency' (quoted in *Patterns of Prejudice* 1967: 23). However, their later Objective 9 appears much more indebted to the BUF's theory of the Corporate State, where they propose: 'To ensure that just profits, salaries and wages, founded on a fair partnership between employers and employees, are guaranteed by maintaining the principle of private enterprise within a framework of national guidance, wherein employees would be genuinely represented in all matters' (ibid.).

Implicit in Webster's article is a third reason why summarising the economic policies of the NF is difficult: they change over time and, in part, reflect the changing attitude of the party towards electoral politics. During the 1970s, when the NF was pursuing power through democratic elections, and party members were (reportedly) more middle class, party economic policy tended towards a more conservative attitude to the capitalist status quo. Following their woeful achievement in the 1979 general election, the party magazines and newspapers through the 1980s show a diminishing interest in popular elections and a corresponding increase in more radical responses to capitalism, partly in order to attract younger supporters 'before they become enmeshed in the system which has trapped their parents' (Webster 1980: 13). However, as I show below, even at their most radical, the ideologues of the NF could not transcend a capitalist political economy, and their attempts to develop 'third way' solutions, in essence, simply recalibrate and rehabilitate capitalism in the service of 'the nation'. This chapter examines two political economies advocated by the NF: during the 1970s, the party drew implicitly on the example of Nazi Germany, and argued for autarky; during the 1980s, the party advocated distributism, as a native rather than imported economic ideology. But first, I will discuss some important historic precursors that lay the groundwork for understanding fascist political economies in general.

Fascist political economies

During the interwar period, it was only really the British Union of Fascists (BUF) that advanced an elaborated political-economic theory, principally in the writings of Alexander Raven Thomson. Emulating Fascist Italy, the 'Corporate State' was proposed by the BUF as the solution to the inequity and inefficiencies of capitalism. Contrary to fantasies of a 'Workers' State' (Wegg-Prosser 1936) or a radical reorganisation of the economy to the benefit of all (Mosley n.d. circa 1933), the corporate state 'would be superimposed upon capitalism, rather than substituted for it' (Benewick 1969: 146). 'Private property, enterprise and initiative would not be eliminated' (Benewick 1969: 145) and nor would profit or exploitation, as long as the fascist government considered it in 'the national interest'. What *would* have been eliminated was dissent. As Mosley (n.d. circa 1933: 5) declared: 'All who pursue a sectional and anti-national policy will be opposed by the might of the organised State.' Unions would have been permitted under the British version of corporatism but, like in Fascist Italy, they would be expected to serve the nation and the state, rather than represent any 'sectional' interests, such as the workers. In Fascist Italy

> the purpose of fascist corporations was [...] to settle disputes between labour and capital, on opposite sides of the class divide. But while organized capital continued to be represented by its own speakers in the CGII [Confederazione Generale dell'Industria Italiana] labour found itself 'represented' by fascist party bureaucrats.
>
> *(Neocleous 1997: 45)*

Baker (2006: 242) argues that all forms of fascist political economy divide 'the world between "good capital" nationally based and orientated to production – and "parasitic capital" – considered international, profit maximizing and anti-nationalistic'. In the more racist and conspiratorial varieties of fascism, such as those that dominate the British tradition, international 'parasitic capital' is tied to Jewish economic activity, Jewish power, and, hence, is a key trope in anti-Semitic conspiracy theories. 'Marxism' is also attacked for its internationalism – indeed, for Hitler, the chief crimes of Marxism were its internationalism and its Jewishness, two qualities that, for him and other Nazi ideologues, spiralled around and mutually reinforced each other (Neocleous 1997: 40). At the core of Nazi economic ideology was an obsession with a strong Germany and, as they saw it, a zero-sum conflict which pitted Germany's interests against that of international companies and investors (Szejnmann 2013: 370) – an obsession that made them visceral opponents of both the politics and economics of 'internationalism'. Indeed, Gottfried Feder, in his works on 'interest slavery', proposed 'a distinction between "rapacious" (*raffendes*) and "productive" (*schaffendes*) capital (or, to put it differently, 'parasitical Jewish finance capital' and 'creative national capital')' (Szejnmann 2013: 358). Such anti-Semitism lay squarely and thoroughly at the heart of the Nazi autarkic economic project. Szejnmann (2013: 360) demonstrates that, in repeated speeches,

> Hitler did not tire of emphasizing the importance of protecting the 'national economy' (the 'honest working economy') with the power of a 'national state' against Jews and Marxist leaders, who he described as the main supporter of 'internationalisation' and the exploitation of Germany.

In more detail, Szejnmann (2013: 359) argues that 'Hitler's economic vision' consisted of two prime directives:

> (a) a replacement of the capitalistic economic system with one that was dominated by state control and planning but allowed private initiative in a 'national economy' that served the common good (re-establishing the primacy of politics) and was free of Jews (racism); (b) opting out of crucial parts of the global free market economy and pursuing autarkic policies and expansion in a quest to secure agricultural land to feed one's own population [not including Jews of course, JER] and to secure raw material for industry.

The point above, that Nazis 'allowed private initiative' acknowledges a key point regarding the Nazi economy that also accords with Fascist Italy's economy: neither during the more radical programmatic phases of fascism in Italy and Germany, nor once in power, when 'both regimes abandoned any attempt to alter radically the structure of economic organization' (Baker 2006: 232), did fascism oppose private property or private ownership of the means of production. True, they were by no means 'capitalist markets' in the conventional sense. Indeed, Buchheim and Schemer (2006: 411) suggest that a way to name/describe the economy of Nazi Germany 'would probably have been "state-directed private ownership economy" instead of using the term "market"'; more forcefully, Baker (2006: 237) suggests that Hitler's *völkisch* economics amounted to 'a genocidal slave and permanent war economy'. However, in both Fascist Italy and Nazi Germany, 'the industrial sector was allowed to remain in private hands but was charged with meeting "national needs"' (Baker 2006: 233).

Fascist conspiracy theorists maintain that both (international and finance) capitalism and communism are tools used by Jews (variously labelled Jewry, International Jewry, Zionism, and in more recent iterations simply 'Internationalists' or 'Globalists') to subvert the power of nation states and, in the case of racial fascists, to undermine white people. One of the more concise examples of this conspiracy explanation was written by William Joyce, in the BUF publication *Fascism and Jewry*:

> The Jews control and actuate alike the decadent democratic capitalism and the hideous fratricidal Communism. Using both instruments they hope to prevent every white people [sic] from achieving the freedom to work out the fullness of their own economic destiny. Only through the defeat of Jewry can Britain be free.
>
> (Joyce n.d.: 7)

This I refer to as the *core conspiracy* of fascism, which has shaped all fascist proposed plans to nationalise the economy and insulate it from perfidious internationalism (Richardson 2017). In fascist discourse, 'the international' is a source of anxiety and threat; it is a nexus of power that threatens to overwhelm Us; a potential usurper of resources that properly belong to Us. For British fascists, the economy should be limited to, and within, the national space and 'those to whom it belongs' (Joyce 1936: 532), to the exclusion of non-national others (including, or perhaps especially, Jews). It should also be structured in a way different to either of the two opposing poles of internationalism – international capitalism and international Communism – and the conspiratorial (Jewish) 'Money Power' that fascists believe lies behind both.

The core conspiracy in NF discourse

The NF Manifesto for the 1979 general election stated baldly that 'We loathe the Communist system' (p.34) and, in their Manifesto for the 1974 elections, that they 'totally reject the idea of "détente" with Communism', since it 'has not abandoned its ambition of destroying the civilized world' (p.26). Britain was, unsurprisingly, frequently cited as a key battleground of this war against the civilised world. One NF leaflet (circa 1976) listed a range of alleged Communist infiltration, from 'burrowing deeper into the Civil Service, betraying defence secrets, making war on independent businessmen, directing public money into the hands of subversives at home and abroad' to 'taking over key positions in the Mass Media [...] to undermine our faith in ourselves, in our race and nation, and in traditional standards of decency' (NF Leaflet, **Reds Under The Bed?**). Despite the extent of such subversion, the leaflet alleges that 'Conservative, Labour and Liberal politicians have done nothing about it [...] *Could it be that even the traditional parliamentary parties have been infiltrated?*' (ibid., emphasis added).

This conspiratorial outlook is discussed at greater length in other NF articles, and frequently in such a way that finishes just short of the 'core conspiracy' and openly declaring '*it's the Jews*'. The full answer, it often seems, is provided in another text. One article in *Spearhead* (1970: 8) argues that it is essential to study communism in order to understand the broad 'scheme of international conspiracy into which communism fits'. The column then directs the reader to a range of anti-Semitic works – including Chesterton's *The New Unhappy Lords*, Knupffer's *The Struggle for World Power* and the *Protocols of the Learned Elders of Zion* – that 'exposes vividly the collusion between communism and high finance' (ibid.). Even John Tyndall was, on occasion, surprisingly coy about the conspirators, leaving calculated blanks in his abbreviated version of the core conspiracy:

> if Communism and capitalism are working together to a common end, what is that end? What is the grand objective of all contemporary policy? [...] the objective is world power, world control [...] But world power for whom? This is the question that is crucial [...] The missing piece in the jig-saw puzzle must for the moment be supplied out of the imagination of the reader.

> *(Tyndall 1972: 7)*

British fascism during the 1970s was still caught in the rhetorical bind that required it to simultaneously present exoteric and esoteric political commitments, to address both credulous and cadre audiences (Billig 1978; Richardson 2011, 2013, 2017; Wodak & Richardson 2013). This meant that even in that most exoteric of political genres, the General Election Manifesto, one can find statements confirming (to those who understand the code) their continued adherence to esoteric fascist conspiracy theories:

> We must understand Communism, not as a system existing on its own, but merely as the visible part of a movement of world-subversion which rests no less on its invisible pillars of support within the West. We must recognize that the object of this wider movement of which Communism is a part is *to subject us to the rule*, not of Russia as such, but *of a cosmopolitan elite* of whose aims Russia is merely an instrument and America an instrument of a different kind.
>
> *(Emphasis added, National Front 1979: 34)*

This statement of official party policy reveals that the NF did not hate Communism merely for what it stood for and executed in the world, but because they considered it a tool 'of a movement of world-subversion', which uses both Communism and (capitalist) America as instruments of global rule. The leaders of this 'wider movement' are referred to as 'a cosmopolitan elite'. The 'cosmopolitanism' of this political-economic elite was also invoked in the (1977) pamphlet *Beyond Capitalism and Socialism*. Here the NF poured 'scorn' on 'utterly phony "patriotism"' the fume of which mingle today with the thick cigar smoke of City boardrooms as cosmopolitan millionaires drape their mercenary consciences with the colours of the flag' (p.2). 'Cosmopolitan' is an important watchword in anti-Semitic discourse, and not simply that of the extreme right. As Miller and Ury (2015: 11) point out, 'the "anti-cosmopolitan campaign" in the Soviet Union (1949–53) singled out writers, artists, scholars, musicians and athletes of Jewish origin for their "anti-patriotic" activities and accused them of slandering "the national Soviet character"'. Similarly, for fascists, Jews are 'often seen as quintessential cosmopolitans – a transnational community that was at home everywhere (and nowhere)' (Miller and Ury 2015: 8).

A slightly earlier article by Bleach (1976: 6) offered an almost identical argument: 'Just as Communism and Capitalism ostensibly appear to be foes, there is much evidence to suggest the existence of a financial power superior to them which frequently uses one or the other, and quite often both, for its execrable ends.' Looking at the 'evidence' in the text, one is struck by the emphasis placed on Jewish-sounding conspirators:

> It is now well-known history that the 1917 Revolution was plotted and financed [...] by international financier based in New York. [...] A wealthy banker called Jivotovsky, whose daughter later married Trotsky (alias Bronstein), had a hand in it too.
>
> *(Bleach 1976: 6)*

Why else, the article insinuates, would the daughter of a wealthy capitalist banker marry the Marxist Trotsky unless they were part of the same cosmopolitan conspiracy? Elsewhere, the article uses the phrase 'New York money power' comprised of, *inter alia*, 'the Schiffs and Warburgs, Morgans and Rockerfellers' as well as Kuhn, Loeb and Company and the Rothschilds, all of whom were apparently involved in bankrolling Communism – *contra* what you would expect capitalists to do.

Jews are also accused of using financial influence over both business and democratic politics in ways contrary to the best interests of Britain and British people. In the discourse of some British fascist parties, this line of argumentation is expressed openly; given their democratic pretentions, this financial power tended to be euphemised slightly in the NF discourse of the 1970s. In its manifesto for the 1974 general elections, for example, the NF strenuously opposed 'the dominant and inviolable position of finance over the economy […] Finance calls the tune, and the potential of industry is ever frustrated by the stranglehold grip of *money power*' (emphasis added, p.3).

Autarky

Autarky is a political-economic theory that advocates national economic independence or self-sufficiency. Autarky is a recurrent feature of fascist economics given the basic assumption, central to all forms of fascism, that economic life should serve 'the nation'. Mosley's inter-war economic proposals, for example, included 'an autarkic system of trade with an insulated home market, which exchanged manufactured goods for essential primary products' within the British Empire (Thurlow 1980: 105). Fielding (1981) argued that, by adopting autarky as its guiding economic principle, the NF followed the 'measures put by Mosley to the Labour Party which later formed part of New Party and BUF policy' (p.67). However, he added, 'this is probably because they have been selected from a general currency of ideas on the Right rather than from any explicit orientation' (ibid.) Before taking leadership of the NF, John Tyndall looked to the autarkic transformation of Germany under Nazism for economic pointers – described as a country where, 'by means of magic, as it were, [Hitler] radically eliminated unemployment' (Tyndall 1969: 4). In this laudatory review of the conspiracy text *Red Symphony*, Tyndall simultaneously argues for the rehabilitation of Hitler and National Socialism – a movement that he argues was only stopped because it opposed the evil of international finance – and draws political-economic inspiration for restructuring British industry. The true accomplishments of National Socialism he argued, combatting both communism and 'the omnipotence of the financial International', were apparently being kept from the masses:

> The masses must never be allowed to see it [National Socialism] in its essentials, as a national revolt against the stranglehold of the world money power and an attempt to re-establish an industrial system based on the physical and technical resources of soil and people.
>
> *(Tyndall 1969: 5)*

In later iterations, and with Tyndall now Chairman of the party, the anti-Semitic underpinnings of their proposed autarky would be hidden behind a veneer of economic rationalisation. In their (1974) manifesto, the NF argued that the 'economy must be wholly transformed in its structure so as to enable the greatest possible immunity from world conditions and the greatest possible national self-sufficiency' (p.3). This transformation would not be so full and complete as to do away with capitalism, however. As John Bean (1970: 4) put it, private ownership and private enterprise are 'healthy and instinctive' parts of our economy. The NF, he argued, needed to show the electorate 'that a prosperous and united Britain requires private enterprise (productive capitalism) to ensure maximum productivity, and a framework of national control to ensure that it is fairly distributed to the benefit of all who contribute to it.' In more detail, the (1974) manifesto argued:

> In the task of restructuring industry to cater for the needs of this [home] market we will apply a combination of free enterprise and state enterprise [...] We will take from capitalist doctrine its best features, which are individual incentive and healthy, bracing competition, but in contrast to the old laissez faire capitalism we intend to ensure that competition is fair and conducted according to a set of rules. This shuts out the foreign competitor who utilizes cheap, sweated labour [...] Private ownership and the profit motive must operate within industry if its dynamism is to be maintained, but private industrial endeavour must serve a higher national and public interest.
>
> *(pp. 4–5)*

The extract above demonstrates that analysis of NF economic reasoning in purely economic terms cannot grasp its specific character. NF political economies are not based on classic economic considerations (import/exports, un/employment, GDP, etc.) but are riven with the national chauvinism that characterises every dimension of their political outlook. They do not detail here what the authoritarian 'set of rules' structuring activities of companies would amount to, other than it would function to exclude 'the foreign competitor'. The 'higher national and public interest' is also under-defined, reduced to national ownership of capitalist enterprises. Capitalist accumulation is similarly reduced to a matter of ethno-nationality: shut out foreign businesses to better advance the national interests. The interests of British *workers* are not spelled out, other than the implicit assumption that labouring for 'British' bosses will somehow be less exploitative than for 'foreign' owners. The enthusiastic support for capitalist entrepreneurialism in the extract, and its apparently vitalistic effect on both the individual and society, has echoes from the past – Otto Ohlendorf, for example, 'an enthusiastic National Socialist and high-ranking SS officer, who since November 1943 held a top position in the Reich Economics Ministry' and considered private ownership of industry to be 'a precondition to developing the creativity of members of the German race' (Buchheim & Schemer 2006: 408). The constant aim of National Socialist economic policy was, he argued, 'to restrict as little as possible the creative activities of the individual. […] Private property is the natural precondition to the development of personality. Only private property is able to further the continuous attachment to a certain work' (quoted in ibid.).

It is in the (1977) pamphlet *Beyond Capitalism and Socialism* that we can read the most extended presentation of the NF's autarkic policies. Its author, John Tyndall, argues 'From capitalism we also take the element of incentive that is contained in the profit motive. Profit is quite legitimate as a variable wage to those who provide the brains and initiative that make for national prosperity' (p.17). However, onto this capitalist mode of production, they

> superimpose our own doctrine of nationalism, which in economic terms means that we seek salvation through the independence and self-reliance of the nation-state, or our own country and people […] we reject the internationalism that stands at the centre of both socialism and contemporary finance-capitalism.
>
> *(Ibid.)*

In a faux-populist nod to the material conditions of British workers, page 1 of the pamphlet acknowledges 'the existence of real grievances in industry', but only in order to argue that 'These grievances arise, almost without exception, out of the iniquities of modern international finance capitalism'. It is the *internationalism* of finance capitalism, rather than the capitalist mode of production *per se*, that Tyndall identifies as the sources of British suffering (p.3) – an 'evil, fraudulent and parasitic' racket which creates 'monstrous injustices within the national economy' (p.12). As he saw it:

> International finance today stands at the centre of the vast jungle of world trade in which Britain is enmeshed. Finance is able by its own operations to cripple national economies […] In any sane world economy the import/export trade of each country would extend to no greater level than that country's resources […] Such a system, however, is not allowed because it would cut the ground from under the feet of international finance.
>
> *(p.5)*

In the extract above, and throughout the pamphlet, finance is given agency to act – calling the tune (p.3), intentionally creating deflation and unemployment (ibid.), calling in loans (ibid.) and, as above, not allowing any challenge to its power and control. Every feature of the modern international market – international tariffs, interest payments, deregulation and everything else – is interpreted as a challenge to the primacy of the nation; and, behind that, is identified a nexus of interests and conspiratorial powers. Commenting on 'the Generalised system of preferences' for example – that is, trade regulations (supported by then-Prime Minister Harold Wilson) that allowed developing countries to pay reduced or no duties on their exports to the EU – Tyndall argued that behind the claims to alleviate world poverty

> there is a motive that is far from as idealistic as it is made to sound. Out of such a policy enormous profits accrue to the international financiers, whose money is shrewdly invested in the very coolie industries that are going to benefit from preferential entry into the British market! Behind the façade of socialist idealism there lurks the leering grimace of money power.
>
> *(p. 12)*

This, and other, passages of the pamphlet reveal that the NF's position on international/finance capitalism is founded – ontologically – on the central, inescapable presence of anti-national conspiracy. And, as in all fascist political economies, this in turn draws on the core anti-Semitic conspiracy summarised by Joyce (1936), amongst many others. Thus, Tyndall claimed that a big business network was behind Labour's 'fight against capitalism', including millionaires Lords Sainsbury and Campbell, Leonard Matchan, Sidney Bernstein, Robert Maxwell and Harold Lever.

It is hardly a coincidence that the majority on this list of donors are Jewish. The exact same list of prominent Jewish businessmen was also included in an earlier article by Tyndall (1972), alleging to expose 'the wealth of facts [...] which prove Communist-Capitalist collaboration' (p.6). The (1977) pamphlet also includes the perennial canard that 'Leon Trotsky (Bronstein) [...] was financed in Russia by foreign capitalists operating from New York' (p.13). At other points Tyndall derides 'cosmopolitan millionaires' (p.2) and 'entrenched Money Power' (p.5), and argues 'the nature of modern-finance capitalism is such that it makes the finance capitalist nothing better than a huge parasite feeding on the body of the national economy' (p.10). Such a rhetorical flourish bears more than a passing resemblance to Tyndall's infamous words, spoken at a National Socialist Movement rally, at Trafalgar Square in July 1962: that 'in our democratic society, the Jew is like a poisonous maggot feeding off a body in an advanced state of decay' (quoted in Walker 1977: 38–39). For Tyndall and the NF, the autarkic solution to international finance capital was little more than a repackaging of the core anti-Semitic conspiracy theory regarding Jewish money power and its global dominance.

Autarky was also the political economy of choice for other British fascist parties during the 1970s, including the National Party (NP), which split from the NF in 1976. Issue 1 of *The British Worker* (1977), the newspaper of the NP, listed the policies that the party stood for in bullet-points. Following the standard racist commitment to 'Stop immigration, start repatriation', the remainder all related to political-economic issues:

> Get Britain out of the common market
> Fight Communism
> Ban foreign imports we can produce ourselves
> Control Investment overseas

Bring British industry under British ownership and control
Halt inflation by reforming our financial system

Ignoring the very vague final political aspiration in this list – tantamount to saying 'halt inflation by doing things better' – the remaining five stake out the commitment of the party to autarky. All policies aim to restrict the national economy
within the borders of 'the nation', restructured to the benefit of 'British workers'.
Across the rest of this first issue of the party newspaper, there were articles celebrat-
ing cases 'where British workers are put first' – e.g. where 'five West Indian nurses'
were denied work permits, and where work permits for hotel and catering indus-
tries were reduced (British Workers First, *The British Worker* 1977, No.1, p.3) – and
articles on international trade, which reported that British companies 'now make
half of their pre-tax profits overseas. […] These figures show how the international
interests of big business are increasingly coming into conflict with the national
interests of this country' (British (?) Capitalism, *The British Worker* 1977, No.1, p.3).
Union bosses were also alleged to be in thrall to international capitalism. Reporting
an incident, where Bill Keys (the General Secretary of the Printers Union) did not
publish a letter from the NP criticising an article in the Union journal which supported 'the capitalist policy of multiracialism', the article stated:

> Multinational capitalism has sought to break down national boundaries and
> national differences to bring about a cosmopolitan 'One World' that is 'One
> Great Market'. The only force that can stop it is nationalism. […] Keys' talk
> about internationalism and the wickedness of discrimination puts him right
> alongside the cosmopolitan capitalist who wants to invest his money wher-
> ever in the world it will make the most profit.

Of course, the obvious question that arises from this argument is why did the
NP believe that nationalism is the only force that can stop international capitalism? Why not a stronger working-class movement? Why not communism? The
answer is suggested in an advert on the back cover of the newspaper. Immediately
above the bullet-points of party principles partly quoted above there was placed an
advert for Raven Books, and amongst the titles on offer were the same conspiracy
texts: Skousen's *The Naked Capitalist*, Chesterton's *The New Unhappy Lords*, Allen's
None Dare Call it Conspiracy and Nesta Webster's *World Revolution*. All these books
advanced more or less explicit variations on the core conspiracy: that Jewish capitalists and Jewish communists were allies and co-conspirators in a plan to achieve
global (Jewish) political and economic power. For the NP, autarky was a means to
insulate Britain from internationalist Jewish power.

Distributism: a 'native' fascist economic model

Distributism (also known as distributivism) is a slightly more marginal economic theory within British fascism, principally because it dominated the political-economic

thinking of the NF during the 1980s, a period when the party was at its most esoteric. Originally, distributism was developed and popularised during the opening
decades of the twentieth century, chiefly by Hilaire Belloc and G.K. Chesterton.
The political-economic theory was first coined by Belloc in *The Servile State*
(1912), developed in his later *An Essay on The Restoration of Property* (1930), and
taken up by G.K. Chesterton in his *GK Weekly* magazine and book *The Outline of
Sanity* (1928). Distributism is not an inherently fascist political-economic theory,
but was adopted by British fascist parties from the 1980s onwards as another 'third
way' alternative to capitalism and socialism. As Brons (1984: 20) put it, 'As a movement, we are only interested in those ideas which form part of, or complement, the
ideology of Racial Nationalism. That ideology *does* form a coherent whole even
if the totality of Belloc's does not' (emphasis in original). Distributism advocates a
wider distribution of land, property and the means of production than is currently
experienced in British society; it is in favour of small businesses and a decentralised
economy, and is opposed to collectivism, trade unions, urbanism, internationalism
and usury. Inspired by the medieval guild system, distributism advocates establishing
small farming and craft communities, where production is based on craftsmanship
and small workshops. As with all fascist political economies, distributism is based on
chauvinistic and exclusionary nationalism, and the 'principle' that 'there must be no
foreign ownership of British industry' (Pearce 1985: 18).

The distributist opposition to moneylending and usury entails a strong dislike of
banks and systems of (international) finance which, particularly when interpreted and
applied by fascist ideologues, frequently spills over into the familiar 'core conspiracy'
anti-Semitic argumentation regarding Jewish 'money power'. However, these anti-
Semitic conspiracies were not grafted onto distributism by fascists, but were present
from the outset by virtue of both Belloc and Chesterton's anti-semitism. Belloc was
convinced that the 'future was in the hands of Jewish bankers and financiers', and
became a supporter of Mussolini (quoted in Veldman 1994: 32). He also wrote the
anti-Semitic book *The Jews*, first published in 1922 and reprinted in 1937 with a new
introductory chapter, which was described by the then-leader of the NF Andrew
Brons (1984: 20) as his 'admirable Yid book'. Belloc's thesis, largely inspired by the
Russian Revolution, was summarised on the book's contents page: 'The Jews are
an alien body within the society they inhabit. [...] An alien body in any organism is
disposed of in one of two ways: elimination and segregation' (Belloc 1922: xi). The
Russian Revolution is referred to as 'the Jewish Revolution in Russia' (1922: xii)
but, precisely reflecting the core conspiracy of fascism, Jews are also assumed to be
the controllers of finance capitalism. Belloc alleges that, until recently,

> Men hesitated to attack the Jews as financiers because the stability of society
> and of their own fortunes was bound up with finance – but when a body of
> Jews also appeared as the active enemies of existing society and of private for-
> tune, the restraint was removed – since the Bolshevist movement open (and
> hostile) discussion of the Jewish problem has become universal.
>
> *(Belloc 1922: xii–xiii)*

His argument is convoluted, but Belloc suggests that, because he views Bolshevism as a 'Jewish movement' this enables him, and others, to debate whether all Jews – not only 'Jewish Bolshevists' but *all Jews* – should be allowed to remain in Britain, or should be 'disposed of' via elimination or segregation.

Belloc's anti-Semitism is widely accepted by his supporters – indeed, for some, it appears to be a primary reason why he has attracted such support (cf. Brons 1980, 1984, 1985). A pamphlet entitled *In defence of Hilaire Belloc*, written by the Church in History Information Centre (n.d.), acknowledged 'Few would deny that as a teenager […] Belloc absorbed anti-Semitic attitudes' (p.7). His political-economic views, and the ways that these meshed with his anti-Semitism, are positively evaluated:

> Belloc detested both international finance, which exploited and manipulated the ordinary working people, and Marxist socialism and communism which, by making the state the owner of all productive wealth, would be destructive of freedom of the spirit. It was widely believed at the time that the leaders of both these forces were small groups of Jews. Because of this, a negative feeling developed towards them.
>
> *(p. 9)*

The rise of distributism in the NF is attributable to the political context of the situation at the end of the 1970s, and a decline in party fortunes. With the collapse of their electoral strategy in 1979, younger and more radical members in the NF looked for alternative ideological foundations to Hitlerite National Socialism that party policy could draw upon. Initially, Strasserism was touted as an option – several articles were published in *Nationalism Today*, the ideological mouthpiece of this new radical leadership, that argued the Strasser brothers should be included in the list of 'people who laid the foundations of Nationalist ideology', or which claimed 'the German National Revolution was betrayed [by Hitler] following [Gregor] Strasser's death' (Holland 1984: 12). Other articles argued that more 'native' traditions in anti-socialist, anti-capitalist politics exist, which were more appropriate for British 'nationalism'. A review of *Yesterday and Tomorrow* (helpfully also on sale in the NF's book shop) approvingly quoted the book's argument that 'Capitalism and its Communist offspring' are 'two alien dogmas', and that people

> […] in the White nations are now looking back to our own ideological and spiritual heritage, *seeking in the ideas of our forefathers a future for our children*. The German National Socialists; the Fascists; the British Distributists and early patriotic socialists; all these and many others have contributed to the great heritage of National Revolutionary thought.
>
> *(Emphasis added, quoted in Acton 1983: 8)*

Brons (1985: 15) argues that whilst some of the ideas of National Socialism and Fascism were 'similar to those of the Distributists', since 'their nationalism sprang, in part, from the same instincts and traditions from which all European nationalism has sprung', with distributism 'the National Front has a lineage of its own' which it was now starting to reclaim. This lineage enabled the NF to articulate a thoroughly anti-Semitic political economy, without it being derived from openly Nazi source material. Thus, in this same article Brons praises the Chestertons and Belloc for attacking 'the Judaeo-Financial clique that dominated not only this country but also the United States and later Bolshevik Russia' (1985: 15). A 'Roots' article on Belloc described him as the author of a 'brilliant expose of Zionism in his book *The Jews*' (*Nationalism Today* 20, January/February 1984, p.9). Issue 4 of *New Nation* (Autumn 1983, p.11) published a half-page extract from this book; in this same issue, Cecil Chesterton was included in the magazine's ongoing 'Great British Racialists' column (p.18). Chesterton, the column informs us, was 'unambiguously [...] on the side of the White Race' (ibid.). He risked 'his freedom as well as the wrath of the Judao-Financial Establishment' with his journalism and, with the publication *Eye Witness*, 'he and Belloc fearlessly exposed tyranny, dishonesty and the power of International Jewry' (ibid.).

By 1985, the Constitution of the party declared that the NF 'is a distributist movement', opposed to both capitalism and communism. The magazines *New Nation* and *Nationalism Today* included multiple articles that offered detailed discussion and passing reference to distributism as the assumed ideological backbone of the party, as well as selling copies of Belloc's and Chesterton's books. When the NF split in 1989, two radical factions broke off, each also subscribing to distributist economic policy. International Third Position, run by Derek Holland, continued to try to put the 'Political Soldiers' ethos of spiritual revolution into practice in its training centre in the UK and by buying property in France. The Third Way, led by Patrick Harrington, supported decentralisation, small businesses and environmental issues, and ideologically fused distributism with social credit – another anti-Semitic economic theory, developed by Clifford Douglas.

We can also detect echoes of distributism in later British National Party discourse. During the first few years of Nick Griffin's leadership, this tended to be most closely associated with opposition to global capitalism (cf. Griffin 2002) though, as Griffin (2005: 4) was to later categorically state, this 'opposition to global capitalism [...] in no way conflicts with our support for private enterprise'. Paragraph 3.2.6 of the 12.2 version of the Party Constitution (2010) demonstrated the BNP's continued adherence to distributism, declaring: 'social stability and contentment is best achieved by the many enjoying a personal stake in the assets and undertakings of their own nation. Accordingly, we believe that private property ownership, including where practicable in the means of production and distribution, should be encouraged and spread to as many members of the nation as possible' (p.8).

In a rare extended mediated endorsement, the BNP magazine *Identity* published a two-part article which purported to discuss distributist economics and its superiority to capitalist economies, where 'currencies always accumulate in the hands of the few' (Holroyd 2003a: 18). Holroyd presents two cases that he believed demonstrate the benefits of distributist economics: the historic example of Wörgl where, in 1932, the Mayor issued his own currency which he required inhabitants to spend rather than the Austrian Schilling (2003a); and the contemporary example of Bali, described as 'a paradise on earth', where 'Virtually every man and woman [...] is an accomplished artist and dancer' (2003b: 13). The implausible examples in the second part of his article (2003b) are closer to a gift economy and bear little resemblance to distributism. The example of Wörgl is more significant, as it is still presented in online neo-fascist discourse as a paradigm case where (Jewish) 'Money Power' was threatened. However the basic principles of distributism, which these cases are claimed to demonstrate, are conspicuous by their absence in both articles, despite Holroyd's conclusion that "The Wörgl scrip was *therefore* a Distributist form of currency" (emphasis added, 2003a: 18). Similarly, the origins of distributism in Chesterbelloc's anti-Semitic arguments are absent, other than a photo-caption of Belloc's portrait which informs the reader: 'Hilaire Belloc: another leading exponent of distributism' (2003a: 19). The two articles therefore act less as a discourse on distributism and more as an indication that the editor of *Identity* was familiar with the existence of the theory – thereby marking a continuity with the more 'radical' 1980s. Readers unfamiliar with distributism are, in turn, provided with the name of an author – Belloc – that they may wish to read more about.

The departure of 'third position' activists from the NF did not signal the end of its commitment to distributism. In the early 1990s, the NF published a booklet called *A look at Britain's only democratic nationalist political party* (1993 or 1994). Organised as a series of questions and answers, the booklet presents party ideology in a condensed and simplified way. For example, asked what the NF would do about companies being bought and sold on the stock exchange, the party answers:

> The National Front believes in a system of distributist ownership. This means that we would strongly encourage workers to directly own the factories, farms or other places of employment where they work. [...] This would break down the traditional divide between workers and management – they would truly be a team.
>
> *(p.22)*

Their motivation for supporting distributism is therefore two-fold: it would ensure national ownership of companies, and it breaks down the class distinction between white collar and blue collar workers. Nowhere in the booklet does the NF argue against capitalism, or suggest that they consider labour in a capitalist system to be alienating. Indeed, the very next Q&A openly states that a capitalist mode of production would still be central in their fantasy economy:

> *56. Does this mean you are against Private Enterprise?*
>
> No, quite the reverse. We are strongly in favour of people setting up and running their own business. As the business grows and the number of employees increases we would encourage the company to become a co-operative venture
>
> *(p.22)*

This is, therefore, still very much a capitalist economy, merely with smaller employers. Over the page the party specifically states that it is the concentration of economic power in advanced capitalism that it finds objectionable: 'Both communism and capitalism concentrate control of companies in the hands of either finance houses or state bureaucrats. Distributism gives direct ownership and direct control to the people' (p.23). However, the companies that the NF imagines here will still employ workers, and these workers will labour, generating surplus value for company owners. It would only be when a company grew to a (vaguely defined) size that it would be 'encouraged' (by indefinite means, again) to include employees in a profit-sharing scheme. Elsewhere in the booklet, the party shows that it is aware of how profit is generated:

> Ever since the days of the British Empire, City of London financiers have been investing British money abroad. [...] The National Front believes it is against the best interests of Britain for these financiers to use the wealth of the British people in such a way. We would ensure that the wealth created by British workers is invested back into Britain to create jobs for our own people.
>
> *(p.21)*

First, needless to say, by 'our own people' the NF means 'white British people' (see Richardson 2017). Second, the NF acknowledges 'wealth [is] created by British workers' (and, one surmises, through workers not being fully compensated for their labour). This is, therefore, a capitalist mode of production, and the only aspect of it that is rendered problematic by the NF is the investment of (British) money abroad by 'financiers' and 'Money Power'.

Whilst some may conclude that this indicates the NF had, by this point, drifted from the anti-capitalist thrust of distributism and that, in contrast, the party in the 1980s held a more radical (and so accurate) interpretation of Chesterbelloc, in fact, earlier articles in *Nationalism Today* and *New Nation* reveal a similarly forgiving attitude to the capitalist status quo in Britain. Brons (1980: 3), for example, openly declares 'Private enterprise is justly praised for providing a profit motive for industry' and that the NF must 'restore to people the rights to private property and the incentives of private profit'. Acton (1984: 13) argues that the nascent economic boom 'achieved under Thatcher's government can only be as superficial as it is short-lived', and that a range of measures are needed, including workers' co-operatives, nationalising banks and the abolition of the Stock Exchange, to ensure stable growth. The conclusion of the article, emboldened for emphasis in the original, voices the petit bourgeois sensibility under the surface of British fascist economics: 'Under the present industrial and financial regime *British industry is virtually the least profitable place to invest money.* Only when a National Front Government is in power [...] can this situated be reversed' (emphasis added, ibid.). Slightly earlier, in issue 16 of *Nationalism Today*, an editorial argued that 'the NF is the only party capable of rescuing British industry', through its policy 'that, *where possible*, large and monolithic organisations [...] be broken down into small private businesses and workers' co-operatives' (Industrial Front, *Nationalism Today* 16, p.18). Not only does the weasel word 'where possible' entail exceptions to this policy – that is, some large, profit-generating companies will not be broken down – elsewhere the article explaining party policy reveals its interpretation of 'small firms' to mean companies of up to 100 employees.

In fact, statistics from the Department for Business Innovation and Skills reveals that the 'revolutionary' changes proposed by distributist fascists already largely exist in capitalist Britain. Data from 1994 shows that there were 3.5 million businesses operating in Britain, and that 99.4 per cent of these employed 99 or fewer employees. Further, of these 3.5 million companies, 72.3 per cent (3 million) employed zero people – they were run by self-employed sole proprietors. Distributists always maintain that 'Under capitalism, the natural and unavoidable trend is always towards more and more mergers and [hence…] towards monopoly control' (Pearce 1985: 18). Actually, the reverse is the case in Britain. By 2015, there were 5.3 million small businesses operating in Britain and now 99.3 per cent of them employed 49 or fewer employers; 1.1 million (20 per cent) businesses had only 1–9 employees; and 4.1 million businesses were run by self-employed proprietors with no employees (76 per cent of all companies, up from 72.3 per cent 20 years previous). In contrast, 0.6 per cent of businesses were 'medium-sized' (with 50 to 249 employees) and only 0.1 per cent of businesses were categorised 'large' (with 250+ employees). The 7,000 large businesses in the UK do make a large contribution to employment, but small and medium employers still account for 60 per cent of UK employment.

Essentially, the proposed 'distributist' policies for the UK economy would have had very little impact on the majority of British workers' employment; Britain already is dominated by small and medium employers and by the widespread ownership of businesses. However, this does *not* mean that fascist distributism would be benign. What fascists propose, in effect, is a continuation of the current capitalist mode of production – but with two key differences. First, Jews and other 'non-nationals' will be denied property rights; the anti-Semitic content of distributism is undeniable and enduring, from those who coined the theory through to its late adopters in the NF. It is another licence for ethnic cleansing, clothed in the literary pretentions of Edwardian aristocracy. Second, distributism re-inscribes the primacy of politics in fascist ideology, and aims to ensure that no institution(s) could challenge the power of the party. As Brons summarises,

> those who accumulate, or benefit from the accumulation of, the largest holdings of capital, are not pursuing the perfectly legitimate drive for profit […] they are active in the pursuit of power […] *A Nationalist state simply cannot tolerate unconstitutional challenges to its power.*
>
> *(Emphasis in original, 1980: 3)*

Thus, distributism would constitute a racial and a political revolution in Britain, but it would have done very little to change Britain's capitalist economy.

Conclusion

Despite its claims to be committed to 'third way' political economies, the NF, like all British fascist parties, never freed itself from capitalism (Richardson 2017). Even at its most radical, during the 1980s, capitalism was very rarely criticised *in toto*. Instead, the National Front's critique of capitalism, during both of the phases discussed in this chapter, took one of three forms: it was directed against 'non-British' or international ownership of companies; against profiteering and exploitative practices frequently associated with 'non-British' owners or employers (what used to be called 'sweating', or 'sweated labour'); or against international finance capitalism and globalisation. Essentially, British fascists only oppose forms of capitalism where profits are enjoyed by 'non-British' capitalists. Profit accumulation – and the corresponding exploitation of workers – is not viewed as being inherently problematic, as long as companies and capitalists are 'British' (that is, white/Aryan). As Neocleous (1997: 43–44) argues:

> Fascism sits comfortably in the tradition of reactionary thought which identifies money and finance capital rather than capitalist commodity production as the 'enemy'. The goal in this tradition is not a classless society and the abolition of exploitation but a 'people's community' in which the excesses of the money-based modern society are curbed. Fascist attacks on 'capital' are always attacks on finance or banking capital rather than capitalist production.

In addition, when fascists use autarkic or distributist policy to attack finance or international capital this equates to an attack on Jewish capitalists – or, more accurately, the fascist attack on finance capital is part of an anti-Semitic conspiracy theory that maintains that Jews control capitalism for their own financial benefit and economic power. This is because fascist conspiracies are not only radical simplifications of complex historic and political-economic processes, they are also personifications: the fault lies with (Jewish) people, rather than systems, and so the solution, for fascists, is to remove them from a position of influence within the nation.

References

Primary sources

Acton, T. (1983) Book Review, Yesterday and Tomorrow, *Nationalism Today* 18, September/October, p.8.

Acton, T. (1984) British Industry – Facing the Abyss, *Nationalism Today* 21, March/April, p.13.

Bean, J. (1970) NF Must Win Labour Voters, *Spearhead* 34 June, p.4.

Belloc, H. (1922) *The Jews*. London: Constable and Company, Ltd.

Bleach, K. (1976) Thatcher's Red Herring, *Spearhead* 93, April, pp.6–8.

Brons, A. (1980) The Economic Threat to National Independence, *New Nation* 2, Autumn, pp.3–4.

Brons, A. (1984) Hilaire Belloc, Andrew Brons reviews A. N. Wilson's Biography, *New Nation* 6, Winter, p.20.

Brons, A. (1985) The Roots of British Nationalism, *Nationalism Today* 26, Jan/Feb, pp.14–15.

Church in History Information Centre (no date) *In defence of Hilaire Belloc.*

Griffin, N. (2002) The Slow Motion Crash, *Identity* 23, August, pp.4–6.

Griffin, N. (2005) Global Capitalism: The Big Picture, *Identity* 51, January, pp.4–6.

Holland, D. (1984) A Revolution Betrayed, Part One, *Nationalism Today* 22, May/June, pp.12–13.

Holroyd, A. (2003a) Time to Think Distributist, *Identity* 28, January, pp.18–19.

Holroyd, A. (2003b) Using Distributism to re-build our Communities, *Identity* 29, February, pp.12–14.

Joyce, W. (n.d. circa 1935) *Fascism and Jewry.* London: BUF Publications LTD.

Joyce, W. (1936) Analysis of Marxism, *Fascist Quarterly*, 2(4) October, pp.530–542.

Mosley, O. (n.d. circa 1933) *Fascism in Britain.* BUF Publications.

National Front (1979) *It's Our Country – Let's Win It Back! The Manifesto of the National Front.*

Nationalism Today (1983) Industrial Front: Small is Beautiful, Issue 16 May/June, p.18.

New Nation (1983) Great British Racialists, No.12 Cecil Chesterton, Autumn, p.18.

Pearce, J. (1985) A Stake in our Country, *Nationalism Today* 26, January/February, pp.18–19.

Spearhead (1970) Communism and Subversion, *Spearhead* 30, February 1970, p.8.

Tyndall, J. (1969) The Real History Makers: A Remarkable Document on the Anatomy of World Revolution, *Spearhead*, 23 (April/May), pp.4–6.

Tyndall, J. (1972) Why Big Money Backs World Communism, *Spearhead* 51, April, pp.6–7.

Webster, M. (1980) The Salvation of Capitalism is NOT a National Front Objective, *New Nation* 2 Autumn, pp.12–13 & 30.

Wegg-Prosser, C. F. (1936) The Worker and the State, *Fascist Quarterly*, 2(2) April: 255–266.

Secondary sources

Baker, D. (2006) 'The political economy of fascism: Myth or reality, or myth and reality?', *New Political Economy*, 11 (2): 227–250.

Benewick, R. (1969) *Political Violence and Public Order.* London: Allen Lane.

Billig, M. (1978) *Fascists: A Social Psychological View of the National Front.* London: Harcourt Brace Jovanovitch.

Buchheim, C. & Schemer, J. (2006) 'The role of private property in the Nazi economy: The case of industry', *The Journal of Economic History*, 66 (2): 390–416.

Fielding, N. (1981) *The National Front.* London: Routledge and Kegan Paul.

Harris, S. (1973) 'Spearhead of British racialism', *Patterns of Prejudice*, 7 (4): 15–20.

Lunn, K. (1980) 'Political anti-semitism before 1914: Fascism's heritage?' in Lunn, K. & Thurlow, R. C. (eds) *British Fascism: Essays on the Radical Right in Inter-War Britain.* London: Croom Helm.

Miller, M. L. & Ury, S. (2015) 'Cosmopolitanism: The end of Jewishness?' in Miller, M. L. & Ury, S. (eds) *Cosmopolitanism, Nationalism and the Jews of East Central Europe.* London and New York: Routledge.

Neocleous, M. (1997) *Fascism.* Buckingham: Open University Press.

Patterns of Prejudice (1967) 'A British fascist programme', 1 (2): 23.

Rees, P. (1979) *Fascism in Britain: An Annotated Bibliography.* Hassocks, Sussex: Harvester Press, Ltd.

Richardson, J. E. (2011) 'Race and racial difference: The surface and depth of BNP ideology', in Copsey, N. & Macklin, G. (eds) *British National Party: Contemporary Perspectives*. London: Routledge.

Richardson, J. E. (2013) Racial populism in British fascist discourse: The case of COMBAT and the British National Party (1960–67), in Wodak, R. & Richardson, J. E. (eds) *Analysing Fascist Discourse: European Fascism in Talk and Text*. New York: Routledge.

Richardson, J. E. (2017) *British Fascism: A Discourse-Historic Analysis*. Stuttgart: ibidem-Verlag.

Sykes, A. (2005) *The Radical Right in Britain: Social Imperialism to the BNP*. Houndmills: Palgrave Macmillan.

Szejnmann, C.-C. W. (2013) 'Nazi economic thought and rhetoric during the Weimar Republic: Capitalism and its discontents', *Politics, Religion and Ideology*, 14 (3): 355–376.

Thurlow, R. C. (1980) 'The Return of Jeremiah: The rejected knowledge of Sir Oswald Mosley in the 1930s', in Lunn, K. & Thurlow, R. C. (eds) *British Fascism: Essays on the Radical Right in Inter-War Britain*. London: Croom Helm.

Veldman, M. (1994) *Fantasy, the Bomb and the Greening of Britain*. Cambridge: Cambridge University Press.

Walker, M. (1977) *The National Front*. Glasgow: Fontana/Collins.

Wodak, R. & Richardson, J. E. (eds) *Analysing Fascist Discourse: European Fascism in Talk and Text*. New York: Routledge.

4

EXPORTING FASCISM ACROSS THE COMMONWEALTH

The case of the National Front of Australia

Evan Smith

Introduction

On Saturday, 2 June 1978, a group of nine people gathered in a room of the Southern Cross Hotel in the Melbourne CBD to launch the National Front of Australia (NFA). According to the Australian Security Intelligence Organisation (ASIO) informant, nine people attended the meeting, including several well-known far-right activists, a 16-year-old schoolboy and an undercover reporter for the newspaper *The Age*.[1] Seven out of the nine listed were already known to the authorities in some regard. The meeting was led by a 23-year-old law student and army reservist, Rosemary Sisson, who had travelled to Britain in 1977 to seek permission from the National Front's John Tyndall to establish an NF in Australia. According to ASIO, Tyndall had appointed Sisson to be Chairwoman of the NFA until a directing body was created. In a report on Sisson by the Victorian Police's Special Branch, Sisson was described in these terms:

> She appears to be intensely sincere in her beliefs but politically naïve and immature. I do not believe that she has the ability to form a political party on her own volition and would most likely be used by other persons taking advantage of her enthusiasm, while maintaining their anonymity.[2]

The meeting, which lasted between two and four hours, commenced with the playing of *God Save the Queen* and passed several motions relating to the outlook of the NFA, the composition of the National Directorate, membership fees and a statement of ambition regarding the contesting of elections in the near future. The 'highlight' of the meeting was listening to a tape recording of Tyndall. The ASIO informant described Tyndall's speech as such:

> Tyndal's [sic] speech included greetings to the newly formed NFA and congratulations and it is encouraging to him that the National Front had extended to Australia ... He pointed out that the National Front had been established for almost 12 years and during this time there had been clashes with the authorities, Police Special Branch and most left-wing groups. In spite of all this, they had conducted massive demonstrations and never instigated violence but violence was forced upon them ... The speech continued with the usual self praises and self congratulations for the National Front.[3]

Tyndall also mentioned in his speech that National Fronts had been established in several other countries, such as New Zealand, Canada, South Africa and Rhodesia. After Tyndall's speech, a letter of congratulations from the leader of the New Zealand National Front, David Crawford, was read out.[4] Sisson saw the connection to the British NF as very important and most of the policies outlined at the meeting centred around maintaining Australia's links with Britain, the Commonwealth and the 'Anglo-Celtic' race. These included the establishment of the Commonwealth National Front (CNF) as a (theoretical) co-ordinating body of the various NFs across the globe and the call for a reconfigured British Commonwealth as 'an exclusive closely-knit association of White states',[5] where there was either a large white population or ruling white elite. This led to the calling for the re-entry of Rhodesia and South Africa into the Commonwealth and support for white rule in both countries. As evidenced by the singing of the old national anthem, loyalty to the British Crown was paramount to the NFA.

This chapter will explore how the growth of the NF in Britain during the 1970s was seen as a blueprint for far-right activists in Australia (and elsewhere in the 'white' Commonwealth) and attempted to draw upon the NF's international reputation to establish a local version of the party. At the heart of this was a commitment to maintaining the links of empire in a post-imperial world and the continued importance of Britain to the Commonwealth. However, in the eyes of the NFA and the various other National Fronts established around the world, the Commonwealth was to be reconstituted as an expression of white supremacist solidarity – particularly as South Africa and Rhodesia were deemed to be on the frontline of a battle between multi-racialist communism and 'white civilisation' in this period of the Cold War. While there has been a wealth of literature about the National Front in Britain, its international links have not been sufficiently researched and the literature on the post-war far right in Australia is also quite limited. In the few studies of the post-war far right, scholars have tended to focus on the Australian League of Rights (ALoR) or the latter National Action and the Australian Nationalist Movement (Moore 1995, 2005; Whitford 2011; Mondon 2012).

This chapter seeks to redress this by looking at the case of the short-lived NFA, with a substantial proportion of the archival material on the NFA coming from the three ASIO files on the group held at the National Archives of Australia in Canberra. These files, although seen through the prism of the security services' surveillance of the NFA, provide a thorough insight into the organisation that is unparalleled amongst other post-war far-right groups, both in Australia and over-seas. From this, this chapter will argue that the attempts to establish the NFA and the wider Commonwealth National Front were not fortuitous from the very out-set, as the notoriety of the British NF severely hindered the attraction of mem-bership and brought the attention of the authorities, the press and the anti-fascist movement from the beginning. Like the NFA, attempts to establish National Fronts in New Zealand and South Africa did not last long and never eventuated in Canada or Rhodesia. The chapter will show that the case of the NFA and the CNF falls into a wider history of a British-styled fascism being exported to Australia and elsewhere within the British Commonwealth, yet failing to thrive outside of its original domestic context.

Earlier examples of British fascism and imperial ties

Paul Stocker (2015: 165) has written recently:

> All fascist movements sought to portray themselves as imperialists, and the true champion of Empire compared to the weak 'old gang' politicians who were throwing the Empire away, but differed in terms of rhetoric and policy substance…

This is particularly true in the relationship between the various strains of British fascism and Australia. Since the British Fascisti (BF) first emerged in Britain in the mid-1920s, the far right in Australia has attempted to replicate these British groups down under. The most infamous of these groups in the inter-war period was the New Guard, led by Lt. Colonel Eric Campbell. Inspired by the BF and the British paramilitary response to the General Strike of 1926, the New Guard was formed by a group of ex-servicemen in February 1931 in Sydney (Amos 1976: 13). Coming out of several paramilitary organisations established in the 1920s, the New Guard opposed the rise of communism, the Labor Party and militant trade unionism during the Depression. Despite being established a year and a half before Oswald Mosley's British Union of Fascists (BUF), in 1933, Campbell and Mosley looked to build the New Empire Union. In August 1933, *The Blackshirt* announced that the BUF was forming a New Empire Union that would bring together the various fascist movements from across the British Empire. While fascist movements were springing up in New Zealand, South Africa and Canada, the BUF concentrated on the New Guard, who allegedly had 100,000 members and was reported to have 'often played a decisive part in Australian politics' (*The Blackshirt* 26 August, 1933). The same article mentioned the negotiations between Mosley and Campbell, announcing that with the New Empire Union:

> we now have a united Fascist drive throughout the Empire, against the great financial interests which have impeded Empire development, and towards the self-contained Empire which is our common objective.

After a brief visit to Europe, where Campbell met Mosley, as well as representatives from Fascist Italy and Nazi Germany, he returned to Australia in 1934 and transformed the New Guard into the Centre Party. Moving from a paramilitary organisation to a political party, Campbell explained in his new manifesto, *The New Road*, that the Centre Party represented a fascist revolution in Australian politics. Campbell (1934: 49) argued:

> I am a Fascist because I am a democrat. I am a democrat because I believe in government by the general will. The only possible form of government for a country like Australia, where … there is no traditional ruling class, is the intelligent selection by the people of the most high-minded and capable of their number to undertake the task of government …
>
> The party system of government is a negation of everything that [democracy] stands for; it is to the ideals of Fascism that we must look for the retention of democracy as the guiding spirit of the people.

This was reinforced in a letter that Campbell wrote to Mosley in May 1934 (intercepted by the British and Australian authorities), in which he stated that the 'principles of the Centre Party are simply an application of the Fascist principles to Australian conditions'.[6]

However, Campbell's conversion to fascism did not convince many of the New Guard's former supporters, and membership dwindled over the next few years. By the time that *The New Road* was published, the material conditions that had allowed the New Guard to appear to be a temporary political force in Australian politics had changed. Much of the political impetus behind the New Guard was opposition to Premier Jack Lang and a fear of the Labor Party's 'socialist' agenda. After Lang was replaced as Premier by the United Australia Party's Bertram Stevens (with the UAP also in power at Commonwealth level under Prime Minister Joseph Lyons), much of this fear dissipated, as these governments at State and Commonwealth level were 'very much similar in ideology and social character to the New Guard' (Moore 2011: 205). At the same time, the economy started to recover after the Great Depression, which had pushed a significant number of Australians to the political extremes, both right and left. And as well as these economic and political conditions, the Centre Party's increasing enthusiasm for German National Socialism alienated many of those who formerly supported the New Guard (although Campbell then moved away from this pro-Nazi position in 1937–1938, saving himself from internment, and a similar fate to Mosley, in the Second World War) (Moore 2010: 109).

Intelligence files from the National Archives of Australia reveal from intercepted letters that a small network of supporters of Mosley remained in Australia in the mid-to-late 1930s and were in contact with the BUF headquarters in London. Some Mosleyite sympathisers in Australia were directed by the BUF in London to a German schoolteacher named W. Erich Meier, who was also in contact with local groups linked to the German National Socialists.[7] Spread between South Australia,

Victoria and Queensland, these handful of fascist sympathisers did not seem to partake in much activism beyond letter-writing to the local media, but they did draw up a programme of the Australian Union of Fascists and National Socialists, announcing:

> 1. The Movement is absolutely loyal to the Crown and the British Empire and maintains the highest ideals of Nationalism and believes in effective government by Leadership.[8]

Most of the programme seemed to apply the policies of the BUF to Australian circumstances, but there were some points specifically tailored to Australia's role within the British Empire. The first affirmed that the Australian Union of Fascists would wholeheartedly take part in the 'reciprocal trade relationships with Britain and the rest of the Empire' as proposed by the BUF, and limit imports 'first and foremost to British Goods'.[9] The second was a pronouncement of the group's immigration and racial policy, which was much more clearly outlined than the BUF's policies concerning 'race'. The programme declared that the group supported:

> 14. Enforcement of the 'White Australia' policy. Immigration to be limited solely to Britishers and members of the British Empire of European stock. Also to Fascist European Races in a limited degree. The cancellation of the existing naturalization laws and of all laws permitting the privilege of citizenship to foreigners and aliens born in Australian Territories and Water.[10]

Despite the drawing up of this programme, it seems that the Australian Union of Fascists did not make much progress beyond this initial stage and the BUF's dreams of establishing a fascist foothold in Australia had petered out with the fortunes of the Centre Party in 1934.

In the post-war period, Mosley still championed the Dominions as the saviour of the British Commonwealth, but now suggested that Britain, alongside the Dominions, should enter the European Common Market. In the early 1960s, Mosley (1961: 33) argued that the Dominions (and Britain) 'fit naturally into united Europe' as they were 'great primary producers' that could supply what Europe, at the time, lacked. Dominions like Canada and Australia were seen as vital food producers for a booming Western Europe, but Mosley also argued that it was necessary for Europe to maintain its colonies in Africa for economic and geo-strategic (i.e. anti-communist) purposes (Mosley 1961: 111–112). However, Mosley was unable to inspire a local following like he had with Campbell's Centre Party in the 1930s and when Mosley publicly announced plans to visit Australia in 1969, ASIO assessed him not to be a security risk, but someone who needed to be watched by the organisation while in the country.[11]

The pro-Britishness of the Australian far right was best demonstrated in the post-war period by the Australian League of Rights, which emerged out of the

'Social Credit' movement of the 1930s, and pronounced a programme of anti-communism, monarchism and anti-Semitism. Its leader, Eric Butler, began the post-war ALoR in South Australia in 1946 and a national ALoR was established in 1960 (Moore 1995: 68). As Aurelien Mondon (2012) explained, during the 1960s the League was anti-communist, supported the Vietnam War, was pro-monarchist and pro-empire, anti-liberal and blended traditional conservative rhetoric with anti-Semitic conspiracy theory. Andrew Moore (1995: 75–79) claimed that the ALoR had some traction at the lowest levels of the Liberal/National Party where there was a transmission of ideas and political action between the far right and the outlier of the L-NP. However, as David Greason (1994: 88) showed in his book, the more youthful sections of the Australian far right eschewed the ALoR for their conservatism and 'stuffiness'.

The ALoR had overlap with Chesterton's League of Empire Loyalists and Butler belonged to an Australian chapter of the LEL, travelling to London in 1962 to meet with Chesterton.[12] Like ALoR, the LEL had a particular following in South Australia and in 1958, the South Australian Police's Special Branch noted connections between those involved in the Social Credit movement (such as Butler) and the local version of the LEL.[13] The aims of the LEL, the Special Branch reported, were:

1) To maintain the name of the British Commonwealth of Nations
2) To restore the British Empire as such
3) To engineer, where possible, the separation of the British Commonwealth from the United Nations
4) To awaken the public to the gradual dissolution of the Empire and to take steps to prevent such dissolution
5) To avert the establishment of a 'World Police Force'.[14]

Despite the close personal connection between Butler and Chesterton, it was the ALoR which was to have longevity, but by the late 1970s, the League was seen by a younger generation of far-right activists as an anachronism from a bygone era. Although it had its origins in the LEL, the British NF seemed to many on the far right across the British Commonwealth to be the dynamic and broad movement needed for the political landscape of the crisis-ridden 1970s.

The National Front and its British context

After the Second World War, Oswald Mosley revived his political activism with the Union Movement (UM), but anti-fascist opposition beat back Mosley's attempts to build a movement in the East End of London and in 1951, he went into self-imposed exile in Ireland until the late 1950s (Renton 2000; Macklin 2007). This can be viewed as the end of 'classical' fascism in the vein of the inter-war movement, with the defining organisation of the post-war fascist movement (before the arrival of the NF) being the League of Empire Loyalists, which attracted disaffected

Conservatives who were worried about decolonisation within and immigration from the British Commonwealth. The LEL became the conveyor belt through which all the major names of British fascism – Colin Jordan, John Tyndall, Martin Webster, John Bean and Andrew Fountaine – passed, but most did not remain in the organisation for long. From the late 1950s to the 1960s, the British far right was characterised by a series of splits into tiny organisations, often featuring the same individual and only superficially distinguishable from each other.[15]

In February 1967, the LEL and John Bean's British National Party, along with several smaller anti-immigration groups, including members of the Racial Preservation Society (RPS), merged to form the National Front. The National Front was 'an attempt to synthesize the mass politics and economic and political programme of the BUF with the ferocious anti-semitism and racial populism of Arnold Leese', the leader of the tiny inter-war group, the Imperial Fascist League, presented in a 'more respectable and seemingly rational guise' (Thurlow 1998: 247). With Chesterton as its chairman, the NF tried to appear as a legitimate political party, although divided between Chesterton's elitism and support for mass politics by John Bean and Andrew Fountaine, two leadership figures from the BNP. Chesterton saw the NF as 'a pressure group, rather than as a potential mass movement', while others, with a more radical position, 'insisted that the NF's sights be set on a mass membership, a nation-wide and popular movement' (Walker 1979: 188). The leadership of the National Front was hesitant to include Tyndall and Webster's Greater Britain Movement, who were viewed as neo-Nazi extremists, but as Martin Walker (1977: 68) explained, amongst the rank-and-file NF members, it had been 'long expected and desired that any coalition of the Right would have to include Tyndall'. The disparate groups involved in the amalgamation brought different membership numbers, properties and finances, along with several publications – *Spearhead* from Tyndall's NSM and GBM; *Candour* from Chesterton's LEL; and *Combat* from Bean's BNP, which merged with *Spearhead* in 1968.[16] Membership numbers were hard to define throughout the existence of the NF, but it is estimated that it had around 1,500 members at its inception (Lewis 1987: 248).

It was also Conservative MP Enoch Powell's 'Rivers of Blood' speech that allowed the National Front to exploit popular racist attitudes as Powell 'brought the language and arguments of the neo-fascist political fringe into the heart of the establishment' (Thurlow 1998: 246). 'There can be little doubt', Richard Thurlow (1998: 249) wrote, 'that the NF would not have survived if Enoch Powell had not unwittingly given it such a helping hand in its infancy'. However Powell was still seen as part of the Conservative establishment, which the NF tried to distance itself from. This led to a clash between Chesterton and the more militant members, who were 'desperate… to capitalize on support for Enoch Powell' – a strategy that Chesterton, who eschewed the populism of Powell, had 'resolutely opposed' (Walker 1977: 94). This clash resulted in Chesterton resigning in October 1970, with John O'Brien, a recent convert from the Conservative right via the National Democratic Party (NDP), becoming chairman in February 1971 (Shipley 1978: 14). O'Brien attempted to purge the NF of its neo-Nazi elements, represented in the leadership by Tyndall and Webster and, throughout 1971, the factional fighting continued, but Tyndall was able to survive. In early 1972, O'Brien and his supporters defected to the National Independence Party (NIP), with Tyndall replacing him as chairman (Lewis 1987: 252).

In 1972, Idi Amin expelled the Asian community from Uganda and as Uganda was a former British colony, many of these Asians had United Kingdom passports. Over the next two years, around 23,000 Ugandan Asians migrated to Britain, with around another 17,000 distributed between India and other Commonwealth countries (Gupta 1974: 321). This caused much outrage amongst anti-immigrant constituency, with the National Front, as well Enoch Powell and the Monday Club, campaigning against this intake of migrants. By criticising the 'soft' approach towards the Ugandan Asians by the Government, the NF appeared to many as an extreme extension of traditional Conservative ideals. This period saw the NF attempt to capitalise on anti-immigrant sentiment amongst 'disillusioned, largely middle-class Conservatives', reinforced by 'growing links with the reactionary Conservative Monday Club' (Eatwell 2003: 336). The attempts at closer ties with the Conservative right brought the NF significant numbers and members, such as Roy Painter and John Kingsley-Read. Membership numbers reached their highest during 1973–74. While not exact, membership was estimated at being between 14,000 and 17,500 (Thurlow 1998: 259). However there was still apprehension amongst the Nazi elements of the leadership, such as John Tyndall and Martin Webster that the NF was becoming too close to the Conservatives. The National Front's strategy with the Monday Club was appropriation of members and infiltration, 'aimed to win over its support and, ultimately, destroy it' (Miles & Phizacklea, 1984: 121). What characterised the NF during the period from 1968 to 1974 was its use of Conservative opposition to black immigration and its extreme position on traditional Conservative ideas. However, when the economic crisis set in after 1974, the NF moved away from trying to appeal to middle-class Conservative voters to attempting to siphon Labour Party supporters and appealing to the working class, exploiting the dire economic situation by blaming black immigration for shortages in employment, housing and welfare.

After its dismal results at the two general elections in 1974, there was another power struggle within the NF, with those who had come to the NF via the Conservatives (described as 'the populists') calling for the resignation of Tyndall as chairman for his neo-Nazi persona (Taylor 1979: 135; Lewis 1987: 252). Throughout 1974 and 1975, Tyndall and the leader of the 'populists', John Kingsley-Read, wrestled for leadership of the NF, before the 'populists' left in early 1976 to form the National Party. Although the NP quickly won two council seats in Blackburn in May 1976, the NF remained the prominent far-right party in Britain during the late 1970s and despite a growing anti-fascist movement against them, Tyndall's party sought to expand across the British Commonwealth.

Laying the foundations for the NFA

The Age journalist who attended the meeting was David Wilson who wrote about the establishment of the NFA in the newspaper the following week. Wilson described the secret meeting of nine people as:

> the culmination of 12 months' work: trips to England by two of the nine, talks with the head of the English movement, Mr John Tyndall, letters to the chairman of the New Zealand division, Mr David Crawford, and weeks of long hours carefully selecting the initial members of the Australian movement, printing, letter writing and telephone calls.
>
> *(The Age, 4 June, 1978)*

The National Front of New Zealand (NFNZ) preceded the establishment of the NFA, and was 'officially' formed in 1977 by B. B. Thompson, Kerry Bolton of the New Zealand Democratic Nationalist Party and David Crawford, who was to become the leading figure of the short-lived NFNZ (Spoonley 1987: 157–158).[17]

According to ASIO intelligence reports, a Birmingham-based NF organiser, Jeremy May (who had previously lived in Australia), had travelled in early 1978 to assist Sisson in setting up the NFA, while Sisson also communicated with Tyndall in writing.[18] In an intercepted letter, presumably between Sisson and Tyndall, written in late November 1977, it was suggested that the NFA would supposedly operate differently than the British NF, writing:

> We agree with your suggestion that an Australian NF body should aim to function – at least initially – as a pressure group concentrating on basic political technique and party organisation, rather than attempting to achieve mass popular appeal and publicity.[19]

This letter was written in the wake of the 'Battle of Lewisham' in August 1977 when the British NF attempted to march through a borough of south-east London with a large African-Caribbean community.[20] The clashes between anti-fascist protestors and the police, as well as with some NF members, brought the NF to the attention of many Australians as the scenes were broadcast on the news (*Sydney Morning Herald*, 15 August 1977; *The Canberra Times*, 15 August 1977). The NF had shifted in their strategy from attempting to gain influence amongst ex-Conservative Party voters and building its membership base to a strategy of 'owning the streets' and gaining as much publicity as possible from these street battles, whilst simultaneously contesting elections and trying to siphon off disaffected Labour voters (Husbands 1988: 66).

It seemed from Sisson's letter that the NFA were not expecting to mimic the British NF's approach just yet – with only a handful of interested people, occupying the streets was beyond their capabilities at this stage. The month before the establishment of the NFA, May wrote an article in Tyndall's journal (aligned to the NF at the point in time) *Spearhead*, titled 'Towards a National Front of Australia'.[21] Like

Oswald Mosley's British Union of Fascists in the 1930s,[22] the NF saw Australia as 'a vast and fascinating country with tremendous social and economic potential' and while the country was 'almost completely self-sufficient in economic resources', it was perceived that Australia was at the mercy of foreign investment and international liberalism. May pointed to the ending of the 'White Australia Policy' as a particular symbol of Australia's despair, lamenting the 'invading hordes' from southern Europe, the Middle East and Asia. Furthermore, May focused on Australia's 'complete absence of protection for almost the entire length of the country's vast coastline' as another example of the country's weakness, with the naval defences, described as a 'bathtub floatilla', unable to prevent 'Chinese drug racketeers, Pacific Islanders and, most recently, Vietnamese refugees' from reaching its shores. Despite this, Australia was still seen as a bastion of the old white Commonwealth at a time when South Africa and Rhodesia seemed on the verge of collapse. May warned *Spearhead*'s readers:

> Let us be clear on one point. Should South Africa ever fall to the forces which threaten to engulf Western civilisation, we can be sure that Australia will be next on the list. Liberalism is a luxury which Australia simply cannot afford, if only for geographical reasons. No protection money will ever be sufficient to dissuade the teeming Asiatic billions from erupting into the island continent once they get their chance.

May declared that the only way to 'safeguard the nation from this fate' was the creation of the NFA, which he described as 'an urgent and imperative necessity'. 'Native Australians', by which May meant white Australians with a British background, 'are a proud, strong-minded and independent people', who also maintained their links to Britain. It was up to the NFA to 'ensure that this distinctive national identity … is encouraged, enforced and politically activated'.

The *Australian Nationalist* and white supremacist solidarity

With this mission in mind, the establishment of the NFA was preceded by attempts to gauge public opinion through the secret distribution of literature across Melbourne. As David Wilson wrote in *The Age*, 'The only indication of the secret spread of the movement was through the carefully circulated newsletter, *The Australian Nationalist*' (*The Age*, 4 June 1978). *The Australian Nationalist* had started appearing from January 1978 and was a mimeographed publication written by Sisson. The first issue called for a united Australian nationalist party and bemoaned that the nationalist movement at that time was 'almost hopelessly and irretrievably fragmented into mutually suspicious, competitive and absurdly idiosyncratic, exclusive little groups.'[23] But Sisson declared:

> IT IS IMPERATIVE THAT WE REGROUP AND UNITE! Only though unity and the strength this gives us can we begin to tap and realise the incalculable political potential of national patriotism within this country.[24]

Sisson pointed to the British NF as the example 'forever before our eyes' of the uni-fication of several different far-right groups.[25] *The Australian Nationalist* expressed a pro-British Commonwealth nationalism and its influences were very much drawn from the British fascist movement, rather than the American far right. Similar to May's article, Australia was portrayed as the bastion of the white British civilisation on the periphery of Asia and Sisson argued that this meant that a strong nationalist movement was needed to maintain this position. The fear of invasion by Asians was long-standing in Australia and Sisson evoked this in a January 1978 article:

> The geographical situation of Australia, with its close proximity to some of the most populous of Asiatic nations, impels us to be very much on our guard against nationally destructive propaganda.[26]

In the editorial to the April 1978 edition of the newsletter, Sisson further champi-oned Australia's links to Britain and the importance of their 'proper ethnic pride'. She argued:

> Australia owes almost everything it has to Great Britain. The conquering and pioneering spirit of our forefathers was British. This can never be denied. If anything, we should seek closer links not only with white Europe, but to a greater extent with our mother country. Even though we are no longer a cluster of colonies, but are fully self-governing and independent, there is no reason why we should forsake our history and clamour for a republic.[27]

One of the recurring themes in *The Australian Nationalist*, which pre-empted the for-mation of the NFA and the CNF, was the importance of the British Commonwealth and solidarity with minority white rule in Africa. By the late 1970s, the Rhodesian civil war had raged for more than a decade and the Smith regime had been brought into negotiations with the Patriotic Front, which represented the two major organ-isations of the Zimbabwean national liberation movement, the Zimbabwe African National Union (ZANU) and the Zimbabwe African People's Union (ZAPU). Many white supremacists and anti-communists saw Rhodesia as a microcosm of the battle against communism and multi-racial democracy in Southern Africa during the Cold War, particularly after the fall of the Portuguese colonies of Mozambique and Angola between 1975 and 1977 (Barclay 1983: Lowry 2007). South Africa supported Rhodesia militarily and also intervened in the Angolan civil war, fight-ing against the Soviet- and Cuban-backed People's Movement for the Liberation of Angola (MPLA) (Polack 2013). Like many on the far right across the globe, Sisson championed the apartheid regime in South Africa, declaring that 'White rule is the only solution to the problem of government' and asserting that the ruling National Party had 'provided a stable government to all of the country's inhabitants, despite opposition, both internally and externally'.[28] 'A strong White government is the solution', Sisson argued, 'not only for South Africa but for every country where White men live'.[29] In another issue, Sisson called for white Rhodesians to be allowed to enter Australia as 'refugees', instead of those who came from Vietnam and Cambodia at the same time. Sisson described these 'refugees' as 'the type of people who can make a great contribution to Australia' as they shared a similar settler colonialist background.[30]

In June 1978, *The Australian Nationalist* became *Frontline: Magazine of the National Fronts of Australia and New Zealand*, with the debut issue dedicated to the formation of the NFA. Unlike the descriptions by ASIO and by David Wilson in *The Age*, the June meeting of the nine people to form the NFA was described in *Frontline* in grandiose terms. Quoting the opening address by Sisson, meeting supposedly 'mark[ed] an important event in the political history of Australia' by forming a new political party that 'represents the future of the Australian people' and 'revive[d] national pride'.[31] The magazine also carried the text of Tyndall's speech heard at the meeting, in which Tyndall described Australia as a *terra nullius* transformed by British settlers into a bulwark of white civilisation on the edges of the British Empire:

> Australia was not so very long ago a wilderness inhabited by a few savages, and it took some very hardy determined, self-reliant and tough pioneers to carve a great country and a great civilization out of that wilderness.[32]

Tyndall enthused about the formation of the Commonwealth National Front, remarking that the 'realisation of the National Front spanning the whole British Commonwealth has always been a dream to me' and with the establishment of the NFA, 'the sight of this dream being fulfilled is enormous encouragement to me'. Tyndall asserted that the NFA was not subordinate to the British NF and there was to be 'equal partnerships' between the NF in the UK and those in Australia, New Zealand and South Africa.[33] In an article in *Frontline*, the CNF was to co-ordinate activities amongst the various NFs across the Commonwealth, but allowed discretion to each NF to function as it desired. The article explained:

> Subject to their adherence to a common set of basic principles and objectives, National Front organisations in various countries are free to determine their own rules of association, to make their own executive decisions and to determine themselves all policies relating to their own countries' domestic political affairs.
>
> The above will include the right to determine whether the National Front in a particular country will function as a fully fledged political party, seeking power in its own right by the ballot box, or whether it will function merely as a pressure group or society for the furtherance of National Front ideals.[34]

The magazine also carried the letter of congratulations from the NFNZ's leader David Crawford, which described the NF as 'the vanguard of the most impelling force ever to strike your country in the last 100 years'.[35] Crawford mentioned that

National Fronts now existed in Australia, New Zealand, South Africa and Canada. The journal *Patterns of Prejudice* noted the announcement of the Commonwealth National Front in mid-1978, but stated that the only NF that had been set up by that time was in New Zealand[36] – although by March 1979, ASIO believed that the NFNZ was 'almost finished'.[37] *Patterns of Prejudice* also stated that NFs in Canada and South Africa were still in development.[38]

Power struggles inside the NFA

The 16-year-old schoolboy who attended the inaugural meeting of the NFA was David Greason. In his autobiography, *I was a Teenage Fascist*, Greason (1994: 168–186) described the meeting as a ramshackle and ill-organised affair, with him moving a motion for the formation of the NFA, even though he had not seen the motion previously. Greason described that in the days following the meeting and the publicity given to the NFA in the mainstream media, several different far-right identities, usually linked to the now defunct National Socialist Party of Australia (NSPA), claimed to be part of the NFA's leadership. This is borne out in the ASIO files, which catalogue that various people in Victoria, Queensland and New South Wales all claimed to represent the National Front in Australia, including Robert Cameron, the NSPA's former leader, and Anton Heintjes, a Dutch migrant and former member of the NSPA.[39] According to Greason and ASIO, the NFA seemed to be limited to Victoria and Queensland, where the Queensland Immigration Control Association (run by John C. A. Dique) had significant influence.[40] The rival to the NFA in Sydney was the Australian National Alliance (ANA), which eschewed the pro-Britishness of the National Front and leaned more towards the white supremacism coming out of the United States, influenced by the infamous newspaper *National Vanguard*. According to Greason, the ANS tried to foster a uniquely Australian nationalism, appropriating the symbolism of the Eureka Flag, and promoted the idea of an Australian republic. Quoted by Greason, the ANA's paper *Audacity* stated, 'Australian nationalism must not become a second fiddle to an overseas conductor who is anxious to make an international reputation orchestrating a group which plays dead-beat Rule Britannia' (cited in Greason 1994: 180). The leading figure of the ANA was Jim Saleam, who had been a member of the NSPA and went on to lead several far-right groups, such as National Action and the Australia First Party (Moore 1995: 120–125).

By 1980, *Patterns of Prejudice* was reporting that the NFA had between 100 and 300 members, but had been subject to in-fighting,[41] particularly as Sisson made trips to the UK to meet with Alan Birtley, a NF member jailed for weapons and explosives offences. The ASIO file carries significant correspondence between Sisson and an NF member named Margaret Swan, with whom Sisson discusses her links to Birtley extensively.[42] In a letter dated 19 October 1979, Sisson admits 'I am in love with Alan although I tried hard to refrain from doing so.'[43] By the end of 1979, Birtley had been released from prison in the UK and had come to Australia to live with Sisson, with the media alerting the authorities after Birtley slipped through Customs at Melbourne Airport (*Sydney Morning Herald*, 30 December 1979).

In the UK general election in May 1979, the British NF contested more than 300 seats and was wiped out at the polls. Similar electoral contests by the NFA in 1980 led to the same results, with Sisson and Viktor Robb both failing dismally in the race for a Senate seat in Queensland during the 1980 federal election. As mentioned in *Patterns of Prejudice* and in Greason's book, by 1980 there had been several defections from the NFA to the National Alliance, but the National Alliance was unable to make any more headway than their rivals. The media also focused less on the National Alliance, which did not have the same name recognition of the 'National Front', the latter infamous across the English-speaking world.

The Commonwealth National Front did not last long into the 1980s. The NFA emerged to a completely hostile media and fared very poorly in its electoral pursuits, but was also not popular enough to take up the strategy of 'occupying the streets'. Besides the production of *Frontline*, Sisson's organisation dwindled and was eventually overtaken by rival groups, namely National Action. *Patterns of Prejudice* also reported in 1978 that the National Front of South Africa was in talks of merging with another small racist group and that the Chairman, Jack Noble, had resigned.[44] The NFSA's other major figure, Ray Hill, also left South Africa in 1980, before returning to the UK to join the British Movement as an undercover antifascist mole for *Searchlight* magazine. According to Hill, the biggest political action performed by the NFSA was a protest at a Johannesburg hotel in January 1979, which was broken up by the police (Hill & Bell 1988: 63–65). Due to this public disturbance, the South African Minister of the Interior refused John Tyndall permission to enter the country, as Tyndall had been invited by Noble and Hill to speak to the local NFSA.[45] Although members of the leading National Party had welcomed both Oswald Mosley and A.K. Chesterton in previous years (Bunting 1986: 70–71; Macklin 2010), Tyndall's attempts to build an opposing force to the ruling party of apartheid ensured that his presence was not welcome in South Africa. Once Hill and Noble left South Africa, the remaining membership was swallowed up by the Afrikaner Herstigte Nasionale Party and the paramilitary Wit Kommando. Meanwhile the National Front of New Zealand also dissolved by the early 1980s, with David Crawford and Kerry Bolton forming the breakaway group New Force, as well as the New Zealand branch of the Church of Odin (Van Leeuwen 2008: 17). According to Paul Spoonley (1987: 161–162), New Force (after 1983 the Nationalist Workers Party) was developed as a cadre party that espoused a seemingly anti-capitalist position, along the lines of the 'political soldier' and Strasserite sections of the British NF in the 1980s.

The British NF, which was seen as the beacon of the CNF, also collapsed after the 1979 election into warring factions. Tyndall formed the New National Front in 1980 and, in 1982, transformed this into the British National Party (BNP). The remnants of the NF in the 1980s became known as the Official National Front and

the NF Flag Group (Copsey 2004: 36–46), which competed with the more outwardly neo-Nazi British Movement and the BNP for support, primarily amongst
football hooligans and skinheads, in the Thatcher years.

ASIO and the Australian far right

In his PhD thesis on the extreme right in Australia, Jim Saleam (1999: 142) suggests that it was the authorities, particularly ASIO, that stifled the development
of the NFA, writing 'two facts were demonstrated: some Extreme-Rightists had
strategies, and the para-State intended they not blossom.' In his review of the
literature on the history of the Australian far right, Andrew Moore (2005: 6)
described Saleam's argument that 'the surveillance and prosecution of right-wing
nationalist groups after 1975 were predicated upon their conflict with the liberal-
internationalist agenda of the state' was 'clearly a case of special pleading'. While
ASIO had infiltrated the NFA from its very inception and monitored it closely,
the hostility it faced from the Australian public and its inability to gain any sort of
traction politically was more to do with the NFA's ideology and the composition
of its membership.

As John Blaxland (2015) has acknowledged in his volume on the official history of ASIO, the security services had monitored the far right in Australia since
the inception of the NSPA in the early 1960s and continued to monitor the far
right throughout the 1970s, even though the various far-right groups did not seem
to present a danger to the parliamentary system and the 'poor quality' of its small
membership. A 1972 report drawn up by ASIO noted that, while the NSPA had
received 'considerable' media attention in 1970 due to its announcement that it
would run candidates in the 1970 half-Senate election, it was a very small organisation, which relied on 'provocative baiting and counter-demonstration action as
a means of gaining publicity'.[46] Based on the increasing conflict between the NF
and anti-fascist protestors in Britain, such as at Red Lion Square in 1974 and the
aforementioned 'Battle of Lewisham', ASIO believed that violence between the
NFA and sections of the left was likely, partly because of the NSPA background
of some involved in the NFA and also because, '[r]ight-wing extremist groups
have tended to attract violent elements whether the leadership welcomes them
or not'.[47] These ASIO files indicate a high level of monitoring, but little intervention, with the agency's Director General writing, 'the NFA seems unlikely to
attract widespread support'.[48] As Steve James (2013: 342) has written, ASIO has
primarily played a pre-emptive role in dealing with right-wing politically motivated violence and has predominantly focused on 'intelligence-gathering' in order
to 'alert the commonwealth attorney general to the likelihood and magnitude of
threatened or perceived violence'. Compared with the British NF, ASIO determined that the threat posed by the NFA to national security was minimal. Troy
Whitford (2013) has shown that when National Action was formed in 1982, both
ASIO and the NSW Special Branch took measures to monitor and infiltrate the
organisation, especially in the late 1980s when NA became increasingly involved

in racist and political violence (as noted in the 1991 national inquiry into racist violence in Australia) (HREOC 1991: 198–199). This level of intervention by the security services does not seem to have been present in ASIO's monitoring of the NFA in the late 1970s.

Conclusion

Paul Jackson and Anton Shekhovtsov (2014: 6) have described the relationship between the British and North American far right since 1945 as one of 'accumulative extremism', where national level activism is augmented by the transnational, reinforcing each other's extremist politics and 'develop[ing] a wider sense of an imagined comradely community'. A crossover of ideas, strategies and personnel between the far right in Britain and the United States has promoted the notion of 'white pride worldwide' and a practical solidarity between different forms of racialised nationalism in the Anglophone world (Jackson & Shekhovtsov 2014: 24). Other scholars have also described this transmission of far-right ideas and practices across the globe as 'transnational fascism', describing far-right allegiances within Europe or between Europe and settler colonial communities around the world (Bauerkämper 2010; Finchelstein 2010). The relationship between the National Front in Britain and the National Front of Australia, as well as those in South Africa and New Zealand as envisaged by the Commonwealth National Front, are another example of 'transnational fascism' or 'accumulative extremism' between the post-imperial metropole and the (former) settler colonies of the British Commonwealth.

The NFA attempted to seize the initiative presented by the British NF, creating an antipodean version of the UK organisation. The NFA had a particular pro-British outlook and saw a white-dominated British Commonwealth as its goal, but equally, like many other white supremacists and far-right activists in the 1970s and 1980s, championed the white minority states in Southern Africa as examples for Australia to follow (particularly with regard to the country's indigenous population).[49] Furthermore the NFA saw South Africa and Rhodesia as symbols of white 'civilisation' being attacked by non-white and communist forces. Solidarity with these former settler colonies was paramount to the NFA's worldview. The NFA sought to capitalise on the international infamy of the British NF and conjure up the populist support for the NF that it had experienced in the UK from around 1972 to 1977, although it was envisioned that the NFA would remain predominantly, in the early years at least, as an extra-parliamentary pressure group, rather than an electoral force.

However, the existence of the NFA was fleeting and did not last long in the 1980s, with a similar experience faced by the National Fronts in South Africa and New Zealand. The three large ASIO files that have been released provide an in-depth view of how the NFA functioned as a political organisation in its first few years and reveal an insight into why the group failed to flourish in comparison with its British sister organisation. The close monitoring by ASIO from late 1977 onwards shows that a number of Australian far-right activists looked to the NF to assist them in unifying the far-right movement, similar to how the British NF had done in the late 1960s, but the model provided by John Tyndall's party was difficult to transpose onto the Australian movement. This was partially due to the fragmentary nature of the Australian far right, where different groups and personalities dominated the scene in Melbourne, Sydney and Brisbane, for example. As the files reveal, soon after the NFA was announced in Melbourne by Rosemary Sisson, other far-right figures in Queensland and New South Wales pronounced that they were indeed leaders of the fledgling group, causing tension between Sisson and others. These tensions did not go away and festered, particularly while Sisson was in the UK, and a number of members switched to the Sydney-based Australian National Alliance.

The files also show that from its inception, the NFA faced a hostile media and a growing anti-racist movement in Australia, which had learnt from a decade of controversy in the UK concerning the British NF, especially with the 'Battle of Lewisham' and the formation of the Anti-Nazi League fresh in the public's mind. The amount of attention that the NFA got from the very beginning hindered its growth and ensured that only dedicated far-right activists became involved with the organisation, with many 'soft' racists put off by the media spotlight. The name of the group was very much a double-edged sword for the NFA. While hoping to ride the wave of infamy afforded by the name 'the National Front of Australia' and enter the public consciousness, the notoriety attached to the moniker of the NF severely curtailed any potential to court wider public support. By the early 1980s, the NFA had disappeared in all but name – even though *Frontline* was still published sporadically until the mid-1980s.

The Australian far right still looks to Britain, as well as the United States and continental Europe, for inspiration, with the latest incarnation, Reclaim Australia and the United Patriots Front, inspired by the English Defence League (EDL) and other anti-Islam social movements. At the time of writing, the loosely based protest model of Reclaim Australia, based on the tactics of the early EDL (before their marches were restricted by the police and anti-fascist counter-demonstrations), seem to have had more short-term success than the NFA in the late 1970s. However, as this chapter shows, many have tried to transport a far-right or fascist movement into Australia, based on British groups, with very limited success.

Notes

1 ASIO Intelligence Report, 'National Front of Australia', 8 June 1978, p. 1, NAA A6122 2553, National Archives of Australia (Canberra, ACT).
2 Special Branch CID, 'SISSON, Rosemary Irena (13.2.55) – Chairwoman of "NATIONAL FRONT of AUSTRALIA"', 13 June 1978, NAA A6122 2553.
3 ASIO Intelligence Report, 'National Front of Australia', pp. 5–6.
4 ASIO Intelligence Report, 'National Front of Australia', p. 6.
5 'The Inaugural Meeting of the National Front of Australia: Annex to the Agenda', NAA A6122 2553.

6   Letter from Eric Campbell to Oswald Mosley, 7 May 1934, NAA A6122 2 vol. 1.

7   Secret Service Report on Nazism and Fascism in Australia, 2 July 1943, D1915 SA19070, National Archives of Australia, Adelaide, South Australia. See also Bird (2014: 18).

8   'Policy of the Australian Union of Fascists and National Socialists', n.d., D1915 SA19070, NAA.

9   'Policy of the Australian Union of Fascists and National Socialists'.

10   'Policy of the Australian Union of Fascists and National Socialists'.

11   ASIO Director General to the Minister for Immigration, 3 February 1969, NAA. A6980 S202516. Mosley eventually reconsidered and did not visit Australia at this time.

12   'Soft Selling Anti-Semitism: *Searchlight* looks at the League of Rights', *Searchlight* 49 (1979) p. 3.

13   'League of Empire Loyalists', SAPOL Special Branch report, 11 February 1958, p. 1, NAA D1918 S3039 (Adelaide).

14   'League of Empire Loyalists', p. 2.

15   These included the White Defence League, the National Labour Party, the British National Party, the National Socialist Movement and the Greater Britain Movement.

16   'Spearhead' was originally the name of a paramilitary elite corps formed by John Tyndall and Colin Jordan in 1962 while both were in the National Socialist Movement. It gained them notoriety when Tyndall, Jordan and two others, Kerr Ritchie and another future NF member Denis Pirie, were jailed for breaches of the Public Order Act, pertaining to the formation of a paramilitary organisation (Thurlow 1998: 237).

17   Thompson had been a follower of Chesterton's League of Empire Loyalists in the 1960s and had established a local chapter of the League. In 1967, Thompson, with other British fascist émigrés, formed a National Front, but this did not last long.

18   ASIO telegram, 'Subject: National Front of Australia (NFA)', 9 June 1978, NAA A6122 2553.

19   Letter to John Tyndall, 25 November 1977, NAA A6122 2553.

20   See Widgery 1986: 45–49; Renton 2006: 51–73; Smith 2009.

21   Jeremy May, 'Towards a National Front of Australia', *Spearhead* (May 1978) p. 17.

22   For BUF descriptions of Australia, see *The Blackshirt*, 30 November 1934; *Action*, 15 May 1937.

23   'Editorial', *The Australian Nationalist* (January 1978) p. 1, NAA A6122 2553.

24   'Editorial', *The Australian Nationalist* (January 1978) p. 2.

25   'Editorial', *The Australian Nationalist* (January 1978) p. 2.

26   'The Western Guilt Complex', *The Australian Nationalist* (January 1978) p. 5.

27   'Editorial', *The Australian Nationalist* (April 1978) p. 1, NAA A6122 2553.

28   'South Africa', *The Australian Nationalist* (April 1978) p. 2, NAA A6122 2553.

29   'South Africa', p. 2.

30   'Rhodesian "Refugees"', *The Australian Nationalist* (March 1978) p. 3, NAA A6122 2553.

31   'National Front of Australia Formed', *Frontline*, 1/1 (June 1978) p. 1, NAA A6122 2554.

32   'Speech by Mr John Tyndall', *Frontline*, 1/1 (June 1978) p. 6, NAA A6122 2554.

33   'Speech by Mr John Tyndall', pp. 4–5.

34   'The Commonwealth National Front', *Frontline*, 1/1 (June 1978) p. 3, NAA A6122 2554.

35   'A Message from the NF New Zealand on the Occasion of the Formation of the National Front of Australia', *Frontline*, 1/1 (June 1978) p. 8, NAA A6122 2554.

36   'National Front's "Global Network"', *Patterns of Prejudice*, 12/2 (1978) p. 12.

37   ASIO Intelligence Report, 'National Front of Australia', 23 March 1979, NAA A6122 2554.

38   'National Front's "Global Network"', p. 12.

39 ASIO Message Form, 'Subject: Antonius Nicolaas Johannes Heintjes', 9 June 1978, NAA A6122 2553. ASIO were also interested in Cameron because members of the Hindu sect Ananda Marga allegedly planned to plant a bomb to kill Cameron and his family, after he claimed in the *Sydney Morning Herald* to be the leader of the NFA. Three Ananda Marga members were charged with the attempted murder of Cameron in late 1978 and went on trial twice in 1979, being convicted after the second trial. Strongly suspected on being involved in the Hilton bombing in February 1978, the three members were pardoned for this crime in 1985. See ASIO press clippings in NAA A6122 2425; Molomby 1986: 52–67; Hocking 1993: 132–137.

40 See the various material of the Queensland Immigration Control Association contained in NAA A6122 2553.

41 'Subversion Down Under', *Patterns of Prejudice*, 14/3 (1980) p. 35.

42 See the correspondence between Sisson and Swan in NAA A6122 2556.

43 Letter from Rosemary Sisson to Margaret Swan, 19 October 1979, NAA A6122 2556.

44 'National Front Setback', *Patterns of Prejudice*, 12/4 (1978) p. 11.

45 'Resistance in South Africa', *Patterns of Prejudice*, 13/1 (1979) p. 15.

46 ASIO, 'The National Socialist Party of Australia', pp. 4–5, NAA A12389 A30 PART 14.

47 Letter from ASIO Director General to the Attorney General, 7 June 1978, NAA A6122 2553.

48 Letter from ASIO Director General to the Attorney General, 7 June 1978.

49 In a 1981 interview with Sisson and Viktor Robb, published in the University of Queensland's student newspaper *Semper*, both praised apartheid as the framework for how Australia should deal with the Indigenous population, rhetorically asking, 'What's wrong with the aboriginals developing the way they wanted to and us developing the way we wanted to and the Asians developing the way they wanted to – but in Asia.' Sisson continued to say,

> Our aboriginal policy is basically that the aborigines should be given land rights. A register should be set up. We work out a compromise of what the aborigines want and they keep their customs ... The national Front, because we're aware of our own race, we believe that we can really understand what the aborigines want – as a race.

> *(Quoted from Henzell 1981, p. 13)*

References

Amos, K. (1976) *The New Guard Movement 1931–1935*, Melbourne: Melbourne University Press.

Barclay, G. (1983) 'Friends in Salisbury: Australia and the Rhodesian Unilateral Declaration of Independence, 1965–1972', *Australian Journal of Politics and History*, 29/1 (April) pp. 38–49.

Bauerkämper, A. (2010) 'Transnational Fascism: Cross-Border Relations Between Regimes and Movements in Europe, 1922–1939', *East Central Europe*, 37, pp. 214–246.

Bird, D. (2014) *Nazi Dreamtime: Australian Enthusiasts for Hitler's Germany*, London: Anthem Press.

Blaxland, J. (2015) *The Protest Years: The Official History of ASIO, 1963–1975*, Sydney: Allen & Unwin.

Bunting, B. (1986) *The Rise of the South African Reich*, London: International Defence and Aid Fund.

Campbell, E. (1934) *The New Road*, Sydney: Briton Publications.

Copsey, N. (2004) *Contemporary British Fascism: The British National Party and the Quest for Legitimacy*, Houndmills: Palgrave Macmillan.

Eatwell, R. (2003) *Fascism: A History*, London: Pimlico.

Finchelstein, F. (2010) *Transatlantic Fascism: Ideology, Violence and the Sacred in Argentina and Italy 1919–1945*, Durham, NC: Duke University Press.

Greason, D. (1994) *I was a Teenage Fascist*, Ringwood, Victoria: McPhee Gribble.

Gupta, A. (1974) 'Ugandan Asians, Britain, India and the Commonwealth', *African Affairs*, 73/292, pp. 312–324.

Henzell, J. (1981) 'A Evening with the National Front', *Semper*, 3 (April) p. 9.

Hill, R. & Bell, A. (1988) *The Other Face of Terror: Inside Europe's Neo-Nazi Network*, London: Grafton Books.

Hocking, J. (1993) *Beyond Terrorism: The Development of the Australian Security State*, St Leonards, New South Wales: Allen & Unwin.

Human Rights and Equal Opportunity Commission (1991) *Racist Violence: Report of the National inquiry into Racist Violence in Australia*, Canberra: Australian Government Publishing Service.

Husbands, C. T. (1988) 'Extreme Right-wing Politics in Great Britain: The Recent Marginalisation of the National Front', *West European Politics*, 11, pp. 65–79.

Jackson, P. & Shekhovtsov, A. (2014) *The Post-War Anglo-American Far Right: A Special Relationship of Hate*, Houndmills: Palgrave Macmillan.

James, S. (2013) 'Policing Political Violence in Australia' in David Lowe et al. (eds) *Examining Political Violence: Studies of Terrorism, Counterterrorism and Internal War*, London: Taylor & Francis.

Lewis, D. (1987) *Illusions of Grandeur: Mosley, Fascism and British Society, 1931–81*, Manchester: Manchester University Press.

Lowry, D. (2007) 'The Impact of Anti-Communism on White Rhodesian Political Culture, ca.1920s–1980', *Cold War History*, 7/2, pp. 186–187.

Macklin, G. (2007) *Very Deeply Dyed in Black: Sir Oswald Mosley and the Resurrection of British Fascism after 1945*, London: I.B. Tauris.

Macklin, G. (2010) 'The British Far Right's South African Connection: A.K. Chesterton, Hendrik van den Bergh, and the South African Intelligence Services', *Intelligence and National Security*, 25/6, pp. 823–842.

Miles, R. & Phizacklea, A. (1984) *White Man's Country: Racism in British Politics*, London: Pluto Press.

Molomby, T. (1986) *Spies, Bombs and the Path of Bliss: Ananda Marga and the Hilton Bombing*, Sydney: Potoroo Press.

Mondon, A. (2012) 'An Australian Immunisation to the Extreme Right?', *Social Identities*, 18/3, pp. 355–372.

Moore, A. (1995) *The Right Road? A History of Right-Wing Politics in Australia*, Sydney: Oxford University Press Australia.

Moore, A. (2005) 'Writing about the Extreme Right in Australia', *Labour History*, 89 (November) pp. 1–15.

Moore, A. (2010) 'The Nazification of the New Guard: Colonel Campbell's Fascist Odyssey, 1933–1938', in Emily Turner-Graham & Christine Winter (eds) *National Socialism in Oceania: A Critical Evaluation of its Effect and Aftermath*, Frankfurt am Main: Peter Lang.

Moore, A. (2011) 'Discredited Fascism: The New Guard After 1932', *Australian Journal of Politics and History*, 57/2 (June) pp. 188–206.

Mosley, O. (1961) *Mosley – Right or Wrong?* London: Lion Books.

Polack, P. (2013) *The Last Hot Battle of the Cold War: South Africa v Cuba in the Angolan Civil War*, Havertown, PA: Casemate.

Renton, D. (2000) *Fascism, Anti-Fascism and Britain in the 1940s*, Houndmills: Palgrave Macmillan.

Renton, D. (2006) *When We Touched the Sky: The Anti-Nazi League 1977–1981*, Cheltenham: New Clarion Press.

Saleam, J. (1999) 'The Other Radicalism: An Inquiry into Contemporary Australian Extreme Right Ideology, Politics and Organization, 1975–1995', unpublished PhD thesis, University of Sydney.

Shipley, P. (1978) 'The National Front', *Conflict Studies*, 97 (July).

Smith, E. (2009) 'A Bulwark Diminished? The Communist Party, the SWP and Anti-Fascism in the 1970s', *Socialist History Journal*, 35, pp. 59–80.

Spoonley, P. (1987) *The Politics of Nostalgia: Racism and the Extreme Right in New Zealand*, Palmerston North, NZ: Dunmore Press.

Stocker, P. (2015) 'The Postwar British Extreme Right and Empire, 1945–1967', *Religion Compass*, 9/5, pp. 162–172.

Taylor, S. (1979) 'The National Front: Anatomy of a Political Movement', in Robert Miles & Annie Phizacklea (eds) *Racism and Political Action In Britain*, London: Routledge and Kegan Paul.

Thurlow, R. (1998) *Fascism in Britain: From Oswald Mosley's Blackshirts to the National Front*, London: I.B. Tauris.

Van Leeuwen, W. (2008) 'Dreamers of the Dark: Kerry Bolton and the Order of the Left-Hand Path, a Case-Study of a Satanic/Neo-Nazi Synthesis', unpublished MA thesis, University of Waikato.

Walker, M. (1977) *The National Front*, Glasgow: Fontana.

Walker, M. (1979) 'The National Front', in H. M. Drucker (ed.) *Multi-Party Britain*, London: Macmillan.

Whitford, T. (2011) 'A Political History of National Action: Its Fears, Ideas, Tactics and Conflicts', *Rural Society*, 20/2 (April) pp. 216–226.

Whitford, T. (2013) 'Combating Political Police: An Overview of National Action's Counterintelligence Program 1982–1990', *Salus Journal*, 1/2, pp. 40–51.

Widgery, D. (1986) *Beating Time: Riot n Race n Rock n Roll*, London: Chatto & Windus.

5

THE DOG THAT DIDN'T BARK?

Assessing the development of 'cumulative extremism' between fascists and anti-fascists in the 1970s

Alex Carter

Introduction

Shortly after midnight on 19 June 2017, Darren Osborne drove his van into a crowd of Muslims outside of the Finsbury Park Mosque, killing one person and injuring many others. The timing of this attack, mere weeks after two deadly Islamist attacks in London and one in Manchester, led some to view it as the result of 'cumulative extremism' (CE).[1] This concept, defined as 'the way in which one form of extremism can feed off and magnify other forms' by Roger Eatwell (2006: 205), first began to gain serious traction amongst policymakers and academics after the English Defence League was formed in response to the actions of Islamists in 2009. Subsequently, CE appeared in iterations of the Governments' Prevent counter-terrorism strategy as well as in further academic studies and articles in the national media (HM Government 2013). Yet for all the increased attention CE has received, it remains a relatively under-studied concept. With a few notable exceptions, there is still a dearth of sustained explorations of historical case studies to better understand the factors which may lead to an escalation or de-escalation of the protest repertoires employed by opposing social movements. The developments between Islamists and anti-Muslim terrorists across the beginning of 2017 only add more urgency for a greater understanding of processes of CE. As Anderson (2013: 42) warns, if counter-terrorism strategies are being informed by a threat that 'is being exaggerated ... the consequence will be unnecessary fears, unnecessary powers and the allocation of excessive resources to the counter-terrorism machine.' On the other hand, an insufficiently nuanced understanding of the factors that influence the development of CE could have the opposite effect and lead to a downplaying of the very real threat of terrorism and political violence posed by the escalation of movement–countermovement (M/CM) contests. The more accurate the understanding of CE the easier it will be to design context-sensitive and effective policy measures by which to manage the interactions of opposing groups within a society.

From 1967 to 1979 an M/CM contest developed between fascists and anti-fascists in Britain. This chapter will assess the extent to which this M/CM contest generated processes of 'cumulative extremism' (CE) leading to tactical escalations between the opposing social movements and to increased mobilisations as the movements' support ebbs and flows.

1967–1975

The origins of this case study lie in February 1967, when the NF was founded. For the first few years of the nascent organisation's existence very little of consequence happened. While there were certainly violent skirmishes between the NF and their opponents, these tended to be localised, often spontaneous and always small-scale, with only a handful of people from each side involved.

There were two major events, during the latter part of the 1960s and the beginning of the 1970s, that helped pave the way for the NF's subsequent growth. The first was the 'Rivers of Blood' speech given by renegade Tory MP Enoch Powell on 20 April 1968. Powell's speech emotively described a near-apocalyptic vision of the UK, its ruin brought about by continued non-white immigration, and it had a huge effect on public debate as well as provoking dramatic displays of public support. The day after the speech, striking dockers marched from East London to Parliament in support of Powell, and there was a string of other strikes around the country with similar motives for the following week (Lindorp 2001). Many scholars argue that Powell's speech, as well as his subsequent anti-immigration campaigning over the next few years, 'effectively dissolved the Conservative and Labour parties' racial consensus'; whether or not this is true he certainly went some way towards politicising the issues of race and immigration, which in turn helped to legitimise racist arguments and by extension the organisations who espoused them (Messina 1989; Trilling 2013).

The second occurred in August 1972, when the Conservative government allowed thousands of Ugandan Asian refugees, who had been exiled by Idi Amin, to enter the country. As the 'immigration' issue was thrust once more into the forefront of public discourse, the NF leadership acted with impressive speed to capitalise on the opportunity: within '24 hours of the first alarming headlines from Uganda, the NF had organized a 100-strong picket of Downing St. in the afternoon of 14 August, followed by the delivery of a petition of protest by John Tyndall [chairman of the NF] to Number 10 that evening' (Walker 1977: 35).

The Front's subsequent anti-immigration campaign was (relatively) successful. Over the last four months of 1972 the Front gained over 800 new members, and their annual Remembrance Day march that year drew 1,500 activists, twice as many as in 1971 (Walker 1977). Martin Webster, National Activities Organiser of the National Front, later remarked that the organisation's real beginnings lay with the arrival of the Ugandan Asian immigrants (*Campaign Against Racism and Fascism*, 1978a).

The following year the NF's good luck continued, as they gained their best parliamentary result with 16.2 per cent of the vote in a parliamentary by-election in
West Bromwich, and had also reportedly grown their membership to 14,000 (Miles
& Phizacklea 1984). Buoyed by their successes, the NF confidently announced that
they would be fielding 54 candidates in the February 1974 general election (Copsey
2017). As the NF went from strength to strength there was an attendant growth in
anti-fascist activities. From 1973 onwards, spurred into action by the advances made
by the NF, many local anti-fascist organisations were formed (*Campaign Against
Racism and Fascism*, 1978a). Indeed, 'the more successful [the NF] became, in local
elections, the more left-wing and liberal bodies throughout the country recognized
the threat and began to mobilize against it. The obvious weapon for them to use, in
leaflets and in speeches, was the political histories of Tyndall and Webster' (Walker
1977: 148).[2] Tyndall and Webster had both previously been members of the openly
Nazi National Socialist Movement (NSM), and incriminating photos of them from
those days had landed in the hands of their enemies. However, the NF's plans to
field 54 candidates in the 1974 election, and the five minutes of free radio and TV
broadcasting time this entitled them to, was an even stronger motivational influence
on the growing anti-fascist movement (Copsey 2017).

From 1974, there was an intensification in the M/CM relationship, in terms of
both the size of anti-fascist mobilisations and the commitment to confrontational
tactics. On 21 May 1974, between 300 and 400 anti-fascists attempted to break up
a National Front meeting at Oxford Town Hall, where Martin Webster was speaking (AJEX 1974). In Canterbury on 8 June, students at an NF meeting 'scuffled'
with police while attempting to interrupt the proceedings. Around 300 students
marched through the streets in protest at the NF meeting, and NF stewards later
attacked this counter-demo with staves, badly injuring some of them, after which
two people were arrested (AJEX 1974).

A week later, on 15 June, the mounting tensions between the fascists and the left
erupted in the biggest clash between fascists, anti-fascists and the police seen in the
UK since the inter-war period. The NF had organised a protest march culminating
in a meeting in Conway Hall, London, and a corresponding counter-demonstration
had been called by the anti-imperialist organisation, Liberation, with the backing of
a broad cross-section of the labour movement (Copsey 2017). It was arranged with
the police that both groups would be allowed to march to Red Lion Square, where
the NF would hold their meeting in Conway Hall, a small number of anti-fascists
would have a meeting in another room of the building which they would access via
a side entrance, and the rest of the counter-demonstrators would hold their protest
outside. These plans were, however, thrown into disarray when during the march
two of the more militant leftist groups, the International Marxist Group (IMG) and
the International Socialists (IS), made a direct assault on the police cordon blocking
the main entrance to the hall.

The incident provoked two short but intense waves of vicious fighting between
the activists and the police, during which time the student Kevin Gately was fatally
wounded (Home Office 1975). Walker has argued that towards the end of the fracas

the police made an unnecessary push through the crowd, an action which 'led to individual acts of police violence against demonstrators and … gave the far left permanent ammunition in its long arguments against the police as the physical weapon of the establishment' (Walker 1977: 162–163). Indeed, as we shall see, interactions between the police and the far left continued to escalate from this point. The NF came through the situation unscathed, having conducted their march in a relatively orderly fashion while obeying any instructions from the police.

Red Lion Square was a major fillip to the anti-fascist movement, causing a spike in M/CM mobilisations. NF marches were opposed by large anti-fascist mobilisations in Leicester in August 1974, and in Hyde Park the following month. In Leicester a large group of around 6,000 anti-fascists peacefully opposed around 1,500 NF marchers, and in Hyde Park 7,000 anti-fascists occupied the NF's planned route, forcing the police to divert their march. At a meeting following the latter incident, NF member Walter Barton declared that 'It's time to turn our young men loose on the Reds' (Walker 1977: 163). Indeed, between 1972 and 1974 the growing violent opposition to NF activities had provoked the development of a defence strategy, whereby groups of men would be positioned around any NF march ready to link arms and repel attacks. These 'defence groups' had become, by the 1974 Remembrance Day parade, an organized body of tough young militants who bore the name of the 'Honour Guard' (Walker 1977: 163). The interactions between the far right and their enemies were beginning to take on the shape of CE: the achievements and actions of the far right invigorated and fuelled the anti-fascist movement, whose militancy and radicalism in turn provoked the formation of marshal bodies and aggressive attitudes and tactics amongst the fascists.

This aggressive attitude became more open and apparent after the October 1974 election, in which the NF polled relatively well. However, with the election over, the need to appear internally united disappeared. Consequently, throughout 1975, as the leadership fought over the reins of the Front, the grassroots members orchestrated a series of violent attacks on left-wing and anti-fascist targets. In August 1975 a group of between 30 and 40 NF members and Loyalists attacked a meeting organised by the Northern Ireland Civil Rights Association (NICRA) in Liverpool. They assaulted the speaker and other attendees with chairs, hospitalising one person and severely injuring several others (Correspondence to Maurice Ludmer 1975). In November 1975, a National Council of Civil Liberties (NCCL) sponsored event at Manchester Polytechnic, at which Northern Irish politician and activist Bernadette Devlin was scheduled to speak, was attacked by a large group of NF and BM activists (British Movement 1975). Six people were badly hurt, with one man requiring 19 stitches after a fascist smashed a bottle into his face (Hann & Tilzey 2003).

The anti-fascists, for their part, maintained constant pressure on the NF. In March 1975, a NF demonstration in Islington, North London, was opposed by around 6,000 anti-fascists. On 6 September, the National Front held a 'March Against Muggers' event through East London, which faced heavy opposition from assorted left-wing activists. Had it not been for a heavy police presence there might have been large-scale fighting between the two groups (Leech 1994; Lux 2006).

The next month the Front's AGM in Chelsea Town Hall faced opposition from an IS and IMG-organised counter-demo with roughly 1,000 anti-fascists present (Copsey 2017). It seems that the relationship between the opposing social movements was providing some kind of succour to both sides; the more they opposed each other, the more they provided motivation. On the other hand, while their clashes may have been generating support for one or both sides – alongside other factors, such as the influx of refugees and Powell's intervention – they do not seem to have had a significant radicalising effect.

Two key theoretical points can be made with regard to the foregoing discussion. First, on the causes of the violence at Red Lion Square, Walker posits that 'both sides had distributed the kind of literature and propaganda in the weeks before the march which made some kind of clash almost inevitable' (Walker 1977: 162–163). While their aggressive posturing no doubt fuelled the violent situation to some degree, another answer may lie in the militant anti-fascists' Trotskyite perspective on the causes of the emergence of fascism in general, and the NF in particular. Deriving their analysis from Trotsky's thesis on fascism, these groups (IS and IMG) thought that, as capitalist society lurched from one economic crisis to another, the increasingly exploited working class would begin to organise with determination for the class war. The ruling class, realising that the powers at their disposal under a liberal democratic regime were insufficient to maintain their dominance and meet the growing threat from the labour movement, would seek the introduction of an authoritarian state. The *petit bourgeoisie* would then feel crushed in the struggle between the Labour Movement and the ruling class, and this 'discontent would be expressed in support for Fascist political parties' (Taylor 1982: 33). Finally, the ruling class would encourage the growth of the fascist movement with the aim of enticing workers to join, thereby splitting the working class and ensuring that their own dominance was secured. The IMG and IS were convinced that this analysis applied to 1970s Britain, and considered that racialism was the tool which would be used to divide the workers. Moreover, they argued that 'the NF was deliberately using the tactics of the organised labour movement to convince workers that it was a working class party' (Taylor 1978: 59). The only conclusion that the Trotskyite groups could draw was that it was necessary to face the fascist threat using physical force (International Socialists 1974).

Second, and in light of the foregoing point, it is clear that the issues of race and class were central to the escalation of this episode. Both the fascists and the far left were competing over the constituency of the white working class, and this fact shaped the tactics of both groups: the Front attempted to co-opt left-wing tactics, like the short-lived Trade Unions Against Immigration (TRU-AIM), and the far left – who were the main violent instigators in the larger-scale clashes – used displays of violence against the Front and the police to demonstrate that they were the true revolutionary force of the working class (Walker 1977; Taylor 1982).

The issue of race was just as key in shaping the tactics and areas of operation of the opposing groups. The fascists hoped to exacerbate existing racial social divisions between white and non-white communities to start a 'race war' and divide the labour movement, an aim which was greatly helped by the arrival of the Ugandan Asians. This was the reason so many of their later marches were through minority communities like the East End of London. The far left hoped to recruit minority communities to aid their revolutionary struggle and to prevent the division of the working class. This analysis is strengthened by the fact that the NF polled noticeably better in the October 1974 election in constituencies in London which were both working class and contained a higher proportion of non-white residents (Husbands 1983). From this perspective, it seems clear that this conflict was not one fuelled by cumulative extremism, at least not largely speaking, in that it was not the 'extremism' of one group fuelling the 'extremism' of another. Rather, it was the relationship the opposing movements had with third-party groups which shaped the escalation and de-escalation of the conflict.

Throughout 1975, a rift had been growing between two camps within the Front, the 'populists' and the 'neo-Nazis', and in November it came to a head, resulting in the populists seceding from the Front to form the National Party (NP). Although the NP was never as successful in terms of total vote share or membership size as the NF (although they were to win two council seats in Blackburn), they did rob their erstwhile colleagues of a number of their most experienced organisers and activists, roughly 2,000 of their members (around one-fifth of the total), as well as the financial backing of the prominent benefactor Gordon Marshall/Brown, and thereby did do some serious damage to the NF (Taylor 1982). The magazine *Campaign Against Racism and Fascism* (*CARF*) later argued that by successfully labelling them as Nazis, 'the NF split in 1975 can in part be attributed to' the anti-fascist movement (*Campaign Against Racism and Fascism* 1978a).

This demonstrates two factors which can inhibit a social movement's momentum and thus interrupt processes of CE from developing. In the first instance, as social movements mobilise they attempt to advance 'collective action frames', 'the interpretive packages that activists develop to mobilise potential adherents and constituents' (Polletta & Jasper 2001). These processes then become the 'subject of intense contestation between collective actors representing the movement, the state, and any existing counter movements' (McAdam et al. 1996: 16). These 'framing contests' are important because how 'successfully groups frame their identities for the public thus affects their ability to recruit members and supporters, gain a public hearing, make alliances with other groups, and defuse opposition' (Polletta & Jasper 2001). Further, social movement organisations that are engaged in an M/CM conflict are not only attempting to frame their own identities and grievances, but also those of their enemies. By highlighting the openly Nazi past of the leaders of the NF, the anti-fascist movement was very successful in framing them as racists and fascists, thus impeding their ability to gain mass appeal and generate more support. The second factor is the degree of internal unity a social movement organisation can maintain: the less cohesive a social movement organisation is, the greater the difficulty it will have in sustaining mass-mobilisations of its members. While this is something which often has more to do with the internal political and social chemistry of an organisation or movement than any external factors, divisions can be created, exacerbated and exploited by counter-movements – as is demonstrated here.

1976–1977

The events at Red Lion Square notwithstanding, the relations between the various groups embroiled in this M/CM contest only really began to heat up during 1976. Anti-fascists clashed with NF members who were walking to an assembly point for a march on Saturday 28 February, during a by-election in Coventry. During the fracas, Andrew Fountaine, John Tyndall and Martin Webster were all assaulted, with Tyndall receiving a brick to the side of his face (*Spearhead* 1976). Two months later, on 24 April, the British Movement (BM) held a 'Patriots' March' in London on the same day that the NF held one in Bradford, an area with a large Asian community. The BM event was heavily policed, and the hundreds of fascists and anti-fascists were kept separate as the BM marched towards Trafalgar Square. However as they entered the Square, the anti-fascists briefly broke through the police lines and exchanged blows with the BM before being forced back again by the police (Lux 2006).

The NF marched through Bradford 'deliberately provoking a violent confrontation with Asian youth' (Farrar 2004: 8). Indeed, young people from minority communities had now begun to engage in the anti-fascist actions with gusto; a development that the NF had no doubt been hoping for, as it leant empirical credibility to the framing devices in their propaganda which painted their enemies as fundamentally un-British and lawless troublemakers (Benford & Snow 2000). Six hundred NF members faced off against between 3–4,000 counter-demonstrators, and as the day wound on groups of young anti-fascists clashed with both the police and the NF. A police riot van was pushed onto its side and a patrol car was turned over; counter-demonstrators also hurled missiles at the police and the fascists. This could not have been a better outcome for the NF: ostensibly violent immigrants and left-wing hooligans attacking the forces of law and order.

Mirroring events in 1972, the NF's fortunes were once again improved by a highly publicised wave of refugees arriving in Britain. The regime in Malawi had expelled its Asian population, many of whom were British passport holders. As the first immigrants arrived in Britain, the mainstream press published highly inflammatory headlines: *The Sun* ran the headline 'Scandal of £600-a-Week Immigrants: Giant Bill for Two Families Who Live in a 4-Star Hotel' on 4 May, with the *Mirror* running the line 'New Flood of Asians into Britain' (*Campaign Against Racism and Fascism* 1977a; Taylor 1982).

This development was a spark which ignited 'the long hot summer of 1976', in which the NF experienced a period of growth while community tensions were increasingly strained (*Campaign Against Racism and Fascism* 1978a). On 4 June 1976, 10-year-old Gurdip Singh Chaggar was killed in what has been widely seen as a racially motivated attack. Chaggar's death provoked a huge reaction from within the local community, while community leaders did their best to rein in the expressions of anger from amongst the Asian youth: 'When the murder took place there was on the one hand a massive reaction amongst the Asian community of insecurity, of anger; there was also a reaction amongst many sections of white people fearful of the possible counter-violence by young Asians' (*Comment: Communist Fortnightly Review* 1976). These concerns were not entirely unfounded, as some young Asians' first response after Chaggar's death and the lack of an appropriate police response, 'was undirected violence and the stoning of cars by Asian youth … as well as attacks on several whites including a Communist Party member and a Newsline photographer' (Ramamurthy 2013). It is highly likely that this was exactly what both the NF and BM were hoping would happen.

The communal leadership of the Asian community struggled to pacify their youth:

> The leaders of the Indian Workers' Association [IWA] were in some difficulty to cope with the rising tide of feeling amongst the Asian community … For instance, several hundred young Asian lads went to an already scheduled IWA meeting on the Sunday two days after the murder, and effectively took it over. In a spontaneous way they initiated a demonstration to the local police station and it was left to one or two of our comrades to go with them to try to contain any wild activity. The IWA leadership did not go with them.
>
> *(Comment: Communist Fortnightly Review 1976: 212)*

The group marched to the police station, blocking the roads around the building. The police's first action was to arrest two of the protesters, one of whom had been with Chaggar when he was murdered. The Youth group proceeded to engage in a sit-in, and ultimately the police released the people that had been arrested. The day after this the Southall Youth Movement (SYM) was formed (Ramamurthy 2013). It is worth quoting Ramamurthy here:

> For Mohsin Zulfiqar, the protests in Southall 'really gave us the basis that direct action [does bring] positive results, hence our own ability to challenge the National Front by saying that we're prepared to fight against you physically, not just have demonstrations and pickets and so on … The authority of individuals in SYM was accepted 'because some of them had reputations as good fighters and organisers against racism in the schools – particularly in the fights with skinhead gangs several years ago.
>
> *(Ramamurthy 2013: 27)*

The SYM went about ensuring that their *modus operandi* really was one of self-defence, rather than aggressive campaigns of political violence. A peaceful march was held in Southall, attended by around 7,000 people. A meeting was also held at the local Sikh temple on the Wednesday five days after the murder, with between 150 and 200 attendees. The IWA, other local immigrant organisations, religious groups, trades unions, Labour and the CPGB, were all represented. At this meeting it was agreed that a demonstration should be held, so as not to create a political vacuum, but it was also widely agreed that the issue of communal 'self-defence' should be avoided, as it was just likely to lead to further 'violence and division in the community' (*Comment: Communist Fortnightly Review*, 1976: 213). So, despite hate crime and fascist provocation, there were still influential moderate communal voices helping to prevent non-white communities from becoming radicalised to the point of using organised and aggressive (as opposed to defensive) violence.

The same month as Chaggar's death, Community Relations officers in Blackburn released a dossier detailing more than 30 attacks carried out on Asian families and their properties. The officers argued that the blame for these attacks lay with the local National Party and their provocative activities (Walker 1977; Hann 2013). On 15 July a group of NF members attacked a West Indian club in Bradford injuring several people (*Campaign Against Racism and Fascism* 1977c). The murder, rising incidence of racist attacks, the growth of the fascist movement and hostility from the police and media all combined to provoke a growing militant attitude amongst Black and Asian youth. Militant immigrant groups in London, Leicester, Blackburn and Birmingham, supported by the Institute of Race Relations, developed self-defence groups within their communities. 'The young Asian militants wanted direct action to protect themselves against racist attacks by individuals and discrimination by the authorities, rather than relying on the State' (Smith 2010: 20). The SYM, and the other Asian Youth Movements (AYM) that followed, were organised and militant in their own way but were not provoked into operating aggressively by their right-wing antagonists.

Drawing a *direct* causal link between the fascist parties' activities and the high incidence of racist attacks, and, by extension, ethnic minority militancy, is impossible. However, as Taylor suggests, the 'existence of widespread support for racism as demonstrated by electoral support for the NF was, it could be argued, an indication to those contemplating such attacks on coloured people that such violence was, if not necessarily socially acceptable, at least more likely to be condoned than other types of violence' (Taylor 1982: 111). This suggestion is lent further weight when one considers that former NF chairman Kingsley-Read made a speech following Chaggar's death in which he claimed 'One down – a million to go' (Taylor 1982). That exacerbating conflict across racial lines was one of the NF's main strategies is lent further credence when one considers that as early as February 1976 the Association of Jewish Ex-Servicemen (AJEX) observed that: 'Webster's idea of direct action is to provoke a Race War' (AJEX 1976). In short, CE was Webster's explicit aim. Further, across the month that Chaggar died, 'It seems likely that ... the NF received over a thousand enquiries for membership' (Walker 1977: 199). Throughout the whole of 1976, the NF gained 4,500 new members, increasing their paid membership to 14,000 (*Campaign Against Racism and Fascism* 1977a).

The first major confrontation of 1977 happened at Wood Green in London on 23 April 1977. Around 1,500 NF members gathered at Ducketts Common to march to Palmers Green, and were opposed by around 3,000 anti-fascists from the IMG, Socialist Workers' Party (formerly the IS), the Labour Party, the IWA and anarchist groups. The more militant sections of the opposition, led by the SWP, broke away from the peaceful counter-demo and laid an ambush for the NF. Notably, ethnic minority groups had clearly been radicalised by the provocative tactics of the fascists, and a large number of local youths from the Cypriot and West Indian communities joined in the militant opposition to the Front. As the NF march neared them, the anti-fascists launched a barrage of missiles at the fascists. In the ensuing fighting 81 people were arrested, and one anti-racist was stabbed (*Campaign Against Racism and Fascism* 1977b; Hann 2013).

The following month the local elections were held, and once again the NF's results were the source of serious concern for the left. This was particularly true of their performance in London, where they received 119,063 votes. When a group of young black people, later dubbed the Lewisham 21, were arrested during early morning raids for suspicion of 'conspiring with each other and persons unknown to rob persons unknown', and their cause was taken up by community and left-wing activists, the NF were presented with an ideal target: ostensibly law-breaking immigrants being defended by both their ethnic minority community and the left. Accordingly, on 17 June 1977 a meeting of the Defence Committee for the 'Lewisham 21' (later the Lewisham 24) was attacked by NF members who beat unconscious one of the women present. The SWP, who were heavily involved in the 'Lewisham 21' Defence Committee, decided it was necessary to escalate the situation and go on the offensive. Central Committee member John Deason organised a group of stewards to defend not only the activities of the Defence Committee, but all the SWP's operations. These groups of stewards became known as the 'Squads': 'Officially sanctioned by the SWP leadership, [the Squads] were tightly organised groups of anti-fascists whose job was to attack NF initiatives, as well as defend anti-fascist events' (Birchall 2010: 36).

The next time the NF attacked the Defence Committee's stall they were ambushed by a Squad who viciously fought them off. This development served to escalate hostilities in the region for a while. The next month, on Saturday 2 July, a group of around 200 National Front members again violently attacked the Defence Committee who had organised a rally in Lewisham. The police arrested 50 people, 23 anti-fascists and 27 fascists (*Campaign Against Racism and Fascism* 1978b; Hann 2013). The high number of anti-fascists arrested, mainly for defending themselves, merely reinforced the view that the police were a racist organisation; indeed, the very operation which had led to the arrests of the Lewisham 24 had been called PNH, which many believed to stand for 'Police Nigger Hunt' (*Campaign Against Racism and Fascism* 1978b; Potter 1977). Shortly afterwards, almost certainly in an attempt to further inflame communal tensions, the NF announced that they would hold an 'Anti-Mugging' march from New Cross to Lewisham.

The day of the march was 13 August 1977. As the Front gathered to march through South London, two different groups of anti-fascists prepared their response. The first, organised by the All Lewisham Campaign Against Racism and Fascism (ALCARAF), was a peaceful affair orchestrated to avoid the NF's march altogether. The second, largely co-ordinated by the SWP, had every intention of physically opposing the NF (Copsey 2017). Between 3 and 6,000 militant anti-fascists, many armed with blunt instruments and knives, waited on the NF's route at Clifton Rise, and as the fascists approached them the anti-fascists hurled a barrage of missiles at their enemies. A strong police presence managed to maintain control of the situation for a while, but eventually some determined anti-fascists broke through their line to attack the NF close up, splitting their march in two (Anon. 1995). This led to extremely vicious fighting between the two sides and the police. The first main point to be made about the riot in Lewisham is that it seems likely that many of the people involved in the fighting enjoyed the thrill of the experience itself, over and above the ideological commitment to defeating their enemies. One anarchist present on the day stated:

> Flying kicks, punches and the clashing of improvised weaponry filled the space around me. A Nazi leapt out yelling, "COME ON THEN, YOU RED BASTARD!" We struggled, me slamming him with a lump of wood. He relaxed his grip, someone had bashed him on the side of the skull with a brick. He caught many a boot as he hit the deck, my own included. I had that glorious novocaine feeling above my upper lip. Pure adrenaline, pure violence.
>
> *(Lux 2006: 62)*

Similarly, Steve Tilzey of the SWP who was also in the thick of the conflict described how 'It was a real buzz, and I felt as if I had been part of something really special' (Hann & Tilzey 2003: 10). Yet another anti-fascist recounted that 'We were at Clifton Rise when the march got split in two by a wedge of anti-fascists. We charged through and threw things at the retreating fascists. It was absolute chaos but incredibly, incredibly exhilarating' (Hann 2013: 268). This all points to the way that highly emotionally charged situations can socialise groups of people into becoming desensitised to violence, and thus perhaps lead to increasingly militant viewpoints. Further, the intense emotions experienced at events such as this can help to maintain activists' commitment to the movement; as demonstrated, many activists enjoy these confrontations and actively seek them out.

The police eventually managed to divert the NF members down side streets to the prearranged meeting held by John Tyndall. The militant anti-fascists, their numbers now swelled by local Black and Asian youths, pressed forward into Lewisham (Lux 2006). Here the main conflict was between the militant anti-fascists and the police, as the former pushed forward in an attempt to attack the police station. As the remaining mob of anti-fascists marched past the Lewisham clock tower, the police numbers having thinned, the militants hurled smoke bombs and other missiles at the remainder of them. The second point to be made about the day's events was the escalation in policing tactics. As the anti-fascists continued towards the police station, they were met with a novel sight:

> Down from where we'd just come, across the wide road, slowly advancing, a line of police with riot shields. It looked spooky, fascinating even, the whole scene made menacing by blackened skies and the distant plume of smoke.
>
> *(Lux 2006: 65)*

It was the first time that the UK police used riot gear and tactics outside of Northern Ireland, demonstrating a mutually radicalising effect between the forces of law and order and militant social movements (BBC n.d.). In their work on 'spirals of violence' between movements and countermovements, Busher and Macklin argue that 'contest escalation often occurred at the intersection with other more violent contests', pointing out that fascists and anti-fascists in Britain who were also politically invested in the Irish Troubles sometimes borrowed the more deadly tactics of the conflict there, with one English anti-fascist even detonating a bomb in London (Busher & Macklin 2015: 60). Here it seems that there is evidence that the police, or state apparatuses in general, are prone to this pattern as well, as the British state took tactics it had developed in the far more bloody conflict in Northern Ireland and used them in the streets of the capital – needless to say, the sight of riot police would become a much more common occurrence at political demonstrations as the years passed.

Shortly after the riot police arrived, the anti-fascists' plan to storm the police station was thrown into disarray by the arrival of even more Special Patrol Group (SPG) officers, and so most of the militants took the opportunity to retreat rather than being arrested. Shortly after the events, Steve Redford wrote in *CARF* magazine that:

> The tactics adopted by the police at New Cross and later in the day in Lewisham High Street both appalled and astounded me ... I am not one of those who believes that the police are a fascist force – not yet anyway – but their actions on August 13 can only strengthen the position of those who do argue this line.
>
> *(Campaign Against Racism and Fascism 1977a)*

The popular narrative amongst the left, which had taken root after Kevin Gately's death, that the major concern of the police was to suppress the forces of the revolutionary left, was gaining traction. However, it should be noted that this narrative did not find acceptance among the general population outside the ranks of the far left. The actions of the (overwhelmingly Protestant) Royal Ulster Constabulary (RUC) in Northern Ireland during the Troubles were often interpreted by the whole Catholic community as unfairly repressive, and thus had a radicalising influence on the broader community as well as activists (Carter 2017). This is largely because the RUC were widely perceived as being biased and on more than one occasion they unnecessarily employed extreme methods. By contrast, when anti-fascists faced the police in Britain they were often the instigators of violence, and as such were not widely perceived as the victims among the broader British population. Thus their interactions with the police, while possibly radicalising already committed activists, did not draw any others into the conflict. The exception to this observation were the Black and Asian minority communities, whose daily experiences of institutional racism led to them viewing the police in much the same way that Catholics in Northern Ireland viewed the RUC.

Which brings us to the third and final noteworthy aspect of the 'Battle of Lewisham': the involvement of minority community members. As Martin Lux (2006: 63) noted:

> knots of young blacks and asians fought the cops ... We were mega-hyped, armed and dangerous ... I pressed ahead, noticing that most of the folk with us now were black and not all of them youngsters. On the other side of the road a dozen beefy middle aged blacks emerged from a minicab firm, some wearing crash helmets, others carrying bin lids like shields. All were tooled up.

This was something the far left recognised and tried to capitalise on. Tim Potter from the SWP wrote that 'It was they [the 'young West Indians'] who gave Lewisham its special character. Traditionally alienated from the revolutionary left, they assembled in the thousands to stop the Front. We must learn what produced that situation and how the strength and militancy of black youth can become a central component in the mass struggle against the fascists and racists in Britain' (Potter 1977: 19). As already noted, both the far left and the far right were trying to radicalise immigrant communities, in a similar fashion to how both sides were competing over the hearts and minds of the working class. The far left wanted the immigrant communities to join their revolutionary cadres, the fascists wanted to provoke a race war. Indeed, it was widely felt by many on the left that 14 August 1977 was, in particular, a turning point in the M/CM contest:

> Lewisham was important since it marks the first point in the clash between these movements; the radicalisation of parts of the black community, a grow-ing fascist movement, attracting attention from the press, and the police adopting a policy of confrontation.
>
> *(Potter 1977: 19)*

In November 1977 the Anti-Nazi League (ANL) was formally launched by Paul Holborow, Peter Hain and Ernie Roberts (Renton 2006). The League's objectives were 'to organise on the widest possible scale against the propaganda and activities of the Nazis in Britain today' (Anti-Nazi League 1977). The formation of the ANL was the result of a confluence of different factors. First, 'the highly publicized electoral advances of the National Front in the 1977 Greater London Council elections ... convinced many left activists, and specifically those within the SWP, to create a broad-based, umbrella movement to combat the Front' (Messina 1989: 110–111), as it was felt that the SWP was too small to 'stem the tide' (Renton 2006).

Second, the SWP were aware that they alienated themselves from the rest of the labour movement with their aggressive tactics, and wanted a specifically anti-fascist organisation to carry on their work without catching the flack for this, demonstrating that the need on the part of a social movement organisation to win votes and garner support from a wider movement may act as a mechanism of de-radicalisation in certain circumstances. Third, and perhaps most importantly, the ANL was a response to what many felt was a lacklustre attempt on the part of Labour to fight the NF (Renton 2006). The ANL was the first-ever national body entirely dedicated to anti-fascism (Copsey 2017).

1978–1979

In 1978 the ANL joined forces with Rock Against Racism (RAR). RAR had been founded between August and December in 1976, by the photographer Red Saunders and others, in response to racist comments made by Eric Clapton, David Bowie and Rod Stewart (Hann 2013). In the battle for the hearts and minds of the working class, as well as British youth in general, urban youth music scenes were a key battlefield, and RAR was a fairly successful initiative in this endeavour. Dave Renton has written widely on this cultural war fought between the far left and far right over parts of the British music scene from the 1970s onwards after the event of punk rock in 1976:

> The quick demise of bands like the Sex Pistols created a space that was partly filled by a revived skinhead subculture, with which the National Front attempted to connect. Here it was helped by the traces of ambiguity that punk displayed towards fascism … The people who organized Rock Against Racism deliberately endorsed the rougher music of bands like the UK Subs or Jimmy Pursey's Sham 69. Sham in particular stressed their street origins. Songs like 'I Don't Wanna' and 'The Cockney Kids are Innocent' were written for an audience of unemployed young workers, the people whom the National Front and RAR both sought … Sham 69 gave anti-racists a route into the minds of young skinheads. In adopting this street music, Rock Against Racism grabbed it out of the hands of white racists.
>
> *(Renton 2006: 36–38)*

This is an important aspect of this episode. For the most part, the 'battle lines', or conflict cleavage, between the far right and far left were non-ascriptive (i.e. ideological) rather than ascriptive (i.e. racial). Both sides wanted to recruit the working class to their cause, and so had to be cautious in their application of violence. When violence was used, it was against members of the minority communities or against committed activists – this necessarily limited the number of people who would be drawn into the conflict. Whereas republicans and loyalists in Northern Ireland detonated bombs which killed Catholics and Protestants not actively involved in the Troubles, thereby creating an impetus for others to join through a drive for revenge or protection, a similar use of mass violence would have gained nothing for the NF or the SWP – indeed, if anything it would have delivered a propaganda victory to their enemies. Rather, their efforts were somewhat channelled in this less violent direction.

On 4 May 1978, the local elections were held, and the results seemed to show that the NF had lost support (Taylor 1982). However, on the night of the local elections, a 25-year-old Bengali called Altab Ali was murdered by three teenage boys as he walked home from where he worked in the East End of London. Even if Ali's murderers were not members of the National Front, many observers felt that following their poor performance at the election in May the NF's tactics changed, with Stan Taylor (1982) arguing that they embarked on a campaign of violence and provocation in the East End. The Bethnal Green and Stepney Trades Council argued that

> The relatively poor showing of the National Front in the local Council elections, on the same night that Altab Ali was stabbed to death, seemed to signal a marked change of tactics by racist groups in the area … Their tactics seem, from May of this year, to have moved over to a much more overtly provocative posturing, their members becoming openly involved in the serious mass outrages which have shocked the East End in recent months.
>
> *(Bethnal Green and Stepney Trades Council 1978: 32)*

Racial attacks on immigrants in the East End were becoming increasingly common, especially towards the Bengali community. It was also strongly felt by many that the Metropolitan Police's attitude towards these events tended to be at best indifferent, at worst openly hostile to the victims (Bethnal Green and Stepney Trades Council 1978).

Soon after Ali's murder, around 7,000 people, largely from the Bengali community, and organised by the Federation of Bangladesh Youth Organisations (FBYO), marched behind his coffin to Hyde Park in a protest against racist violence (Ramamurthy 2006). The next month, on 12 June, around 150 white youths 'went on a "racialist rampage" in Brick Lane in Hackney during which they smashed the property of Bengalis and attacked them with stones, bricks and bottles' (Taylor 1982: 155–156). A 55-year-old man was knocked unconscious due to the group throwing rocks through his shop window.

> This was by far the biggest group to have threatened the Asian community in [the] area, and heralded a new and frightening escalation of racial incitement. Some Asians and anti-racists fought off the attackers. It was perhaps ten minutes before the police arrived.
>
> *(Bethnal Green and Stepney Trades Council 1978: 41)*

On 25 June another Bengali, Ishaque Ali, was murdered in Hackney, East London. The murders provoked days of protests, which culminated in the full-scale occupation and shutting down of Brick Lane (Hann 2013). Another result of racist attacks was the development of a hardened cadre of Bengali men eager to clash with their fascist antagonists:

Now, however, a new attitude is developing among the young men of the Asian community in the East End. The ability to fight, the martial arts, the language of 'self defence' and an aggressive self-awareness has taken over from the gentler approach of their elders. Karate takes precedence over the traditional Bengali cultural activities of theatre, music, dance and poetry.

(Campaign Against Racism and Fascism 1977b)

Once again, the police's reaction, or lack thereof, towards black and Asian murders acted as a radicalising agent:

we went to the police and the police took the attitude that, 'What can we do?' ... and there was the time when we said 'Right if you can't defend us, then we will have to defend ourselves' ... Police indifference was an experience that was witnessed again and again.

(Ramamurthy 2013: 46)

After June the escalating tactics of the fascists were becoming more obvious. Attacks on members of the Black and Asian communities were increasing, even on children. A 'whole series of arson attempts were made on the Immigrants Advice Bureau and on the Asian premises in its vicinity in Hanbury Street' (Bethnal Green and Stepney Trades Council 1978: 42). Further, a Black man was stabbed by two white youths in Mile End Road. In early July, a group of Bengali workers were leaving their shift at a bottling plant in East London when they were attacked by around 30 white men armed with bottles and bricks. Eight of the Bengalis were hospitalised over the attack. The police issued a statement claiming this was a fight over a car, despite the Bengali men emphatically stating that it was an unprovoked racist attack (Bethnal Green and Stepney Trades Council 1978).

Around this time a man named Fred Challis and three accomplices were jailed for admitting to 300 racially motivated attacks in Tower Hamlets, as well as the murder of a homeless man. Challis smashed the man's face in with a gas cylinder, before scrawling 'NF rules OK' on the wall in blood; Challis was not actually a member of the NF but felt that the party would appreciate this act (Bethnal Green and Stepney Trades Council 1978). Taylor has argued that these developments cannot be

divorced from the presence of the NF in the East End of London, both indirectly in that racism was given a 'legitimate' outlet, and directly insofar as it was alleged that not only were NF members involved in violence but that the NF's leadership was turning a blind eye to such behaviour.

(Taylor 1982: 156)

His arguments were given some weight by Granada TV's World in Action series which aired an investigation of the NF in July 1978. The programme included the alleged testimony from a Special Branch undercover operative who claimed that the systematic use of violence to terrorise political opponents and ethnic minorities was at least tacitly accepted by the national leadership. The programme was viewed by over 10 million people (YJAR 1979). The same month, on 15 July, three of the largest British Asian organisations – the Standing Conference of Pakistani Organizations in Britain, the IWA, and the Federation of Bangladeshi Associations – all asserted the need for Asian 'self-defence' groups, and encouraged their members to join the ANL. This was a clear sign of the growing militancy within the Asian community, who had formerly been affiliated with the much more moderate Joint Committee Against Racialism (Taylor 1982).

Meanwhile, the more militant elements of the anti-fascist movement were continuing their aggressive campaign against the Front. Towards the end of 1978, the SWP Squad in Manchester learned that the NF were forming a football team, the 'Lillywhites', and were playing in the 1978–79 Sunday Football League. They soon discovered that the NF were using a van parked behind a pub as an ersatz changing room, and so on Sunday 8 October 1978 the Squad ambushed the Lillywhites, chasing some off and trapping the rest in their van which the anti-fascists then pushed on to its side (Hann & Tilzey 2003). After a few weeks of an ongoing campaign of disruption waged by the anti-fascists, the League stopped the Lillywhites' involvement.

After they had shut down the Lillywhites, the same Squad observed the National Front members selling papers in Manchester city centre every Sunday. After watching them for a number of weeks, they planned to ambush them on the way to their pitch. On the day, the Squad attacked them with a range of blunt weapons and knives, hospitalising several of them (Hann & Tilzey 2003). At the same time, some NF members began looking for more extreme means to use against their political foes. At the end of 1978, two prominent NF members were imprisoned for possession of explosives. James Tierney from Devon, and Newcastle branch 'Security Officer' Alan Birtley both received three years for the offences, with Birtley admitting in court that several members of his branch were capable of making explosives and they had intended using them against their opponents (Association of Jewish Ex-Servicemen & Women 1979). On Friday 19 and Saturday 20 January 1979 at their Annual General Meeting, the National Front's John Tyndall said that it

> hasn't been the National Front that's been obliterated. The obliteration has been of the red mobs who declared war against the National Front – the red mobs whose members, as they nurse their scars and bruises, are now perhaps wiser than before.
>
> *(Campaign Against Racism and Fascism 1979)*

Two years of feuding between the fascists and anti-fascists finally erupted in what would be the last large-scale fracas of the decade. On 23 April, in Southall, Ealing, the NF booked a meeting at Southall Town Hall. This action faced opposition from both the IWA and the ANL. The former suggested closing down local business on that particular day in protest and encouraged people to ignore the event, while the latter suggested a more confrontational approach (Copsey 2017). Activists from the

SYM, ANL and other anti-fascist groups congregated around the Southall Town Hall prior to the NF meeting. As the counter-demo grew, around 3,000 police, including the now notorious SPG, horses, dogs and a helicopter descended onto the area (Fryer 1984). The police

> split the demonstrators into distinct groups thereby preventing the possibility of a peaceful sit-down protest. Serious disturbances between police and demonstrators then followed at various locations. Missiles were thrown at police from the anti-fascist side, including flares, smoke-bombs and a petrol bomb, which was hurled at a police coach.
>
> *(Copsey 2017: 142)*

At some point during this chaos the activist Blair Peach was killed due to a blow to the head, widely believed to have come from an SPG officer. Copsey (2017: 142) has highlighted the fact that having refused to run an official inquiry into Peach's death, many felt that the state had absolved the police of all guilt, the result being that 'the actions of the police at Southall represented a crucial moment in the anti-fascist struggle, with the state now replacing the NF as the main adversary'.

On 3 May 1979 the general election was held, and the National Front 'captured two British electoral records: that for the largest number of candidates (303) put up by an insurgent party since 1918 … and that for the smallest average share of the total vote per candidate (1.6 per cent)' (Taylor, *New Society* 1981). Indeed, the NF's results were disastrously low, with a 'drop in the NF vote which varied between 25 per cent and 75 per cent in the constituencies which were contested in both 1974 and May 1979' (*Spearhead*, No. 128, May/June 1979). Although over 190,000 people voted for them, this result nonetheless effectively sounded the death knell for the NF (Copsey 2017). After their failure, the NF descended into both sectarian in-fighting and more vicious street-fighting against the left. It also saw a fault line widen within the ANL and SWP, with some of those urging the need for violent anti-fascist means being expelled from the SWP (Anon. 1995).

Conclusion

As with any contentious episode, the group actors in this case study were all involved in a process of 'coevolution' (Oliver & Myers 2002). The interactions between the two movements and the state did lead to some degree of escalation in terms of each of their 'collective action repertoires' (Beckwith 2000): the SWP's Squads and the NF's Honour Guard, martial bodies who used violence for defensive and offensive purposes; the Bengali groups trained in karate and the SYM and AYMs, who were organised to defend themselves and their communities with more skill; and the introduction of the riot police by the state, measures which had been developed through interaction with the lethal paramilitaries of Northern Ireland and which were then employed to quell the rising militancy of the far left and far right in Britain. Yet even though there is evidence of each of these groups being radicalised to some extent, these processes were limited and clearly affected them at different rates and to different extents.

The fascists and the far-left anti-fascists coevolved in a much more closely symbiotic, or tightly and symmetrically 'coupled', fashion. Both the Squads and the Honour Guard were formed as a result of interactions between the two movements, and the actions of one (such as protests or carnivals) were highly likely to provoke a response from the other. However, despite many large-scale mobilisations, several of which descended into relatively serious cases of public disorder, the levels of violence employed by both movements remained relatively stable across the case study, and gradual escalations (increases in attacks on the enemy's events for instance) occurred more or less evenly on both sides. Walker has addressed the question as to why the fascists' and anti-fascists' conflict during this period did not escalate further:

> In neither body was there any sign of overall determination to take their opposition to the extreme of street warfare. The real cause of their hostility was that they both saw themselves as revolutionaries against the liberal capitalism of the British state. They each desired passionately to win the allegiance of the working class, and to destroy their opponents ...
>
> The passionate vocabulary of the Left, and the equally passionate speeches of Tyndall and Webster suggested that they were unsuccessful rivals for the support of the same social groups – neither Tyndall nor the Trotskyists had made any real headway within the mass of the British Labour Movement, and until they did the violence of which they spoke was unlikely to materialize.
>
> *(Walker 1977: 173)*

This is an astute observation, which accurately describes how the escalation of the conflict was, at least in part, contingent on the success of one or the other group in gaining hegemonic dominance over the social group whom they both sought to court. Further, as stated above, the competition over a social base had a limiting effect on the levels of violence employed, in that groups were obviously less likely to use violence indiscriminately for fear of alienating their target constituency. Although it is likely this dynamic would only remain if the conditions that the movements found themselves in throughout this case study did not change significantly; were one or the other to become widely popular and gain mass support then it is possible that this could provoke communal polarisation and the situation could then escalate violently.

The minority communities and the social movement organisations which sprang from them, however, were much more reluctant to engage directly with the far right. Unlike the fascists and leftist anti-fascists like the SWP, they were not engaged in a struggle for ideological dominance of the working class but rather were concerned with 'self-defence' and campaigning for 'black rights on a variety of levels' (Ramamurthy 2013). While they were organised in opposition to the fascists – indeed, they arguably had a much more pressing motivation to do so than the far left – they were just as concerned with tackling racism and improving the lot of their communities. For them to organise with an eye to being aggressively involved in large-scale violent conflicts, as the far left and far right did, would have been a counterproductive move that may well have reinforced racism at the local and state levels while possibly bringing about repressive measures from the state and impeding their efforts to 'promote the cause of equal rights and social and economic opportunities' (Ramamurthy 2013: 40).

It is likely that both the National Front and the SWP would have both been pleased with a more militant and confrontational attitude developing amongst the British minority communities. The far left were interested in how 'the strength and militancy of black youth can become a central component in the mass struggle against the fascists and racists in Britain' (Potter 1977: 19). For their part, the NF wanted the social boundaries between white and non-white communities to become more pronounced and for animosity to develop across them. As Joe Pearce, editor of the Young National Front magazine *Bulldog*, explained:

> The strategy was simple. We had to stir up enmity and hatred between black and white youths, thereby making multiculturalism untenable and a race war inevitable. The newly formed Young National Front … would become an army of race warriors, a new *Sturmabteilung*, the stormtroopers of the New Order.
>
> *(Pearce 2013: 62)*

This is very similar to McCauley's concept of 'JuJitsu Politics'. McCauley writes that a group may intentionally provoke an enemy into attacking their target constituency so that in response they will be radicalised into joining them. McCauley cites the actions of the terrorists involved in the 9/11 attacks on America as being an example of this strategy, in that their ultimate goal was to provoke counter-attacks from the US in order to radicalize the wider global Muslim population (which, to a greater or lesser extent, it did). McCauley writes:

> Terrorists count on the response of the state to mobilize those who sympathize with the goals of the terrorists. State response, to the extent that it hurts or outrages those less committed than the terrorists, does for the terrorists what they cannot do for themselves. This is jujitsu politics: using the enemy's strength to mobilize against the enemy.
>
> *(McCauley 2006: 49)*

Obviously this theoretical concept needs some revision if it is to be applied to this case study. Whereas for Al-Qaeda this was a 'weapon of the weak' in their war against an overwhelmingly superior force, for the NF it was an attempt to mobilise the majority population and the state against minority communities. Actions such as their 'Anti-Muggers March' through Lewisham and their physical attacks on groups like the Lewisham 21 Defence Campaign were intended to radicalize the Black and Asian communities so as to foster communal animosity. The ultimate hope was that the white British population would come to see the National Front as the best channel through which to express their group interests. However, these groups that the NF attempted to provoke were motivated by a 'desire to be accepted as equal citizens and to belong in Britain', and had little interest in fighting a war on the streets (Ramamurthy 2013: 2). The NF employed similar tactics with the far left. By the second half of 1977 they had begun to rely on provoking left-wing opponents in order to get publicity (Taylor & Layton-Henry 1977). Here, at least, it did seem the tactic produced some support for them. They garnered both media attention and, it seems, votes through their clashes with the far left; although it is not clear the extent to which their association with violence was ultimately off-putting to the electorate.

As was demonstrated, the development of collective action frames by the fascists and anti-fascists had a significant impact on the extent to which the movements were capable of generating and mobilising supporters. In the first instance, political developments such as Powell's 'Rivers of Blood' speech and the large influx of Ugandan refugees in 1972 created conditions which were conducive to the National Front being able to disseminate their narratives of racial competition. However, the anti-fascists' 'counterframes' that painted the National Front as fascists and their policies as racist, which were lent empirical credibility by the pictures documenting the explicitly Nazi past of Tyndall and Webster, gave them the upper hand in the 'framing contest' and seriously hindered the NF's progress (Benford & Snow 2000). Interestingly, the National Front both benefited from and was damaged by the media's involvement with these framing processes. The incendiary headlines that were published by the tabloid press following the arrival of the Malawi Asian refugees in 1976 created fertile soil for the NF's xenophobic ideology, yet by the same token the media's explicit hostility towards the fascists was one of their greatest barriers to success.

Notes

1 See McDuff 2017.
2 John Tyndall and Martin Webster had both been members of the Nazi National Socialist Movement (NSM) in the early 60s, and journalists had obtained pictures of them wearing Nazi uniforms (see Walker 1977).

References

Primary sources

AJEX (1974) *AJEX Defence Bulletin*, No. 1, July *Searchlight* Archive – SCH/01/Res/AF/04/003, University of Northampton, Northampton.

AJEX (1976) *AJEX Defence Bulletin*, Vol. 2, No. 1, February *Searchlight* Archive – SCH/01/Res/AF/04/003, University of Northampton, Northampton.

Anderson, David. (2013) *The Terrorism Acts in 2012: Report of the Independent Reviewer on the Operation of the Terrorism Act 2000 and Part 1 of the Terrorism Act 2006*, TSO: London.

Anti-Nazi League (1977) *Anti-Nazi League Founding Statement*, November.

Association of Jewish Ex-Servicemen & Women (1979) *Action Briefing*, Issue No. 11 *Searchlight* Archive – SCH/01/Res/AF/04/003, University of Northampton, Northampton.

Bethnal Green and Stepney Trades Council (1978) *Blood on the Streets: A Report*, Bethnal Green and Stepney Trades Council: London.

British Movement (1975) *'British Tidings' Bulletin of British Movement*, No. 51, November *Searchlight* Archive – SCH/01/Res/BRI, University of Northampton, Northampton.

Campaign Against Racism and Fascism (1977a) Issue 1, May.

Campaign Against Racism and Fascism (1977b) Issue 7, August/September.

Campaign Against Racism and Fascism (1977c) Issue 8, October.

Campaign Against Racism and Fascism (1978a) April.

Campaign Against Racism and Fascism (1978b) August/September.

Campaign Against Racism and Fascism (1979) Issue 8.

Comment: Communist Fortnightly Review (1976) 10 July.

Correspondence to Maurice Ludmer (1975) *Searchlight* Archive – SCH/01/Res/SLI/02/001, University of Northampton, Northampton.

HM Government. (2013) *Contest: The United Kingdom Government's Strategy for Countering Terrorism: Annual Report*, London: TSO.

Home Office. (1975) *The Red Lion Square Disorders of 15 June 1974*, London: Her Majesty's Stationery Office.

International Socialists (1974) *National Front: The New Nazis*, London *Searchlight* Archive – SCH/01/Res/AF/09/003, University of Northampton, Northampton.

Spearhead (1976) No. 92, March.

Spearhead (1979) No. 128, May/June.

YJAR (1979) *YJAR Mag: Young Jews Against Racialism*, No.1 April.

Secondary sources

Anon. (1995) *Anti-Nazi League: A Critical Examination 1977–81/2 and 1992–95*, London: The Colin Roach Centre.

BBC. (n.d.) *BBC On This Day:* '1977:Violent Clashes at NF March' [http://news.bbc.co.uk/onthisday/hi/dates/stories/august/13/newsid_2534000/2534035.stm], Accessed 23/03/2015.

Beckwith, Karen. (2000) 'Hinges in Collective Action: Strategic Innovation in The Pittston Coal Strike', *Mobilization: An International Quarterly*, 5 (2): 179–199.

Benford, Robert D. & David A. Snow. (2000) 'Framing Processes and Social Movements: An Overview and Assessment', *Annual Review of Sociology*, 26: 611–639.

Birchall, Sean. (2010) *Beating the Fascists: The Untold Story of Anti-Fascist Action*, London: Freedom Press.

Busher, Joel & Graham Macklin. (2015) 'The Missing Spirals of Violence: Four Waves of Movement–Countermovement Contest in Post-war Britain', *Behavioral Sciences of Terrorism and Political Aggression*, 7 (1): 53–68.

Copsey, Nigel. (2017) *Anti-Fascism in Britain*, Macmillan Press Ltd: London.

Carter, Alexander J. (2017) 'Cumulative Extremism: Escalation of Movement–Countermovement Dynamics in Northern Ireland Between 1967 and 1972', *Behavioral Sciences of Terrorism and Political Aggression*, 9 (1): 37–51.

Eatwell, Roger. (2006) 'Community Cohesion and Cumulative Extremism in Contemporary Britain', *Political Quarterly*, 77 (2): 204–216.

Farrar, Max. (2004) 'Social Movements and the Struggle Over 'Race' in *Democracy and Participation: Popular Protest and New Social Movements*, edited by Malcolm J. Todd & Gary Taylor, London: Merlin Press.

Fryer, Peter. (1984) *Staying Power: The History of Black People in Britain*, London: Pluto Press.

Hann, Dave. (2013) *Physical Resistance: A Hundred Years of Anti-Fascism*, Alresford: Zero Books.

Hann, Dave & Steve Tilzey. (2003) *No Retreat: The Secret War Between Britain's Anti-Fascists and the Far Right*, Lytham: Milo Books.

Husbands, Christopher T. (1983) *Racial Exclusionism and the City: The Urban Support of the National Front*, London: George Allen and Unwin.

Leech, Kenneth. (1994) *Brick Lane, 1978: The Events and Their Significance*, London: Stepney Books.

Lindorp, Fred. (2001) 'Racism and the Working Class: Strikes in Support of Enoch Powell in 1968', *Labour History Review*, 66 (1): 79–100.

Lux, Martin. (2006) *Anti-Fascist*, London: Phoenix Press.

McAdam, Doug, John D. McCarthy & Mayer N. Zald. (1996) 'Introduction: Opportunities, Mobilizing Structures, and Framing Processes: Towards a Synthetic, Comparative Perspective on Social Movements', in *Comparative Perspectives on Social Movements: Political Opportunities, Mobilizing Structures, and Cultural Framings*, edited by Doug McAdam, John D. McCarthy & Mayer N. Zald, Cambridge: Cambridge University Press.

McCauley, Clark. (2006) 'JuJitsu Politics: Terrorism and Responses to Terrorism', in *Collateral Damage: The Psychological Consequences of America's War on Terrorism*, Edited by Paul R. Kimmel & Chris E. Stout, Westport: Praeger Publishers.

McDuff, Phil. (2017) 'Are we more at risk of terrorism than ever, or does it just feel like that?', *Guardian* [www.theguardian.com/commentisfree/2017/jun/21/us-and-them-extremism-terror-attacks], Accessed 30 June 2017.

Messina, Anthony M. (1989) *Race and Party Competition in Britain*, Oxford: Oxford University Press.

Miles, Robert & Annie Phizacklea. (1984) *White Man's Country: Racism in British Politics*, London: Pluto Press.

Oliver, Pamela E. & Daniel J. Myers. (2002) 'The Coevolution of Social Movements', *Mobilization: An International Quarterly*, 8 (1): 1–24.

Pearce, Joseph. (2013) *Race with the Devil: My Journey from Racial Hatred to Rational Love*, Charlotte: Saint Benedict Press.

Polletta, Francesca & James M. Jasper. (2001) 'Collective Identity and Social Movements', *Annual Review of Sociology*, 27: 283–305.

Potter, Tim. (1977) 'Lessons of Lewisham', *International Socialism*, 1 (101): 19–23.

Ramamurthy, Anandi. (2006) 'The Politics of Britain's Asian Youth Movements', *Race & Class*, 48 (38): 38–60.

Ramamurthy, Anandi. (2013) *Black Star: Britain's Asian Youth Movements*, London: Pluto Press.

Renton, David. (2006) *When We Touched the Sky*, Cheltenham: New Clarion Press.

Smith, Evan. (2010) 'Conflicting Narratives of Black Youth Rebellion in Modern Britain', *Ethnicity and Race in a Changing World*, 2 (1): 16–31.

Taylor, Stan. (1978) 'Race, Extremism and Violence in Contemporary British Politics', *New Community*, 7 (1): 56–66.

Taylor, Stan. (1981) 'The Far Right Fragments', *New Society* (n.v.; n.p.).

Taylor, Stan. (1982) *The National Front in English Politics*, London: Macmillan Press Ltd.

Taylor, Stan & Zig Layton-Henry. (1977) 'Race at the Polls', *New Society* (n.v.; n.p.).

Trilling, Daniel. (2013) *Bloody Nasty People: The Rise of Britain's Far Right*, London: Verso.

Walker, Martin. (1977) *The National Front*, Glasgow: Fontana Paperbacks.

6

WHITE YOUTH

The far right, punk and British youth culture, 1977–87[1]

Matthew Worley and Nigel Copsey

Introduction

On 18 August 1979, the Conway Hall hosted the inaugural London concert of Rock Against Communism (RAC), a movement conceived within and supported by the far-right National Front (NF). Reports of the evening provide mixed accounts. For anti-fascists keen to oppose the gig, a sizeable police presence – supported by strategically placed vans belonging to the London Met's Special Patrol Group – ensured protesters were soon escorted to the nearest tube station (Ellen 1979: 17; Goldman 1979a: 9). For Joe Pearce of the Young National Front (YNF), the failure of the relatively well-known Skrewdriver to play tempered expectation that the gig would kick-start an 'anti-commie backlash' against 'left-wing filth in rock music', particularly Rock Against Racism (RAR) and the Anti-Nazi League (ANL) initiated by members of the Socialist Workers' Party (SWP).[2] Skrewdriver, a punk band from Poulton-le-Fylde (near Blackpool) that released two singles and an album on Chiswick Records in 1977, had amassed something of a skinhead following on their move to London in the same year, among whom was a small core of NF and British Movement (BM) activists. The band's singer, Ian Stuart, had in turn joined the NF in early 1979, thereby becoming a well-known 'face' in far-right circles prior to the Conway Hall gig. Come August, however, and Stuart stayed away, stating 'record company pressure' as an excuse for his no show (Brazil 1979: 18–19; Stuart 1979: 17).[3]

In the event, only two bands performed – The Dentists from Leeds and White Boss from Coventry.[4] According to Vivien Goldman, who reported on the gig for *Melody Maker*, the crowd was overwhelmingly male (Goldman counted five women) and relatively young. About 150 people attended, with pictures of the gig revealing skinheads, punks, mods and assorted hairy youngsters bouncing around to sets that included odes to the 'Master Race' and protestations of Nazi innocence

(Verrall 1981: 12). In between, a teddy boy DJ – Mike's Bluejean Bop – flew the confederate flag but reportedly played mainly punk tunes by the Sex Pistols, Devo and, most surprisingly, the Tom Robinson Band, best-known as RAR stalwarts and releasing 'Glad to be Gay' on an EP in 1978. For her own part, Goldman chatted to Tony Williams, the NF's Ipswich organiser, about Britain's imminent descent into racial chaos, resisting his request to come back to her place after last orders. Apparently, Goldman's Jewish origins were no longer an issue for Williams if she renounced Zionism (Goldman 1979a: 9).

At first glance, the lacklustre nature of RAC's launch may seem simply to demonstrate the limited nature of the far-right's appeal to British youth in the 1970s (Shaffer 2013: 458–482). Dig deeper, however, and it provides a way into, first, a significant juncture in far-right politics; a 'cultural turn' that eventually spawned a global network of Nazi-aligned music scenes. Beyond the NF's White Noise Club distributing records throughout Europe by the mid-1980s, the Blood & Honour franchise launched by Ian Stuart and others in 1987 soon boasted divisions in Germany, Scandinavia, the US, Australia and elsewhere (Shaffer 2014: 111–124; Langebach and John Raabe 2013: 249–264; Brown 2004: 157–178; Lowles and Silver 1998). Second, the emergence of RAC reveals the contested and politicised nature of British youth culture in the late 1970s and 1980s. This, after all, was a time when the left organised ANL–RAR carnivals to combat the influence of the far right and gigs were often broken up by mobs of NF and BM supporters (Worley 2012: 333–354). Just a month before the RAC gig, Sham 69's performance at London's Rainbow theatre had been brutally cut short by a BM assault headed by its notorious Leader Guard.[5] In the weeks after, a Crass gig at Conway Hall and a 2-tone revue at Hatfield Polytechnic saw the appearance of anti-fascist 'squads' organised to physically beat the fascist threat wherever it arose.

The objective of this chapter, therefore, is to denote the moment, site and practice of the far-right's attempt to colonise and cultivate British youth culture. The first section will outline the political and socio-economic context in which British fascism developed into the 1970s, locating the moment of 'crisis' that allowed far-right appeals to gain traction. The second section will delineate sites of far-right recruitment among young people; in particular, it will explore attempts to claim youth cultural styles and forms of popular music as conduits for fascist politics. Finally, the chapter explains the practical expression of far-right engagement with British youth culture, outlining its contingent strategies and approaches. By drawing from a mixture of archival and relatively obscure material, the chapter seeks to demonstrate just how and why the far right utilised the cultural spaces associated with punk to propagate racism and fascism. It serves also to complement the more typical focus on leftist efforts to channel punk towards politically progressive ends (anti-racism, anti-war etc.), suggesting that the far-right's appropriation of punk and skinhead styles forged a distinct subculture aligned instead to the politics of Nazism and ultra-nationalism. That fascist efforts were limited and repelled should offer succour. But the cultural mediums it sought to claim and the initiatives it developed from the 1970s remain pertinent at a time when the threat of far-right resurgence continues to resonate.

The moment: is Britain dead?

The 1970s saw British fascism emerge from the doldrums in which it had laboured since Sir Oswald Mosley's hey-day during the 1930s.[6] Its principal vehicle was the National Front, formed in 1967 from an amalgam of far-right sub-sects. John Tyndall, a former member of the National Socialist Movement and Greater Britain Movement, served – with some interruption – as chairman from 1972 to 1980, overseeing a fluctuating membership of around 15,000 in the mid-1970s and a series of notable local and by-election results. In 1977, the NF registered some 119,000 votes (5.3 per cent) in the Greater London Council elections and almost 250,000 votes in municipal contests held across the country. There was even talk of the NF supplanting the Liberals as the third party of British politics behind Labour and the Conservatives (Walker 1978; Fielding 1981).

In terms of policy, the NF platform centred mainly on issues of immigration and racial identity. The Front's manifesto for the October 1974 general election promised a ban on all non-white immigration into Britain and repatriation of 'all coloured immigrants' (National Front 1974: 17–19). Such demands were typically wrapped in the language of patriotism, moral conservatism and strict social discipline (law and order, capital punishment), fusing events such as the arrival of Malawi and Ugandan Asians into Britain with questions of economic and socio-cultural development. Scratch beneath the surface, however, and the NF's ideological basis revealed itself to be informed by a crudely racist worldview imbued with conspiratorial anti-Semitism. Though not openly National Socialist, many of its leaders – including Tyndall – took their inspiration from Nazism; Hitler's route to power, via a mix of electoral politics and street-level mobilisation, formed the NF's basic *modus operandi* (Pearce 2013: 81–82).[7] As for the NF's 'rank and file', disgruntled Conservatives and empire loyalists would mingle with unabashed Nazis and the virulently racist (Billig 1978). Disillusionment with the Labour governments of 1964–70 and 1974–79 (combined with a growing sense by which 'the left' was associated with students and middle-class intellectuals) served to open up a political space for the NF amongst what had previously been Labour's core working-class vote.

The NF was not the sole voice of British fascism. A tradition of far-right factionalism continued even as progress appeared to be made in membership and electoral terms. The National Party, founded in December 1975 by John Kingsley-Read following a schism in the NF leadership, stood on a platform of racial populism propagated by an unstable mix of erstwhile Tories from the Conservative Monday Club, and 'Strasserites' opposed to John Tyndall (Copsey 2004: 17–18).[8] It too threatened briefly to become an electoral presence in the mid-1970s, winning two council seats in Blackburn and competing against the NF in London and elsewhere. On the streets, meanwhile, the BM propagated an openly neo-Nazi political brand that prioritised physical confrontation over the ballot box. Led by Michael

McLaughlin, a Liverpool milkman who took charge from Colin Jordan in 1975 (following the latter's arrest for stealing women's knickers), the BM developed a reputation for violence that recruited pockets of support in places such as London's East End (Hill and Bell 1988: 135). Other smaller groupings existed, among them the League of Saint George, before the NF's disappointing general election performance in 1979 occasioned a round of splits and divisions that threw up the New National Front, the British Democratic Party, the Constitutional Movement and, in 1982, the British National Party (BNP). More generally, and amidst bouts of intra-fascist conflict, membership boundaries blurred across what was a constantly evolving and mutating fascist terrain.

The relative visibility of the far right in this period had multiple causes, primarily relating to the mood of 'crisis' and 'decline' that hung over Britain in the 1970s. Loss of empire, entry into Europe, mounting economic problems and the IRA's mainland bombing campaign ensured a resonance for far-right appeals to patriotism and national revival. Immigration, of course, provided a simplistic and prejudicial explanation for rising unemployment and related social issues, while the assertive militancy of the British trade union movement lent credence to the idea of political power no longer being the preserve of parliament. This, after all, was a decade of weak and minority governments, of sustained industrial unrest, high inflation, an unstable currency 'rescued' by the International Monetary Fund (IMF) in 1976 and slowing economic growth that slipped in and out of recession (Tomlinson 2000; Hickson 2005). In short, the political and economic 'consensus' that had underpinned Britain's post-war reconstruction appeared to be crumbling as the general optimism of the 1960s gave way to the gloomy prognoses of the 1970s.

Given such a context, the preoccupations of the far right – racial and cultural specificities, immigration, nationalism, social order, anti-communism – bound themselves to questions of national sovereignty, identity and economic performance. Indeed, the ten years that separated Enoch Powell's evocation of the River Tiber foaming with blood and Margaret Thatcher's stated concern as to Britain's being 'rather swamped by people with a different culture' saw racial politics find a ready echo towards the shifting centre of British polity.[9] As mainstream political and media voices began to flirt with the language of the far-right fringe, so the tenets of fascism fed on the anxieties of a nation seemingly convinced of its ongoing decline. In the event, Thatcherism's more constitutional expression of 'popular authoritarianism' served to curb the march of British fascism (Hall 1979: 14–20). Simultaneously, however, the presumptions and prejudices that fuelled the NF's growth made in-roads into British youth culture, seizing on the aggressive oppositionism of punk to construct a vehicle for fascism that rolled into the 1980s and beyond.

The site: on the streets

The 1970s saw the NF become a recognisable thread within Britain's socio-political fabric. Electoral broadcasts were transmitted in 1974 and 1979; interventions in local and by-elections brought media attention. Beyond the hustings and associated electoral paraphernalia, NF paper sellers took up position on street corners as the NF's insignia became a graffitied staple of the urban landscape. Processional marches, replete with drums, banners and rows of union flags, grew to be commonplace under the direction of Martin Webster, the NF's national activities' organiser. These, in turn, were typically met by anti-fascist protestors, paving the way for set-piece confrontations such as in Lewisham in August 1977. Though played down in the NF's public literature, the 'battle for the streets' provided an integral part of the Front's strategy. Racially motivated attacks increased in accord with the far-right's influence, ranging from petty-vandalism and arson to physical assault and murder (Bethnal Green and Stepney Trades Council 1978; Renton 2006: 11).[10]

Essential to the NF's growth was the recruitment of disaffected working-class youth (Billig and Cochrane 1981: 3–15). Writing in the summer of 1977, Derek Holland noted the NF's need to counter the influence of left-wing parties mobilising 'youth' in support of causes such as anti-racism and anti-imperialism. For Holland, at least, himself a young student, the main 'battle ground' was education, meaning a focus on technical colleges, universities and schools via recruitment drives and leafleting against 'Marxist' teachers (Holland 1977: 9) – or 'political paedophiles', to use the language of the NF's annual conference. To this end, a Young National Front (YNF) was soon established, through which football tournaments and social events (NF discos) were organised in tandem with the dissemination of NF literature aimed specifically at young people (Pearce 1978: 5).

More effectively, perhaps, September 1977 saw the launch of *Bulldog*. Run, initially, as a 'one boy operation' by the teenage Pearce, the youth-orientated paper featured articles on local NF activism alongside crude cartoons, pieces on sport and, somewhat belatedly, music. Sales were undertaken at football matches, gigs and outside school gates, with appeals made to 'skins, mods, punks and teds' to lend their support against 'long-haired lefty poseurs'.[11] Fortuitously, too, the selling of *Bulldog* to school kids elicited media attention, making Pearce's claim that circulation 'increased ten-fold, from several hundred copies per issue to several thousand' instructive, if somewhat exaggerated (Pearce 2013: 62).

Hitherto, Britain's post-war fascists had struggled to connect with teenage youth. In 1956, at the first meeting of the youth wing to Sir Oswald Mosley's Union Movement, the speaker's message had been an impossible sell: 'We, the youth of Britain, have finer, more noble things in our lives than rock and roll'. As may be imagined, the sounds emanating from radios and Dansette record players across the country drowned out the fascist call, leaving Mosley with a youthful cadre of approximately ten active members (Grundy 1998: 102 & 127). Two years later, in the wake of the 1958 Notting Hill race riots, Mosley also appealed directly to the racist proclivities of white working-class teddy-boys, claiming to admire their virility and masculinity. His sons, Alexander and Max, even adopted the ted-style. Again, however, such advances brought little-to-no lasting response (Dack 2015: 8–26).

Far-right appeals to youth fared no better in the 1960s. In 1964, when commenting upon seaside clashes between mods and rockers, an earlier incarnation of the BNP had detected 'a strong feeling of protest against coloured immigration'. Believing that it could harness such 'healthy' instincts to the cause, the BNP recommended pointing young people's attention towards groups such as The Bachelors, whose music is 'Western and tuneful, in contrast to the scruffy twitchings of the "Rolling Stones" type'.[12] Come 1970, and John Tyndall responded to reported incidents of 'Paki-bashing' by opining that the majority of first-generation skinheads were like 'lost sheep wandering in the city wilderness, desperately seeking some kind of leadership that they can look up to and some kind of cause in which they can believe'. His solution was simple: discipline, compulsory boxing, wrestling, judo and other combat sports. But if truth be told, and for all their supposed racist potential, this was not a constituency that Tyndall was minded to exploit. 'The fact is', Tyndall wrote without recourse to a crystal ball, 'that no group of people could be less politically or ideologically motivated in their actions than Britain's skinheads'.[13]

Come the mid-1970s, however, and more concerted attention on youth coincided with Holland's recommendations and Pearce's *Bulldog* initiative. Pearce himself had noted the presence of hundreds of young people on the NF's demonstration at Lewisham in 1977, many of them football hooligans, but also a 'smattering' of second generation skinheads. As an avid Chelsea fan, Pearce knew only too well that Chelsea supporters had the worst reputation for football hooliganism in the country; he also knew that many were aggressively racist. Pearce, therefore, deliberately targeted this terrace culture, initiating a 'league of louts' in *Bulldog* whereby hooligans were encouraged to send in reports of racist chants at football matches. The worst offenders were typically supporters of Chelsea, Leeds, West Ham and Newcastle. By the late 1970s, the NF was apparently selling several hundred copies of *Bulldog* at Chelsea (to crowds of around 9,000) with sales at West Ham a close second (Pearce 2013: 117–122).[14]

Parallel developments were ongoing in Leeds, where the NF's regional organiser for Yorkshire, Eddy Morrison, similarly recognised the need to channel youthful discontent towards political ends. Throughout 1976 and much of 1977, Morrison headed his own variant of the British National Party, attacking left-wing meetings and organising 'vigilante groups' to combat what he termed 'negro violence', before joining the NF at the turn of the year.[15] Unlike Pearce, however, Morrison was a seasoned political activist by 1977, aged in his late 20s and entrenched in the factional world of the far right (Morrison 2003: 10–17). As a David Bowie fan, he was also attuned to the political implications of popular music. Bowie, after all, had alluded to fascism in interviews over the mid-1970s and thereby prompted – after Eric Clapton's drunken pledge of support for Enoch Powell at a concert in 1976 – the establishment of RAR (Widgery 1986: 42–43; Goodyer 2009: 10–13; Buckley 2000: 289–291). Accordingly, Morrison interpreted RAR as a 'carefully orchestrated campaign motivated by the Socialist Worker Party' [sic], writing to the music paper *Sounds* in April 1977 to urge a 'racist backlash' against RAR and envisioning a 'Rock For Racism' concert of 'all-white bands' headlined by Bowie but co-ordinated by punk rockers, hell's angels, teds and 'Bowie youth'. These youth cultures, Morrison reasoned, were 'the storm-troop stewards of the racism you'll never take out of the young' (Morrison 1977).[16] From such daydreaming, RAC would emerge in 1978 (see below).

In effect, both Pearce and Morrison began to grope towards the idea of youth culture and popular music providing a political medium for the far right. In rather basic terms, they presented a response to the 'cultural turn' ongoing across leftist politics through the 1960s into the 1970s, whereby growing emphasis was placed on 'new' spheres of struggle – race, gender, sexuality, culture, language, consumption – beyond the traditional concentration on class and socio-economic production (Kenny 1995; Dworkin 1997). The early 1970s, for example, saw a protracted debate take place in *Marxism Today*, wherein the political meaning of the 1960s counter-culture and youth culture more generally fed into the Communist Party of Great Britain's attempt to reimagine itself (Jacques 1973: 268–280). And while no such heavyweight theoretical musings emerged from the British far right, the movement's relationship to youth and youth culture did prompt at least some reflection. Thus, writing in 1980, Morrison urged 'white nationalists' to learn from the left's extending 'the revolution' into 'every area of society'. A youth movement, he insisted, was a means to counter this, to build an 'alternative society' within the system via bookshops, social clubs and amenities (Morrison 1980: 15, 19). Not dissimilarly, Pearce's response to what he perceived as the left's adoption of popular culture was to contest it, applying crude claims to various musical forms and youth cultural styles.[17] Most notoriously, the YNF's recruitment drive made in-roads into the resurgent skinhead culture of the mid-to-late 1970s, fostering an aggressive image that simultaneously reconciled territorial loyalties and socio-economic concerns with racial identity and a sense of purpose. In addition, the BM cultivated a core of young activists around the likes of Glen Bennett, Nicky Crane, Gary Hitchcock, Gary Hodges and Charlie Sargent, skinheads whose youthful presence did much to align the revived subculture with racial politics and neo-Nazism.

Again, the context is important. The far right's turn to youth coincided with the emergence of punk, a musical form, style and culture that appeared, ostensibly at least, to embody a reaction to the contemporaneous socio-political climate and prospective (no) future. Political symbols, slogans and signifiers of 'crisis' formed a core component of punk's iconography. Where the early designs of Malcolm McLaren and Vivienne Westwood comprised swastikas, images of Marx, situationist references and quotes from Buenaventura Durruti, so the Sex Pistols' first release, 'Anarchy in the UK' (1976), coincided with the government's application to the IMF – the song's title providing both a totem of the country's sense of decline and a cry for self-emancipation. As for The Clash, they delivered songs of barbed social commentary that referenced 1976's Notting Hill riot, unemployment, boredom, hate and war. Not surprisingly, therefore, punk could be – and was – read in political terms, be it to align the use of the swastika to incipient fascism or find a proto-socialist consciousness in punk's urbanity, DIY approach or lyrical focus. Amidst punk's cultural assault, the 'progressive' and the 'reactionary' often intermingled (Sabin 1999: 199–218).

Certainly, on the far right, younger activists such as Pearce and Morrison saw in punk the 'frustration of white working-class youth' (Morrison 1981: 20). Pearce, who shared Morrison's Bowie fixation, acknowledged RAR's ability to use music as a means to politically mobilise young people and began to feature punk bands in *Bulldog*; Morrison attended punk gigs in and around Leeds and sought out bands to support the NF (Pearce 2013: 128; Morrison 2003: 10–17).[18] Subsequently, as punk fractured and fragmented over the turn of the decade, so particular bands and scenes (2-tone, Oi!) were seen to represent a suitable fusion of aggressive rebelliousness and working-class authenticity akin to the self-perceived image of young NF and BM recruits. Or, to quote the BM's Chris 'Chubby' Henderson, 'the lads fought on a Saturday afternoon, and new punk bands sung about it later in their raw unrefined lyrics […] now the boys would smash up a pub to the sound of The Clash or Generation X instead of the Four Tops' (Ward and Henderson 2002: 60–62). In particular, the blunt social realism of bands such as Sham 69 and those formed in their wake was described by Pearce as 'music of the ghetto. Its energy expresses the frustrations of white youths. Its lyrics describe the reality of life on the dole'.[19]

We should note that the NF's and BM's incursion into punk-informed youth cultures was controversial. Not only did it provide grist to the mill of RAR and provoke music press exposés of fascist attempts to corrupt young minds, but the shift towards young fascists attending gigs and listening to popular music proved contentious within the far right. Though the BM's *British Patriot* included a 1977 article wondering if swastikas and iron crosses signalled punk's embrace of racist or nationalist politics, the far right's standard cultural position was far less circumspect ('Critic' 1977: 3–4). In simple terms, 'classic' art forms were associated with 'classic civilisations'; that is, culture was seen to reflect the strength and vitality of a nation or race. For both the NF and the BM, this meant a veneration of non-modernist art forms rooted in the European or British past. Wagner, Elgar, Purcell and Vaughan Williams were the musical 'heroes' of a John Tyndall or a Colin Jordan; pop music, by contrast, was an 'alien' and 'degenerate' cultural form that served only to distort Britain's true identity (Woodbridge 2003: 129–144). Thus, where Jordan looked upon punks as 'freaks' who shared nothing with 'real and radical racialism', so the *NF News* accused Johnny Rotten of being both culturally and politically a 'white nigger' (Jordan 1977: 3).[20] In 1978, it seems, a few young skins were even expelled from the BM for their 'degenerate' taste in music, while 'elders' in the NF reportedly baulked at the growing skinhead presence on marches and at organised events (Bushell 1980: 27; Jordan 2011: 64–73; Bean 1999: 223).[21] By the early 1980s, Tyndall was calling for 'white folk music' and classical records to replace the 'negroid-style' tunes played previously at YNF discos; the fragmentation of the NF in the early 1980s was even blamed on the movement's being infiltrated by 'gays, the punks and the racial Trotskyites'.[22]

Partly as a result of this, the far-right's youth cultural activities gained a momentum of their own. Those involved cut across organisational divisions, paving the way for Stuart and Crane's Blood & Honour initiative that eschewed any formal affiliation to an established far-right party or organisation. Simultaneously, many of those who aligned to the NF and BM in the late 1970s comprised youngsters whose connection to fascist politics was vicarious, temporary or simply borne of personal association. As Suggs (Graham McPherson), a young London skinhead friend of Ian Stuart at the time and lead singer of a band – Madness – that included NF/BM members among its audience, pointed out:

> [You] go round all these kids houses and they've got, like, Union Jack jackets and British Movement shirts, and it's all this game of going down Brick Lane every Sunday marching for the British Movement and it all gets a bit heavy […] It gives them something. "WE ARE SOMETHING" […] There's a lot of horrible perverts backing all these things, but the average punter doesn't know what the fuck's going on. He sees the Union Jack, hears the national anthem, remembers what his old man was saying about the war.
>
> *(Goldman 1979b: 1927)*

Read this way, joining or supporting the NF appeared a desperate grasp to retain some kind of cultural or personal identity in a changing world. Read another, it served as a wilfully anti-social gesture guaranteed to offend, provoke and intimidate (Walker 1982: 7–17).

For others, far-right politics became a vocation that found cultural expression in music and style. In effect, young fascists began to enter into youth cultural spaces, recruiting a smattering of punk-fans and skinheads to give political focus to their disaffection and territorialism. Hitchcock, speaking in 1980, remembered not being able to relate to punk at first, but 'all the clubs were either disco or punk and the discos never let us in, so we used to go to punk clubs to meet and have a beer' (Bushell 1980: 27). Bands, be it Sham 69, The Lurkers, The Jam, Madness or Skrewdriver, were adopted and followed; gigs, clubs, shops and pubs became contested spaces into which politics were projected as a result of left-wing and right-wing claims to their meaning or significance. Even the music press served as a site of political debate, as young NF members were encouraged to challenge the cultural politics of *Melody Maker*, *NME* and *Sounds*.[23] Though it took time for an explicitly 'white power' scene to emerge in Britain, the early 1980s saw the likes of Skrewdriver, Brutal Attack and The Ovaltinees performing at punk gigs in and around London.

Things had changed by 1984. The far right had all but moved away from contesting youth cultural forms and styles towards forging its own particular variant, releasing its own records by its own bands to an audience defined by a stylistic off-shoot of a skinhead culture that resisted claims to its identity. Black MA1 jackets, high-boots, fully-shaved heads, Celtic crosses and Nordic symbols became the 'uniform' of a Nazi-skin some way from the more polished look of the 'sussed' or 'traditional' skinhead (whose musical tastes lent towards soul, ska and early reggae).[24] For a time, however, the far right encroached into mainstream sites of youth cultural expression, appropriating its forms and endeavouring to colonise its spaces. The results were ugly, with gigs broken up and bands tarnished with political stains that often proved hard to remove.

The practice: we are white noise

RAC was conceived in Leeds but raised in London. The Leeds punk scene was closely associated with bands such as Gang of Four and The Mekons, both of whom openly supported RAR and comprised part of a vibrant leftist milieu gathered around the university and polytechnic (O'Brien 2011: 27–40). In response, Morrison targeted punk gigs as sites of recruitment and provocation, exploiting 'town versus gown' animosities to rally a small-but-violent 'Punk Front' of young NF supporters buoyed by punk's energy and anger but dismissive of left-wing (or 'student') claims to its political potential. A short-lived fanzine, *Punk Front*, was produced; gigs, especially those organised by RAR, were attacked; claims were made to the punk nights held at the city's F-Club.[25] In the event, such activities led to Morrison's arrest following a violent altercation between NF and ANL supporters at The Fenton pub in 1978, though not before The Dentists and The Ventz had formed to provide the nucleus of RAC.

The Dentists were led by Mick Renshaw, a close associate of Morrison in the Leeds NF; The Ventz by Alan Peace, who gave an interview to *British News* in September 1978 describing RAC as a reaction to SWP attempts to manipulate punk for its own ends through RAR. Though organisation was rudimentary, Peace revealed plans for a magazine, 'anti-communist' gigs and a record designed to 'let people know that there are bands around who won't be brainwashed'.[26] Just who those bands were remained a moot point. Beyond The Dentists and The Ventz (who soon withdrew, renaming themselves Tragic Minds), only White Boss from Coventry fully committed to the RAC cause. A few others – The Crap, Column 44 – were subsequently listed as due to appear at a cancelled RAC gig scheduled for early 1979, but Morrison's arrest and drawn-out prosecution all but curtailed RAC's Yorkshire operation (Brazil 1979: 18–19). For this reason, RAC effectively relocated to London, featuring in *Bulldog* for the first time in mid-1979 as preview to the Conway Hall gig in August.

RAC's transferral to London was not by chance. The presence of far-right contingents at punk gigs had long been a source of controversy, resulting in music press and leftist criticism of bands such as Sham 69 for not doing more to distance themselves from sections of their audience. Indeed, it was Sham's decision to play an RAR gig with the reggae band Misty in Roots in early 1978 that provoked a schism in their following, paving the way for right-wing 'shows of strength' building up to the infamous 'last stand' at London's Rainbow theatre in 1979.[27] Just as Morrison's 'Punk Front' disrupted gigs in Leeds, so punk gigs in London occasionally saw territorial and subcultural skirmishes take on a political sheen – as when a group of BM skinheads flexed their muscles at The Lurkers' appearance at Woolwich Polytechnic in late 1978, or at Crass gigs in the capital in 1979. In and around the ANL–RAR carnivals of 1978, so NF and BM reprisals were meted out against 'the left' as punk and 2-tone gigs became increasingly politicised over the course of 1978–80.

Some of this was covered in *Bulldog*. Attacks on 'reds' made it clear that 'white power had taken over', Pearce wrote in 1980, listing examples of occasions where

NF or BM mobs had infiltrated or broken up benefits organised by the left.[28] Details of *Bulldog* paper sales at gigs were given; the presence of NF supporters at concerts ranging from Bad Manners and Madness to UK Decay and Siouxsie and the Banshees were reported; incidents of racial or NF slogans being chanted were documented.[29] Simultaneously, the music press regularly bemoaned the repressive atmosphere brought to bear by far-right interventions at punk gigs in the capital, a mood captured in essence on singles by The Jam ('"A" Bomb in Wardour Street') and The Ruts ('Staring at the Rude Boys').

And yet, despite the presence of a young fascist milieu at London's punk gigs, it took a while before any bands openly aligned to the far right. Skrewdriver only broke cover in 1982, with Stuart relaunching his band at a series of London gigs and issuing the single 'White Power' in 1983 on the White Noise Records label financed by the NF (Pearce 1987). In the meantime, RAC continued to exist more in name than in substance. *Bulldog* included an 'RAC News' page from 1979, featuring short articles on bands and an 'RAC Chart' compiled by Pearce or readers. An RAC fanzine, *Rocking the Reds*, also emerged, proffering a similar mix of features and reviews. In both cases, the political allegiance of a band or the intended meaning of a song was less relevant than the trigger response accorded to words such as 'white', 'England', 'riot' or images that evoked violence, fascism and ultra-nationalism. Thus, The Skids' *Days of Europa* (1979) was featured for its cover imagery of the 1936 Olympics and choice quotes about European pride and nationalism were attributed to the band's singer, Richard Jobson. Alternatively, a song such as the Angelic Upstarts' 'Guns for the Afghan Rebels' – which condemned the Soviet intervention in Afghanistan – was extolled for its anti-communist sentiment.[30]

Nor was RAC firmly committed to punk. Given their penchant for David Bowie, both Pearce and Morrison wrote enthusiastic articles about the new romantics and synth pop inspired by the Thin White Duke. To this end, Bowie was presented as the pioneer of 'white European dance music', with Morrison claiming to detect 'strains of classical and traditional Aryan music' within the songs of Spandau Ballet and Ultravox (Morrison 1981: 20).[31] Arguably, the 'highpoint' of the far right's attempt to claim and colonise the youth cultural spaces opened up by punk came in 1981, when a gig held by three Oi! bands at the Hambrough Tavern in Southall precipitated a riot. Oi! was a term coined by the *Sounds* journalist Garry Bushell to describe 'a loose alliance of volatile young talents, skins, punks, tearaways, hooligans, rebels with or without causes united by their class, their spirit, their honesty and their love of furious rock 'n' roll' (Bushell 1981: 11). The inclusion of skinheads in the Oi! milieu, however, ensured that a gig held in an area with a relatively large proportion of Asian inhabitants brought concern manifested in the venue being firebombed by local youths wary of the skins' association with racial politics. There followed a media-stoked moral panic, enflamed by the attention drawn to a compilation album, *Strength Thru Oi!* (1981), that combined a title reminiscent of the Nazi slogan *Kraft durch Freude* with a cover image depicting the BM's Nicky Crane. In truth, Oi!'s politics were contested and its primary focus one of class (Worley 2013: 606–636). Most of the bands associated with it denounced racism and Bushell garnered the wrath of the far right by deliberately not covering RAC or skinhead bands that expressed racist or fascist viewpoints. Nevertheless, the fact that some Oi! band members harboured right-wing pasts and its audience included a core of young NF or BM followers ensured Oi! was tarred with the 'Nazi' brush.

As this suggests, blunt punk rock remained RAC's music of choice. Beyond *Bulldog*'s coverage of punk and Oi! bands unconnected to the far-right, a few young fascists began to join or form their own groups. The BM's Glen Bennett and, occasionally, Nicky Crane, played in The Afflicted; Henderson became the singer of Combat 84; Hitchcock helped his erstwhile BM comrade Gary Hodges form the avowedly apolitical 4-Skins. By the early 1980s, moreover, a smattering of bands – Brutal Attack, The Diehards, London Branch, The Ovaltinees, Peter and the Wolf – began to write ultra-nationalistic and explicitly racist songs that lyrically moved some way from punk/Oi!'s occasionally patriotic dystopianism. Most of these bands had BM-roots or tendencies, thereby explaining perhaps their absence from the NF-aligned *Bulldog* prior to RAC's official relaunch in 1983. Nevertheless, it was they who combined with Skrewdriver to form the nucleus of a distinctly nationalist, 'white power' scene in the UK. The clandestine gig in Stratford (east London) that marked RAC's return featured Skrewdriver, The Ovaltinees and Peter and the Wolf; the White Noise Club organised by the NF – but ostensibly non-aligned[32] – was showcased on an EP that featured Skrewdriver, Brutal Attack, The Diehards and ABH from Lowestoft.[33]

In terms of performing, Britain's nascent RAC bands were soon forced underground. For a time, support slots and the occasional headline gig enabled Skrewdriver, Brutal Attack and others to perform at relatively mainstream venues such as the 100 Club in Oxford Street. The Blue Coat Boy in Islington (Skunx, then Streets) also put on regular punk gigs in the early 1980s that attracted a far-right audience. The Agricultural pub nearby was a regular for young NF and BM skinheads in the 1980s. Over time, however, as the politics became more overt, so bands found gigs harder to come by. The music press steered clear beyond the odd exposé of a particular band's Nazi sympathies; anti-fascists organised as Red Action (later Anti-Fascist Action) mobilised to physically disarm the far-right threat (Red Action n.d.; Hayes 2014: 229–246). Ultimately too, an audience baying for songs that extolled white pride and race hatred was a limited one that few bands wanted anything to do with. Some, including the Cockney Rejects, literally beat BM and NF elements out of their gigs.

The result of such marginalisation was paradoxical. On the one hand, the banishment of RAC to the cultural and political fringe enabled cultivation of a distinct music-based subculture. From 1983, RAC gigs were necessarily held in secret to avoid censor or anti-fascist reprisals – a state of affairs still ongoing today. Directions to meeting points were circulated surreptitiously; venues were often not known until the day of the event or found far from the usual music circuit. The RAC/ White Noise Club's summer festivals, for example, took place on a Suffolk farm belonging to the father of future BNP leader Nick Griffin. Not dissimilarly, inability to access either the major or independent record industry necessitated RAC forge its own labels, media and distribution networks. Beyond the NF's White Noise Records, The Ovaltinees – formed as White Youth in Crayford and led by BM Leader Guard member Micky Lane – self-released their *British Justice* EP in 1983, before Skrewdriver negotiated a deal with the German Rock-O-Rama label that provided opportunity for others (Brutal Attack, Public Enemy) to make and distribute records across Europe and into the US. Fanzines also began to flourish in the mid-1980s, with titles such as *England's Glory* (Berkshire), *The Truth at Last* (Kent) and *The Voice of Britain* (Midlands) supplementing the more formal publications of *White Noise* and, from 1987, *Blood & Honour*.

In effect, a self-contained micro scene developed, with a growing collection of bands playing regularly together in Britain and abroad. Over the mid-to-late 1980s, the likes of British Standard (Glasgow), Last Orders (Grimsby), New Dawn (Greenock), No Remorse (South London), Prime Suspects (Reading), Skullhead (Newcastle) and Sudden Impact (Croydon) became staples of the RAC circuit. Partly as a result, Blood & Honour morphed into its own music-based political movement ('the independent voice of Rock Against Communism'), nominally distinct from any recognised far-right party but replete with its own internal rivalries, financial disagreements and sex scandals.

On the other hand, therefore, punk's fascist outgrowth became consumed within a subterranean world of internecine political wrangling that simultaneously spread wider as it retreated underground. Not only did divisions on the far right break the connection between a dwindling NF and Skrewdriver in the mid-1980s, but the subsequent history of the White Noise Club and Blood & Honour was fuelled by money-squabbles and personal tensions that led, ultimately, to murder (Lowles 2001: 221–253).[34] Concurrently, all lack of pretence as to working through established cultural channels led the politics of RAC to become ever more extreme. If 'White Power' (1983) had seen Skrewdriver segue easily from songs of national pride to slogans of racial supremacy, then *Blood & Honour* (1985) and *White Rider* (1987) saw Stuart openly endorse the politics of National Socialism. By the same token, connections to far-right milieus on the continent helped transform the aesthetic and texture of RAC. So, for example, Nazi symbols and Nordic imagery began to predominate over the Union Jack (Raposo 2012). The 'voice of Britain' became 'music for Europe'; RAC's punk-informed emphasis on social reportage and political commentary gave way to mythical fantasies of race and Viking warriors (Sabin and Raposo 2015).[35]

That punk inspired a fascist variant should not really surprise. From the outset, its utilisation of the swastika and fascination with all things abject revealed dark impulses that led all-too-easily beyond the provocative or voyeuristic (Duncombe and Tremblay 2011). Punk's urbanity, combined with a skinhead revival that related to punk's social realism but envisaged itself to be a more authentic expression of street-level culture, further provided opportunity for the far right to connect to Britain's inner-city white youth. '[The] bully-boy sex-power of Nazism/fascism is very attractive', Jon Savage noted in 1976, 'an easy solution to our complex moral and social dilemmas […] the cult of the powerful' (Savage 1976: 8–12). For these reasons also, the industrial music pioneered by Throbbing Gristle from 1975 likewise accommodated those whose interest in extremes led to Nazism, while in between emerged a neo-folk sound from the likes of Death in June, Above the Ruins and Sol Invictus through which the more esoteric roots of fascism were explored (Alexander Reed 2013; François 2007: 35–54). Ultimately, however, RAC forged a world of its own, flirting first with ideas of infiltration before constructing an underground Nazi subculture that wallowed in obscurity whilst simultaneously exerting a global reach.

Conclusion: hail the new dawn (or a new dawn fades)?

The far right's engagement with youth culture from 1977 comprised three overlapping processes designed to contest, colonise and construct. These, in turn, took a variety of forms, but all centred on utilising cultural mediums to propagate racial or fascist politics of various stripes. Initially, young activists within the far right contested the political meanings projected onto punk by RAR and within the music press. They rejected any notion that punk's protest or intent was inherently 'progressive' or 'leftist', preferring instead to find affinity with the social realism and musical excitement generated by groups such as The Clash, Sham 69 and others. Bands, records and youth cultural signifiers were given alternative meanings; politics were refracted through the language, imagery and aesthetic of punk's early stirrings.

By 1978, as claims to punk's development were played out in competing musical forms and youth cultural styles, so the far right sought to colonise the spaces opened up over the course of 1976–77. Gigs were disrupted; stages, pubs and clubs were commandeered both physically and for paper sales. Perennial rivalries of style and territory took on political implications amidst the heightened socio-economic climate of the late 1970s into the 1980s. In other words, the far right moved to penetrate aspects of youth culture, subverting its sounds and styles to propagate its politics. Most obviously, punk, 2-tone and Oi! were each – in slightly different ways and to varying degrees – claimed as the preserve of the far right, while a skinhead image was adopted through punk to embody the imagined persona of the young white nationalist.

Ultimately, of course, such claims were resisted, countered and overwhelmed. As a result, the far right necessarily constructed its own variant of punk/Oi!, reconfiguring the skinhead image into a recognisable but distinct sub-sect of the broader subculture and establishing alternative networks of communication. Though organised interventions occasionally reoccurred – as at the Greater London Council's 'Jobs for a Change' festival in June 1984 (Forbes and Stampton 2014: 101–105)[36] – the visibly fascist presence at gigs receded over the mid-1980s. Similarly, while antagonisms between left and right continued at street-level, culminating in the infamous 'Battle of Waterloo' in 1992 whereat anti-fascists mobilised against those travelling to a Blood & Honour gig in Eltham, the politicised youth culture propagated by RAC ploughed an ever-deeper furrow as it evolved into the 1990s. Many of its original 'core' members journeyed also to the furthest-flung margins of British (and Irish) politics via connections to crime, hooliganism and the brutal terror-tactics of Combat 18 (in which Hitchcock and Sargent were integral).

Thirty years on, and Blood & Honour has finally fallen victim to the ageing process. Though its name was taken from the slogan that appeared on the daggers of the Hitler Youth (*Blut und Ehre*), decades of internal wrangling, splits and division have left a British rump comprised mainly of heavily tattooed men in their fifties reliving their 'glory days' at occasional gigs in back-room pubs. As this suggests, connections to youth culture are now little more than nostalgic; no longer is there even a sense of mobilising a new generation of 'storm troopers' to the Nationalist cause. The English Defence League (EDL) may have briefly flourished amidst a climate of Islamophobia, building support on the remnants of the far-right's football hooligan connections.[37] But it, too, descended into internecine disarray as it sought to deny its Nazi draw. UKIP, intolerant but not fascist, is now the principal vehicle of racial populism; a party with little in the way of youthful demeanour. Music no longer retains a dominant position within youth cultural identity.

To sum up, political and cultural alignments during the 1970s allowed the far right opportunity to contest and intervene into sites of British youth culture. The sense of 'crisis' and 'decline' that permeated the decade gave shape to politicised cultural forms seized upon by young activists in the BM and NF. That they were cultivated 'from below' is important, and explains how RAC transformed into Blood & Honour to develop its own political form and practice. And while it would be overstating matters to suggest that this in any way corresponded with the 'cultural turn' ongoing across the left during the 1960s–1980s, it nevertheless marked an attempt by the far right to forge a cultural politics that related to the lives of those it wished to influence, mobilise and recruit. If not quite a 'new dawn', then, RAC proved a far more stubborn and nefarious influence than its ramshackle origins ever appeared to warrant.

Acknowledgements

This chapter stems from a Leverhulme Trust funded project on 'punk, politics and British youth culture'. Thanks must also go to Russ Bestley, Tim Brown, Jon Garland, Stewart Home, Chris Low, Lol Pryor, Ana Raposo, Lucy Robinson, Roger Sabin, Ryan Shaffer, John Street, Tiffini Travis, Tim Wells, David Wilkinson and Steve Woodbridge for their comments and insights.

Notes

1 This chapter was originally published as an open access article in JOMEC Journal, 9, 2016: 27–47.
2 'Rock Against Communism', *Bulldog*, No. 14, 1979, 3. In 'Rock Against Communism Hits the Headlines', *Bulldog*, No. 15, 1979, 3, the event is nevertheless reported to have been a success.

3 'Record company pressure' probably related to Rough Trade's decision to stop distributing Skrewdriver's records on hearing of the band's NF association. So the story goes, Rough Trade staff spent the day of the gig smashing every copy of every Skrewdriver record kept in their warehouse.

4 The *NME* mistakenly reported that a band called Homicide played. They did not.

5 'Nazi Nurds Wreck Sham's Last Stand', *Sounds*, 4 August 1979, 10; 'Rudie Bam Bam', *Sounds*, 3 November 1979, 10.

6 The term 'fascism' is used to refer to a generic concept. The authors understand fascism as the most extreme point on the far-right of the political spectrum, a fundamentally anti-democratic position that advocates aggressive forms of ultra-nationalist politics and often includes virulent racism.

7 Pearce admitted: 'Although the NF's position was always to deny strongly that it was a neo-Nazi party, one could not graduate to the inner-sanctum of the cognoscenti within the Party without tacitly accepting Nazi ideology [...]'.

8 'Strasserism' refers to a strand of fascism named after Gregor and Otto Strasser that placed emphasis on anti-capitalism and mass action. Within the NF, it was propagated in the publication *Britain First* (edited by Richard Lawson).

9 On 20 April 1968, the Conservative MP Enoch Powell caused controversy with a speech suggesting that immigration and proposed anti-discrimination legislation would lead to social conflict and racial violence. The River Tiber reference was drawn from Virgil's *Aeneid*. Margaret Thatcher's quote was given in an interview to the television programme *World in Action* on 27 January 1978 in relation to concerns about immigration.

10 According to Renton, 31 suspected racial murders took place in Britain between 1976 and 1981, as the NF marched and the BM mobilised to claim ownership of the streets. See also 'The Nazi Party' documentary shown on *World in Action*, ITV, 3 July 1978.

11 *Bulldog*, No. 14, 1979, 3.

12 'The Answer to Mods and Rockers', *Combat*, No. 17, 1964, 5.

13 *Spearhead*, April 1970, 3. Organising 'youth' had formed one of the NF's original objectives in 1967, but little progress was made until the mid-1970s. Thanks to Ryan Shaffer for this information.

14 *Bulldog*, No. 16, 1979, 4.

15 *British News*, January and February 1977 and March 1978.

16 Thanks go to Jon Savage for providing a copy of the letter.

17 *Bulldog*, No. 14, 1979, 3 and No. 18, 1980, 3.

18 Pearce's personal preference was for 'futurist' bands such as The Human League and Cabaret Voltaire. His brother, Stevo (Steve), who DJ-ed at the Chelsea Drugstore pub on the King's Road, established the Some Bizarre label that specialised in signing electronic and industrial bands to major record companies. Stevo regularly denounced the politics of his brother.

19 'We are the New Breed', *Bulldog*, No. 21, 1981, 3.

20 *NF News*, No. 10, 1977, 1.

21 *NF News*, No. 23, 1980, 2. See also *National Socialist*, No. 3, 1981, for Jordan's take on skinheads: 'mindless oafs [...] tonsured, nihilistic hooligans being against all order, old or new, and for violence for violence's sake and the pure pleasure of damage and destruction' (reprinted in Jordan 2011: 69).

22 'NF and BM link up in "Gay" Axis', *Spearhead*, May 1981, 17. The 'gay' reference was to Martin Webster, who had not followed Tyndall (who ran *Spearhead*) into the New National Front. It may also refer to Nicky Crane, the BM Leader Guard member.

23 *British News*, No. 43, 1978, 10; Letters, *NME*, 18 March 1978, 62; Letters, *Sounds*, 8 April 1978, 63, 15 July 1978, 51 and 21 October 1978, 63.

24 This battle for skinhead identity was played out in various ways, but see fanzines such as *Hard as Nails*, *Backs Against the Wall*, *Bovver Boot*, *Croptop*, *Skinhead Havoc*, *Spy-kids*, *Stand Up and Spit* and *Tell Us The Truth* for a rejection of the far-right's claims to the culture.

25 'Gang of Three/Quarters', *Temporary Hoarding*, No. 9, 1977, 11–14. 'Town versus gown' tensions were evidently exploited by Morrison in Leeds.

26 Interview with Alan Peace of The Ventz, *British News*, September 1978, 6–7.

27 Sham's 'last stand' took place on 18 July 1979, ostensibly a farewell gig before Pursey formed a new band with Steve Jones and Paul Cook from the Sex Pistols. Instead it provided a rallying point for London's far right to finally shut down a group they perceived to have used and betrayed them. Violence permeated the evening, culminating in a stage invasion amidst right-arm salutes and shouts of 'sieg heil'. In the short-term, the Sham Pistols came to nothing and Pursey continued to play and release records with Sham 69 for another 12 months. But the event served as a pivotal moment in the band's history.

28 *Bulldog*, No. 18, 1980, 3.

29 *Bulldog*, Nos. 19–28, 1980–82.

30 *Bulldog*, No. 16, 1979, 3 and No. 25, 1981, 3; *Rocking the Reds*, no number, 1982. The Skids' song 'Blood and Soil' also made the RAC chart in *Bulldog*, No. 26, 1982, 3.

31 'White European Dance Music', *Bulldog*, No. 25, 1981, 3.

32 A White Noise circular insisted 'Our purpose will be, not to push party politics as such, but to promote the bands all over the world who have had the courage to come out and declare their Nationalist loyalties'. 'White Noise' leaflet, undated (circa 1984).

33 *Bulldog*, No. 33, 1983, 3. The EP was titled *This is White Noise* and released in 1984.

34 On 10 February 1997, Chris Castle was murdered by Martin Cross (ex-Skrewdriver) and Charlie Sargent following a schism in Combat 18 relating, in part, to the subscription list for Blood & Honour.

35 'Voice of Britain' was the title of a Skrewdriver single released on White Noise Records in 1984; the slogan 'Music for Europe' appeared on the cover of White Noise Club's magazine *White Noise*, No. 3, 1987, 1. By the 1990s, connections to Tom Metzger's US-based White Aryan Resistance had also brought Klansman imagery into the fold.

36 At the event, a group of BM-led activists – among them Paul Burnley (Public Enemy/ No Remorse), Adam Douglas (Skrewdriver), Chris Henderson (Combat 84) and Mick McAndrews (head of the 'Wolfpack' that followed Peter and the Wolf) – broke up a performance by The Redskins. As their name suggests, The Redskins (previously known as No Swastikas) were left-wing skinheads and active members of the SWP whose songs and style challenged far-right and media perceptions of skinhead culture and politics. Nicky Crane, who was also due to join in the disruption, arrived late, deciding instead to intervene during a set by Hank Wangford.

37 We may note here how increases in ticket prices, health and safety regulation and the transition to all-seater stadia have restricted the 'space' for political intervention into football and, indeed, music. Thanks go to Stewart Home for making this point.

References

Alexander Reed, S. (2013) *Assimilate: A Critical History of Industrial Music*, Oxford: Oxford University Press.

Bean, J. (1999) *Many Shades of Black: Inside Britain's Far Right*, London: New Millennium.

Bethnal Green and Stepney Trades Council (1978) *Blood on the Streets: A Report by Bethnal Green and Stepney Trades Council on Racial Attacks in East London*, London: Bethnal Green and Stepney Trades Council.

Billig,M.(1978) *Fascists: A Social PsychologicalView of the National Front*,London: Academic Press.

Billig, M. and R. Cochrane (1981) 'The National Front and Youth', *Patterns of Prejudice*, 15:3, 3–15.

Brazil, D. (1979) 'Spittin' Hate at the Future of Rock 'n' Roll', *The Leveller*, October, 18–19.

Brown, T. S. (2004) 'Subcultures, Pop Music and Politics: Skinheads and "Nazi Rock" in England and Germany', *Journal of Social History*, 38:1, 157–178.

Buckley, D. (2000) *Strange Fascination: David Bowie, the Definitive Story*, London: Virgin.

Bushell, G. (1980) '(Sk)in the Beginning ...', *Sounds*, 2 August, 27.

Bushell, G. (1981) 'Oi! – The Column', *Sounds*, 17 January, 11.

Copsey, N. (2004) *Contemporary British Fascism: The British National Party and the Quest for Legitimacy*, Basingstoke: Palgrave Macmillan.

'Critic, A'. (1977) 'Rock and the Reich', *British Patriot*, January–February, 3–4.

Dack, J. (2015) 'Cultural Regeneration: Mosley and the Union Movement', in N. Copsey and J. E. Richardson (eds) *Cultures of Post-War British Fascism*, London: Routledge.

Duncombe, S. and M. Tremblay (2011) *White Riot: Punk Rock and the Politics of Race*, London: Verso.

Dworkin, D. (1997) *Cultural Marxism in Post War Britain: History, the New Left and the Origins of Cultural Studies*, North Carolina: Duke University Press.

Ellen, M. (1979) 'No Fun with the Front', *NME*, 25 August, 17.

Fielding, N. (1981) *The National Front*, London: Routledge.

Forbes R. and E. Stampton (2014) *When the Storm Breaks: Rock Against Communism, 1979–1993*, London: Forbes/Stampton.

François, S. (2007) 'The Euro-Pagan Scene: Between Paganism and Radical Right', *Journal for the Study of Radicalism*, 1:2, 35–54.

Goldman,V. (1979a) 'Seeing Red at RAC', *Melody Maker*, 25 August, 9.

Goldman,V. (1979b) 'Only Rock 'n' Roll?', *The Leveller*, December, 27.

Goodyer, I. (2009) *Crisis Music: The Cultural Politics of Rock Against Racism*, Manchester: Manchester University Press.

Grundy,T. (1998) *Memoir of a Fascist Childhood*, London: Heinemann.

Hall, S. (1979) 'The Great Moving Right Show', *Marxism Today*, January, 14–20.

Hayes,M. (2014) 'Red Action – Left-Wing Pariah: Some Observations Regarding Ideological Apostasy and the Discourse of Proletarian Resistance', in E. Smith & M. Worley (eds) *Against the Grain: The British Far Left from 1956*, Manchester: Manchester University Press.

Hickson, K. (2005) *The IMF Crisis of 1976 and British Politics*, London: I.B.Tauris.

Hill, R. and A. Bell (1988) *The Other Face of Terror: Inside Europe's Neo-Nazi Network*, Glasgow: Grafton.

Holland, D. (1977) 'The National Front – A Youth Wing?', *Spearhead*, June, 9.

Jacques, M. (1973) 'Trends in Youth Culture: Some Aspects', *Marxism Today*, September, 268–280.

Jordan, C. (1977) 'Letter', British *Patriot*, May/June, 3.

Jordan, C. (2011) 'National Socialism: World Creed For the Future', in *National Socialism: Vanguard of the Future: Selected Writings of Colin Jordan*, Gresham Publishing.

Kenny, M. (1995) *The First New Left: British Intellectuals After Stalin*, London: Lawrence & Wishart.

Langebach, M. and J. Raabe (2013) 'Inside the Extreme Right: The "White Power" Music Scene', in A. Mammone, E. Godin and B. Jenkins (eds) *Varieties of Right-Wing Extremism in Europe*, Abingdon: Routledge.

Lowles, N. (2001) *White Riot: The Violent Story of Combat 18*, London: Milo Books.

Lowles, N. and S. Silver (eds) (1998) *White Noise: Inside the International Nazi Skinhead Scene*, London: Searchlight.

Morrison, E. (1977) Letter to Sounds, 1 April.

Morrison, E. (1980) 'Why the Left is Winning', *Spearhead*, May, 15 and 19.

Morrison, E. (1981) 'Don't Condemn Pop!', *Spearhead*, April, 1981, 20.

Morrison, E. (2003) *Memoirs of a Street Fighter: A Life in White Nationalism*, London: Imperium Press.

National Front (1974) *For a New Britain: The Manifesto of the National Front*, London: NF.

O'Brien, L. (2011) 'Can I Have Lick of Your Ice Cream?', *Punk & Post-Punk*, 1:1, 27–40.

Pearce, J. (1978) 'The Importance of the Young National Front', *Spearhead*, February, 5.

Pearce, J. (1987) *Skrewdriver: The First Ten Years*, London: Skrewdriver Services.

Pearce, J. (2013) *Race with the Devil: My Journey from Racial Hatred to Rational Love*, St Benedict Press: North Carolina.

Raposo, A. (2012) '30 Years of Agit-prop: The Representation of "Extreme" Politics in Punk and Post-Punk Music Graphics in the United Kingdom from 1978 to 2008', PhD diss., University of the Arts London.

Red Action (undated) *We Are … Red Action*, London: Red Action.

Renton, D. (2006) *When We Touched the Sky: The Anti-Nazi League, 1977–81*, Cheltenham: New Clarion Press.

Sabin, R. (1999) '"I Won't Let That Dago By": Rethinking Punk and Racism', in R. Sabin (ed.) *Punk Rock: So What? The Cultural Legacy of Punk*, London: Routledge.

Sabin, R. and A. Raposo (2015) 'Designing British Neo-Fascist Rock, 1977–1987: From "Rock Against Communism" to "Blood and Honour"', in Fabian Virchow (ed.) *Visual Politics of the Far Right*, New York: Springer.

Savage, J. (1976) London's Outrage, No. 1, 8–12.

Shaffer, R. (2013) 'The Soundtrack of Neo-Fascism: Youth and Music in the National Front', *Patterns of Prejudice*, 47:4–5, 458–482.

Shaffer, R. (2014) 'From Outcast to Martyr: The Memory of Rudolf Hess in Skinhead Culture', *Journal Exit-Deutschland*, 2:4, 111–124.

Stuart, I. (1979) Letter to Melody Maker, 29 August, 17.

Tomlinson, J. (2000) *The Politics of Declinism: Understanding Postwar Britain*, London: Pearson.

Verrall, R. (1981) *We Are National Front*, London: NF, 1981.

Walker, I. (1982) 'Skinheads: The Cult of Trouble', in P. Barker (ed.) *The Other Britain: A New Society Collection*, London: RKP.

Walker, M. (1978) *The National Front*, London: Fontana.

Ward, C. and C. Henderson (2002) *Who Wants It?* Edinburgh: Mainstream.

Widgery, D. (1986) *Beating Time: Riot 'n' Race 'n' Rock 'n' Roll*, London: Chatto & Windus.

Woodbridge, S. (2003) 'Purifying the Nation: Critiques of Cultural Decadence and Decline in British Neo-Fascist Ideology', in J. Gottlieb and T. Linehan (eds) *The Culture of Fascism: Visions of the Far Right in Britain*, London: I.B. Tauris.

Worley, M. (2012) 'Shot By Both Sides: Punk, Politics and the End of "Consensus"', *Contemporary British History*, 26:3, 333–354.

Worley, M. (2013) 'Oi!, Oi!. Oi!: Class, Locality and British Punk', *Twentieth Century British History*, 24:4, 606–636.

7

NEW VISUAL IDENTITIES FOR BRITISH NEO-FASCIST ROCK (1982–1987)

White Noise, 'Vikings' and the cult of Skrewdriver

Ana Raposo and Roger Sabin

Introduction

In getting the political message across, design and the utilisation of 'the visual' were always crucial to the neo-fascist rock scene.[1] This chapter will address the graphics and other visuals associated with the British far right from 1982–1987, a foundational period. The focus will be on content encompassing periodical publications (magazines, fanzines, newspapers, etc.), badge designs, ephemera and – primarily – record sleeves. The argument will explore how punk aesthetics (a DIY approach, spontaneity, and use of collage) meshed with skinhead obsessions (boots, violence, and 'martyr images') and tropes derived from far-right political culture (swastikas, runic symbols, and Aryan ideal body-types) to produce an aesthetic that became a new kind of subcultural language.

We will also explore how this language evolved, from a previous emphasis on 'anti-communism' in the late 1970s, to more overtly racist rhetoric in the mid-late 1980s. This story involves a move away from a close association with the main neo-fascist party, the National Front (NF), and towards a looser, international-facing approach guided by a skinhead faction. The central position of the band Skrewdriver is a secondary theme; undoubtedly the most iconic and influential band in the neo-fascist movement. The essay therefore complements existing work on far-right youth (see Worley and Copsey, Chapter 6, this volume; Shaffer 2013; Lowles and Silver 1998) and sign systems (Collins and Gable 2003) to offer fresh perspectives based on close visual readings of hitherto underexplored sources.

Radicalisation

If the period between 1979 and 1982 was a period of hiatus for neo-fascist rock in Britain, it was followed by a burst of renewed energy marked by a flurry of records.[2] This happened under the aegis of a new NF formation, the White Noise Club, which in time gave rise to White Noise Records; a label which would set the tone for all future neo-fascist rock releases. Along the way, connections with the wider European far right were forged, and a deal with German label, Rock-O-Rama Records, facilitated wider distribution. Now, the visual identity of British neo-fascist rock became associated less with union flags and nationalist nostalgia, and more with a melding of neo-fascist skinhead culture and Nazi-era symbolism.[3]

This was, in short, British neo-fascism taking a more radical white supremacist direction. Although the movement was ostensibly still being helmed by the NF, nobody was under any illusion that youth initiatives were being guided by the skinhead faction, whose allegiances were more in alignment with the neo-fascist skinhead subculture in general; and a split looked more inevitable over time.

The context goes back to the 1979 election, in which the NF had taken a battering. Instead, the British people had elected Margaret Thatcher, leader of the most right-wing (Conservative) government the country had yet seen. How far she had stolen the NF's fire is a matter for debate among historians; as is the question of how far anti-fascist campaigns were successful in stemming the NF's rise; though they did have effect.[4] The early Thatcher years were marked by rises in unemployment and poverty levels, coupled with urban riots in Birmingham, Leeds, Liverpool, Manchester and London, and a general elevation of 'racial' tensions; immigration often providing a prejudicial explanation for the nation's ills by the right.

Increasingly, politics became polarised at the fringes, with the rise of more radical-left groups providing a counterpoint to the rise of the white supremacist right. Anarchism in particular became popular, and was the engine behind a revitalised Campaign for Nuclear Disarmament: it was epitomised on a grass-roots level by anarcho-punk, another offshoot from punk. Meanwhile, political groups that were on the radical left such as Red Action and later the socialist/anarchist Anti-Fascist Action were heirs to the Anti-Nazi League tradition (though critical of it), and took the fight to the neo-fascists on the streets ('the reds' continued to be the main enemy in this regard). 'Red' music came to be associated with bands like the Redskins (whose existence gave the lie to the idea that all skins were neo-fascist), and, later, bands associated with the 'Red Wedge' movement.

The NF's reaction to its crisis was to take stock and regroup; 1979–82 is generally seen as a wilderness period for the party, marked by internal squabbling and financial woes. The British Movement (BM), a 'newer', more hardline party, was a concern and stealing support, and the NF needed to decide how to react.[5] So far as youth initiatives were concerned, *Bulldog*, the magazine, was kept going, Rock Against Communism, the brand that had been created in response to Rock Against Racism, was kept going, and the Young National Front was also kept going; but now the skins had much more traction. What this meant for the NF was that it was even more unelectable than before. Any hope of mainstream acceptance was thrown to the wind: whereas previously it might have been possible to make excuses for the 'barmy fringe', this was no longer credible (if it ever had been). Now it was a different kind of party, with a struggling minority in favour of getting back to a state of 'electability', and an ascendant faction preferring a revolutionary path.

This change was all the more significant because skinhead culture itself was by now more extreme. The neo-fascist wing was no longer content to identify itself as 'hard-punks-with-an-attitude-against-immigrants', but in the early 1980s moved more towards a self-image that might best be described as street-fighting 'stormtroopers' (as some publications were putting it). Similarly, their look became associated with a 'uniform': black MA-1 jackets, decorated with patches, with black straight-leg trousers and 12- or 18-hole Dr Martens. As NF and BM support among skins swelled, racist and homophobic violence increased; and insofar as urban street battles with leftists and anarchists became more common, it all started to look a little reminiscent of London and Berlin in the 1930s (though, obviously, on a much smaller scale).[6]

We should note briefly that the neo-fascist skinhead scene was developing in other ways, too, and that *skinzines* of this persuasion continued to be the vehicle for community-building and empowerment. In the 1980s, these publications offered a vision of a scene obsessed with 'free speech' (i.e. the skins as the only people telling the truth about the 'race problem') coupled with a sense of victimisation (i.e. 'nobody likes skins because we're the only people telling the truth' and 'there's a conspiracy against us'). They also indicate the growing fashion for Nazi symbolism and amateur artwork; both of which would be co-opted by NF products, as we shall see.[7]

Towards a new visual culture

In terms of a discernibly new attitude to visuals, we can identify two areas in particular that took on a grass-roots popularity after 1979: typography and graphic symbolism. Regarding the former, there was increasing use of gothic (or 'blackletter') fonts. The gothic 'family' of fonts had significant links with the Third Reich, though obviously had other connotations (e.g. religious scripts in the Middle Ages). In 1933 the Nazis identified it as the people's typeface – the '*völk* script' – and used it in their propaganda.[8] Since then, pop culture adopted the script with glee, often precisely because of the 'danger' hinted at by its Nazi associations, and the perception of it as having a 'threatening' aesthetic – with its sharp edges and varying levels of legibility: for example, witness its use in comic books, on the covers of novels, and on movie posters. Inevitably, it was taken up in pop and rock music design – during punk, bands as varied as The Damned, Blitz and The Users were adopters, while in heavy metal it seemed to be everywhere (think of AC/DC, Motorhead, etc.). To be clear: in these contexts, there was no overt political message, in contrast to the usage by neo-fascists, who were clearly looking back to a specific time and a specific place (Bain and Shaw 1998).

Simultaneously, other imagery associated with Nazi Germany became fashionable, such as runes, death's heads, eagles and the very occasional swastika (Collins and Gable 2003).[9] In particular, pre-Christian symbols became a kind of fetish. In the 1930s and 1940s, the Nazis had glorified a romanticised 'Aryan/Norse' heritage, based on the superiority of the 'race', and therefore symbols from pagan Europe had been appropriated – including, for example, Celtic crosses, sun crosses, Odal runes, sun wheels and lightning bolts. In the 1980s, these symbols were now re-discovered and re-promoted by the neo-fascists, even though they continued to have 'another life' in other areas of society: for example, neo-pagans continued to wear decorated jewellery, while Christians were fond of 'cross' designs for obvious reasons (in fact, the cross started out as pagan symbolism for the dividing of the year into four seasons).

For neo-fascists, the Celtic cross, in particular, became a statement of ideological intent – not least because it was a bold, powerful symbol and easy to graffiti. So, just as the circled 'A' had become the calling-card of the anarcho-punks, so the Celtic cross was the riposte. (Thus, for example, the band name 'No Remorse' became 'N★ Rem★rse'.) It would eventually become the most widely recognised symbol of global neo-fascism, and today is the logo for the Stormfront website, the internet's leading 'hate site'.[10]

The reason swastikas were not more in evidence (in early 1980s Britain) is difficult to explain. It was not unusual to see graffitied swastikas on the streets, but in terms of neo-fascists actually wearing swastika patches, badges, armbands, etc. this was rarer – and certainly less fashionable than the above-mentioned Celtic crosses. Possibly the swastika (incidentally, itself a pre-Christian symbol) remained taboo, and in the early 1980s was still considered 'too much'.[11] It had been made 'uncool' by anti-fascists back in the punk days of the 1970s, and there was a certain reluctance by even hardliners to use it: one view was that neo-fascism should be 'neo', and that they should avoid glorifying a German regime that had possibly killed family members in the war (an attitude which chimed with 1970s NF policies to distance the party from Nazism).[12] This meant that the Celtic crosses were sometimes adopted as a code to get around not using swastikas (though, of course, such a move could be interpreted as motivated less by reticence than by pragmatism). Whatever the case, by the late 1980s, swastikas were becoming much more visible – as we shall see.

In Europe, the situation regarding swastikas was more complex. And this was something that had to be taken into account if British neo-fascists were ever going to merchandise records and other products there. In countries that had been occupied during the war, the symbol had deeper resonances than in Britain (it was noticeable, for example, that during punk, European bands and fans had not adopted the symbol with nearly so much gusto as their British counterparts). In post-war Germany, the swastika was banned, and the same was true of many other countries, along with other symbols deemed to 'incite racial hatred'. This was another dimension to neo-fascist efforts to 'keep things in code' (and to use less inflammatory symbols), and it is hardly irrelevant that Rock-O-Rama, who we'll hear more about in a moment, was a German label.

Finally, as a sidebar, and getting away from the Nazi heritage, there were other graphic symbols that became more popular – though these were less evident – for example, imports from the neo-fascist scene in the USA: white power 'Aryan' fists, Ku Klux Klan symbols, Dixie flags, etc. Similarly, from the pro-Apartheid movement in South Africa (particularly the Afrikaner Resistance Movement). Finally, and more rarely, there were examples of détourning anti-fascist imagery in a neo-fascist cause. Bricolage, as ever, was the order of the day.

Thus, the new UK visual identity was a grass-roots phenomenon, and took shape after 1979. It is possible to trace its development via skinzines, underground political magazines, and − especially − in fashion. What was different about the large-scale adoption of this kind of imagery was not that it was 'new' (such symbols had been circulating for some time), but that it started to be promoted and distributed in a much more systematic fashion. Now, market stalls in the capital and other urban centres became places for neo-fascists to pick up the latest patches, badges, t-shirts and paraphernalia; and reports in the *skinzines* attest to how young skinheads from all over Europe would descend on London's Portobello Road or Brick Lane at the weekends.[13]

What the new visual identity signified was 'membership of a clique'. Neo-fascists could now identify each other more easily, and the sense of community being fostered by the '*zines*' was solidified. Knowledge of the 'correct' symbols denoted subcultural capital − which in turn contributed to an individual's 'authenticity'. In other words, to be an 'ace face' in the neo-fascist skinhead community, it might mean that you were good at fighting, and knew about music; but it might also mean you knew a Celtic cross when you saw one − and where to buy a t-shirt with the symbol on it. Finally, the look was also useful in that it functioned in opposition to other looks − notably that of the anarcho-punks, whose visual identity was similarly based on strong symbols and a different kind of 'uniform'. (The socialist bands, and fans, never developed quite the same visual brand. Hammers-and-sickles and red stars, although they were part of youth culture, never caught on to quite the same degree.)

Thus, in terms of subcultural studies, this neo-fascist 'club' could be oppositional in the sense described by Dick Hebdige (1979) ('anti-establishment', 'anti-high street', etc.), but could also encompass a sense of taste distinction and one-upmanship among peers, as theorised by Sarah Thornton (1995). And the simple appeal of having fun should not be neglected: for example, it IS certainly possible to detect an element of revelling in the 'naughtiness' of it all − an aspect that went back to punk, and the idea of being as offensive as possible in order to goad 'straight' society. (Neo-fascist skins often knew that there was something ridiculous about wearing the fashion and *sieg-heiling* in a country that had fought the Nazis, but were prepared to do it anyway to prove a point − that being, their anger at the 'race' situation − and for the sake of a bit of liberal-baiting amusement.)[14]

The NF responds

For the National Front − already in turmoil − the new situation now existing in neo-fascist skinhead culture meant it was faced with a choice. It could either embrace what was happening or eschew it. More out of desperation than anything else, it chose the former course. Many members felt it had nowhere else to go, even if this meant turning its back on its former policies. So, for example, by becoming more firmly associated with the skins – indeed, allowing itself to be led by them in many ways – the NF was saying goodbye to its more 'inclusive' pre-1979 stance, and goodbye to its old (nostalgic) appeal to Second World War 'verities'. In other words, the skinhead adoption of symbols pertaining to Nazi Germany was not likely to chime with the old NF's appeal to ex-servicemen and women from the war era.

The NF's new attitude was made manifest by the creation of the White Noise Club in 1983 – which would remain the most visible face of neo-fascist rock until 1987. Since the petering out of the original RAC bands in 1979, the flame of neo-fascist rock had been kept alive by *Bulldog*'s RAC News column (and the efforts of editor Joe Pearce), which became increasingly strident over time.[15] It didn't have much to report on, however, and apart from a few 'RAC discos', it could only complain weakly that, 'At the moment it's only the fans who have got the guts to stand up and fight. But soon many of the bands will start to join the Rebellion [sic] as well' (*Bulldog* 19, 1980, 4). To fill the void, the column became increasingly desperate in its efforts to claim any band for the racist cause: a 1982 edition offered a rave review of a bootleg tape which almost surreally included tracks by Sparks and Steve Harley.

This lack of neo-fascist bands would change, however, with the founding of the White Noise Records label (1983). The initiative followed the model of 'indie labels' that had blossomed during punk, with the two main differences (apart from content) being that it was clandestine in the sense of having no means of mainstream distribution, and that it was founded to make money for a political party (the NF). Indeed, to secure a greater level of financial viability, a deal was struck with German label Rock-O-Rama in 1984, in order to facilitate distribution through Europe. (Rock-O-Rama had been famous as a punk label in the late 1970s, but now increasingly took on far-right material.)

In terms of White Noise Records' underground nature, no commercial record chain was interested, and any overt selling was likely to attract the attention of anti-fascists and the police. Therefore, the records were sold by mail order (via *Bulldog* and elsewhere), at gigs – though, again, the gigs were few in number due to clampdowns – and via the very few commercial outlets that existed. Of course, for fans, the fact that the records were 'covert' made them all the more glamorous, and the reality that they were so despised by the mainstream media only went to prove that the politics they espoused represented 'the truth'.

The label's main inspiration seems to have been the anarcho-punk model, though this is speculation and other precedents are identifiable.[16] On one level, this can be seen in terms of financial strategies. Just as Crass and their ilk used profits from gigs and record sales to support political causes – feminist groups, animal rights organisations, striking miners, and so on – so the neo-fascist bands were expected to funnel profits towards the NF. Also, just as Crass used money to support fledgling bands with similar views, so the neo-fascist bands would do the same.

This relationship was also reflected in the visuals. For the neo-fascists, agit-prop was now taken to a new level, with coded symbols and gothic lettering the order of the day – reflecting anarcho-punk strategies of communicating via black and white symbolism, and using sleeves as propaganda vehicles.[17]

Thus, to simplify: although the (physical) 'dialogue' on the streets was perceived to be mainly with socialist/leftist groups like Red Action, the (aesthetic) dialogue of the White Noise label was with anarcho-punk. We should note, however, that not all anarchists were Crass-style pacifists, and the street war was much more complex – typically involving a cross-section of the anti-fascist left. (Some anarchist factions embraced an 'any means necessary' approach, while anarcho-pacifists took varying stances in relation to neo-fascism, which could involve passive protest, for example, to attempt to stop gigs or close down distribution centres, and violence in the name of 'self-defence'. In the later 1980s, the movement would split into a pacifist wing and a more violent strand, typified by Class War.)

The White Noise Records/Rock-O-Rama initiative birthed 16 records in our chosen period, between 1983 and 1987. Not all the music was punk, though this was the dominant mode (rockier, bluesier fare became more evident later). The visuals, not unexpectedly, co-opted the grass-roots fashion for gothic lettering and Nazi symbolism, and meshed this with more 'traditional' skinhead imagery. The execution of the sleeves and the PR around the records was lo-tech and amateur in nature, not least because no overground design agency would go near the material. Most of this work remained anonymous.

Skrewdriver

The key band in the White Noise plan was Skrewdriver. They had been founded in 1977, as a punk band, and courted a skinhead following: they 'came out' for neo-fascism in 1982. In their early career, they had not been political in any overt sense, but had been one of those punk bands that flirted with swastikas. Their leader, Ian Stuart Donaldson, was the person who took the band in a rightwards direction, changing personnel along the way: he joined the NF in 1979, and became a 'youth organiser' for the party.[18] He was also responsible for the band's look, which moved from punk to skinhead, and then to neo-fascist skinhead (black shirts and MA-1 jackets, union flag patches, and so on). Skrewdriver were evidently meant to play at the 1979 RAC festival in London, but had not shown up: now, in 1983, it was time for them to step into the limelight.[19]

The first batch of White Noise releases were Skrewdriver records, and the sense of relief in 'RAC News' was palpable –

> The fact is that the music business is dominated by middle-class trendies and rich capitalists who support multiracialism. It therefore takes a band with real guts to stand up for the White working class in such a hostile environment.
>
> *(Bulldog 33 1983, 2)*

Henceforward, any new release by Skrewdriver would shoot to Number 1 in the RAC charts – helped, no doubt, by the band's strong friendship with Joe Pearce.[20] From the point of view of the visuals (our main concern in this essay) three releases were key, and here we look at them in turn:

White Power (1983)

The sleeve for this EP featured the title in gothic lettering below a white power Aryan fist, in stark black and white. The reverse was a photo of the band onstage, with details of band members, and bits of additional information (Joe Pearce is thanked for backing vocals). The main song on the record was the eponymous 'White Power', and the b-side consisted of 'Smash the IRA' and 'Shove the Dove' (an anti-CND rant, and clearly a riposte to anarcho-punk band Crass).[21]

To say more about the fist itself: it had been visible in neo-fascist circles in the late 1970s, and became more popular with time, eventually appearing with frequency in *Bulldog*. It probably originated in the USA as a retort to the Black Power movement (the Black Power fist salute would first have become widely known to the British public via the televised gesture by athletes during the 1968 Olympics).[22] Thus, we can say that just as Rock Against Racism begat Rock Against Communism, so Black Power begat White Power.

The fist, as a symbol of defiance, has a much longer history, of course, going back to the start of the nineteenth century, and including political causes of all kinds.[23] Within late twentieth-century popular culture, it could be found every-where. For example, the confrontational black-and-whiteness of the *White Power* sleeve is reminiscent of the merchandising for Motorhead, a band that Donaldson was always very interested in, and who were erstwhile labelmates back in the punk days. (When Motorhead would do 'secret' gigs, they'd call themselves 'Iron Fist and the Hordes from Hell', with accompanying t-shirt designs featuring a clenched fist and gothic lettering.) Similarly, within punk, fists in various guises were com-mon, and could be found on record sleeves by – for example – the Tom Robinson Band and the Anti-Nowhere League.

White Power was thus a statement of intent. When histories of record sleeves talk about 'the most provocative sleeve ever produced', they usually mean something like the Stones' *Sticky Fingers* or the Pistols' *Never Mind the Bollocks*. But *White Power* is obviously in another category altogether. It would be tempting to say that it is also the vilest sleeve ever produced – but, alas, the neo-fascist scene of the 1990s would prove otherwise.

'Invasion' (1984)

The sleeve for this single again features heavy gothic script, with a cover image in black and white: this time of a figure – possibly a skinhead – crucified on a hammer-and-sickle. The reverse features a photo of the group, with Donaldson at the front, in full 'battle dress' with black MA-1 jackets and patches (Donaldson sports a union flag patch on one arm, and a lightning bolt rune patch on his chest – making 's' for Skrewdriver).

The cover image is especially interesting, in that it is, in fact, a détourned anti-fascist poster from Germany in 1932. In the original version, the figure is crucified on a swastika. (To be specific, the poster was designed by Karl Geiss as an election poster for the Social Democratic Party, and was called 'The Worker in the Reich of the Swastika'.)[24] This poster itself was paid homage to by John Heartfield in a much better-known poster of 1934, and had inspirations going back to Christian images in the Middle Ages of saints being crucified upon a wheel. There would have been other associations, too, because the image of a 'crucified skinhead' had become a visual trope within the skin subculture – a design usually attributed to Mick Furbank, produced for the shop 'Last Resort' in London's East End, a skin-head emporium that welcomed adherents of all political persuasions.

Thus, the cover for 'Invasion' spoke to a particular strain of neo-fascist para-noia – the idea that skins were 'martyrs' and that the people responsible for the martyring were 'reds'. The record itself is about the Russian invasion of Afghanistan (and not about an 'invasion of immigrants', as is commonly supposed), and therefore the hammer-and-sickle has another, specific, meaning. As for the reverse image of the band in 'stormtrooper' mode, this fits with the narrative about 'the only band with guts', and echoes the photos of bands like The Clash during the punk era – offering an image of a gang standing up for 'what's right' (a trope usefully theorised by Simon Reynolds and Joy Press (1996) as signifying a kind of 'adventure rock'[25]).

This is White Noise! (1984)

The sleeve for this EP has no script at all, but simply a Celtic cross design, in black and white. The title of the EP appears on the reverse, along with details of the songs – one by Skrewdriver, and three by other bands (the Diehards, Brutal Attack and ABH). The image on the reverse is a photo of two children next to a Young National Front standard – kids being symbolic of the 'future that has to be defended', and standards of a particular kind of Nazi-friendly neo-fascism.[26]

This record, then, was a kind of manifesto for White Noise and the NF. It made several statements at once: a) that White Noise was a 'scene' with many bands involved, and not just Skrewdriver, b) that the NF was still very important as a driving force, and c) that a stand-alone symbol on the sleeve was enough to sell the record. On this latter point, we have already talked about the meaning of the Celtic cross, but in the context of sleeves, it is worth noting that the nearest comparator in the world of more mainstream alt-rock music was the marketing of the aforemen-tioned Crass. They, too, had the confidence that a stand-alone symbol would speak to their fans (see, for example, the multiple uses of their snake-head circle design, along with the circled 'A'). Once again, bands at different ends of the political spec-trum mirrored each other.

Thus, it's clear the period of the early 1980s saw neo-fascist rock becoming more hardline and taking roughly the form we are familiar with today. With the founding of White Noise, the 'scene' could finally be claimed to be real, as opposed to the fantasy previously espoused by *Bulldog*. By using punk as a model, neo-fascist rock now had an 'indie label', and a press to report on records and gigs. Of course, it was still on a small scale: when *Bulldog* boasted of the 'dozens' of albums sold by White Noise, this didn't really compare with the thousands of records that were being sold by Crass Records, or with the hundreds of thousands by Virgin. But nevertheless, it represented a perverse Thatcherite success story in terms of small business entrepreneurialism (albeit at the edges of legality).

At the centre of this new vision was Skrewdriver, a gang of 'men on a mission', led by Ian Stuart Donaldson. It is clear that this period sees the start of his 'heroisation', and although it wasn't clear at the time, his celebrity would ensure his martyrdom after his death (in 1993). This meant that neo-fascist rock now had a figurehead, which was a step forward in propaganda terms from the anonymous and fragmented nature of RAC in the late 1970s. The fact that his views moved ever-rightwards over time both encouraged and reflected the new mood of the scene – and especially its embrace of Nazism.

Into Europe

After 1984, the scene gathered further momentum; with new bands, new publications and new elements being added to the visual mix. In particular, images of 'Vikings' became popular. The quotation marks are important because the relationship to real Viking culture was tenuous: instead, the idea was to channel old neo-fascist fixations with masculinity and warrior culture into new and appealing imagery. But at the same time, the act of looking back to a Nordic/Viking past had political ramifications, and reflected a new desire to champion a European heritage rather than a specifically British one. Thus, a mythology developed whereby white Europeans were seen as Aryans with a common bloodline, and with common enemies (black and Asian immigrants, Jews, etc.). The concomitant re-imagining of history posited that the two world wars were tragic mistakes, and that there should be 'no more brothers' wars'.

This re-orientation towards Europe was also rather convenient because this was where the money was. If distribution of neo-fascist rock records and paraphernalia could be achieved here on a greater scale, then potentially the financial rewards could be high. Already, Rock-O-Rama had made inroads, and Skrewdriver had done successful tours of Germany and Scandinavia (*Bulldog* 38, 1984, 4).[27] In time, White Noise Records would release compilations of European bands – an obvious next step. The only problem with this inclusive pan-European policy, that included as a priority 'making friends with Germany', was that it exacerbated the retreat from the pre-1979 NF strategy.

The background to this reorientation was a newly energised press for neo-fascist rock. *Bulldog*'s 'RAC News' had done its job, and was now overtaken by other more focused publications. *Rocking the Reds* (1980–84) was a relatively obscure supplement that was eventually subsumed into *Bulldog*, while *New Dawn* (1986) was the name of the publication that took over from *Bulldog* when it was prosecuted for breaking the laws against incitement to racial hatred.[28] But most importantly, there was *White Noise* (1986–88) which touted itself as the 'fanzine' for the eponymous label. It was not a real fanzine, of course, because it was still an NF publication, but it did have more 'credibility' than the other titles because it was closer to the *skinzines* of the period.[29] Its logo was a fist with a lightning bolt, and although it covered all the neo-fascist bands, it was clear that Skrewdriver were the main attraction (Donaldson's face graced the cover to issue 1).[30] *White Noise* was enthusiastic about the new pro-Europe direction, and one cover featured an illustration of a skinhead graffiti-ing the words 'White N★ise' across a map of the continent, with a sub-heading 'Music for Europe' (*White Noise* 3, 1987, 1).

The obsession with Vikings was most evident on the record sleeves. The 1984–87 period saw a continuation of old tropes (Celtic crosses, skinhead imagery, etc.) but with the addition of some relatively elaborate illustrations. The sleeves for the albums by Skrewdriver (*Hail the New Dawn*, 1984; and *Blood and Honour*, 1985), and Brutal Attack (*Stronger than Before*, 1986) seem to be of a piece. They all represent hyper-masculine warriors (supposedly) 'fighting for their race': and all seem to be looking back to a mythologised Viking or Norse/Teutonic past. By implication, the neo-fascist skins were heirs to this genetic heritage.

In more detail: a) Skrewdriver's *Hail the New Dawn* (1984) features an amateurish but detailed drawing of a Viking ship landing ashore, with the lead warrior clad in furs and a helmet with wings, brandishing a huge flag with a version of the sun cross. The illustration is in black and white, and framed by the title of the LP and the band's name in gothic lettering. The sleeve was drawn by Nicky Crane, another key figure in the neo-fascist firmament;[31] b) Skrewdriver's *Blood and Honour* (1985) has a warrior, semi-naked, with a horned helmet and axe dripping with blood, surveying a rocky landscape at sunset or sunrise. It is a poorly rendered ink drawing, in colour, framed by the title of the LP and band name in gothic script. The warrior design appears to be a swipe from a 1970s Conan comic book (of the era associated with artist Barry Windsor Smith) and, as such, we might wryly suggest that the reference is less to a Viking past than to Hyborea. The sleeve is the work of a tattooist (and is signed 'Bugs Tattoo'), which could be interpreted as a coded encouragement to fans to visit the parlour to get their (neo-fascist) tattoos done; c) Brutal Attack's *Stronger Than Before* (1986) has an illustration of a Viking-style figure, with winged helmet, upon a horse, that is most likely appropriated from a book illustration or a nineteenth-century etching. In fact, closer inspection reveals that the figure is Odin on his eight-legged steed Sleipnir – a Norse god with a helmet in the shape of an eagle.[32]

For sure, these images were meant to evoke a Nazi connection. Along with the aforementioned runes and symbols, the Nazis had been interested in other aspects of their supposed Norse/Teutonic heritage, and this included idealised images of 'Aryans' and Vikings, often by way of reference to Wagner's operas. Himmler in particular was fascinated by Norse paganism and had even started an organisation in 1935 to research the heritage of the German people, and to educate them about their genetic Aryan superiority: he also controlled the SS and modelled them on a Nordic knightly order.[33] The actual science behind these ideas was nonsense, and debunked even at the time; but, as Himmler and his fellow devotees knew, it made for a strong visual brand.

The 'Vikings' on the record sleeves were thus meant to signify bravery and physical superiority, but also sacrifice, honour and dying for the cause. When used in conjunction with death imagery (SS-style death's heads, etc.) the message was underlined. It all fitted perfectly with the previously explained skinhead narrative of martyrdom, and provided another (glossier, more spectacular) angle on the old theme of legitimising and inciting violence against enemies.

But there are other ways to think about these images. In a British context, they do not make much sense on any historical level (indeed, no more so than Himmler's ideas). For example, it does not help us to explore the exact sources for these images, because the 'Vikings' are based on Victorian notions of what they looked like: today historians are sceptical of the 'burning and pillaging' stereotype, and prefer to see them as farmer-settlers. So, for example, there is no evidence of 'winged' or 'horned' helmets. The ultimate historical irony is that the Vikings were themselves 'immigrants' to, and invaders of, the British Isles.[34]

Thus, perhaps it is more helpful to think about these images as being filtered through a 'fantasy' imagination. It is clear that in the twentieth century, Viking and Norse imagery and mythology had become part of pop culture as never before – in comics (*Thor*, etc.), movies, literature, computer games, and so on. Very often, such preoccupations meshed with other influences from fantasy and 'sword and sorcery' literature – such as Tolkien's *Lord of the Rings* and the aforementioned Conan stories, by Robert E. Howard (both of which drew from Norse myth). It all amounted to a fantasy 'soup' of pumped-up warrior mythology that made sense in its own terms. (As a sidebar, the politics of fantasy and sword-and-sorcery literature have often been criticized for being right-wing. For example, both *The Lord of the Rings* and *Conan* have been characterised as 'racist' for the way they focus on bloodlines and stratify various tribes according to 'racial' characteristics. We might pause, therefore, to consider further the significance of the *Blood & Honour* sleeve featuring a Conan clone, or, indeed, the fact that Ian Stuart Donaldson was a big fan of *Lord of the Rings*.)

This idea of a 'fantasy lens' leads us to the influence of heavy metal. At the same time that the Viking imagery was becoming popular in neo-fascist circles, heavy metal was going through a renaissance, with a significant part of its visual armoury being made up of similar artwork, typically mixed with gothic lettering. Specifically, for a British context, we need to take account of the New Wave of British Heavy Metal (NWOBHM), which dates roughly from 1979–86, and which mixed metal preoccupations with punk. Thus, the music was faster and less polished, and the sleeves were often amateur in nature, along punk DIY lines. Bands like Iron Maiden, Diamond Head and Vardis took metal back to sweaty pubs and gave it a new lease of life. In the same way that the new guitarists were not necessarily Jimmy Pages or Ritchie Blackmores, so the new sleeve artists were not Roger Deans. It amounted to an aesthetic that was aping the mainstream, but at the same time not.

This seems to chime with what was going on in the sleeves we have highlighted from the neo-fascist tradition – not just in terms of their content (choice of pictures and of typeface) but also in their studied amateurishness. Of course, the neo-fascists had to work with what they had: no mainstream design agency was going to take on the job, so they had to rely on 'mates'. But at the same time, a certain level of amateurishness was acceptable in the context of the surrounding pop culture, especially with reference to the NWOBHM. (To take one example, and to be slightly cruel for a moment, the Viking on the cover of *Hail the New Dawn* is rather dwarf-like, with an impossible body posture and strange musculature – hardly the image of Aryan perfection that was undoubtedly hoped for.)

This connection seemed to be solidified by the fact that certain bands were moving away from a punk sound and more towards metal and blues (Skrewdriver among them – Donaldson had never hidden his liking for this kind of music), and that the neo-fascist press was now giving space to metal bands.[35] One publication, for example, covered the (non-fascist) NWOBHM band Tank, who had just released a record titled – rather conveniently – *Honour and Blood* (*White Noise* 7, c.1988, 5).

In other words, the codes could be easy to mistake, if you were not part of either particular 'club'. An anecdote about the researching of this essay underlines the point. When Ana was in the early stages of her groundwork, she showed a few of the neo-fascist sleeves as slides to a student seminar. Afterwards, one of the more mature students approached her and explained that she was ashamed to say that her son had been a fan of neo-fascist music, but was now 'over it', and invited Ana to see his record collection. Delighted to have located a stash of these rare items, Ana duly met with him; only to find that they were, in fact, metal records.

Yet, having said all this, for the neo-fascists, there was a political point to the emphasis on this kind of imagery. As we've suggested, the 'Viking' can be a British image, but it is more likely to be a symbol of a European past – a shared heritage with the 'white races' on the continent. This was a re-orientation of neo-fascist perspective from the early days of RAC, and a long way from the 1979 days of riffing on images of union flags, bulldogs and Churchillian associations. The title of a track on *Hail the New Dawn* summed things up: 'Europe Awake!' (to quote the lyrics: *What has happened to the heritage that once was yours and mine/…A capitalistic economy, the communists roam the streets/The old people aren't safe outside, what solution do we seek?/ [Chorus] Europe awake, for the White man's sake!…*).

As previously explained, the fact that Germany now had the thumbs-up (with Rock-O-Rama and Skrewdriver both doing good business there) underlined the new outlook. Increasingly, bands would refer to the tragedy of internecine conflicts between the European nations – especially between Britain and Germany. A sleeve that would appear outside our time frame, but which perfectly sums up the new mood, was No Remorse's *This Time the World* (1988), which featured a Viking, an SS infantryman and a skinhead, all fighting for the same cause.

For the same reason, there were increasing references to Rudolf Hess. To briefly explain: Hess had been Deputy Führer until 1941, when he flew to the UK in an attempt to make peace. He was then taken prisoner, tried for war crimes and imprisoned until his death in 1987. For neo-fascists, therefore, he was an ideal 'martyr' to the idea of 'no more brothers' wars'. A track on Skrewdriver's *Blood & Honour* is devoted to him, and entitled 'Prisoner of Peace'.[36]

However, the move into Viking art was also heralding a more insular future for neo-fascist rock. It was less aggressive than the stark black and white sleeves of the early White Noise period, and might be interpreted as representing a retreat from agitprop and into spectacle and fantasy. This was about a community that was no longer as interested in reaching out to disenfranchised youth – a community that was becoming a kind of semi-religious cult. Thus, followers were meant to know their martyrs (Hitler, Hess, etc.), to worship gurus like Donaldson, and to be prepared to 'sacrifice themselves' in the battle against non-believers. In other words, as neo-fascist philosophy became more 'fantastical', so images from fantasy became more evident. This philosophical retreat was also undoubtedly an acknowledgement that the efforts of civic society and anti-fascists to suppress neo-fascism had succeeded, at least in keeping it from going overground. Simplistically speaking, an image of a Viking served a purpose – but it was harder to graffiti than a Celtic cross.

Such visuals did start a trend, however, and Vikings continued to be a trope within neo-fascist rock until the present day. In terms of a British context, they can be seen on future Skrewdriver releases (*Warlord*, *The Strong Survive*, etc. – again using amateurish art, which was probably the point); the three *Gods of War* compilation LPs; Lionheart's *A New Beginning*, and many more. There would even be a neo-fascist label called Viking Records, and in 2011, a 'Viking Fest' in the north of England, featuring international neo-fascist bands.

Conclusion

Changing visual obsessions between 1984 and 1987 tell a story of new influences (Nordic myth, heavy metal) and of new priorities (European unity). With the distribution of records becoming more sophisticated, and the press becoming more focused, so neo-fascist rock was starting to make big money: in *White Noise*, the 'shop' section now consisted of a whole page of records, t-shirts, badges and posters. Things were moving to another level: no wonder the European Parliament felt compelled to commission an anxious report on the rise of the phenomenon (Ford 1991).

The story after 1987 takes a new path, which is not a focus of the chapter here, as the tensions that had been building between the skinhead-led music scene and the NF through the 1980s finally came to a head, with the result that a split, led by Skrewdriver, saw the formation of an independent organisation – 'Blood & Honour'. It also marked the point at which European aspirations turned to global aspirations – with an increasing emphasis on 'cracking the States' (in time-honoured rock 'n' roll fashion). Now, fresh visuals would be emphasised, including the 'triskelion', a three-pronged version of the swastika that was the symbol used by South Africa's Afrikaner Resistance Movement (and which also happened to have once been the symbol of an SS regiment). Ever alert to self-branding, the movement did not stay still.

What is striking about our broad-brush survey of the visuals of neo-fascist rock in this period is the way that they, and the neo-fascist philosophy they reflect, are so often backward-looking, whether that means to Second World War era Britain, Nazi Germany or Viking Europe. For all the movement's talk of 'a new dawn' and a 'glorious tomorrow', it was profoundly nostalgic, and obsessive in its search for 'roots'. The yearning for a prelapsarian moment is evident in just about every example we have discussed. At a time in the 1980s when many intellectuals have argued that culture was entering a postmodern phase, when certainties were no longer certain, this can be seen as one more reaction to the zeitgeist. Neo-fascism, then as now, could not deal with a society that was multicultural, tolerant of sexual orientation, democratic and open to change. The response was paranoia, violence, hate – and badly drawn pictures of hairy men with horned helmets…

Notes

1 The word 'scene' here is being used to denote 'the context in which clusters of producers, musicians, and fans collectively share their common musical tastes and collectively distinguish themselves from others' (Bennett and Peterson 2004: 1).

2 An expanded version of this essay can be found in Fabian Virchow (ed.) *The Visual Politics of the Far Right*, Springer VS, Germany, forthcoming. Its roots are in Ana Raposo's PhD thesis *30 Years of Agit-prop: The Representation of 'Extreme' Politics in Punk and Post-Punk Music Graphics in the United Kingdom from 1978 to 2008* (University of the Arts London 2012). The corpus of images discussed is based on Ana's collection, supplemented by other private collections (primarily that of Toby Mott – with gratitude). The zine archives at the V&A (National Art Library) and Liverpool John Moore's University are excellent, and the British Library has good holdings of both zines and political publications. The Bodleian is also useful for political material.

3 The key source on this symbolism is another *Searchlight* publication: *Signs of Hate* (Collins and Gable 2003) though, as reviewers pointed out, it sometimes mistakes the symbols of neo-fascism for those of skin culture more generally.

4 For an in-depth survey of political currents, see Harrison (2011). On the far right specifically, see Copsey and Richardson (2015).

5 Undoubtedly the existence of the BM ('Britain's National Socialist Party') was a factor in the NF's increasingly rightwards turn. However, the relationship between them was complex: there were policy differences, but members co-mingled on marches and were prepared to work together for a common cause.

6 The key figure in the BM was Nicky Crane – see below.

7 Paul Burnley, later of No Remorse, produced the zine *The Truth at Last!* (c.1985–87) which was notable for the way it attempted to cram in as many symbols as possible.

8 In post-war Germany, the font was largely considered taboo.

9 Here, we might also mention numerical codes referring to Nazism – for example, 18 (for the first and eighth letters of the alphabet – hence Adolf Hitler) and 88 – for Heil Hitler.

10 The cross could sometimes be interpreted, and used, in different ways – for example, as a gun sight or as a Cross of Saint George.

11 Again, we should note that the symbol continued to be used in many parts of the world without any fascist connotations, for example, as a Hindu symbol.

12 Airfix briefly banned swastika decals for its model kits in 1978, partly out of nervousness that they'd end up where they shouldn't.

13 Later, Carnaby Street became a focus.

14 This kind of observation is hard to corroborate, but anecdotal evidence suggests that even some (no doubt bored) non-political skins would sometimes *sieg-heil* in the service of 'upsetting students'.

15 None of the first wave of bands – the Ventz, The Dentists, etc. – ever recorded anything.

16 'Hate rock' *per se* has a long history – for example, Ku Klux Klan-sponsored music in the 1920s; and American Nazi Party-sponsored music, and the records of Johnny Rebel, in the 1960s. See the special edition of *Popular Music and Society: Hate Rock* (2007).

17 For more on Crass, and how they were inspired by corporate branding, see Bestley and Ogg (2012). This book is recommended as a general background to the importance of sleeve design.

18 He is referred to as 'Donaldson' in this text, though he sometimes went by the name 'Ian Stuart'.

19 The 1979 RAC festival information is from several web sources (e.g. www.ainaskin. com/history/1980–1982.htm and http://en.metapedia.org/wiki/Skrewdriver): they may not be reliable, but do cite Vivien Goldman, the *Melody Maker* journalist who covered the festival.

20 Pearce went on to write their biography *Skrewdriver: The First Ten Years*, in 1987.

21 An apology was published in the 'RAC News' section of *Bulldog* –

> There is a mistake on the back of the Skrewdriver White Power record cover. Skrewdriver's drummer is called Geoff and not Mark as was printed on the cover. Sorry Geoff! White Noise records will try to get it right next time!
>
> *(Bulldog 35, 1983, 3)*

– revealing that the band possibly had little participation in the sleeve design process.

22 It was a phrase that became associated with George Lincoln Rockwell and the American Nazi Party. He had written a book with the title *White Power* in 1966.

23 Left-wing examples included the designs for the Red Front in 1920s Germany, and the International Brigade in Spain in the 1930s.

24 The image had previously been used by Skrewdriver on the back of their single *Voice of Britain* (1983), and before that, had featured in *Bulldog* (since 1981).

25 Such band photo-shoots, and 'band identities', have a much longer history, of course (for a punk context, see Bestley and Ogg (2012)).

26 It also became a poster.

27 *Bulldog* 38 pointed out that the most fervent pockets of Skrewdriver fandom included Hanover, Wuppertal and Hamburg.

28 'White Noise' was the name of the RAC section, which now took up four pages.

29 Even though it was printed on newspaper stock and was a small tabloid, rather than being A4.

30 The new fist symbol, with the addition of the lightning bolt, could have referred both to the lightning bolts of the SS logo, but also to the symbol of the British Union of Fascists.

31 See Sabin and Raposo (2018).

32 The artwork is attributed to John Field, but the cover is clearly not an original drawing.

33 To this day, pagan sites remain gathering places for neo-fascists.

34 See Wawn (2002) and Frank (2000).

35 Concurrently, other (non-fascist) bands that had their roots in punk were turning towards metal (including the Cockney Rejects, GBH and Discharge) and were being influenced by the NWOBHM (which some historians credit with being a significant step towards the development of 'hardcore').

36 Joy Division (in their guise as 'Warsaw') had also referenced Hess, see Sabin (1999, 216). For more on the Hess connection with neo-fascism, especially as it developed post-1987, see Shaffer (2014).

References

Bain, Peter and Paul Shaw (eds.). *Blackletter: Type and National Identity*. New York: Princeton Architectural Press, 1998.

Bennett, Andy and Richard A. Peterson (eds.). *Music Scenes: Local, Translocal and Virtual*. Nashville TN: Vanderbilt University Press, 2004.

Bestley, Russell and Alex Ogg. *The Art of Punk*. London: Omnibus Press, 2012.

Collins, Matthew and Gerry Gable (eds.) *Signs of Hate*. Ilford: Searchlight Information Services, 2003.

Copsey, Nigel and Richardson, John E. (eds.) *Cultures of Post-War British Fascism*. London: Routledge, 2015.

Ford, Glyn. *Report Drawn Up on Behalf of the Committee of Inquiry into Racism and Xenophobia*. Brussels: Office for Official Publications of the European Communities 1991. http://bookshop.europa.eu/en/report-drawn-up-on-behalf-of-the-committee-of-inquiry-into-racism-and-xenophobia-on-the-findings-of-the-committee-of-inquiry-pbAX5990815/ (accessed 22 February 2013).

Frank, Roberta. 'The Invention of the Winged Helmet.' *International Scandinavian and Medieval Studies in Memory of Gerd Wolfgang Weber*. Rome: Edizioni Parnaso, 2000.

Harrison, Brian. *Finding a Role? The United Kingdom 1970–1990*. Oxford University Press, 2011.

Hebdige, Dick. *Subculture: The Meaning of Style*. London: Routledge, 1979.

Pearce, Joe. *Skrewdriver: The First Ten Years*. London: Skrewdriver Services, 1987.

Popular Music and Society. 30, 4. Routledge, 2007.

Raposo, Ana. *30 Years of Agit-prop: The Representation of 'Extreme' Politics in Punk and Post-Punk Music Graphics in the United Kingdom from 1978 to 2008*. PhD thesis, University of the Arts London, 2012.

Reynolds, Simon and Joy Press. *The Sex Revolts: Gender, Rebellion, and Rock 'n' Roll*. Cambridge, MA: Harvard University Press, 1996.

Sabin, Roger. 'I Won't Let the Dago By: Rethinking Punk and Racism,' in Roger Sabin (ed.), *Punk Rock: So What?*, 199–218. London: Routledge, 1999.

Shaffer, Ryan. 'The Soundtrack of Neo-fascism: Youth and Music in the National Front'. *Patterns of Prejudice*, 47, 4–5, 2013.

Shaffer, Ryan. 'From Outcast to Martyr: The Memory of Rudolf Hess in Skinhead Culture', *EXIT journal, Special Issue: Music and Radicalism*, Ausgabe, 3, 2014.

Thornton, Sarah. *Club Cultures: Music, Media, and Subcultural Capital*. Middletown: Wesleyan University Press, 1995.

Wawn, Andrew. *The Vikings and the Victorians: Inventing the Old North in Nineteenth-Century Britain*. London: Boydell and Brewer, 2002.

Periodicals

Blood & Honour 2. London: Blood & Honour, 1987.
Bulldog 19. London: National Front, 1980.
Bulldog 33. London: National Front, 1983.
Bulldog 35. London: National Front, 1983.
Bulldog 38. London: National Front, 1984.
White Noise 3. London: White Noise Club, 1987.
White Noise 7. London: White Noise Club, c.1988.

8

THE 'OBNOXIOUS MOBILISED MINORITY'[1]

Homophobia and homohysteria in the British National Party, 1982–1999[2]

George J. Severs

Introduction

> I took a party ten years ago which said that homosexuality should be out-
> lawed, people should be driven underground and persecuted. The British
> National Party position now is that what people do in the privacy of their
> own homes is absolutely up to them.

These were some of the last words spoken by Nick Griffin, then a Member of the
European Parliament and leader of the British National Party (BNP) (1999–2014),
on the BBC's flagship political programme *Question Time* on 22 October 2009.
This, along with the rest of Griffin's speech against 'militant homosexuals', led many
commentators to label him and his party homophobic (Czyzselska 2009). However,
this statement did not spark the scholarly attention it warranted, which is surprising, given the major question it arouses: how did the BNP go from being a party
unashamed and unreserved in its opposition to homosexuality to one content for
homosexuals to exist in private? This chapter aims to establish the party's attitude
towards gay men under John Tyndall, former leader of the National Front (NF) and
the BNP's founding leader (1982–1999), thus serving as a starting point for those
seeking to answer this question. In that vein it will examine anti-gay sentiment in
the 'early' BNP, from its founding in 1982 to Griffin's election as leader in 1999,
at which point a period of 'modernisation' began (Thompson 2004; Copsey 2007;
Rhodes 2009).[3]

Not to be confused with the British National Party founded in 1960 by John
Bean, a group which went on to merge with several other fascist parties to form
the National Front in 1967, the 'modern' BNP with which this chapter is concerned emerged from the NF. Founded in 1982 by John Tyndall, the party situated
itself on the extreme-right wing of British politics. Among its key concerns was a

committed opposition to immigration (and the integration of migrant/minority ethnic people with what it saw as 'indigenous white British' communities), feminism and homosexuality. The party remained belligerently nostalgic towards the British Empire, advocated a policy of compulsory repatriation, and constantly articulated passionate support for the nuclear family as a bastion of national reproduction. Whilst it is true that, following its emergence from the NF, many BNP leaders and members were concerned with distancing themselves from previous fascistic associations, the party remained part of a neo-Nazi ideological tradition (Eatwell and Mudde 2004: 65).

The BNP has received a great deal of scholarly attention over the last few decades, and there now exists a wealth of secondary literature on the party, ranging from broad surveys of its ideology and political activity, to comparative and transnational studies (Copsey 2008; Goodwin 2011; Mammone, Godin and Jenkins 2012; Trilling 2013). Far fewer in number, however, are studies concerning British fascism's explicit and trenchant opposition to homosexuality. Julie V. Gottlieb provides a thoughtful analysis of 'Britain's new fascist men', in a refreshing contribution which successfully seeks to 'gender the history of British fascism' by examining the levels and depictions of male hegemony in the propaganda of early British fascism (Gottlieb 2004: 83). Gottlieb's work provides a framework for understanding the gender history of early British fascism, specifically focusing on the British Union of Fascism (BUF) led by Sir Oswald Mosley (b. 1896 – d. 1980). Specifically, we glean that the BUF held a materialist, physical conception of masculinity, centred on the male body and framed by what Gottlieb terms the 'fascist-Futurist paradigm', that is, one which married fascism's propensity for seeking examples of the ideal masculine form in the past with its newly discovered penchant for science, technology and 'progress' (Gottlieb 2004: 90). Whilst the BUF operates largely outside the scope of this chapter, it is worth noting that the Union's gender politics operated within a sexual binary, with male and female bodies existing in political opposition to one another. Fascist new men were recognised as such through their 'healthy male bodies', whilst women, though often depicted as strong defenders of the fascist cause, were confined to 'single-sex gang formation' and often sexualised in propaganda in order to recruit young men (Gottlieb 2004: 91–92). There is a necessary lack of emphasis on the sexuality of fascist new men, but Gottlieb makes it clear that, from its inception, British fascism was inherently concerned with masculinity and the binary relationship between masculinity and femininity. This gendered conception of fascist masculinity has been central to the political and gendered identity of individual fascist men, as well as to ideological fascism itself.

Similar themes emerge in Martin Durham's article 'Gender and the British Union of Fascists' (Durham 1992). By examining how a future fascist Britain was being imagined by, and in the 'interests' of, women, Durham's study reveals that early British fascism was indeed engaging in discourses which propagated a sexual binary, though this is not discussed explicitly by the author. There was a place for women in the BUF during the 1930s, yet Mosley was keen to emphasise that their roles would 'be different from that of the men: *we want men who are men and women who are women*' (Durham 1992: 515). Though not concerned with sexuality, this chapter does begin to highlight a nascent fear of forces which might blur these gendered sexual boundaries, as well as a dislike for the individuals who did not embody the ideologically prescribed sexual norms. James Drennan, an early fascist chronicler of the BUF, singled out 'the womanish man' as a particularly urban phenomenon and as an obvious group for the movement to oppose (Durham 1992, 522). Alexander Raven Thompson, editor of the BUF periodical *Action*, believed that democracy bred 'more sissies than it does Empire builders', echoing Drennan's statements about the effect of liberal democratic modernity on the masculinity of British men (Durham 1992: 523). Though Durham was not interested himself in the dynamics of the sexual binary fostered by this discourse, it is clear that there was one, and that evidence of gendered lines becoming blurred was opposed by the BUF, even thirty years before the Sexual Offences Act 1967 partially legalised homosexuality in Britain.

More attention has been paid to twenty-first-century fascism's engagement with sexuality. Matthew J. Goodwin includes an analysis of homophobia in the BNP in his book *New British Fascism*, whilst studies from the University of Oregon and *Expo* have given the issue independent evaluation in a European and North American context (Commerer 2010; Goodwin 2011; Hannus 2012). Most recently, the journal *Patterns of Prejudice* released a special issue in 2015 dealing with 'gender and the populist radical right'. All of these have proved useful and illuminating contributions to our understanding of contemporary far-right European and North American parties, yet they do little to aid our understanding of fascism's thinking about gay men during the 1980s and 1990s. The *Patterns of Prejudice* special issue, for example, tracks the tendency of contemporary fascists to defend homosexual rights in order to add to their arsenal of Islamophobic rhetoric. Tjitske Akkerman writes, '[a]lthough radical-right parties may generally not be very much inclined to defend the rights of homosexuals, in some cases they may do so in the context of immigration', whilst the editors point out that post-9/11 far-right parties in Europe have argued 'that Islamic values are at odds with liberal democratic values, such as … emancipation of homosexuals and women …' (Akkerman 2015: 43; Spierings, Zaslove, Mügge and de Lange 2015: 8–9). Attention is starting to be paid to the ways in which far-right parties engage with issues of sexuality, though they remain overwhelmingly confined to the contemporary political scene.

Homosexuality's place within late twentieth-century British fascism was briefly discussed in Nigel Copsey's recent chapter concerning the representation of the British far right in popular culture. Copsey uses the novel *Children of the Sun* by Max Schaefer (2010) to highlight the presence of gay British neo-Nazis within the popular press, as the book 'intersperses narrative text with actual cuttings from far-right periodicals and newspaper reports' (Copsey 2015: 115). This is just one of Copsey's contributions to the beginnings of a wider understanding of the British far right's engagement with homosexuality in the post-war period, upon which this chapter is able to build.

This chapter seeks to fill the vacuum of historical attention paid to British fascism's interaction with homosexuality. By examining the documents produced by the NF and the BNP from 1981 (the year before the party's founding) and 1999 (the year in which Griffin defeated Tyndall to become party leader), this chapter will address the themes of anti-gay sentiment prevalent in party discourse and policy. It focuses specifically on the material published by the BNP during this period, namely *Spearhead* and *British Nationalist*, though the former is Tyndall's own publication used for party political purposes. Other sources were consulted during the research process, such as *The Thunderer: The Newsletter of the British National Party Christian Fellowship*. However, this chapter is overwhelmingly concerned with the two major party publications of the period as, by engaging with the anti-gay rhetoric evident within them, it is possible to begin to discern the prejudicial attitudes being articulated and consumed by BNP writers and readers.

Specifically, it aims to make three central arguments. First, that the BNP emerged from a homohysteric milieu and thus established itself as a homophobic party (the differences between these two terms is discussed below). The party's unique selling point to members in 1982 was that it was opposed to (and supposedly devoid of) gay men – it became *the* anti-homosexuality party of choice for would-be fascist members in the early 1980s. Second, that homophobia and homohysteria operated symbiotically throughout the period, largely due to the party's response to the HIV/AIDS epidemic. Third, that the BNP's anti-gay sentiment manifested itself in positioning gay men within fascism's traditional conspiratorial discourse. The Jewish-Bolshevik-Masonic conspiracy was made to accommodate gay men.

Though the party was vocally opposed to lesbianism in its literature throughout the period, the vast majority of its attention was paid to gay men, stemming from the party's belief that the 'conspiratorial' nature of gay men threatened the British nationalist movement, as well as a perceived biological threat posed by HIV/AIDS. For this reason, the overwhelming majority of what follows will focus on the BNP's opposition to gay men.[4] Fascist writers are varied in their terminology when referencing sexual minorities, with 'gay', 'queer' and 'homosexual' being the most common. In what follows, I refer to both 'homosexuality' and 'gay men'. 'Homosexuality' because often the party uses this (and 'queer') as a 'catch all' term for sexual minorities, including but not limited to gay men. I endeavour to refer to 'gay men' when it is this group specifically being targeted or discussed by the sources.

Homophobia and homohysteria

Insofar as the BNP's opposition to gay men is mentioned in the secondary literature, two assumptions are made: first that it existed as a present, though peripheral force in the minds of the party's leaders and members, and second that it can be described as 'homophobia'. This chapter argues that both of these presuppositions are largely inaccurate and betray the glib indifference with which anti-gay sentiment in the British far right has been treated to date. Even Commerer's laudable work which focuses exclusively on Europe's far-right opposition to homosexuality makes the mistake of narrowly discussing the attitude in terms of 'homophobia' (Commerer 2010).

The reason that 'homophobia' is unsatisfactory as a term to describe the attitudes and behaviour of the BNP towards gay men during the period becomes apparent when it is defined alongside 'homohysteria'. The common sense (and widely accepted) definition of 'homophobia' is a fear or hatred of homosexuals, and it seems that writers such as Trilling and Goodwin accept this definition in their employment of the word (Goodwin 2011: 116; Trilling 2013: 70). A cursory glance at almost any BNP publication which discusses homosexuality, however, suggests that this term is insufficient given the party's opposition to homosexuality both socially and politically. The BNP was arguing that homosexuality should be outlawed, rather than simply articulating an aversion towards an 'alternative sexuality'. In short, the party demonstrated more than just a general disdain for homosexuals, but rather a desire to see their erasure from Britain.

Homohysteria, however, is far more applicable. Coined by the sociologist Eric Anderson, homohysteria 'is characterized by the witch-hunt to expose who they [homosexuals] are. When one adds homophobia, to the social understanding that homosexuality exists in great numbers … we have homohysteria' (Anderson 2012: 86). Anderson points out that homohysteria was at its 'apex' in the 1980s, writing that '[t]he public's awareness that homosexuals looked normal (even if still believing that they were not), and that they lived among us' was most pronounced during that decade, not least because of the outbreak of HIV/AIDS which, during the early 1980s, appeared to be affecting gay men in isolation (Berridge 1996: 5-6; Anderson 2012: 86).

There has been some confusion about the term 'homohysteria'. Two of the leading scholars working on studies of homohysteria set out to clarify it more concretely in 2014, and these definitional efforts serve to lay some of the theoretical foundations of this chapter (McCormack and Anderson 2014). The authors were keen to emphasise that homohysteria is a sociological measure of the impact of changing levels of homophobia on heterosexual men's gendered behaviour, especially towards each other (McCormack and Anderson 2014: 154–155). When levels of homophobia spiked, and when gay men were obvious *en masse* rather than erased from society because of a homophobic culture, then homohysteria became more palpable. In short, 'homophobia conceptualizes the nature and effects of prejudice and discrimination on sexual minorities' whilst 'homohysteria conceptualises the contexts when homophobia effects (or is used to police) heterosexual men's gendered behaviours' (McCormack and Anderson 2014: 153).

It is just such a context that this chapter addresses. Namely, the homohysteric culture out of which the BNP was born. From its genesis, as we shall see, the party was engaged in what can be seen as a witch-hunt to expose gay members, as well as writing, organising and agitating in opposition to gay men. This, alongside the party's role in the homohysteric backlash which accompanied the AIDS crisis, clearly marks out a shift in the behaviour and attitudes of the heterosexual men of the British far right, both at the top and the grass roots. As these themes are expanded on below, the homohysteric credentials of the early BNP will become apparent. It will be argued that the BNP emerged from a culture of homohysteria, making homophobia a defining and central feature from its outset, whilst the AIDS crisis ensured that, for the rest of the period, homophobia and homohysteria co-existed in the party's policies and rhetoric.

Anti-gay sentiment in the British far right

The BNP was not alone on the far right in harbouring opposition to homosexuality. As will be outlined later, the BNP emerged out of a debate within the NF about the 'problem' of homosexuality, and how best to deal with it. There was, though, an historical pedigree out of which this debate, and indeed the BNP itself, emerged.

It is worth remembering that homosexuals, and gay men in particular, were victims of the Holocaust. Arrests of gay men began in 1933, the year Hitler became Chancellor of Germany, with these numbers increasing following the extension of state powers to persecute homosexuals in June 1935. In all, 100,000 men were arrested in the period leading up to 1945, with between 5,000 and 15,000 ending up in concentration camps (United States Holocaust Memorial Museum, 2016). This is significant because a great many post-war British fascists maintained a passionate nostalgia for Nazi Germany. Historians have noted that Hitler was often seen 'as a divine being within a cosmic order', whilst Combat 18's connection to Hitler has been well noted ('1' and '8' referring to Hitler's initials, 'A' being the first letter of the alphabet and 'H' the eighth) (Jackson 2015: 91; Shaffer 2015: 149). BNP sources from the period do not tend to use the Nazis' assault against homosexuality as a form of historical justification, though this early example of fascist opposition to gay men should not be ignored. Whether the 'gay holocaust' should be spoken of as homohysteria requires attention elsewhere. For the purposes of this chapter, it suffices to say that there was a precedent of far-right anti-gay sentiment taken to its most violent extreme, one of which many BNP members and leaders were aware.

Before homosexuality was largely decriminalised in Britain in 1967, fascist parties were less concerned with issues of sexuality than those of the later post-war period. A cursory glance at the publications of the British Union of Fascists (BUF) or its leader Sir Oswald Mosley betrays this, with party concerns being much more centred on issues of empire and race (Mosley 1970). This is unsurprising, given the fact that homosexuality's criminalised status necessarily confined gay and lesbian activity to 'underground' cultural spaces, resulting in a blinkered visibility of homosexuals both to contemporaries and to historians of the period (Houlbrook 2005: 19–21).

Absence of evidence, though, is not evidence of absence, and historians of British fascism would be wrong to assume that the writings of early British fascists were not gendered. Indeed, the BUF's 'new man' has significant implications for notions of masculinity within official party dogma. Early British fascism, though gendered, was not overly concerned with questions of sexuality. As the period went on, especially into the 1970s, this began to change. There were, for example, smaller parties on the far right which became especially concerned with opposing homosexuality. The National Democratic Freedom Movement (NDFM), active in Leeds in the mid-to-late 1970s, is particularly worthy of note here, not least because there are anti-fascist activists who initially opposed the NDFM because of the party's intense anti-gay stance.[5]

Though homosexuality was not necessarily the central issue of the NDFM, accounts from former members do emphasise both the revulsion they felt at the perceived homosexuality within the NF, as well as their street-based opposition to gay anti-fascists. In particular, Eddy Morrison, a prominent figure in the British far right having been involved in the NF, New National Front and the BNP before establishing his own short-lived National Action Party, mentions the party's opposition to 'Transsexuals against Nazis', as well as 'a bunch of red weirdos' (Malatesta 2010; Morrison 2013). Of course, this group did not attract the hatred of people like Morrison based solely on their sexualities. Their anti-fascist politics was always going to be a source of conflict with members of the far right. What is crucial, though, is Morrison's description of the group as 'weirdos' and later as 'filth' (Morrison 2013). It seems that the 'different' genders and sexualities of this group aroused a particular kind of attention in Morrison and others like him in the NDFM, and he singles them out for that reason. In short, the sexual identity of this particular anti-fascist group generated an additional layer of hatred from the far-right groups with which it was already in conflict.

Furthermore, the NDFM's co-founder David Myatt's written work is believed to have influenced the right-wing bomber David Copeland, who targeted the gay district of London, blowing up the Admiral Duncan pub in Soho in April 1999, as well as black and Asian areas in the same year. Following the explosion, a copy of Myatt's *A Practical Guide to Aryan Revolution* was discovered in Copeland's flat, a fact which, though arguably tenuous, does link the leaders of the NDFM to a right-wing terrorist who targeted gay men (Kapiris 2014).

Copeland himself clearly represents a special case of far-right hatred for gay men, and one of the most active examples of homohysteria. Graeme McLagan and Nick Lowles argue that his attack on the Admiral Duncan, and on gay men especially, was more 'personal' than his other targets, due to frequent assumptions from his family and peers that he might not be heterosexual. 'In denying any homosexual leanings', they write, 'his hatred towards gay men became even more bitter' (McLagan and Lowles 2000: 149–150). Here we see a particularly extreme example of the way in which homohysteria can (and does) affect male behaviour. Copeland is useful here in demonstrating that the BNP were not alone during the period in harbouring an extreme hatred for gay men, though it should be noted that he was a member of the party (McLagan and Lowles 2000: 20). This far more extreme example of homohysteria, stemming from Copeland's belief that 'homosexuals were degenerates, with no place in society', his desire to 'kill and maim' gay men, as well as to terrify others into heteronormative conformity, ought to be born in mind during discussion of the BNP's homohysteric polemic which follows, as one possible result of this particular brand of political rhetoric (McLagan and Lowles 2000: 150).

Finally, the NF's 'homosexuality debate' requires attention. Though this period of internal in-fighting has been well studied, the centrality of homosexuality to the schism often goes unappreciated. Nigel Copsey is one notable exception to this, having identified the link between the 'schism at the "gay" National Front and the birth of the British National Party', though it remains surprising how limited the attention has been to homosexuality as a factor in the history of this dispute (Copsey 2008: 21).

NF publications from the period demonstrate homosexuality's centrality to the party division. Initially latent, as the party leadership appear to have been keen to under-emphasise its importance for fear of alienating its membership, homosexuality soon became the major piece of political capital in use between rival factions in the NF. Andrew Fountaine, a founding member of the NF, became a prominent critic of the party elite and led a faction in leaving the party after failing in his bid to challenge Tyndall for the NF leadership, citing endemic homosexuality within the party elite and the 'symbiotic' relationship between Tyndall and Martin Webster, National Activities Organiser for the NF and himself a gay man, as his primary motivation (Copsey 2008: 21). This is perhaps most clear in John Tyndall's discussion of homosexuality in *Spearhead*. In the December 1979 edition, one which was keen to emphasise the party's unity and to foster the notion that the schism had ended, Tyndall was asked in a printed interview whether allegations made by Fountaine 'that he attempted to bring certain matters of members' misconduct, including matters of a homosexual nature, to the attention of the Directorate and that [Tyndall] would not allow this' were true. Tyndall dismissed the claims as nonsense, though he claimed that Fountaine was interested in the issue 'as one to be exploited so as to *cause* embarrassment to the party' (emphasis in original). In the next edition (January 1980), however, Tyndall resigned from the National Front, offering a whole-page explanation in which he clarified:

> As I predicted to the Directorate, its failure to remove the taint of homosexuality from the party's leadership has caused widespread defections from the party, particularly in the West Midlands.

Clearly, then, whether it was suppressed or highlighted, homosexuality was the major 'political football' of the internal debate, largely capitalised on by Fountaine and his fellow defectors. The gay men at the top of the Directorate, largely assumed to be led by (or exclusively) Webster, were discussed in a wholly pejorative discourse and positioned as the 'enemy' within this Manichean narrative.

In his analysis of the schism, Copsey notes the fact that homosexuality within the NF was used by Tyndall (amongst others) for the purposes of political point scoring, but maintains that the split can be more aptly attributed to the dispute between Tyndall and the NF Directorate, the former having resigned following the Directorate blocking multiple attempts to vest 'dictatorial powers' in himself.

The New National Front, he argues, was essentially Tyndall's 'pressure group for wrestling control from the NF Directorate', and as a result 'remained committed to the political ideas of the original NF... [whilst offering] an alternative leadership to disaffected Front members' (Copsey 2008: 23). Of course, Copsey is right to emphasise the point that homosexuality was not the only issue at play during the schism, and that the power rivalry between Tyndall and the Directorate could more aptly be described as 'the reason' for the NF's split. However, the fact that opposition to homosexuality was used as the political tool of those leaving the NF (from Fountaine in November 1979 to Tyndall in January 1980) cannot be overlooked. Even if homosexuality was not the overwhelming reason for Fountaine's exit, the fact that he broadcasted it in such terms set the tone of future discussions of the movement's direction. Party publications from the period consistently discussed the schism in these anti-gay terms, both in leading articles and members' contributions (*Spearhead* February 1982: 7; *Spearhead* May 1982: 6). Thus, though the NNF and later the BNP may have nominally subscribed to the same political project as the NF, the schism which marked the split between them ushered in a new culture of anti-gay sentiment. The BNP inherited the homophobic culture of the NF (Copsey 2008: 22), but was established during a period of intense opposition to gay men, and one in which they were being actively sought out and removed.

With this in mind, it is fair to say that the BNP was established within a culture of homohysteria. The British far right at the time was concerned with the reality of the presence of gay men within its midst and were organising new political organisations which would exclude them. Take, for example, Eddy Morrison's article for *Spearhead* in February 1982 'Time for a Name Change' in which he writes '[l]et's face it, members of the New National Front – Webster's NF, with all its stigmas of homosexuality and punk nationalism is not going to pack up and go home!' (Morrison 1982, 7). Indeed, in the edition of *Spearhead* published in March 1982, a month before the BNP was founded, one commentator described the NF leadership as 'that preposterous collection of clowns, babies, queers and crypto-marxists', once again placing homosexuality at the centre of the schism between the NF and the BNP, though as this quote suggests, homosexuality within the NF was not the only reason for the split. The conclusion of these articles and many like them from the time was that homosexuality within the NF had been too widely reported in the mass media and was too embedded in the party elites for the NF to ever 'recover'. A new party was needed, one which would not tolerate homosexuality.

The BNP, therefore, came into being both during and because of the far right's homohysteric culture, and could justly be described as a homohysteric party. If we revisit Anderson's definition from *Inclusive Masculinity* this seems much clearer:

> fundamental to the creation of a culture of homohysteria is the necessity of public awareness that reasonable and 'normal' people could also be gay. [...]

When one adds homophobia to the social understanding that homosexuality exists in great numbers, and that it is not easily identifiable ... we have a culture of homohysteria.

(Anderson 2012: 86)

The BNP became a political necessity for people like Morrison and other members because of the recognition that homosexuality existed within the existing hierarchies of the British far right and the desire not to coexist with them. What follows will discuss the ways in which homophobia and homohysteria operated symbiotically within BNP discourse and policy orientation during the period. The point remains, however, that the party was born out of a homohysteric culture, and that homohysteria was therefore at the heart of the party at the moment of its founding.

It is crucial to note, moreover, that this was not only an issue for the BNP at the moment of its founding, but was continuously central to the party's rhetoric for the entirety of the period. Before he became leader of the party, Nick Griffin had contributed to many BNP publications, and in one notable *Spearhead* article from June 1999, wrote about David Copeland and the nail bombs he had planted across London. Concerning the bomb placed in the Admiral Duncan gay pub in Soho, Griffin wrote that '[t]he TV footage of dozens of "gay" demonstrators flaunting their perversion in front of the world's journalists showed just why so many ordinary people find those creatures so repulsive'. Much can be extrapolated here, from Griffin's dehumanising of gay men by describing them as 'creatures', to his positioning of homosexuals as a group separate from 'ordinary people'. What is of immediate importance, though, is that the anti-gay polemic represents an escalation from the 1982 discourse. Rather than arguing for political organisations devoid of gay men, Griffin was revelling in the fact that a far-right bomber had succeeded in killing several homosexuals. Removing gay men from far-right political parties had been the primary objective in 1982; the homohysteric scope seems to be broader and more insidious at the end of the period. Indeed, a special April 1994 issue of *British Nationalist* in preparation for the local elections in May listed as its penultimate election promise:

OUTLAW HOMOSEXUALITY: The BNP believes that homosexuality should be outlawed, to prevent the further spread of AIDS, and to protect our young people from corruption.

This is quite clearly the language of homohysteria, and can be situated comfortably in the party's discourse on homosexuality.

When the BNP was founded, the polemic against gay men was specific to those within its own ranks and looked towards an internal purge. The language evident in publications from 1994 and towards the end of Tyndall's tenure, however, speaks of proscribing homosexuality nationally. Interestingly, there is one article in *Spearhead* from the period (June 1996) which does not call for express outlawing of homosexuality, though the Australian author does recommend that it 'should be firmly, though compassionately, discouraged in society' (Jackson 1996). With this in mind, it is not without grounding to define the polemic of the BNP as homohysteric, given that it was this language which founded the party and which remained consistent throughout the period.

HIV/AIDS and the BNP

When attempting to understand the AIDS crisis and the BNP, 1982 is a seminal year. First, as we have seen, the BNP formed in 1982 and was actively seeking out gay members in something of a purge after splitting with the NF and identifying themselves in opposition to the NF's 'gay' image. Yet 1982 was also the year in which cases of HIV/AIDS were first identified in the UK. The leading historian of the British AIDS crisis, Virginia Berridge, writes that, thanks to the crisis, '[g]ay men were more publicly visible, their sexuality more discussed and accepted than ever before' (Berridge 1996: 56). Of course, Berridge is not concerned with the far right here, and though her assertion that gay men became more accepted during the epidemic is contentious, the point that gay men became increasingly obvious (if not ubiquitous) is vital in understanding the climate of popular homohysteria which fostered the BNP's attitudes towards them.

BNP literature from the period consistently conflated male homosexuality and the AIDS virus, a trait by no means exclusive to the BNP but one which it in particular capitalised on. Indeed, there was an explicit polemic of homohysteria present in BNP publications throughout the period which drew heavily on the AIDS epidemic. Writing retrospectively in his autobiography, John Tyndall described the 'effeminate looking men' he encountered in London in 1954 as 'the advance guard of the "gay" plague that was later to sweep through society like a poisonous virus', clearly referencing the virus in this polemic against gay men (Tyndall 1998: 42). Indeed, once this 'plague' became apparent to the party, as it did to Britons in general in 1984–1985, the BNP placed AIDS at the heart of its homohysteric discourse (Berridge 1996: 56). The party began anchoring its commitment to 'outlawing' homosexuality to a belief that the logical conclusion of such a policy would be the 'wiping out of AIDS', and printed this as official policy every month in *British Nationalist*, a trend which was only curtailed with the advent of Griffin's modernisation process. Even when lamenting the state of the education system, party authors included homohysteric arguments prejudiced on a conflation of gay men as necessarily being HIV/AIDS carriers. 'Now the Labour Government is making it legal again for education authorities to promote and encourage homosexuality', wrote Carol Garland, a BNP lay member, in a *Spearhead* article in December 1999, 'not seeming to understand that the best possible protection against AIDS is not to indulge in it'. Here, as with other examples, Garland is writing under the assumption that gay sex necessarily leads to AIDS, a belief which was central both to her thinking and the homohysteric attitudes of the BNP more widely.

For much of the period it was possible for supporters to purchase stickers from the party which read '[p]rotect us from AIDS: Outlaw homosexuality!' Party material such as this suggests that the BNP was involved in an active campaign against homosexuality. Though not as active as 'gay bashing', a tactic which had been favoured by the NF (Kelly 2013), the process of displaying such a sticker was by no means passive. It required its user to make a public declaration that they were both against homosexuality being tolerated (agreeing that it ought to be 'outlawed') and that they believed male homosexuality to be the cause of the AIDS virus. Of course, the sticker alone is not reflective of when and by whom it was displayed, the data for which would be virtually impossible to accrue. However, it permits historians of the BNP to determine that the party was campaigning actively against gay men, that the party leadership was aiming to disseminate homohysteric material to grass-roots activists (potentially because of demand, though this is unclear), and that the outlawing of homosexuality, specifically male homosexuality, was a central tenant of the BNP agenda 1982–1999, primarily because of the AIDS crisis.[6]

Much of the language employed around the issue of homosexuality in BNP publications from the period can be read as implicitly linking gay men with the spread of AIDS. Articles were consistently published describing homosexuals as 'destructive' and 'threatening', with 'ordinary' people posited as in need of protection from this group. Many of these referenced AIDS explicitly, but we can clearly see the virus's influence on the authors who do not anchor their argument in it. In May 1994 Linda Miller, a BNP organiser based in London, wrote in *Spearhead* of homosexuality: 'today it is one of the most sinister and destructive forces in society', going on to suggest that homosexuals were 'more likely to wage psychological warfare against the family and heterosexual society'. Clearly, Miller was not concerning herself with a discussion of the AIDS crisis, but she buys into the language and view of gay men as posing a biological threat to nuclear white 'indigenously British' families. Indeed, she goes on to compare heterosexual and homosexual men with red and grey squirrels in Britain, making her belief in a biotic danger emanating from the gay community palpable. Homohysteria from the period which did not explicitly reference AIDS, then, was clearly influenced by the discourse of homohysteria which did associate gay men with AIDS, suggesting just how pervasive this conflation was in party discourse.

As a case study of party attitudes towards gay men, the AIDS crisis is useful in demonstrating the ways in which homophobia and homohysteria functioned symbiotically during the period. As has been argued above, the BNP emerged in a culture of homohysteria, but this did not necessarily mark it out as a homohysteric party by default. With gay men seemingly erased from party ranks, the BNP could have become a quietly homophobic party; one which was not supportive of homosexuality or gay rights but not one involved in active anti-gay politics. The advent of AIDS in Britain, though, ensured that the BNP was a homohysteric party throughout Tyndall's premiership. Anderson has argued that HIV/AIDS ushered in a heightened wave of homohysteria as it meant that the 'ubiquitous presence of gay men could no longer be denied', as well as pathologising gay men as a biological threat (Anderson 2012: 87). This seems to have been the case in the BNP.

Homophobia was an underlying current in the BNP since its founding as the anti-gay far-right party, yet the AIDS crisis meant that homohysteria operated alongside homophobia throughout the period.

The 'queer plot'

These two examples (the origins of the party and HIV/AIDS) are vistas into the homohysteria of the BNP, but they should not be viewed in isolation. Homohysteria was not just a factor of the BNP during its genesis or in reference to the AIDS crisis, but was instead a consistent train of thought throughout the period. This becomes most clear when one realises that the BNP viewed homosexuals as a conspiratorial people, placing them alongside Jews, Masons and communists who are the traditional groups believed to be working against nationalists and/or the state by fascist groups, usually termed the 'Jewish-Masonic-Bolshevik conspiracy'. In one notable *Spearhead* article in May 1994, Linda Miller made the case for viewing gay men in the same light as the party's traditional conspiratorial 'enemies'. In it, she argued that a parallel existed between gay men and Masons, both being a 'society, which excludes women, and which has some odd rituals of the kind that only certain types of men would find particularly appealing'. A tenuous link, perhaps, but the connection is one with particular resonance in BNP thought. Miller goes so far as to compare gay men with Jews, a traditional enemy of the 'old' BNP and their Mosley-led predecessors, arguing that homosexuals were infiltrating powerful Zionist groups, whilst the Zionists thereafter blackmailed gay men into adhering to their global programme for fear of being 'outed'. The 'queer plot', therefore, is aptly named, as BNP writers placed gay men at the heart of fascism's traditionally conceived conspiratorial network.

Another explicit link drawn between homosexuals and a conspiratorial 'underground' movement was made by Ellen Strachan, described by Anti-Fascist Action in 1997 as the BNP's 'in-house "trained psychologist"' (*Fighting Talk* March 1997: 16). In September 1996, Strachan argued in *Spearhead* that gay men tended to be 'free market internationalists' (an obvious enemy of the British nationalist movement, especially one with its roots in National Socialism) because of their 'strong group loyalty and high disposable income'. Though not as trenchant in her homohysteric rhetoric as Miller, Strachan clearly believed that gay men were involved in a conspiratorial agenda which was mobilising against nationalism in a manner particular to homosexuals. This article was so well received by the BNP that John Tyndall gave it outright endorsement in an article written for the same edition of *Spearhead* on the subject of 'authority's collapse', alluding to both the omnipresence and legitimacy of this idea within the party.

Moreover, as with many homophobes, the BNP saw gay men as paedophiles. The aforementioned 1994 election promise that '[t]he BNP believes that homosexuality should be outlawed, to prevent the further spread of AIDS and to protect our young people from corruption' is relevant here also. This quote is one of many which suggest that much of the BNP's homohysteria was grounded in a belief that gay men were predatory and paedophilic. Indeed, this election promise was juxtaposed with a caricatured election promise of the 'main parties': '[t]he Lib/ Lab/Con parties have legalized queer sex at 18, and are now pressing for it to be practised by 16-year-olds', and later in the same April 1994 edition of *British Nationalist*:

> [i]t is no coincidence that many Lib/Lab/Con politicians are campaigning for sex with sixteen-year-old boys. Many are queers themselves! The Establishment is riddled with queers and paedophiles who would love to indulge their filthy practices with our children.

Quite clearly, the polemic of homohysteria here is one which attempted to establish a link between gay men and paedophilia, paedophilic homosexuality and the main parties and gay men as a direct and impending threat to the children of British families, furthering the assertion of gay men as a threatening 'other' or outsider group.

Throughout the period, gay men were viewed by the BNP as an enemy in a number of ways. The biological example has already been discussed in reference to HIV/AIDS, yet party authors were notably concerned about the political threat they believed gay men posed to their movement. In her May 1994 *Spearhead* article, Miller concluded that '[w]hen the BNP achieves victory, we must remember that the queers will always be a fifth column. They must be found out and removed from any position of influence.' This extreme passage situates gay men (to whom the word 'queer' invariably refers throughout the literature) in direct political opposition to the BNP. Indeed, description of them as a 'fifth column' conjures imagery of an 'enemy within' during wartime, a point with stark connections to the BNP's conception of gay men as a threat to both themselves and to the nation, but also to the way in which the AIDS virus attacks the body. It is uncertain whether Miller was aware of this connection, as her article does not appear to be reflective of the nuanced authorship that such a subtle comparison would require. However, as we have seen, other BNP authors certainly do make the connection, often unwittingly. Gay men were not only being written about by BNP authors as part of the Jewish-Bolshevik-Masonic conspiracy during the period, but also as an organised group threatening British nationalism in particular.

It is clear to see that contributors to BNP publications throughout the period accepted the view of gay men as a minority which existed outside the national 'norm', which goes some way in explaining the small but regular articles which vent a degree of anger that gay men (and, less frequently, lesbians) were receiving 'special treatment' from government. One notable example from the December 1999 *Spearhead* had it that:

> [p]rostrate [sic.] cancer kills 10,000 men a year in Britain, yet just £47,000 annually is spent on researching it. AIDS, on the other hand, kills a mere 400 a year. And how much is available for AIDS research? £18 million!

What this illustrates, besides the conflation of AIDS as a disease affecting and propagated by gay men (as has been outlined above), is the ubiquitous belief that homosexuals were receiving special treatment over the interests of the heterosexual 'British' populous. Accepting this parallel, the outcry that homosexuals were having more public funds spent on them unnecessarily which is so visible in the BNP literature, places homohysteria even more centrally into the BNP's agenda, so much so that it almost exactly mirrors one of the ways in which the party famously bemoaned asylum seekers (Kushner 2003; Schuster 2003; Trilling 2013: 94–99). Though this is less conspiratorial in the orthodox sense of the term, it does point to the BNP's belief that homosexuals were receiving special treatment from the government, a fact which undoubtedly contributed to the paranoia-fuelled sense of the group as an 'obnoxious mobilised minority' which was extracting more than its fair share from local and national government.

Conclusion

This chapter set out to challenge the pre-existing suppositions present within the literature regarding the British National Party's engagement with gay men. Current scholarship contends that anti-gay attitudes were peripheral and that, where they were present, they could be defined as homophobia. Yet by examining the ways in which the party wrote about gay men, and how it shaped its policies towards them, it is clear that these premises were inaccurate. The BNP itself was born out of a culture which anchored the party in opposition to gay men, opposition which extended to a belief that the group should be nationally proscribed. When AIDS became a major issue in Britain in the mid-1980s, the BNP's polemic against gay men took on a more vitriolic tone; one which adopted a viral discourse and which conflated gay men with the dissemination of the disease. The party also placed gay men within its orthodox conception of the underground anti-nationalist conspiratorial movement, a fact which prompted more homohysteric rhetoric and which offers a new dimension to how the BNP viewed gay men, namely as a dangerous, mobilised minority. In short, a thorough reading of BNP documents 1980–1999 reveals that the party's opposition to gay men was a central and continuous doctrine.

Had it not been for the advent of the AIDS crisis, it is entirely possible that the BNP would have reverted to an NF model of intense homophobia. Yet the backlash which the HIV/AIDS epidemic prompted cemented homohysteria's place in the party's policies and rhetoric for the duration of the period. Homophobia was extant from the outset of the BNP's political life, and the circumstances in which the party had come into being set its early days aside as homohysteric. What the AIDS epidemic and the accompanying backlash ensured was that homophobia and homohysteria operated symbiotically within the BNP. It was not enough to hate gay men, the party made it official policy to erase them.

Both the AIDS crisis and the widespread belief that gay men were organising against the nationalist movement by undermining the NF added weight to the notion that homosexuality was part of the anti-fascist underground conspiracy.

This belief, developed by party writers during the period, situated gay men within the Jewish-Masonic-Bolshevik conspiracy, contributing to a mounting belief that gay men were a political enemy to the British nationalist movement. Not only does this add to our understanding of the way BNP prejudice operated against gay men, it also begins to question the rigidity of orthodox fascist discontents. As we increasingly recognise the extent to which modernity has disturbed received wisdoms of all kinds, it is crucial to continue to question the ways in which traditionally conceived prejudices functioned. As this example has shown, gay men can very easily be overlooked, despite their centrality within the BNP's particular world view.

Though not alone in discussing the ways in which gender and sexual minorities have been engaged with by British fascism, this chapter has begun to fill a sizable lacuna of knowledge. Very little had previously been written about the ways in which British fascism located itself in opposition to homosexuality, nor the ways in which that prejudice operated. By analysing the BNP's anti-gay sentiment and policy in terms of homohysteria, this chapter has sought to challenge the current thinking on fascism's 'homophobia', and to set out some of the ways in which its anti-gay sentiment functioned in reality.

It is hoped that this study of the BNP's homohysteria will help to facilitate and stimulate future scholarly endeavours, and that it has, to a certain extent, challenged traditional notions of how the party situated itself in opposition to gay men. The gender history of British fascism has been well served over the last few decades, yet despite a few brief but trailblazing efforts, its sexuality history has been overlooked. As one of the first studies dedicated solely to examining the ways in which British fascism engaged with homosexuality, it is hoped that others will see the merit in pursuing a sexuality history of fascism, and begin to question the place of homosexuality within their own histories of the far right.

Acknowledgements

For their assistance in reading earlier drafts, I wish to thank Sophie Syms, James Somper, Julie Severs, Ruby Ellis, Andrea Mannone and especially Joe Mulhall. As this chapter deals primarily with men, I dedicate it to the women who have most encouraged me: Dr Elizabeth Batters, Roz Bundy, Julie Severs, Alison Severs, Ruby Ellis, Sophie Syms, Katie Ball and Sinéad Jein.

Notes

1   The title is taken from the caption of a picture of gay men kissing on a demonstration: Obnoxious mobilised minority (1996).
2   This chapter first appeared as an article in *Gender and Education*, 2017, 29: 2, 165–118. We would like to thanks the editors of *Gender and Education* for their kind permission to reprint it.
3   One should be cautious of the fact that the far right, especially in times of modernisation, was keen to change its image to the electorate, whilst not necessarily changing its core

beliefs or fascist dogma. Cas Mudde has referred to this as 'the front stage of the extreme right parties' (Mudde 2000: 21).

4   Virtually nothing has been written on the BNP's opposition to gay or queer women. For initial primary material on this issue, see 'Labour Fat Cats Stalked by "equality"' and 'Queers on Top!', *British Nationalist* (August 1993), p. 2 and p. 4 respectively, and Nigel Jackson, the Australian fascist and supporter of the Holocaust denier David Irving, 'In Search of Well-being', *Spearhead*, No. 328 (June 1996), pp. 12–13.

5   The NDFM was brought to my attention initially by one such activist, Terri, at the launch of Fred Leplat (ed.) *The Far Right in Europe* (London, 2015) in December 2015 at Housmans Book Shop, London. I am grateful to her for taking the time to enlighten me.

6   I am grateful to Dr Joe Mulhall (*Hope Not Hate*) for sourcing these stickers for me. The interpretation of the source is my own.

References

Primary sources

British Nationalist. August (1993) British Library: Zk.9.d.774.

British Nationalist. April (1994) British Library: Zk.9.d.774.

Garland, C. December (1999) 'Wanted: A new breed of men with old ideas'. *Spearhead* 370: 20–21. British Library: Rh.9x.23.

Griffin, N. June (1999) 'Stranger things have happened'. *Spearhead* 364: 14–17. British Library: Rh.9x.23.

Jackson, N. June (1996) 'In search of well-being'. *Spearhead* 328: 12–13. British Library: Rh.9x.23.

Miller, L. May (1994) 'A queer plot'. *Spearhead* 303: 10–11. British Library: Rh.9x.23.

Morrison, E. February (1982) 'Time for a name change'. *Spearhead* 160. British Library: Rh.9x.23.

Mosley, O. (1970) *My Life.* London, Thomas Nelson and Sons Ltd.

Spearhead 161. March (1982) British Library: Rh.9x.23.

Spearhead 163. May (1982) British Library: Rh.9x.23.

Spearhead 370. December (1999) British Library: Rh.9x.23.

Strachan, E. September (1996) 'Internationalism in the 1990s'. *Spearhead* 331. British Library: Rh.9x.23.

The Thunderer: The Newsletter of the British Nationalist Party Christian Fellowship, July/August (1994) British Library: Zk.9.a.3635.

Tyndall, J. September (1996) 'When authority collapses'. *Spearhead* 331. British Library: Rh.9x.23.

Tyndall, J. (1998) *The Eleventh Hour: A Call for British Rebirth.* London: Albion Press. British Library: Yc.1993a.1613.

Secondary sources

Akkerman, T. (2015) 'Gender and the radical right in Western Europe: A comparative analysis of policy agendas', *Patterns of Prejudice* 49.1–2: Special Issue: *Gender and Populist Radical Right Politics*: 37–60.

Anderson, E. (2012) *Inclusive Masculinity: The Changing Nature of Masculinities.* London: Routledge.

Berridge, V. (1996) *AIDS in the UK: The Making of Policy, 1981–1994.* Oxford: Oxford University Press.

Copsey, N. (2007) 'Changing course or changing clothes? Reflections on the ideological evolutions of the British National Party 1999–2006', *Patterns of Prejudice* 41.1: 61–82.

Copsey, N. (2008) *Contemporary British Fascism: The British National Party and the Quest for Legitimacy*. Basingstoke: Macmillan.

Copsey, N. (2015) 'When popular culture met the far right: Cultural encounters with post-war British fascism', in Copsey, N. and Richardson, J. E. (eds) *Cultures of Post-War British Fascism*. London: Routledge.

Durham, M. (1992) 'Gender and the British Union of Fascists', *Journal of Contemporary History* 27.3: 513–529.

Eatwell, R. and Mudde, C. (eds) (2004) *Western Democracies and the New Extreme Right Challenge*. London: Routledge.

Goodwin, M. J. (2011) *New British Fascism: The Rise of the British National Party*. London: Routledge.

Gottlieb, J.V. (2004) 'Britain's new Fascist men: The aestheticization of brutality in British Fascist propaganda', in Gottlieb, J.V. and Linehan, T. P. (eds) *The Culture of Fascism: Visions of the Far Right in Britain*. London: I.B. Tauris & Co Ltd.

Houlbrook, M. (2005) *Queer London: Perils and Pleasures in the Sexual Metropolis, 1918–1957*. London: University of Chicago Press.

Jackson, P. (2015) 'British neo-Nazi fiction: Colin Jordan's *Merrie England – 2000* and *The Uprising*', in Copsey, N. and Richardson, J. E. (eds) *Cultures of Post-War British Fascism*. London: Routledge.

Kushner, T. (2003) 'Meaning nothing but good: Ethics, history and asylum-seeker phobia in Britain', in *Patterns of Prejudice* 37.3: 257–276.

Leplat, F. (ed.) (2015) *The Far Right in Europe*. London: Resistance Books.

Mammone, A., Godin, E. and Jenkins, B. (eds) (2012) *Mapping the Extreme Right in Contemporary Europe: From Local to Transnational*. London: Routledge.

McCormack, M. and Anderson, E. (2014) 'Homohysteria: Definitions, context and intersectionality', *Sex Roles* 71.3–4: 152–158.

McLagan, G. and Lowles, N. (2000) *Mr Evil: The Secret Life of Racist Bomber and Killer David Copeland*. London: John Blake Publishing Ltd.

Mudde, C. (2000) *The Ideology of the Extreme Right*. Manchester: Manchester University Press.

Rhodes, J. (2009) 'The Banal National Party: The routine nature of legitimacy', *Patterns of Prejudice* 43.2: 142–160.

Schuster, L. (2003) 'Common sense or racism? The treatment of asylum seekers in Europe', *Patterns of Prejudice* 37.3: 233–255.

Shaffer, R. (2015) 'British, European and white: Cultural constructions of identity in post-war British fascist music', in Copsey, N. and Richardson, J. E. (eds) *Cultures of Post-War British Fascism*. London: Routledge.

Spierings, N., Zaslove, A., Mügge, L. M. and de Lange, S. L. (2015) 'Gender and populist radical-right politics: An introduction', *Patterns of Prejudice* 49.1–2: Special Issue: *Gender and Populist Radical Right Politics* 3–15.

Trilling, D. (2013) *Bloody Nasty People: The Rise of Britain's Far Right*. London: Verso.

Web links

Anti-Fascist Action. March (1997) *Fighting Talk* 16: 1–24, https://libcom.org/files/FIGHTING%20TALK%20-%2016.pdf (accessed 15 September 2016).

Commerer, B. (2010) 'Populist radical right homophobia'. *APSA 2010 Annual Meeting Paper*. http://papers.ssrn.com/sol3/papers.cfm?abstract_id=1657658## (accessed 18 July 2014).

Czyzselska, J. (2009) 'I thought we got past this homophobia'. *The Guardian*, www.theguardian.com/commentisfree/2009/oct/24/nick-griffin-bnp-homophobia (accessed 21 March 2015).

Hannus, M. (2012) 'Expo: Threatening visibility – Radical right homophobes in European Parliaments 2012'. http://expo.se/www/download/res_threatening_visibility_EN_w_1.2.pdf (accessed 20 July 2014).

Kapiris, M. (2014) 'Myatt: Theoretician of terror?' https://regardingdavidmyatt.wordpress.com/tag/a-practical-guide-to-aryan-revolution/ (accessed 10 January 2015).

Kelly, J. (2013) 'Nicky Crane: The secret double life of a gay neo-Nazi'. *BBC News Magazine*. www.bbc.co.uk/news/magazine-25142557 (accessed 19 March 2015).

Malatesta (2010) 'Eddy Morrison and the NF split' https://malatesta32.wordpress.com/2010/08/12/eddy-morrison-the-nf-split/ (accessed 12 September 2016).

Morrison, E. (2013) *Memoirs of a Street Soldier*. http://memoirsofastreetsoldier.blogspot.co.uk/ (accessed 10 January 2015).

Thompson, K. J. (2004) 'All change on the British 'extreme right'? Nick Griffin and the 'modernization' of the British National Party (BNP)'. PhD Diss., Univ. of Bath. http://ethos.bl.uk/OrderDetails.do?uin=uk.bl.ethos.402101 (accessed 25 February 2015).

United States Holocaust Memorial Museum. 2016 (?). Persecution of Homosexuals in the Third Reich. www.ushmm.org/wlc/en/article.php?ModuleId=10005261 (accessed 15 September 2016).

Audio-visual sources

Question Time [television programme, online], Prod. credit n.k., Prod. company n.k., Prod. country n.k., 22:35 22/10/2009, BBC ONE, 63mins. http://bobnational.net/record/17143 (accessed 24 February 2015).

9

CLOSING THE GENDER GAP

Women and the far right in contemporary Britain

Hannah Bows

> Far right political activists are not all men, there are also women among them. This very simple statement has not received enough attention from activists and educators who are combating against far right politics.
>
> *(Andrea Pető n.d.)*

Introduction

The far right has been of increasing interest to academics and policymakers since the 1980s when support for the far right started to increase, particularly in France, and then later with the Freedom Party in Austria. A plethora of studies emerged which examined membership of far-right parties, drawing theoretical links between gender, socio-economic status and far-right activism. However, some areas remain under-researched and there is a notable gap in relation to women's involvement in far-right groups. The salient image of the angry white, working-class male dominates the discourse around far-right movements in Britain. Revealingly, the cover image for Daniel Trilling's (2012) book, *Bloody Nasty People*, featured no females but four young angry white men, alongside Nick Griffin dressed in a suit. Research has consistently shown that women support the far right in significantly fewer numbers than men and as a result their involvement has often been overlooked. Rarely are they considered as active agents in the construction of far-right ideology or the mobilisation of right-wing movements (Blee and Deutsch 2012).

As Bacchetta and Power (2002: 1) point out, it is 'something of an understatement to remark that historically and currently studies of the right overwhelmingly focus on men', which has led to an incomplete picture of the gender politics of the far right in Britain as elsewhere. As a recent analysis of the British case aptly put it (Dauber 2017: 60) 'British women in the far right deserve more scholarly attention than they have been given. Even after reviewing existing data and research, we know painfully little about women in the British far right'. For even if they are smaller in number, women can assume important roles. In the British case, the roots in female activism stretch back to the 1920s. As Julie Gottlieb's (2003: 269) pioneering study of inter-war British fascism revealed, women did exert influence at every stage of the British Union of Fascists' life-cycle. In more contemporary times, Martin Durham's (1998) work on the 1970s National Front (NF) demonstrated the presence of women on local branch committees and as election candidates. In 1977, in the London County Council elections, for example, twenty out of ninety-one NF candidates were women. There were also female members of the NF's National Directorate, the NF's pre-eminent organisational body.

This chapter aims to provide an overview of the small pool of existing empirical and theoretical work in relation to women and the contemporary far right, highlighting gaps in knowledge and suggesting future directions for research.

Definitions, terms, explanations

Needless to say, there is no universally agreed definition of the far right. The term has been used varyingly to describe extreme groups, fascist groups, populist radical right groups, or 'single-issue' anti-immigrant groups. As Allen (2014: 356) points out 'although "far right" is a convenient umbrella term, the reality is that those who exist within it are rather more disparate, diverse and divergent'. However, despite the different groups incorporated within the use of the term, a number of core ideological principles are shared across the strands, namely a 'nativist' ideology 'which holds that states should be inhabited exclusively by members of the native group ("the nation") and that non-native elements (persons and ideas) are funda-mentally threatening to the nation-state's homogeneity' (Mudde 2007: 19). In this chapter, the term 'far right' will be used interchangeably with the 'radical right' and 'extreme right' to identify groups or movements (Kitschelt 1995; Hainsworth 2000; Ignazi 2000; Roxburgh 2002; Carter 2005) that are rooted in the ideological commitments identified by Mudde (2007).

The term 'gender gap' has been used to characterise the over-representation of men in the far right. Research to date has shown that women are signifi-cantly under-represented across the far-right spectrum, from relatively moderate/liberal radical right parties to the most extreme neo-Nazi groups (Mudde 2014). Although traditionally women have been more likely to vote 'conservatively', the rising level of education and their increasing role in the labour market in addition to the growth of women's rights and improvement in equality legislation and policies strongly linked to feminist movements have gradually brought women closer to left-wing parties (Barisione and Mayer 2013: 3). Consequently, Barisione and Mayer (2013: 3) argue that 'the electoral growth of far-right parties has brought about a third cleavage, women appearing more reluctant to give their votes to these parties'.

Some academics explain this gap with reference to the dominant 'masculine' character of far-right organisations (Kimmel 2007; Treadwell and Garland 2011) while others suggest that the underlying reasons relate to differing levels of religiosity between men and women (Gidengil et al. 2005); differences in anti-immigrant attitudes; and/or women having lower levels of political interest (Fontana et al. 2006). Gidengil et al. (2005) suggest that the fundamental values and beliefs (and how these differ) between men and women are critical factors to explaining the gender gap in support for the far right. Research by Barisione and Mayer (2015) provides further support for this idea. Using the 2014 European Election Studies dataset they analysed gender as a predictor of vote choice for radical-right parties across six European countries: Austria, Belgium, Denmark, France, the Netherlands and Sweden. They found that, while the gender gap persists, once controlled for education, age, religion and occupation, the interaction of gender with political attitudes and left–right ideology significantly affects electoral support for radical right parties in the six cases studied. Thus, the gap does not depend on education, religion or occupation factors but rather differences in political attitudes among women compared to men; women are less likely to agree with the ideological and political stances of radical far-right parties.

What Gidengil et al. (2005) argue is that men's anti-statist views (broadly defined as opposite to the state and state intervention in socio-economic affairs), their greater preoccupation with questions of law and order and their penchant for a get-tough approach all contribute to the gender gap in far-right support. Harteveld et al. (2015) suggest there are two mechanisms that might explain the gender gap: *mediation* (women's attitudes and characteristics differ from men's in ways that explain the populist radical right vote) and *moderation* (women vote for different reasons than men). They conclude that it is a combination of both mechanisms; women do not generally differ from men in their level of nativism, authoritarianism or discontent but their attitudes are less strongly related to the radical-right vote.

Examining this in more detail, Barisione and Mayer (2013) suggest there are four key lines of argument which attempt to explain this gender gap:

- First, men dominate industrial blue collar, manual occupations and have seen a reduction in employment opportunities as they increasingly compete with immigrants for low-skilled jobs and social housing. Men are more likely to be the 'losers of modernity' (Betz, 1994) or 'globalisation losers' (Ford and Goodwin 2010) and are therefore more prone to supporting the far right than women (who tend to occupy jobs in the public sector and have generally held more economically secure positions). Rapid socio-economic changes lead to factual or perceived disintegration in local communities (Goodwin et al. 2013). Men may be more directly impacted by these changes than women and thus more likely to vote for far-right groups.
- The second line of argument suggests that women may be more religious than their male counterparts and the widespread condemnation of anti-immigration messages from the far right by the Christian Churches in particular may be

heard by women as they attend church in higher numbers. However, in the British context, data from the British Social Attitudes surveys in 1983 and 2012 (NatCen 2012) reveals a steep decline in women attending religious services. In 1983, 48.5 per cent of women did not attend services compared to 64 per cent of men but in 2012 that figure had risen to 63.8 per cent of women and 69.5 per cent of men. The gender gap in religious service attendance has thus closed and the vast majority of men, and women, do not attend services. Consequently, the argument that women are less likely to support the far-right because of religious commitments does not hold in Britain. It may, in fact, work the other way: several far-right groups have situated their ideology within Christian morals and values – the British National Party's (BNP) launch of a Christian Council of Britain in 2006, for example, which Woodbridge (2010) recognised as an attempt to appeal to what it regarded as the Christian majority in Britain. More recently, Britain First, who have arguably stepped into the gap left by the disintegration of the BNP and EDL, have specifically situated the movement within Christianity, with their explicit aim to protect British and Christian morality (Allen 2014). Britain First claims that Christianity is integral to Britain, arguing that it forms the foundation of British society and culture (Allen 2014: 357). Britain First have incorporated Christianity into their demonstrations, holding self-titled 'Christian Patrols' through areas in London where they carried crosses and handed out newsletters and information about the organisation. Thus, the far right has in some cases mobilised support from Christians and therefore the suggestion that religion might be a barrier to supporting far-right movements is not necessarily persuasive. Rather, these groups are using religion as a way of legitimising their ideology.

- The third strand of research points to the gradual diffusion of feminist ideas across all levels of society. This, coupled with increasing numbers of young women who are highly educated, may prevent women from supporting far-right movements which reflect traditional patriarchal ideologies and gendered expectations of women. Research has consistently shown that support for the far right goes down as levels of education rise (Goodwin 2013). However, this is true when holding for gender, thus higher levels of education not only reduce female support, but male support as well. Therefore, this argument does not explain lower levels of support among women.

- Finally, socialisation of girls and boys into gendered roles which reflect stereotypes around masculinity (physically strong, aggressive, violent) and femininity (demure, ladylike, non-violent) may explain the lower numbers of women supporting the far right, which is characterised by traditional masculine traits of aggression and violence, particularly groups which have emerged from previous football hooligan movements (Treadwell and Garland 2011). In the British context, 'new' far-right movements like the EDL are deeply rooted in masculine frameworks, in particular 'hegemonic masculinity' (Connell 1987). 'Hegemonic masculinity' is a concept used to describe normative practices that embody the most honoured way of being a man, based on socially constructed

scripts. According to the 'hegemonic masculinity' model, men should be heterosexual, white, dominant, physically and mentally strong – the ultimate
'Alpha male'.

This is illustrated further in a study by Trickett (2014) which examines young
men's membership of gangs which perpetrated hate crimes against Muslims.
Participants in the study drew distinctions between themselves as men and the
'others' who were invading their indigenous territory. Their discourses were based
on masculinity and whiteness which were inherent to their British identity. The
resentment they felt about the socio-economic strains they experienced was redi-
rected onto Muslims who they perceived to be taking their jobs and eroding their
identity. As Trickett (2014: 256) explains, the respondents' resentment about these
strains 'and their enactment of hate crimes as "doing difference" were both partly
as a result of prejudice but also linked to the respondents' reflections on their own
masculine identities'. Similarly, Treadwell and Garland (2011: 632) argue that 'it is
this connection between anger, marginalization, alienation and frustration felt by
so many young men in deprived white working-class communities' that far-right
groups like the EDL can exploit. However, as discussed later in this chapter, the
masculine frameworks of these groups may not be as much of a barrier to women's
involvement as traditionally thought.

Although in some cases the above factors may have some impact on the gender gap, they cannot fully explain the phenomenon (Immerzeel et al. 2015; Félix
2015). Thus, the current understandings of women's under-representation in far-
right movements is not well understood. Unfortunately, there has been a lack of
research examining women's involvement and the existing studies are limited by
small sample sizes and varying methodology.

With the far right's relatively recent embrace of Islamophobia, it is unsurprising
that some research has found that women's motivations for joining or supporting
far-right groups is bound up in this Islamophobia. Both Pettersson (2015) and
Félix (2015) have found that the anti-Muslim rhetoric/narrative internalised by
female members was key in terms of their attraction to far-right groups. In Britain,
anti-immigration and Islamophobia have been dominant tropes in the ideological
discourses and narratives of far-right movements. As Allen (2014: 354) argues,

> the British National Party and English Defence League forged new frontiers
> in British political spaces in relation to anti-Islam, anti-Muslim ideologies.
> Whereas the former sought to do so in formal political arenas, the latter did
> so as a street-level movement. With the subsequent waning of both, Britain
> First has emerged seemingly to fill the political void they left.

Islam is presented as the major threat facing the West (Goodwin 2013). Both the
English Defence League (EDL) and Britain First built their movements around anti-
immigrant and anti-Muslim rhetoric. Britain First states that the 'fightback' against

the rapid growth of Islam in Britain (Islamification) needs to continue and that they alone will be the ones providing the 'frontline resistance' (Allen 2014: 357).

A number of recent high-profile child sexual exploitation (CSE) cases involving gangs of predominantly Asian men have fuelled the narratives of the far-right organisations that have used this to declare their protection and support for (white) British women. As Miah (2015: 55) argues, the racial politics of CSE allows the far right to make an entry point from the 'margins of society to the mainstream on the back of media reporting to publicly defend the victims of "grooming" cases'. Some far-right movements have capitalised on these cases in mobilising support (Cockbain 2013). For example, the then-leader of the BNP Nick Griffin focused heavily on the Asian grooming and paedophile rings in Keighley, claiming this was rooted in Islam and the Muslim culture, citing the Koran as evidence and scaremongering at a party speech delivered in the town in 2004, that these gangs would spread across Britain, for which he subsequently was charged with hate speech offences (Stokes 2006). This discourse was linked to immigration and 'othering' of Muslims, despite the majority of Muslims in Keighley being born in Britain. These scandals were used to support two dominant narratives: that the Asian population was rapidly taking over and that there was a lack of social cohesion – the conclusion of both was the same: the Asian community is a problem that must be tackled (Bunting 2005). More recently, in response a similar Asian paedophile ring scandal in Rotherham, the EDL, made camp outside the police station and held a number of marches and demonstrations, demanding action was taken against the Asian community, and accusing anyone who did not support their campaign as condoning paedophilia, whilst simultaneously remaining mute on the multiple cases involving white men (Anti-Fascist Network 2014).

The EDL also focused heavily on alleged Muslim over-representation in the sexual grooming of these (white) girls (Kassimens et al. 2015). They used this to create a moral panic about Islam and the 'risks' to women. However, the ways in which these risks are perceived by women and men may be different and may impact their motivations for supporting the far right in different ways. Durham (1998: 179) suggests that 'for women on the extreme right, racism is often linked with a feeling of threat', whereas for men 'it can be deeply imbued with dread – and an anticipation – of a life-and-death struggle not only for territory but for the right to possess "our women"'.

Estimating the number of female supporters and members

It has always been difficult to predict the number of female supporters or members of far-right groups, as many do not have formal membership processes and/or they do not publish information about their membership demographics. A small number of studies have examined gender differences in the membership of far-right groups and have generally reported lower numbers of female supporters compared to male. For example, a study by Ford and Goodwin (2010) found that 69 per cent of British National Party supporters were male and 31 per cent were female.

A further analysis of the leaked membership details of BNP members in 2008 showed between 10 and 15 per cent of members were female. According to a second membership leak in 2009, the BNP had 2,034 female members from a total listed membership of 11,811. This equates to around 17 per cent. Busher (2016: 17) observed around 20 per cent of participants at EDL events were women. In a study by Demos (Bartlett and Littler 2011) examining online support for far-right groups, 75 per cent were men. Furthermore, they report that in no country do females make up more than 36 per cent of online supporters. Even when compared against the national demographics of Facebook users in each country, supporters of populist parties and movements (PPAMs) are younger, and more likely to be male. Furthermore, there is some evidence that women are less likely to even be aware of far-right groups. In a study by YouGov (2012) it was reported that only 26 per cent of women were aware of the EDL compared to 40 per cent of men. Meanwhile, the percentage of women who had never heard of the movement (26 per cent) was over two-fold higher than the equivalent figure among men (10 per cent).

Outside of Britain, research reports similar findings. Among voters for two far-right groups, the Norwegian Progress Party and the Danish People's Party (which have been both led by women for the last four and 15 years respectively), about two-thirds are male (Heidar and Pedersen 2006). In France, the Front National won 34 per cent of the male vote compared to 27 per cent of the female vote in recent regional elections in 2015 (although in France, under Marine Le Pen, there has been increasing gender symmetry, see Dubslaff, 2017). In one poll carried out by Insa for the newspaper *Bild* in Germany in January 2016, support for the far-right anti-immigration party Alternative for Germany hit a record high of 13 per cent, which made it the third most popular political party in Germany. The party is said to have the widest gender divide among voters – whilst the majority of supporters were men, 37 per cent were women. In terms of members, 81 per cent are men. Similarly, the far-right party Sweden Democrats won the votes of 10 per cent men and 6 per cent of women according to one exit poll data (Nardelli 2016).

Thus, across the full spectrum of the far-right, from moderate to extreme parties, women are under-represented (Mudde 2014). However, it has been argued that this may be an oversimplification of the facts – whilst women may vote or support such parties in smaller numbers than men, this may reflect lower levels of political engagement more generally (Spierings and Zaslove 2015) which may account for the gender gap in far-right support. As Mayer (2013: 163) points out, 'women are late comers on the electoral scene; they still pay less attention to politics, seen as a man's world, and would be less prone to support outsiders than long established parties'.

Moreover, whilst the gender gap undoubtedly exists, some research has suggested this gap is closing, or is not as big as was once thought. There has been increasing recognition by scholars that the characteristics that may have once put women off far-right movements: neo-Nazi symbolism, racist positions, gender inequality and anti-abortion rhetoric (Blee and Linden 2012), have largely been left behind by many far-right parties who now incorporate gender equality and gay rights platforms 'into an anti-Islam or anti-multiculturalist ideology that extends their potential appeal to women and LGBT communities' (Akkerman and Hagelund 2007: 199). In Britain, examples of this include the dedicated LGBT division within the English Defence League. Furthermore, whilst Britain First do not have such specific divisions, they frequently attempt to mobilise support for the party through propaganda around homophobia and violence against gay people in Islamic communities.

Whilst once such groups were underground, many far-right parties have now become mainstreamed and as such, the stigmatisation associated with supporting such groups which may have acted as a barrier for women's participation has down reduced (Blee and Linden 2012) and the representation of women, more visible including leadership (Pilkington 2016). Furthermore, it has been argued that the 'masculinity' of far-right parties has been over-emphasised and their ideological direction of travel likely to attract more women in the future (Spierings and Zaslove 2015a: 159–160).

Women in the far right – characteristics and roles

> In the past decade a new group of women have been mobilized to the far right who are not losers of the economic situation, but well educated women with jobs, who are looking at far right as an anti-modernist option to the present emancipation policy and rhetoric.
>
> *(Andrea Pető n.d.)*

Consistent across the research is that supporters of the far-right are male, young–middle-aged, working-class with low levels of education and often living in deprived areas and/or those characterised by high levels of immigration (Ford and Goodwin 2010). Blee and Linden (2012: 98) argue that the experience of participation by men and women in the extreme right is highly gendered (Pilkington 2016). Very little is known about the socio-economic characteristics and demographics of women who vote, support or are members of far-right groups, and the research that does exist is based on small samples. Some research has found links between class, poverty and support of the far right (Power 2010). In a study by Arzheimer and Carter (2003) class was not a strong predictor for women voting for right-wing parties, however education was a positive predictor, with women aged under 24 and with a low level of education attainment associated with higher likelihoods of voting, echoing similar previous findings by Mayer (1999). Lubbers and Tolsma (2011) also suggest that anti-immigration attitudes are less frequent among highly educated voters and therefore education is a better predictor of electoral support than traditional variables such as class or religion. However, Blee (2001) challenges the stereotype that female (and male) members are always from troubled or broken families that were racist. In her study of white supremacist skinhead groups in the US, Blee found many of the women active in these movements were from stable homes that were racially tolerant.

In terms of the role of women in far-right movements, there is some research shedding light on their involvement although normally anecdotally, however their involvement has *generally* been overlooked. This is surprising, as women have always held roles in the British far right. The first fascist movement was formed in 1923 by a woman, Rotha Linton-Orman. But since then, the leadership of fascist and far-right organisations has been dominated by men. Indeed, the frameworks of these organisations were built around traditional gender roles and patriarchal frameworks.

Traditionally, the NF and BNP views held that women should be largely confined to domestic life, and bringing up children. In one pamphlet produced by Veronica Ware, the dominant views of the National Front at the time (the 1970s) were outlined. Drawing on the available literature from the party such as the monthly magazine *Spearhead*, the strongest concerns of the time were around fertility, contraception and women's (lack of) reproductive rights. White women were actively encouraged to produce large families and offered financial incentives to do so. A woman's status was thus to be measured by her performance as a mother. Consequently, women are defined by their ability and choice to have children – women who choose not to, are unable to or are lesbians would be seen as failures and not tolerated. The view on abortion was that it should be absolutely illegal, as it was in direct opposition to the NF's ambition to grow the population of white people.

Contemporary far-right groups in Britain continue to retain traditional standpoints on gender, although some have distanced themselves from the extreme viewpoints around gender, specifically women's roles that the NF had, and have sought to develop a softer edge than their predecessors. However, Durham (2015) notes that the BNP continued to cultivate discourses around the 'problems' of feminism and the problems of women having access to abortion, which was held to be a threat to Britain's survival, although the focus on such issues reduced significantly over the last decade, evident particularly in the 2010 manifesto which focused predominantly on immigration and the alleged 'Islamification' of Britain. Similarly, Britain First, though mainly focused on immigration and anti-Islamic discourse, is rooted in the history of its founder, James Dowson, who was a prominent anti-abortion campaigner.

Although largely dominated by men, women have had a role in these movements. The literature on women's activism in the extreme right has generally suggested women, if present at all, are 'the girlfriends or wives of members' performing 'traditional supportive roles' often associated with the 'emotional work' (Duncombe and Jessop 2002) of talking men down from potentially violent exchanges (Pilkington 2016). As Blee (2001) notes, the images of white women found in far-right racist group propaganda (wife, mother, activist) are used to encourage women to join these groups, however women who become active in the movements often find themselves playing roles less important than they were promised.

However, a number of studies have challenged these assumptions. As far back as 1970, Martin Durham reported women in the National Front held roles ranging from administration to stewards and event organisers. This is still the case in contemporary far-right groups. Pilkington's (2016) study on the EDL found women held a range of roles from administration, stewards and speakers or as local/regional organisers. Whilst many of these roles were supportive in nature, this did not make women feel unequal to their male counterparts. When asked whether their minority position in the EDL concerned them, women activists in this study said they felt comfortable, accepted and equal in a male environment and that having men around made them feel safer. However, Pilkington argues that their roles are fundamentally undermined by claims that their participation is motivated by sexual relations with male partners.

A documentary aired on Sky 1 in 2008 presented the views, opinions and experiences of women in the BNP. This documentary followed the lives of women who married into and worked for the BNP, including the party's South-East regional secretary Lynne Mozar, and Marlene Guest, an activist in Rotherham, who described herself as a believer in the Holocaust – 'just not sure about the numbers'. Throughout the documentary, all three women assert their opinions as their own and refute suggestions that their beliefs and roles are purely based on their husbands or partners.

One of the few insights into women in the EDL was through a BBC documentary aired in 2014. The documentary, titled 'EDL Girls: Don't Call Me Racist' followed three women who were involved, to varying degrees, in the EDL: Gail, Amanda and Katie. All three women had become involved in the EDL for different reasons, or had different motivations, yet they shared a number of commonalities: all had experiences of violence, isolation and deprivation. Of particular interest was Gail, who led the women's division of the EDL, the 'EDL Angels' who had experienced physical violence by a number of Asian men which acted as the trigger for her joining the party. The disillusionment with the existing socio-political landscape was also consistent across the three women. This mirrors the work of others, including Treadwell and Garland (2011) who see this broader disillusionment as a key driver in support for the EDL.

It may be assumed that women are less likely to be involved in the violence associated with movements like the EDL, and instead that they may act as pacifiers of male violence. However, there is some evidence of women's violence in online contexts. An analysis by Copsey et al. (2013) of the 'Tell MAMA' (Measuring Anti-Muslim Attacks) project which monitors street-based and online incidents of hate crime against Muslims through self-reporting, revealed women were responsible for 18 per cent (n=78) of online incidents. Copsey et al. (2013: 23) report that 18 of the cases had a link with the EDL. In seven cases the women were allegedly advocating offline violence against Muslims, which included burning Muslims, killing Muslim babies, blowing up mosques and smearing buildings associated with Muslims with dog faeces. A range of religiously offensive comments were also recorded including references to Mohammed as a paedophile and Satan's prophet, Islam being a cult, and insulting remarks about the Koran. Racist comments were mainly anti-Pakistani comments and references to dirt and filth and included comments accusing Muslims of rape, paedophilia, incest, interbreeding, being terrorists and killing Jews.

Theorising women's involvement in the far right: a feminist perspective

Unsurprisingly, the paucity of research examining women's support of, and involvement in, the far right has resulted in an almost total lack of theoretical developments. Research has recently begun to show increasing interest in the role of women in the far right (e.g. Köttig et al. 2017; Meret 2015; Mulinari and Neergaard 2014), yet the topic still remains under-studied and there is a lack of theory underpinning the existing literature.

Explaining the relationship between women and the far right is not straightforward. Durham (1998: 165), writing about women and fascism in Britain, points out that examining the relationship involves more than one question: 'it is concerned not only with the policy that fascism espouses towards women but with what role they play in fascist movements, both as members and as voters'. The dominant theories explaining far-right voting, support and activism are largely based on men's involvement in such groups. As described earlier in this chapter, scholars have made links between masculinity and social class as key indicators or predictors (Treadwell and Garland 2011). Clearly, these theories do not lend themselves well to explaining women's involvement. There have been some attempts to analyse women's involvement from a feminist perspective. However, feminist scholars have had difficulty in reconciling women's involvement in the far right and the fundamental concepts of feminism, specifically patriarchy and agency.

Consequently, the relationship between feminism and right-wing movements has been described as 'vexed' (Bedi 2006: 51). It is perhaps for this reason that there has not been a systematic effort to examine women in the far right from a *feminist* standpoint. However, as Bedi (2006: 52) points out, the rise of these movements is important for feminist theory and activism. The fact that women in these movements have generally been ignored as 'historically significant in both scholarly and popular narratives has made their examination almost an imperative for feminist scholars'. The increasing participation of women in the far-right means that the 'problem' of right-wing women cannot be ignored (Pateman and Gross, 1986 cited in Bedi, 2006).

One of the primary issues feminists have grappled with is the ideological, patriarchal structures of right-wing movements which affirm women's oppression and are centred on gendered norms which place women firmly as homemakers and mothers, lacking agency independent of their fathers or husbands. As Blee and Deutsch (2012: 262) highlight

> extreme right women's relationships to the gender ideologies of the movements to which they belong are often fraught with complexities, in part because of the double standard but also because they often understand themselves as working against the gender inequality within their own parties.

As such, it is difficult to decipher women's participation in right-wing movements as conscious, independent action or choice (Bedi 2006: 54). However, despite notions of agency and choice sitting seemingly in conflict with the ideological underpinnings of far-right movements, some scholars have drawn parallels between feminism and right-wing agendas. As Bedi (2006: 54) argues:

> The position of feminist scholars gets to be doubly contradictory since both feminism and right-wing women's movements are far from monolithic in their forms of organization, their ideological make-up or their methods of agitation. In fact, feminist and right-wing agendas often find themselves uncomfortably close.

Furthermore, the traditional masculine traits of the far right may not serve to preclude women's agency the way it has been assumed. It may be that women join the masculine movement but negotiate their way through and around the dominant constructions of masculinity and femininity within the boundaries of the movement. An example of this could be drawn from Pilkington's (2016) ethnographic analysis of young EDL members which included eight women members. These so-called EDL 'Angels' were active members and supporters of the EDL and challenged the dominant stereotype of the white, working-class angry male, not least by the symbolic appropriation of the label 'Angel'. However, Pilkington argues that rather than this being seen as the feminisation and virtuousness of the female members, the term was not symbolic of an angelic figure but rather was demonstrated through attaching angel wings to the EDL logo. Pilkington thus argues that within the EDL space, angel does not connote conservative femininity.

However, in relation to women's involvement, theories of why the numbers of women remain so low compared to men remain underdeveloped. Juris (2008) suggests one explanation may be that women are excluded from the 'affective solidarity' developed during activism with predominantly male members. Because women often enter the movements through their male partners or friends, they may not develop strong ties with the organisation (Blee and Linden 2012).

Ultimately, little is known about women in the far right and, consequently, there have been few attempts to theorise women's involvement. However, as Durham (1998: 182) argued, we can no longer believe that the extreme right is 'to be seen as by definition a masculine movement pursuing a misogynist agenda'. Whilst it may often show these characteristics, it is 'capable of winning over significant numbers of women and being influenced by both electoral imperatives and internal dissent to take positions that are incompatible with our usual understanding'.

Conclusion and future research directions

Despite increasing research and policy attention in far-right groups and activism, women supporters are under-researched. It has long been stated that there is a gender gap in relation to the far right, as the majority of members are male and women are less likely to vote for radical right parties than men. However, other research suggests this gap is closing, or may not be as big as originally thought. As Pilkington (2016) pointed out, whilst there are significant obstacles to women's participation in the far right, including childcare and other family responsibilities, this does not necessarily thwart ambition nor isolation within the movement.

Although the existing research remains limited, this chapter has demonstrated that while men remain numerically dominant in support and activism in the far right, these groups are no longer closed to women and the traditional ideologies of the far right are shifting. The existing research documents women in a range of roles within far-right movements, ranging from supportive roles through to leadership. Their motivations for joining remain under-researched, however the existing literature suggests the strong anti-Islam rhetoric of most of the 'new' far right is a dominant factor.

There remains a lack of theoretical contributions to understanding women in the far right, despite the phenomenon being an important issue for feminist scholars. This may in part be down to the difficulties feminists have in reconciling the key principles of feminism with women's involvement in inherently patriarchal frameworks. However, whilst two of the core tenets of feminism – equality and agency – may seem at odds with the far right, important insights by some feminist scholars highlight the ways in which feminism and the far right make (un)comfortable bedfellows.

As far-right groups actively reach out to recruit women, it is increasingly important to examine the gender-specific appeals that draw women to, and maintain their interest in, these movements (Blee 2001). There is a need for research across the West which actively engages female members of the far right in order to understand their histories, motivations for joining and methods of recruitment, their roles within these organisations, how gender and feminism is constructed within the boundaries of individual groups and wider far-right frameworks and the extent to which feminist theory can assist with understanding women in the far right.

Future research should include men and women, girls and boys in their samples in order to develop an evidence base from which to inform policy and practice. Moreover, given the dearth of research on women's involvement, studies which specifically address women's motivations for joining, their trajectories and roles, are needed. In addition to feminist perspectives, there is a need for scholars to examine the usefulness of other theories in explaining women's involvement and develop new theoretical explanations based on empirical research.

References

Akkerman, T. and Hagelund, A. (2007) '"Women and children first!" Anti-immigration parties and gender in Norway and the Netherlands', *Patterns of Prejudice*, 41(2), 197–214.

Allen, C. (2014) 'Britain First: The "frontline resistance" to the Islamification of Britain', *Political Quarterly*, 85(3), 354–361.

Anti-Fascist Network (2014) 'Anti-Fascist Network statement on the far-right and the Rotherham scandal'. *Anti-Fascist Network*, 13 September 2014. Available from: https://antifascistnetwork.org/2014/09/13/anti-fascist-network-statement-on-the-far-right-and-the-rotherham-scandal/ (accessed 20 June 2017).

Arzheimer, K. and Carter, E. (2003) *Explaining Variation in the Extreme Right Vote: The Individual and the Political Environment*, Staffordshire: Keele University. Available from: www.keele.ac.uk/media/keeleuniversity/group/kepru/KEPRU%20WP%2019.pdf (accessed 20 June 2017).

Bacchetta, P. and Power, M. (2002) *Right-wing Women: From Conservatives to Extremists Around the World*, edited by Paola Bacchetta and Margaret Power. London: Routledge.

Barisione, M. and Mayer, N. (2013) 'The transformation of the Radical Right Gender Gap: The case of the 2014 EP Election'. Available from: https://spire.sciencespo.fr/hdl:/2441/vartr994d8sk8l005sgt63hpo/resources/barisione-amp-mayer-2015-the-transformation-of-the-radical-right-gender-gap-1.pdf (accessed 20 June 2017).

Bartlett, J. and Littler, M. (2011) *Inside the EDL – Populist Politics in a Digital Age*. London: Demos.

Bedi, T. (2006) 'Feminist theory and the right-wing: Shiv Sena women mobilize Mumbai', *Journal of International Women's Studies*, 7(4), 51–68.

Betz, H. G. (1994) *Radical Right-Wing Populism in Western Europe*. London: Springer.

Blee, K. (2001) *Inside Organized Racism: Women in the Hate Movement*. Berkeley and Los Angeles, CA: University of California Press.

Blee, K. M. and Deutsch, S. M. (2012) *Women of the Right: Comparisons and Interplay Across Borders*. University Park, PA: Pennsylvania State University Press.

Blee, K. M. and Linden, A. (2012) 'Women in extreme right parties and movements', in Blee, K. and Deutsch, S. (eds) *Women of the Right: Comparisons and Interplay Across Borders*. University Park, PA: Penn State University Press, pp. 98–114.

Bunting, M. (2005) 'Blame it on the Asians'. *The Guardian*, 14 February 2005. Available from: www.theguardian.com/politics/2005/feb/14/immigration.immigrationandpublicservices (accessed 20 June 2017).

Busher, J. (2016) *The Making of Anti-Muslim Protest: Grassroots Activism in the English Defence League*. Oxon: Routledge.

Carter, E. (2005) *The Extreme Right in Western Europe: Success or Failure?* Manchester: Manchester University Press.

Cockbain, E. (2013) 'Grooming and the "Asian sex gang predator": The construction of a racial crime threat', *Race & Class*, 54(4), 22–32.

Connell, R. W. (1987) *Gender and Power*. Oxford: Polity Press.

Copsey, N., Dack, J. and Feldman, M. (2013) *Anti-Muslim Hate Crime and the Far Right*. Available from: http://faith-matters.org/images/stories/antimuslim2.pdf (accessed 20 June 2017).

Dauber, A. S. (2017) 'The increasing visibility of right-wing extremist women in contemporary Europe: Is Great Britain an exception?', in Köttig, M., Bitzan, R. and Petö, A. (eds) *Gender and Far Right Politics in Europe*. Cham, Switzerland: Springer Nature Palgrave Macmillan.

Dubslaff, V. (2017) 'Women on the fast track: Gender issues in the National Democratic Party of Germany and the French National Front (1980s–2012)', in Köttig, M., Bitzan, R. and Petö, A. (eds) *Gender and Far Right Politics in Europe*. Cham, Switzerland: Springer Nature Palgrave Macmillan.

Duncombe, J. and Jessop, J. (2002) '"Doing rapport" and the ethics of "faking friendship"', in Mauthner, M. (ed.) *Ethics in Qualitative Research*. London: Sage.

Durham, M. (1998) *Women and Fascism*. London: Routledge.

Durham, M. (2015) 'Securing the future of our race: Women in the culture of the modern-day BNP', in Copsey, N. and Richardson, J. E. (eds) *Cultures of Post-War British Fascism*. Oxon: Routledge.

Félix, A. (2015) 'The other side of the coin: Women's participation in far right parties and movements in Greece and Hungary', *East European Journal of Society and Politics*, 1(1), 166–182.

Fontana, M., Sidler, A. and Hardmeier, S. (2006) 'The "new right" vote: An analysis of the gender gap in the vote choice for SVP', *Swiss Political Science Review*, 12(4), 243–271.

Ford, R. and Goodwin, M. J. (2010) 'Angry white men: Individual and contextual predictors of support for the British National Party', *Political Studies*, 58(1), 1–25.

Gidengil, E., Hennigar, M., Blais, A. and Nevitte, N. (2005) 'Explaining the gender gap in support for the new right: The case of Canada', *Comparative Political Studies*, 38(10), 1171–1195.

Goodwin, M. (2013) 'The roots of extremism: The English Defence League and the Counter-Jihad Challenge'. Available from: www.chathamhouse.org/sites/files/chatham-house/public/Research/Europe/0313bp_goodwin.pdf (accessed 20 June 2017).

Goodwin, M., Ford, R. and Cutts, D. (2013) 'Extreme right foot soldiers, legacy effects and deprivation: A contextual analysis of the leaked British National Party (BNP) member-ship list', *Party Politics*, 19(6), 887–906.

Gottlieb, J. (2003) *Feminine Fascism: Women in Britain's Fascist Movement, 1923–45*. London: I.B. Tauris.

Hainsworth, P. (ed.) (2000) *The Politics of the Extreme Right: From the Margins to the Mainstream*. London: Pinter Publishers.

Harteveld, E., Van Der Brug, W., Dahlberg, S. and Kokkonen, A. (2015) 'The gender gap in populist radical-right voting: Examining the demand side in Western and Eastern Europe', *Patterns of Prejudice*, 49(1–2), 103–134.

Heidar, K. and Pedersen, K. (2006) 'Party feminism: Gender gaps within Nordic political parties', *Scandinavian Political Studies*, 29(3), 192–218.

Ignazi, P. (2000) *Extreme Right Parties in Western Europe*. Oxford: Oxford University Press.

Immerzeel, T., Lubbers, M. and Coffé, H. (2015) 'Competing with the radical right: Distances between the European radical right and other parties on typical radical right issues', *Party Politics*, 22(6), 823–834.

Juris, J. (2008) 'Performing politics: Image, embodiment, and affective solidarity during anti-corporate globalization protests', *Ethnography*, 9(1), 61–97.

Kassimeris, G. and Jackson, L. (2015) 'The ideology and discourse of the English Defence League: "Not racist, not violent, just no longer silent"', *The British Journal of Politics and International Relations*, 17(1), 171–188.

Kimmel, M. (2007) 'Racism as adolescent male rite of passage: Ex-Nazis in Scandinavia', *Journal of Contemporary Ethnography*, 36(2), 202–218.

Kitschelt, H. (1995) *The Radical Right in Western Europe: A Comparative Analysis*. Ann Arbor, MI: University of Michigan Press.

Köttig, M., Bitzan, R. and Petö, A. (eds) (2017) *Gender and Far Right Politics in Europe*. Cham, Switzerland: Springer Nature Palgrave Macmillan.

Lubbers, M. and Tolsma, J. (2011) Education's impact on explanations of radical right-wing voting. Available from: https://cream.conference-services.net/resources/952/2371/pdf/MECSC2011_0218_paper.pdf (accessed 20 June 2017).

Mayer, N. (2013) 'From Jean-Marie to Marine Le Pen: Electoral change on the far right', *Parliamentary Affairs*, 66(1), 160–178.

Meret, S. (2015) 'Charismatic female leadership and gender: Pia Kjærsgaard and the Danish People's Party', *Patterns of Prejudice*, 49(1–2), 81–102.

Miah, S. (2015) 'The groomers and the question of race', *Identity Papers: A Journal of British and Irish Studies*, 1(1), pp. 54–66.

Mudde, C. (2007) *Populist Radical Right Parties in Europe*. Cambridge: Cambridge University Press.

Mudde, C. (2014) 'Introduction. Youth and the extreme right: explanations, issues, and solutions', in Mudde, C. (ed.) *Youth and the Extreme Right*. New York, London and Amsterdam: IDebate Press.

Mulinari, D. and Neergaard, A. (2014) 'We are Sweden Democrats because we care for others: Exploring racisms in the Swedish extreme right', *European Journal of Women's Studies*, 21(1), 43–56.

Nardelli, A. (2016) 'Rightwing parties are on the rise – but they won't win power without women, *The Guardian*. Available from: www.theguardian.com/news/datablog/2016/jan/26/rightwing-parties-are-on-the-rise-but-they-wont-win-power-without-women (accessed 20 June 2017).

NatCen (2012) British Social Attitudes 29. London: NatCen. Available from: www.bsa.natcen.ac.uk/latest-report/british-social-attitudes-29/key-findings/introduction.aspx (accessed 20 June 2017).

Petö, A. (n.d.) Far right mobilization and gender. Available from: http://eurogender.eige.europa.eu/sites/default/files/EWC%20Statement_peto_2%20(2).pdf (accessed 20 June 2017).

Pettersson, K. (2015) 'Ideological dilemmas of female populist radical right politicians', *European Journal of Women's Studies*, 24(1), 7–22.

Pilkington, H. (2016) *Loud and Proud: Passion and Politics in the English Defence League*. Manchester: Manchester University Press.

Power, M. (2010) *Right-wing Women in Chile: Feminine Power and the Struggle Against Allende, 1964–1973*. Pennsylvania, PA: Pennsylvania State Press.

Roxburgh, A. (2002) *Preachers of Hate: The Rise of the Far Right*. London: Gibson Square Books.

Social and Community Planning Research (1983) British Social Attitudes Survey [data collection]. UK Data Service. SN: 1935, http://dx.doi.org/10.5255/UKDA-SN-1935-1 (accessed 20 June 2017).

Spierings, N. and Zaslove, A. (2015) 'Gendering the vote for populist radical-right parties', *Patterns of Prejudice*, 49(1–2), 135–162.

Stokes, P. (2006) 'White society is now a hell-hole, said BNP boss on race charges'. *The Telegraph*, 18 January 2006. Available from: www.telegraph.co.uk/news/uknews/1508079/White-society-is-now-a-hell-hole-said-BNP-boss-on-race-charges.html (accessed 20 June 2017).

Treadwell, J. and Garland, J. (2011) 'Masculinity, marginalization and violence: A case study of the English Defence League', *British Journal of Criminology*, 51(4), 621–634.

Trickett, L. (2014) 'Reflections on gendered masculine identities in targeted violence against ethnic minorities', in Hall, N., Corb, A., Giannasi, P. and Grieve, J. (eds) *The Routledge International Handbook of Hate Crime*. Abingdon: Routledge.

Woodbridge, S. (2010) 'Christian credentials? The role of religion in British National Party ideology', *Journal for the Study of Radicalism*, 4(1), 25–54.

YouGov (2012) Views on the English Defence League. Available from: https://yougov.co.uk/news/2012/10/08/views-english-defence-league/ (accessed 20 June 2017).

10

'THERE'S A VITAL LESSON HERE. LET'S MAKE SURE WE LEARN IT'

Transnational mobilisation and the impact of Greece's Golden Dawn upon extreme right-wing activism in Britain

Graham Macklin

Introduction

The sudden, shocking and spectacular rise to prominence of the Greek neo-Nazi group Chrysi Avgi (GD – Golden Dawn) after it won 21 seats – 6.97 per cent of the vote – in Greece's May 2012 elections has inspired extreme-right militants across Europe. Its political ascent was viewed with a mixture of admiration and awe. Following three decades languishing at the margins of Greek politics, GD, an overtly national socialist party with a paramilitary structure, directed in accordance with the *Führerprinzip*, which exhibited an 'exuberant anti-Semitism', and whose activists committed racist 'pogroms' against immigrants whilst also violently attacking political opponents, had been propelled into the Greek Parliament by a profound and multifaceted economic crisis (see Psarras 2013 and Vasilopoulou & Halikiopoulou 2015 for overviews).

In Britain, extreme right-wing activists were similarly enthused and enthralled by the rise of GD. They were inspired by its uncompromising 'model' but also by the 'persecution' of the party that followed: the GD leadership was arrested in 2013 and put on trial by the Greek government following a politically motivated murder of an opponent which, in turn, led to the 'martyrdom' of two GD activists, murdered in response by left-wing militants. This chapter offers the first detailed exploration of the interactive diffusion of ideas and strategies that has taken place between GD and the British National Party (BNP), Britain's largest extreme right-wing party until its collapse in the aftermath of the 2010 general election. It explores and contextualises the impact that GD had upon the ideological (re)radicalisation of the BNP as well as elaborating upon the national and international constraints that both facilitated and inhibited its shift towards increased political militancy.

Golden Dawn – a short overview

Formed in 1980, though not formally established until 1985, GD was marginal to Greek politics for much of its existence. In June 2009, shortly before the nation's credit rating was downgraded, GD won a mere 19,624 votes (0.29 per cent) and had no parliamentary representation. Its breakthrough, tied to the perilous state of the Greek economy, came shortly afterwards when the Greek government agreed a second bailout from the EU and IMF in February 2012. In May that year the party polled 440,966 votes (6.97 per cent), winning 21 seats in the Greek parliament, a total that was cut to 18 in re-run elections in June. GD subsequently polled 536,910 votes (9.39 per cent) in the European elections – gaining three seats in the European Parliament – and came third during the 2015 elections with 388,447 votes (6.3 per cent), gaining 17 seats despite many of its candidates, including its leader, still being behind bars.

Academic research exploring the party's meteoric rise has, to date, focused upon its history and immediate antecedents (Bistis 2013; Ellinas 2013); the socio-demographic profile of its supporters (Georgiadou 2013; Halikiopoulou and Vasilopoulou 2013); youth support (Koronaiou et al. 2015); the place of women in its ideology (Koronaiou and Sakellariou 2017); how GD has organised at a local, community-based level (Koronaiou and Sakellariou 2013); and the semiotic space in which its xenophobic politics operates (Dalakoglou 2013); around which, other studies argue, exists an entrenched 'national consensus' wherein xenophobic populism in Greece represents a 'mainstream ideology' (Doxiadis and Matsaganis 2013). Less developed is scholarship exploring the impact that GD had at an international level (Psarras 2013: 28–32 and Tipaldou 2015 are notable exceptions). Rather than focusing directly on GD, however, this chapter seeks instead to investigate its influence upon the broader arc of right-wing extremism in Europe, through a detailed case study of its effects upon British militants. Extreme right-wing ideas are often simultaneously diffused and re-contextualised in two distinct and dynamic ways: through 'impersonal' and 'interpersonal' channels, the former facilitating cultural and ideological emulation and the latter, strategic learning (Van Hauwaert and Perrineau 2013). The chapter examines these dual diffusion mechanisms by exploring GD's transnational impact in a country well beyond its immediate Mediterranean environs.

GD has consciously sought to spread its own influence and to 'create cells in every corner of the world' (Smith 2013). Though its actions have not lived up to the hyperbole, nevertheless activists within Greek diaspora communities in Astoria, New York; Melbourne, Australia; Montreal, Canada; and Nuremberg, Germany, have indeed established such 'cells'. To date there has been little academic investigation of these forms of inter-ethnic organising except for an examination of the party's links with, and influence upon, its Mediterranean counterparts in Cyprus, through which GD hopes to 'restore' the territories of the Byzantium Empire to Greece (Katsourides 2013).

Organisational outreach aside, GD's ideology has also been diffused indirectly through the extreme rights' own counter-cultural networks. Groups like Blood and

Honour, the international neo-Nazi music network, sell GD banners and symbols whilst also offering downloadable copies of the openly Nazi Greek-language magazine, *Omerta: Terror Machine*.[1] Music represents a powerful vector through which the cultural transfer of GD's message to the international audience is effected. Bands aligned with, or supportive of, the party, perform in Europe, including Der Stürmer, a Greek national socialist black metal band who performed in London in June 2013 with support from British bands March or Die and Whitelaw (Sadurni 2013a).[2]

For extreme right-wing activists outside of the Greek diaspora, GD has served an exemplary role. Groups of militants have adopted the name 'Golden Dawn' as a means of aligning themselves with its achievements. Mimetic movements sprang up in Trieste, Italy, where a former member of Forza Nuova, a party with close links to GD, formed 'Alba Dorata' (Pasqua 2012); in Spain where former activists from the Alianza Nacional in Valencia registered 'Amanecer Dorado' as a political party (Olivepress.es 2014); and in Hungary where activists from the Jobbik Magyarországért Mozgalom (Jobbik, Movement for a Better Hungary), who viewed their own party as having gone 'soft', formed Magyar Hajnal (Hungarian Dawn), the more virulent politics of GD serving as their new muse.[3]

Murder and martyrdom

To understand how GD emerged as an exemplar within 'impersonal' extreme-right counter-cultural networks, and how this process of cultural diffusion accelerated, one should begin at the end, or rather the end as the Greek government envisaged it at the time. On 18 September 2013, shortly after GD reached a new high in opinion polls, one of its supporters, Giorgos Roupakias, stabbed to death a left-wing musician, Pavlos Fyssas, in the western Athens district of Keratsini. This incident quickly engulfed the GD's upper echelons. Its leader, Nikolaos Michaloliakos, and five GD parliamentarians were arrested and charged with a range of offences including assault, money laundering and belonging to a 'criminal organisation'. Others were subsequently taken into custody. The following week the Greek parliament voted to suspend state subsidies to the party. GD shed roughly a third of its support, according to one opinion poll, in the aftermath of this crackdown.[4]

The arrest of GD's leadership led to an outpouring of support for the party from extreme right-wing groups across Europe who typically sent letters of protest to, or demonstrated outside, their local Greek Embassies in solidarity or, in the case of numerous football 'ultras', unfurled banners of support at football matches (Tipaldou 2015: 208).[5] Shortly afterwards, on 2 November, two GD activists, Manos Kapelonis and Giorgos Fountoulis, were shot dead outside the party's offices in Athens in retaliation for Fyssas's murder. A third man, Alexandros Gerontas, was severely injured. Greece is a country with a long history of left-wing terrorism (Kassimeris 2013) and, shortly afterwards, the 'Fighting Popular Revolutionary Forces' – a previously unknown 'urban guerrilla' group – claimed responsibility for the killings.[6] Opinion polls conducted in the aftermath recorded a surge in support for the GD, rising from 6.6 to 8.8 per cent in the polls, though this was still below the 10.8 per cent it had enjoyed in June before the Greek government moved against it.[7]

GD staged a candlelight vigil and a protest march for their two slain activists in Athens. Internationally, the killings spurred a second 'wave' of extreme-right protests. In Italy, Forza Nuova activists held a silent torchlight parade in Milan[8] whilst Casa Pound activists demonstrated outside the Greek consulate in Firenze.[9] In Dortmund, Germany the (banned) Nationaler Widerstand Dortmund (NWDO – National Resistance Dortmund) staged a small, silent ceremony outside the town's station.[10] In Stockholm, Sweden, however, a march organised by Svenska Motståndsrörelsen (SMR – Nordic Resistance Movement) ended in violent clashes with police and anti-fascists.[11] In the United States GD activists demonstrated outside the Greek consulate in New York[12] and in the antipodes, the Australia First Party, which had welcomed the arrival of a GD franchise in Melbourne, demonstrated outside the Greek consulate in Sydney in December 2013 to protest the continued imprisonment of GD MPs.[13]

Such demonstrations drew attention to the party's plight and the supposed perfidy of the Greek state but were also indicative of the fact that extreme right-wing groups, despite their ineliminable 'nationalist' core, envisage themselves as part of a broader 'international' community of interest. For such organisations, these events provide the necessary 'emotional energy' which their activists depend upon to galvanise themselves to survive as 'activists' (Collins 2004). Though, at first glance, these actions may appear isolated, disparate or indeed futile gestures of solidarity, in fact they constitute a fluid, multilayered process through which geographically dispersed extreme right-wing activists forge collective identities at an international level. Whilst their actions are not co-ordinated *per se*, this 'joint political action' provides an important mechanism for the transmission of experiences, strategies and ideologies. Such emotional and physical acts of solidarity, together with the provision of logistical support, material or financial, are often crucial for the 'emergence, maintenance and dynamic' of political movements at a local, national and even transnational level (Virchow 2013: 196–213).

The commemoration and memorialisation that followed in the wake of the killing of Kapelonis and Fountoulis reflected a central component of the extreme-right 'action repertoire' of which the Nazis' beatification of Horst Wessel as a 'martyr' (Siemens 2013) is the most famous historical example, though contemporary examples would include the veneration of figures like Rudolf Hess (Shaffer 2014) or Ian Stuart Donaldson, singer of the 'white power' band Skrewdriver. These ritualised actions, which are not of course unique to the extreme right, help forge a 'collective identity moment' wherein past mobilisations are rearticulated and repopulated with new issues and perspectives, providing for the revitalisation of activist identities (Dufour and Giraud 2007).

One way groups sympathetic to GD sought to achieve this 'moment' was through the circulation of CCTV footage of the killings across various social media platforms. Blood and Honour uploaded it to their website with a statement proclaiming Fountoulis and Kapelonis 'martyrs' 'shot dead by [a] Greek government death squad' alongside the motto: 'where the Warrior falls a hundred will rise!'[14] The purpose of circulating these gruesome images was to generate 'moral shock' and the sort of 'outrage' that galvanises activists to action because of such a 'trigger'. Equally importantly, such imagery can serve to facilitate the recruitment into such groups of individuals, 'with or without the network of personal contacts emphasised in mobilisation and process theories'. Organisers work hard to generate and harness the 'emotional energy' released by such events, channelling it into 'righteous indignation' or collective political activity (Jasper 1997: 106–107).[15]

Whilst social movements are unlikely to seriously diverge from established movement cultures, or adopt behaviours and tactics that undermine its collective identity (Meyer 2004: 167–197), the use of such imagery helps 'frame' conflicts. In doing so it can also intensify the beliefs and emotions of those already politically engaged to the extent that they can 'break' these frames, prompting more radical forms of mobilisation. The use of 'grotesque' images as a recruiting tool for the uninitiated is a double-edged sword, however. Whilst some will be motivated by the 'moral shock' of viewing them, others will turn away or see those activists employing them as prurient or manipulative (Halfman and Young 2010: 1–24). The complexity of such responses is captured in the divergent reaction of the two families themselves; the father of Giorgos Fountoulis (subsequently elected to the European Parliament for GD in May 2014) has sacralised his son's death and believes 'we have a sacred obligation to continue'[16] whilst the parents of Manos Kapelonis took the party to court to stop it using their sons' image in its propaganda (Uladh 2014).

Solidarity with Golden Dawn in Britain

In Britain, numerous groups expressed solidarity with GD. Members of the minuscule national socialist British Movement, which had a long history of networking with GD, staged a candlelight vigil for the two murdered activists on 7 November 2013 outside the BBC headquarters in Leeds.[17] More prominently, the New British Union (NBU) mobilised activists from several organisations for a demonstration outside the Greek Embassy in London two days later. The demonstration had originally been called to protest the 'outrage' of the arrest of GD's leadership but, in the intervening period in which its two activists were murdered, the protest was reorientated to reflect this development. Having marched to their destination, the small group were addressed by veteran extreme right-wing activist Peter Rushton who placed the killing of these 'martyrs' into a broader international context for his audience, one in which 'a battle for truth, a battle for identity' was being waged, not just by GD, but by all of them, warning that their opponents sought to silence that 'truth' and 'destroy that identity', the 'ultimate solution' being, he argued, the murder of its activists.[18]

This inclusive, grievance narrative, which encouraged participants to identify with the 'persecution' of GD and other activists being 'silenced' (in particular holocaust 'revisionists') also pointed to the rise of GD who 'in so many ways, have been a sign of hope for us' as giving succour to their own isolated and localised activism.

'Yes we hail the GD as a dawn for us,' proclaimed Rushton, 'as a dawn for all Europeans in their efforts to maintain their identity, in their efforts to maintain their freedom.' Identification was deepened through a ritualised minute's silence for the 'martyrs' during which those present were asked to 'reflect upon our own commitment to our people' and to strive for a 'true democracy' which recognises that 'we do exist as a [white] people'. Grievance, combined in narratives of persecution and martyrdom, was being used as an integrative mechanism to foster a common identity amongst activists, compounded through the speech's defiant climax in which Rushton asserted,

> despite all the efforts of the corrupt academics and media, political establishment, we assert our existence as a people; we assert our identity; we assert our right to be Europeans in Europe … we are with you, brother and sister Europeans, we will stand by you, we will support your fight for Europe. And we will win!'[19]

Identification with GD in the wake of the demonstration was further reflected in the formation of 'New Dawn' which, though it barely existed beyond the Internet, represented a further symbolic act of solidarity with GD inspired by a belief in the common struggle (Sadurni 2013b).

The increasingly complex transnational nature of such activism was mirrored in the actions of Narodowe Odrodzenie Polski (NOP – National Rebirth of Poland), the Polish extreme right-wing group, whose British section was then led by Michał Lewandowski. British-based NOP activists have organised several activities aimed at highlighting the plight of 'our comrades' in GD, including a picket of the Greek Embassy in London on 6 October, a month before the NBU demonstration.[20] The previous day its activists had joined a BNP demonstration against 'illegal, non-European immigration' in an effort 'to help the BNP overcome mainstream media's manipulations which constantly portray this British party as being supposedly "anti-Polish"'.[21] Continuing their activism in support of GD, on 16 October, the same group, carrying NOP and GD banners, handed out bilingual flyers, written in English and Polish, in support of the party in Norwich, Norfolk.[22] Other NOP activists have taken part in GD rallies in Athens.[23]

Though there have been several subsequent demonstrations outside the Greek Embassy in London such actions have, so far, failed to produce the sort of annual set-piece events that occurred in Salem in Sweden, Wunseidel in Germany or Budapest in Hungary – regular fixtures in the extreme right-wing 'demonstration calendar'. Small demonstrations, like that of the NBU, remain important, however. Regardless of whether they are a 'one-off' – in terms of their thematic content – such activities play an equally important role in the mobilising, socialising and integrating of extreme right-wing militants into the 'life' of the movement. They provide a means through which participants imbibe the cultural and political symbols, myths and narratives of the group, internalising the parameters of its collective identity as they do so.

Identities are not constructed in isolation as a matter of ideological self-assessment by activists; they are 'a fluid contingent social process' forged 'in action' and common 'struggle' (Caiani et al. 2012: 103–132). 'Only in action does it become clear who belongs', to such a community, observes Virchow (2013: 200). Public, outwardly expressive demonstrations of solidarity, such as those in support for GD, serve to connect seemingly isolated pockets of local activists to broader, internationalised collective identities, which interact with, and often come to underpin, their own. This interconnection between the micro and macro level, through which local and transnational spheres of activism mutually reinforce one another, is especially evident when one examines the response of the BNP to the travails of GD.

The BNP and Golden Dawn

The NBU demonstration testified to the increased fragmentation of Britain's extreme right-wing milieu. But it also highlighted that despite the increasing miasma of different groups available to activists, the right-extremist 'scene' retains a certain coherence capable of energising activists from disparate groups for joint political action around a 'worthy' cause. In this instance, the suppression of GD and the subsequent killing of two of its activists provided that 'cause' and was used to build and to reinforce this 'community' of activists. 'You killed the men *not* the idea', stated one extreme-right blog.[24]

Nick Griffin, BNP chairman between 1999 and 2014, denied any connection with the NBU, denouncing it as 'a pathetic fancy dress club of pro-Zionist fascist cranks.'[25] Griffin's disdain had nothing to do with its stance on GD, however. Indeed, prominent amongst the NBU demonstrators were several London BNP activists including Kevin Layzell, a leading member of the party's youth wing who marched to the Greek Embassy with the NBU carrying a GD flag.[26] Layzell subsequently addressed a BNP meeting surrounded by Union flags and GD flags, footage of which was uploaded to the main party website, thus tacitly endorsing his message. 'I am standing with the Golden Dawn flag in the back ground', Layzell told his audience after a two-minute silence for its two murdered activists (and other victims of 'white genocide'), 'because the nationalist battle is bigger than us, bigger than our borders, all of Europe is at war and we must stand with our Brothers if we stand any chance of succeeding.'[27]

Though 'impersonal' party networks and media channels helped to diffuse certain tropes about GD, BNP support for their Greek counterparts was dictated by core, racial ideological concerns. The Greeks 'are white Europeans just like us' a BNP fundraising e-mail stated though 'Turks, Kosovans, Albanians and Roma are definitely not'.[28] The BNP also used its own social media platforms to propagate the importance and influence of GD to its own cadres and beyond. It had eulogised GD's electoral advance, reporting of its popularity in opinion polls (which, it claimed, 'the Zionist slaves don't want to see and try to fight') that: 'The Social Nationalist Movement' in Greece 'has set sail to eliminate the local and international usurers with support from every Greek!!'[29]

Perpetuating the grievance narrative, the BNP continually claimed that 'controlled media' (i.e. the Jews) unfairly maligned GD, which had 'even overtaken the BNP in the dehumanisation stakes.' Thus the BNP reproduced a lengthy article taken from GD's English language website that gave readers the 'truth' about the party.[30] Its website also provided supporters with inspiring accounts of GD activities and marches, including the IMIA march in February 2013, an annual event staged in Athens that attracts extreme right-wing activists from across Europe to commemorate the 'immortals', as they are venerated in party literature: three Greek soldiers who died during a clash with Turkey in 1996 over the disputed sovereignty of the islet of Imia (Kardak for Turkey) in the Aegean Sea, 'a result of Greek government treason', according to GD.[31] The BNP publicised the spectacle not simply to inspire its own activists but also to assist GD in 'spreading the flames of the Social Nationalist Revolution.'[32]

It is important to recognise that BNP support for the overtly neo-Nazi GD was also a matter of timing and context. When the BNP was in the ascendant open support for GD would have been unthinkable. Indeed, this had been the case until comparatively recently. During the 2009 European elections the BNP had polled 943, 598 votes (6.2 per cent), gaining two seats in the European Parliament, including one for party chairman Nick Griffin. In the general election the following year 338 BNP candidates polled a total of 564,331 votes (1.2 per cent). Despite increasing its share of the vote the party failed to win a seat and, moreover, during local elections held the same day it lost every single council seat in its east London stronghold of Barking and Dagenham. Recrimination and intrigue followed, tearing the party apart. Five years later, during the 2015 general election, 8 BNP candidates polled a mere 1,667 votes, thereby confirming its descent into electoral oblivion and political irrelevancy.

Now, with its electoral strategy in ruins, the party's leadership wrestled with the reality of how to re-energise a fractured and demoralised membership. Eulogising GD's success provided ideological sustenance and, equally importantly, inspiration for renewed action. 'We can write, intellectualise, and philosophise forever and a day', argued one BNP activist,

> but political action and inventive real life schemes are our only hope now. Golden Dawn activists in Greece have shown us how it can happen. Let us put all our hands to the mast, and guide our nation back from disaster, and into our own Golden Dawn … Right here, starting with Britain and the British now.[33]

The same BNP activist called for his party to go 'back-to-basics' and to emulate what their Greek counterparts were doing but 'with added value'.[34] To enthuse its activists, the BNP website began highlighting GD's own multi-media efforts, linking to video clips of their activism, websites and podcasts all of which, they asserted, are 'helping to break the controlled media's Iron Curtain of Lies over events in Greece'.[35]

The BNP advertised GD activism to enthuse its own activists, offering them opportunities for emulation, though again context is key. GD is notable not simply for the violence deployed against immigrants and political opponents but also for its 'Greek-only' community organising initiatives, including the distribution of food to economically disadvantaged Greeks, the opening of a blood bank and other health services, and an employment agency. Such activities were combined with less attributable, though equally important actions, aimed at 'protecting' Greeks from immigrants. This included evicting 'undesirables' from overcrowded Greek-owned tenements which, true or not, when taken together with other 'urban myths' about the organisation's activities, functioned to build the party's profile, increased its electoral support and allowed it to implant itself in certain communities (Koronaiou and Sakellariou 2013). GD also sought to internationalise this 'local' paradigm. Australian GD activists tried to leverage the country's émigré community as a source of funds though an unregistered charity called Voithame Tin Ellada (VTE – We are Helping Greece). It also tried to bolster its profile amongst the Greek diaspora by dispatching a GD MEP to Australia in 2014, though, ultimately, he was not granted a visa (Safi 2014).

The racialisation of charitable activism as a mechanism for building and embedding support is nothing new or unique to Greece, or indeed for the extreme right historically. It represents a recognisable component of the extreme-right 'repertoire' notably in France, where in 2006 the Bloc Identitaire – a group well known to Greek extremists[36] – opened soup kitchens that pointedly served sandwiches and soups featuring pork as its principal ingredient to discriminate against Jews and Muslims who might have been moved to draw upon the kitchens' 'charity' until the authorities banned them (Willsher 2006). For the BNP, which once prided itself on its own brand of 'community-based activism', the publicity given to such GD activities pointed the way to how it might recapture past glories which had underpinned its local electoral breakthrough in 2002 (Goodwin 2011: 71–76), hence their reproduction within BNP media.

Though BNP activism has not yet developed the same complement of community-based social welfare programmes that GD implemented, its activists, particularly in outer East London, have operated 'food banks' in a bid to establish a reputation and *ergo* local legitimacy as a social service provider. The BNP hoped to use the resultant publicity as a means of entrenching political support for racial nationalist principles in key electoral wards.[37] 'For the avoidance of doubt', noted Griffin, 'our BNP food banks are for indigenous [white] Brits only. "Minorities" all have their own (taxpayer funded) charities.'[38] This exclusionary principle was evident even in the local BNP campaign to support the initiative. Donations were solicited door-to-door by canvassers. Asked if he would make such aid available if a Black or Asian voter answered the door Griffin stated: 'We won't be knocking on their doors – we use the electoral register … we're not apologising for it, we're saying it very proudly, "This is for our people"'.[39]

It is important not to exaggerate the limited extent of this sporadic, local campaign. Between April and September 2013, 350,000 people drew on supplies from 400 food banks operated nationwide by just one charity, the Tressell Trust, which receives no taxpayer funding. Against this the efforts of the BNP seem puny indeed.[40] Political opponents have also alleged the BNP could be breaching electoral law and, more specifically, the provision on 'treating' under which it is an offence to provide before, during or after an election, food, drink or entertainment 'to corruptly influence any voter to vote or refrain from voting', though proving 'corrupt intent' would undoubtedly be challenging.[41]

Nevertheless, Griffin considered such activities 'vital experiments in creating the foundation stones of our future National Revolution.' This was not passive welfare but a means of teaching 'our people' that 'nationalism' was about racial cohesion. Informed by the experience of GD who used 'disciplined cadres' to distribute food, Griffin exerted his personal authority as party leader to implant the strategic and tactical lessons of such actions which, he hoped, would forge similarly committed militants for the BNP. This was politically important since many experienced BNP activists had abandoned the party since 2010. To 'sell' the idea to its activists the BNP uploaded video footage to its website of GD activists running their own (regimented) food and clothing distributions together with a GD document entitled 'the trampling of dignity' which featured further footage of a similar activity run by 'independent producers' spiralling out of control as desperate people fought one another for food. 'Isn't the contrast stunning?' observed Griffin.

> That's a key reason why nationalism in Greece is not only resisting oppression and the violence and hate of the old parties and their leftist militias, but growing in popularity every day. *There's a vital lesson here. Let's make sure we learn it.*[42]

Translating inspiration into action is easier said than done, however. To help its activists learn this 'vital lesson' the BNP offered a practical guide detailing how to launch such ventures in their own wards. 'While many of us find the sight of thousands of penniless Greeks being fed by GD inspirational, a small group of 3 or 4 activists in some forgotten corner of Britain may, possibly, find it all too much', sympathised the author.[43] What is important about this episode is not that the BNP are 'copying' the community-based approach of GD but that they were re-contextualising and repackaging a strategy they had previously used, filtering it through an international lens in order to enthuse anew its own dwindling pool of activists.

The BNP and the 'persecution' of Golden Dawn

Testifying to the importance of 'inter-personal' networks, Nick Griffin has been at the forefront of an international (extreme right-wing) chorus of disapproval protesting the 'persecution' of GD. The BNP was holding its annual conference in Blackpool, Lancashire, on the day that the GD leader, Nikolaos Michaloliakos, was arrested. Hearing the news Griffin took to the platform to address his activists flanked by two NOP activists, Michał Lewandowski and Daniel Dyduk, who

were there as guests. Griffin denounced Michaloliakos' arrest before reading a statement – drafted 'at the suggestion of our Polish comrades' – pledging 'full solidarity' with GD. The statement was then uploaded to the websites of the BNP, the
NOP and GD to ensure an international audience and to demonstrate their unity.[44]
Whilst the 'controlled media' supressed the 'truth' about GD's 'persecution', the
BNP began reproducing GD propaganda on its own website, including interviews
with its leadership, urging 'all nationalists the world over to pass this on' and diffuse
its message further.[45]

The following month, on 23 October, Griffin used his position as an MEP to
raise the question of GD's plight in the European Parliament contrasting the outrage
that greeted Russia's detention of Greenpeace activists with the silence he claimed
greeted the arrest of GD's leadership.[46] Michaloliakos was suitably impressed, writing to Griffin from his prison cell to express his gratitude. Griffin read the letter
out to his followers at a subsequent BNP meeting.[47] GD subsequently re-broadcast
Griffin's speech through their website and social media channels with Greek sub-
titles to communicate that the beleaguered party did not stand alone.[48]

In tandem with declaring solidarity with GD the BNP became increasingly
voluble in naming the forces it believes responsible for 'our Golden Dawn brothers and sisters in Greece suffer[ing] horrors not seen in Europe since Hitler came
to power in 1930s Germany.'[49] This allusion to the depredations of the Nazis to
describe the actions of the Greek government aside, the more common 'frame' was
to depict GD as the victim of a Jewish conspiracy. Publicly returning to a brand
of anti-Semitism largely repressed since 1999, the BNP website featured an article claiming that Michaloliakos had been 'arrested on the orders of international
Zionists'. This was illustrated with a photo of him being taken into custody by
Greek police, transposed in front of a still taken from F. W. Murnau's film *Nosferatu*
(1922), featuring the looming shadow of actor Maximillian Schreck playing the
vampire 'Count Orlok'. It was entitled 'Transnational Judenstadt'. Invoking this
image of 'the Jew' as a bloodsucking vampire, which, incidentally, was taken from
an overtly anti-Semitic website,[50] has a long historical pedigree dating back to the
early medieval period. It also gave stark visual representation to other allusions
in party propaganda as to who and what stood behind the international financial
architecture that the BNP blamed for the austerity measures impoverishing ordinary Greeks.

Far older anti-Semitic prejudices were voiced in the comments section of
the article. One prominent activist claimed, 'since the murder of Jesus, Zionists
have been staging show trials to persecute Christians'. Clearly some party militants viewed the arrest of GD's leadership as a form of crucifixion signalling that
'Zionists' were viewed as the lineal descendant of 'the Jew' as 'Christ Killer'. Such
images intermingled with those of a modern vintage. The article also featured a
photograph of GD MP Illias Panayiotaros being arrested by police whom the caption denounced as 'servants of the Zionist occupational government'. This anti-
Semitic terminology frequently abbreviated to its acronym 'ZOG' was popularised
by the neo-Nazi underground in the United States during the 1970s and 1980s.[51]

Griffin subsequently emerged at the epicentre of a transnational effort by extreme right-wing militants to gain publicity and build support for GD. He addressed a meeting in Moscow on 27 November 2013. Russia was deliberately chosen as the venue to symbolically highlight the supposed hypocrisy of the European Union for criticising President Putin's human rights record whilst refusing to speak up for imprisoned GD activists. Griffin shared a platform with GD MP Artemios Matthaioploulos, Roberto Fiore, leader of the Italian Forza Nuova group, and Russian lawyer Mikhail Kuznetsov, described as a 'Christian rights activist'. The event was live web-streamed to 2,500 viewers.[52]

Griffin's speech again sought to highlight alleged EU hypocrisy over GD, contrasting the outrage that greeted Pussy Riot's arrest for performing their 'punk prayer' in Moscow's Cathedral of Christ the Saviour, with the supposed silence over those who questioned the 'new secular Western pseudo-religion of the Holocaust'. Unlike the 'vulgar' and 'provocative' methods used by Pussy Riot, these individuals, claimed Griffin, used 'scientific analysis and the techniques of standard historical debate', singling out prominent Holocaust deniers like Ernst Zündel, Wolfgang Frölich and Horst Mahler, not to mention 'thousands' of other 'prisoners of conscience' who had been jailed in Germany for what he depicted as the 'thought crime' of challenging 'accepted history'. Griffin was quick to aver, however, that he was not asserting that such ideas were 'correct', for to do so, even in Moscow, he claimed, would mean that upon returning to the EU he would be arrested and 'shipped off to Germany' – a reference to the country's laws against Holocaust denial. To cover himself legally, Griffin claimed to believe 'unquestioningly every last detail of the unquestionable Holocaust story' but added 'I believe that it is the most rank hypocrisy for Western politicians and journalists to condemn Russia for defending the dignity of the Christian Church while ignoring or applauding the persecution of thousands who offend the dignity of the Jewish Holocaust.'[53]

Returning to England, Griffin explained to supporters that he spoke in Russia because the 'attack' on GD was also 'an attack on us'. Situating recent events within the history of the European extreme right, Griffin argued that the ban on the Flemish separatist party Vlaams Blok in 2004 represented a similar message being sent by a 'corrupt liberal elite' to their native populations: should they step out of line, their political organisations would, like GD, be crushed by the state.[54]

The diffusion of skills and resources through such interpersonal networks was perhaps best reflected in Griffin's assistance to GD in preparing a legal challenge to its 'liberal, totalitarian repression' to be presented to the European Court of Human Rights (ECHR). This development was announced at a press conference in Athens on 10 January 2014. Chaired by GD MP Artemios Matthaioploulos with whom he had shared a platform in Moscow the previous month, Griffin spoke alongside Ilias Kasidiaris, GD's spokesman who had been released from prison on bail. Proceedings began with the wife of imprisoned GD leader Nikolaos Michaloliakos reading out a statement from her husband extending his greetings to the militant patriot and great member of the European Parliament Nick Griffin who has staunchly defended the political movement of GD … It is with the same faith that Mr Griffin is struggling daily under adverse conditions for the independence of the British people against bankers and usurers. Our common fight continues.

The BNP published this statement on its website, no doubt to enhance Griffin's standing within his own party which had suffered a public blow the previous week when he was declared bankrupt, for a second time.[55]

Framing the 'persecution' of GD as a 'free speech' issue rather than one of criminality, Griffin again invoked a narrative of grievance, of a party supressed by 'powerful outside vested interests', which diminished the right of the Greek people to choose a 'radical nationalist alternative.' Claiming the treatment of GD was 'illegal', 'immoral' and amounted to 'collective punishment', Griffin again ended his speech with a defiant call to solidarity and common struggle: 'Long live freedom! Victory to Golden Dawn! And on behalf of the real nationalist opposition all over Europe, I tell friend and foe alike, our time will come.'[56]

Griffin's speech failed to intimidate the Greek government. The following day two more GD MPs were remanded in custody, followed by a third the day after. At the peak, up to 72 GD activists, including its leader and all its parliamentarians from the previous parliament, were awaiting trial.

The importance of BNP solidarity for GD was reflected in the fact that it not only broadcast the press conference live on the Internet, but repeatedly featured it on its website and circulated DVD copies of it free with its newspaper, *Chryssi Avgi* (*Golden Dawn*). Ourania Michaloliakou, the party leader's daughter, told the press: 'It fills us with hope to see an MEP from sister-nationalist movements be interested in the case of Golden Dawn and to help us in this difficult struggle we have chosen.' Echoing their sense of isolation, particularly from broader political currents of the populist right in Europe, Griffin stated: 'I'm one of the few friends they have got' (Waterfield and Tzafalias 2014). Demonstrating this, Griffin mobilised his own political resources as an MEP to act as a tribune for GD in the European Parliament, using this platform to directly attack the Greek President Antonias Samaras who assumed the EU presidency for six months in January 2014. During a debate on the programme of activities for the Greek presidency, Griffin denounced Samaras for betraying the Greek nation to 'your bankers' occupation government' – a variation on the 'ZOG' theme discussed earlier – branding him and his fellow politicians the 'real criminals'.[57]

Transnational support in its international context

Transnational networking, and the importance of both 'impersonal' and 'interpersonal' diffusion through such channels, must be understood within its international context and indeed the realignment of right-wing populism on the continent. When the BNP was ascendant its 'modernisation' strategy might have prohibited overt support for GD, which in 2007 it dubbed 'neo-fascist' and *ergo* outside the 'modern' nationalist camp in which the BNP situated itself. Now that it was beginning to atrophy domestically, however, the 'modernisation' strategy was abandoned and more extreme elements courted, in part because of the changing international context. The BNP had been a prominent component of the Alliance of European Nationalist Movements (AENM), an umbrella organisation for numerous extreme right-wing groups that was founded in Budapest in October 2009. Though dominated by the French Front National (FN), within this grouping, the BNP considered Jobbik its 'main partner'.[58]

Griffin desired the AENM to facilitate the homogenisation of its adherents' respective party programmes around 'a common core set of values' which included 'opposition to mass immigration from the Third World, defence of Christian traditional values, the eventual breakup of the European Union, as quickly as possible, and opposition to globalism.' Griffin told one interlocutor:

> To an extent I am [taking the lead] but Jobbik is very seriously involved as well. Jobbik tends to work with people in Central and Eastern Europe whereas I tend to do Western and Southern Europe – it's a joint effort.

Ideological sympathy aside, such a division of labour might explain why Griffin has been at the forefront of publicly supporting GD, though he conceded their relationship is 'still very much in its infancy' (Savaricas and McDonald-Gibson 2014).

International networks are never static let alone ideologically homogeneous, however. Márton Gyöngyösi, deputy leader of Jobbik's parliamentary faction and vice-chairman of the Foreign Affairs Committee, claimed in 2014 his party 'never had any contact' with GD. He was also less effusive than Griffin about their party's respective links. 'Our judgment on the EU is converging. But once again I think their [the BNP] anti-Islamic position is something very difficult to match with our outlook on the world', which was then orientated towards anti-Semitism in the guise of anti-Zionism. 'We are looking for an alliance of traditionalism across the world', Gyöngyösi told the media (White 2014).

Strategically, BNP bridge-building with GD also reflected internal political calculations. Griffin, then facing re-election as an MEP, had scant prospect of re-election. Moreover, the alignment of the extreme-right and right-wing populism was also undergoing a serious makeover ahead of the 2014 European Elections, which the BNP, for several reasons, were not privy too. Marine Le Pen, the FN leader since January 2011, and Geert Wilders, leader of the Partij voor de Vrijheid (PVV – Party for Freedom), forged a new alliance – under the auspices of the European Alliance for Freedom (EAF), a recognised (and funded) EU grouping comprising of individuals rather than parties, which she had joined in October 2011.[59]

The BNP, Jobbik and GD were not invited to join and Le Pen cut herself and her party off from the AENM. Despite long-standing historical links between the FN and the BNP, Le Pen ordered her father, party founder Jean-Marie Le Pen, and Bruno Gollnisch MEP to disengage from this network despite the latter being its President to make the FN path 'perfectly clear'. 'This is being done,' she told journalists. 'We will not have Jobbik in our group, we will not have Golden Dawn' (Waterfield 2013). Therefore, when GD published an article on its website in the run-up to the 2014 European elections stating that Marine Le Pen was 'mulling sending a congratulation letter [if GD polled well themselves], a fact that will result in advancing a flirt that has already started between the French far-right and Greek Golden Dawn', her office issued a furious denial (Michalopoulos 2014). Putting further distance between herself and GD, ahead of the 2015 Greek elections Le Pen went so far as to voice her support for the radical-left Syriza coalition – which won the election – calculating no doubt that Syriza's victory would also strengthen Eurosceptic support in Europe (*France24* 2015). This international purge of poten- tially embarrassing partners was part of Le Pen's broader strategy to 'de-toxify' the FN, to divorce it from the 'extreme-right' appellation and thus to pave the way for further electoral advance, a strategy which, at present, also appears to have stalled.[60]

Whilst publicly applauding Le Pen's own domestic electoral progress, Griffin lamented that 'her alliance with the neo-con #GertWilders and his ultra-Zionist backers won't end well.'[61] For Griffin a different set of political calculations was in operation. His own 'modernisation' strategy had failed to propel his party into the electoral mainstream, its limited electoral gains had been reversed and his activist base had deserted him. Seeking to shore up his support, Griffin adopted a more mil- itant approach, which aligned him more closely ideologically with GD. Excluded from the 'formal' EAF network Le Pen was forging, Griffin allied himself with palpably more extreme groups like Jobbik and GD who were then fashioning new 'informal' networks.

Transnational activism played an important role in bolstering these networks. To build, demonstrate and sustain international support for GD within the broader extreme-right firmament, Griffin spoke regularly alongside GD activists at interna- tional events. In 2014, for instance, he addressed a meeting in Italy in March along- side GD MP Antonis Gregos (prior to which many delegates attended the annual commemoration for another deceased Greek militant, Mikos Mantakas, shot dead by a left-wing activist in Italy in 1975).[62] In September, Griffin addressed a pro- test outside the Greek Embassy in Brussels together with activists from Germany, France, Belgium, Flanders and GD itself.[63] In December he was back in Italy again, speaking at a meeting in Milan alongside GD MEP Eleftherios Synadinos who conveyed the 'greetings' of his imprisoned leader, Michaloliakos, making clear 'the urgent need for solidarity not only for Golden Dawn and Greece, but for the entire West.' Those present renewed their efforts to publicise the 'persecution' of GD and agitate for Michaloliakos' release, recorded the GD website.[64]

Whilst activists at these gatherings represented a plethora of different parties they had already begun to coalesce under the banner of the Alliance for Peace and Freedom (AFP), a new pan-European umbrella group founded in late 2015 as a successor to the defunct European National Front to which GD had previ- ously been aligned (Tipaldou 2015: 205). The AFP president, Italian extreme-right activist Roberto Fiore, had long cultivated his own relationship with GD. He was also a long-standing political colleague and friend of Nick Griffin, the AFP vice-president. Since its foundation, the AFP has sought to provide concrete support to GD, organising a 'fact finding' delegation comprising extreme-right MEPs who travelled to Greece to meet with GD activists, including its imprisoned leader. It also issued a statement condemning the 'undemocratic repression' of GD as being 'in blatant breach of European human rights laws'. The AFP promised to report its findings 'at both legal and institutional level' within the EU in a bid to orchestrate a common, pan-European defence of GD.[65]

As well as serving as a nodal point for activism in support for GD, the AFP has also played a leading role elevating and internationalising the 'cult of martyrdom' around the two murdered GD activists to inspire future commitment and sacrifice. In an act of homage, the AFP officially consecrated its Brussels offices as the 'Georgios and Manos Centre' in April 2016. Opening the centre, which they indicated would serve as 'the symbol of nationalism in the otherwise Eurocratic city', Fiore and Griffin spoke alongside GD MEP Georgios Epitideios.[66]

Conclusion

'That Griffin thinks the way to rebuild the BNP is to build links with the neo-Nazi Golden Dawn in Greece – who are linked to murder and attacks on migrants – speaks volumes', observed Matthew Goodwin (2014) of Griffin's descent into 'political' irrelevancy. What this verdict fails to capture, however, is the intended audience. Griffin did not emphasise the link with GD to rekindle *public* support for the BNP. He did it to try and re-establish his own battered credentials *within* the extreme-right milieu and to woo 'hard core' support for his leadership at a time when 'popular' electoral support for the BNP had all but evaporated, leading to a protracted period of declining organisational capability and diminishing political saliency from which it is unlikely to emerge any time soon.

Ivarsflaten (2006) argues persuasively that right-wing populist parties succeed when they successfully construct a 'reputational shield' to insulate themselves against accusations of racism or extremism. Following the BNP's electoral collapse, which demolished its 'modernisation' strategy, Griffin had to rethink the utility of such an approach. The political collapse of the BNP undermined his credibility as a leader, in terms of both public support but also amongst his activist base, many of whom now considered him a liability. Griffin's decision to align himself publicly with the GD constituted part of his broader strategy to develop an *internal* reputational shield. He appears to have calculated that brazenly supporting GD could serve as a backstop to his waning influence and relevancy, both nationally and internationally, and provide a stable bedrock upon which to rebuild his tarnished credibility amongst the hard-line activists whom he had previously renounced for matters of domestic political exigency. 'We are all being demonized and dehumanized … so I think it's only logical that the "devils" have to stand together,' Griffin stated indicating that, politically at least, he no longer felt he had anything to lose from such associations.[67]

The emphasis of this case study, upon the transnational context in which domestic ideological radicalisation can occur, highlights the agency of individual activists (or small political cliques). It also underscores the importance of understanding how these processes can be facilitated by, and tailored towards, addressing distinct political needs within such groups. It is a politically controlled process, and decisions to emphasise certain ideological facets at certain junctures, whilst suppressing them at others, are sensitive to the broader domestic *and* international concerns. The ideological (re)radicalisation of the BNP, which took place between 2012 and 2014, was undertaken from a point of political weakness by a politically besieged leader of a party with plummeting electoral saliency.

It was a reputational gamble that failed to pay dividends. Presiding over a party increasingly torn apart by internecine conflicts and under increased internal pressure to staunch the flow of votes, members and activists, Griffin reluctantly stepped down as Chairman under duress. His refusal to go quietly led to his expulsion from the party itself in 2014. With Griffin gone, the effort to ideologically (re)radicalise the BNP ceased. The new leadership purged the party website and publications of open association with GD, reverting to its mainstay of 'populist' anti-Muslim politicking in a singularly unsuccessful attempt to avert its near terminal atrophy.

Research on extreme right-wing mobilisation and its effects upon identity construction at a grass-roots level is still in its infancy. This study of how British extreme right-wing *groupuscules* have responded to the 'persecution' of GD highlights just one episode in a fluid, multilayered process of diffusion between extreme-right groups (see Macklin 2013). It is through such practices that 'local' national identities and strategies are articulated and re-articulated into broader, collective ones that are forged in 'action'. Giving due regard to the myriad examples of seemingly isolated micro-mobilisations, and conceptualising them within their wider transnational context, can illuminate a good deal with regard to their impact upon identity construction, as well as the broader processes of ideological and political development taking place within the extreme right-wing milieu.

Notes

1 www.skrewdriver.net/index2.html.
2 For the broader role of such musical genres in its ideological cosmology see 'Golden Dawn and Black Metal': http://ethniko.net/blog/golden-dawn-and-black-metal/.
3 'Hungary's "Magyar Hajnal" assert far right identity against others', 31 October 2013: www.euronews.com/2013/10/31/hungary-s-magyar-hajnal-assert-far-right-identity-against-others/.
4 'Greek neo-Nazi group Golden Dawn climbing back up in opinion polls', 17 November 2013: www.thecommentator.com/article/4367/greek_neo_nazi_group_golden_dawn_climbing_back_up_in_opinion_polls.
5 'European Solidarity', 4 December 2013: http://golden-dawn-international-newsroom.blogspot.co.uk/2013/12/european-solidarity.html.

6 'Η προκήρυξη της εκτέλεσης', 16 November 2013: www.zougla.gr/greece/article/ i-prokiriksi-tis-ektelesis-819462.

7 'Greece's Golden Dawn gains support after members killed – poll', *Reuters*, 16 November 2013: www.reuters.com/article/2013/11/16/us-acw-greece-poll-idUSBRE9AF0AD 20131116.

8 'Milano, 4/11/13: I Camerati ricordano Manos e Giorgos!' 5 November 2013: www. youtube.com/watch?v=Wt4AUlKq594#t=16.

9 'Firenze Per Giorgos E Manolis', 3 November 2013: http://cpfirenze.blogspot.co.uk/ 2013/11/per-giorgos-e-manolis.html.

10 'Germany: Golden Dawn solidarity protest in Dortmund', 8 November 2013: www. youtube.com/watch?v=E-dBfQKDxps.

11 'RIOTS: Support Golden Dawn demonstration – Υποστήριξη Χρυσή Αυγή επίδειξης', 15 November 2013: www.liveleak.com/view?i=497_1384522335.

12 'Golden Dawn New York Demonstrates in Midtown Manhattan for Giorgios and Manolis!' 9 November 2013: http://xaameriki.wordpress.com/2013/11/09/golden- dawn-new-york-demonstrates-in-midtown-manhattan-for-giorgos-and-manolis/. There were other demonstrations across the US for example 'FAR Project Stands with Golden Dawn', 16 December 2013: http://freeamericarally.org/rally/golden-dawn/#more-1535.

13 'Sydney demo in support of GD', 18 December 2013: http://neoskosmos.com/news/ en/sydney-demo-in-support-of-Golden-dawn.

14 www.bloodandhonour.com/.

15 A range of reactions to the killings can be seen on extreme right-wing forums, for instance 'Shocking video shows the murder of 2 Golden Dawn members': www.storm- front.org/forum/t1003578/.

16 'Lambros Fountoulis: "We Have A Sacred Obligation to Continue"', 3 November 2014: www.youtube.com/watch?v=DbKqfZ7k-7o

17 'British Movement Stands with Golden Dawn', 20 November 2013: www. britishmovement.info/. GD reprinted the writings of BM founder Colin Jordan in its magazine, for instance *Χρυσή αυγή*, Maioc-Ioynioc 1981 [*Golden Dawn*, May–June 1981].

18 'Pro Golden Dawn Nationalist Demonstration', 17 November 2013: www.youtube. com/watch?v=aqcS3HEsBqI.

19 Ibid.

20 'National Rebirth of Poland – English Division in offensive', 18 October 2013: http:// en.nop.org.pl/2013/10/18/national-rebirth-of-poland-english-division-in-offensive/.

21 Ibid.

22 'Division England: polski nacjonalizm w Norwich', 16 October 2013: www.nop.org. pl/2013/10/16/division-england-polski-nacjonalizm-w-norwich/. They repeated this action in January 2015.

23 'Athens: 50,000 nationalists against the System', 5 December 2013: http://en.nop.org. pl/2013/12/05/golden-dawn-50-000-nationalists-against-the-system/.

24 'Golden Dawn America Podcast Episode 13: The Working Class is Awake', 25 February 2014', http://birminghamnationalist2.blogspot.co.uk/2014/02/golden-dawn-america- podcast-episode-13.html.

25 Nick Griffin, Twitter, 25 November 2013: https://twitter.com/nickgriffinmep/status/ 404987421504602112.

26 'New British Union (NBU) Solidarity protest at Greek Embassy in London 2013' – photograph 41: www.flickr.com/photos/grey-photography/10847584453/in/photo- stream/.

27 'The Invasion of ideas – Kevin Layzell YBNP', 21 December 2013: www.bnp.org.uk/ news/national/invasion-ideas-kevin-layzell-ybnp.

28 The distinction is not always clear cut for ideologically committed racial nationalists. In *March of the Titans: A History of the White Race* (Ostara: Burlington Iowa 2006): 276–278, essential reading for BNP activists whilst its author was a member, Arthur Kemp argued that the Greeks were a 'biracial' population having mixed with Middle Eastern and African slaves which had, he argued, 'cause[d] the downfall of Classical Grecian civilization'. Kemp was equally keen to emphasise, however, that 'many modern Greeks still retain their original unmixed White European racial identity'.

29 'Everyone collapses, the Golden Dawn prevails', 15 April 2013: www.bnp.org.uk/news/national/everyone-collapses-golden-dawn-prevails.

30 'Golden Dawn – dangerous extremists or long overdue national revival? Make up your own mind!' 23 January 2013: www.bnp.org.uk/news/national/golden-dawn-dangerous-extremists-or-long-overdue-national-revival-make-your-own-mind.

31 'Livestream Now: Imia 2014 Demonstration', 1 February 2014: http://xaameriki.word-press.com/2014/02/01/thousands-begin-to-gather-for-imia-2014-demonstration/.

32 'IMIA 2013 – The Greatest March', 3 February 2013: www.bnp.org.uk/news/national/imia-2013-greatest-march.

33 'Special Air Service, or System Against Soldiers?' 15 July 2013: www.bnp.org.uk/news/national/special-air-service-or-system-against-soldiers.

34 'Christianity and Britain's Slide Towards Cultural Marxism', 8 July 2013: www.bnp.org.uk/news/national/christianity-and-britains-slide-towards-cultural-marxism.

35 'Truth at Last!' 4 October 2013: www.bnp.org.uk/news/national/truth-last.

36 Bloc Identitaire's widely watched 'Declaration of War' video has been translated into several languages including Greek, see, 'Γενιά της ταυτότητας – Déclaration de guerre – Génération Id', 12 October 2012: www.youtube.com/watch?v=TrDL9RUXp2A. Bloc Identitaire activists have also given interviews to Greek extreme right-wing publications, see *We Are Generation Identity* (Arktos: London 2013): 32–41.

37 'East London and Havering Food Bank Success', 5 September 2013: www.bnp.org.uk/news/regional/east-london-and-havering-food-bank-success.

38 See https://twitter.com/nickgriffinmep/status/450606823838863362.

39 'Nick Griffin: "UKIP is a pale carbon copy of the BNP"', 1 April 2014: http://uk.sputniknews.com/voiceofrussia/news/2014_04_01/Nick-Griffin-UKIP-is-a-pale-carbon-copy-of-the-BNP-6512/.

40 'Numbers relying on food banks triple in a year', *BBC News*, 16 October 2013: www.bbc.co.uk/news/business-24536817.

41 See www.electoralcommission.org.uk/__data/assets/pdf_file/0005/149729/List-of-electoral-offences.pdf.

42 'Our Time Will Come', 13 December 2013: www.bnp.org.uk/news/national/our-time-will-come (emphasis in original). See also 'Practical Idealism', 23 July 2013: http://bnptv.org.uk/2013/07/practical-idealism/. Other extreme right-wing groups, including the British branch of the NOP and activists from the now banned National Action, also adopted this tactic.

43 'Food Banks for Small Groups', 8 January 2014: www.bnp.org.uk/news/national/food-banks-small-groups.

44 'Breaking News: Golden Dawn Arrest – a BNP statement', 28 September 2013: www.bnp.org.uk/news/national/breaking-news-golden-dawn-arrest-bnp-statement; 'BNP i NOP wspólnie w obronie greckiego Złotego Świtu', 28 September 2013: www.nop.org.pl/2013/09/28/bnp-i-nop-wspolnie-w-obronie-greckiego-zlotego-switu/ and 'Ανακοίνωση συμπαράστασης υπέρ της Χρυσής Αυγής από τον Βρετανό ευρωβουλευτή Νικ Γκρίφιν', 18 October 2013: www.xryshaygh.com/index.php/enimerosi/view/anakoinwsh-sumparastashs-uper-ths-chrushs-aughs-apo-ton-bretano-eurwbouleut.

45 'Media Blackout regarding Golden Dawn – Break the Chain – Pass This On', 21 October 2013: www.bnp.org.uk/news/national/media-blackout-regarding-golden-dawn-break-chain-pass.

46 'Detention of Greenpeace activists in Russia (debate)', 23 October 2013: www.europarl.europa.eu/sides/getDoc.do?pubRef=-//EP//TEXT+CRE+20131023+ITEM-017+DOC+XML+V0//EN&language=en&query=INTERV&detail=3-302-000.

47 'A Golden Dawn breaking over the Golden Mile', 15 December 2013: http://bnptv.org.uk/2013/12/a-golden-dawn-breaking-over-the-golden-mile/.

48 'Ο ευρωβουλευτής Nick Griffin καταγγέλλει την σκευωρία εις βάρος της Χρυσής Αυγής – ΒΙΝΤΕΟ', 6 January 2014: www.xryshaygh.com/index.php/enimerosi/view/o-eurwbouleuths-nick-griffin-kataggellei-thn-skeuwria-eis-baros-ths-chrushs.

49 'Samaras and Hitler March as One', 18 January 2014: www.bnp.org.uk/news/national/samaras-and-hitler-march-one.

50 'Greece: Jews kill Two Golden Dawn Members in Drive-By Shooting – Ελλάδα: Εβραίοι σκοτώσει δύο Χρυσά Μέλη Dawn Σε', 1 November 2013: http://endzog.wordpress.com/2013/11/01/jews-kill-two-golden-dawn-members-in-drive-by/.

51 'Golden Dawn, Amnesty International and Charitable Status', 23 January 2014: www.bnp.org.uk/news/national/golden-dawn-amnesty-international-and-charitable-status.

52 Nick Griffin, Twitter, 27 November 2013: https://twitter.com/nickgriffinmep/status/405669503654453248.

53 'For those who cannot speak!' 7 December 2013: www.youtube.com/watch?v=XvwvrjSxfAw.

54 'A Golden Dawn breaking over the Golden Mile', 15 December 2013: www.youtube.com/watch?v=3DUnlZQK-8M.

55 'Nick Griffin stands by persecuted Golden Dawn', 21 January 2014: www.bnp.org.uk/news/national/nick-griffin-stands-persecuted-golden-dawn.

56 'Nick Griffin (MEP) – Golden Dawn Party will win the Human Rights trial in the Euro Court', 11 January 2014: www.youtube.com/watch?v=0vwfZHeVC7E.

57 'Programme of activities of the Greek Presidency (debate)', 15 January 2014: www.europarl.europa.eu/sides/getDoc.do?pubRef=-//EP//TEXT+CRE+20140115+ITEM-005+DOC+XML+V0//EN&language=en&query=INTERV&detail=3-029-000. Golden Dawn immediately uploaded footage of the speech onto its websites, see 'Nick Griffin vs Samaras in EU Parliament Circus. Samaras talks "Extremism"', 16 January 2014: http://xaameriki.wordpress.com/2014/01/16/nick-griffin-vs-samaras-in-eu-parliament-circus-samaras-talks-extremism/.

58 'Jobbik's London visit', 24 January 2014: www.bnp.org.uk/news/national/jobbik-london-visit.

59 'Marine Le Pen en Autriche', 27 January 2012: www.frontnational.com/2012/01/marine-le-pen-en-autriche/.

60 'Marine Le Pen: France's National Front is not Right-Wing', *AFP*, 3 October 2013: www.telegraph.co.uk/news/worldnews/europe/france/10353008/Marine-Le-Pen-Frances-National-Front-is-not-Right-wing.html.

61 Nick Griffin, Twitter, 22 November 2013: https://twitter.com/nickgriffinmep/status/403829187351695360.

62 'Golden Dawn Representatives Attend Commemoration of Mikis Mantakas and National Conference in Italy', 4 March 2014: https://xaameriki.wordpress.com/2014/03/04/golden-dawn-representatives-attend-commemoration-of-mikis-mantakas-and-nationalist-conference-in-italy/.

63 https://alliancepeacefreedom.wordpress.com/2014/09/26/golden-dawn-protest/

64 'Golden Dawn Joins Nationalists in Forza Nuova Hosted Conference in Milan', 23 December 2014: www.xryshaygh.com/en/view/golden-dawn-joins-nationalists-in-forza-nuova-hosted-conference-in-milan#ixzz4lJ1AmtvR.

65 The delegation consisted of MEP's Udo Voigt (NPD); Lampros Fountulis and Georgios Epitideios (GD); Roberto Fiore (FN), the president of the APF and a former MEP; Mikhail Kusnetsov, a Russian lawyer; and Michele Saponaro, an Italian lawyer.

66 'Grand opening of the Georgios and Manos Centre in Brussels', 25 April 2016: https://apfeurope.com/2016/04/grand-opening-of-the-georgios-and-manos-centre-in-brussels/.

67 'British far-right leader courts European allies', *Associated Press*, 10 January 2014: www.washingtonpost.com/world/europe/british-far-right-leader-courts-european-allies/2014/01/10/3271b084-7a36-11e3-a647-a19deaf575b3_story.html.

References

Bistis, G. (2013) 'Golden Dawn or Democratic Sunset: The Rise of the Far Right in Greece', *Mediterranean Quarterly*, 24 (3): 35–55.

Caiani, M., della Porta, D. and Wagemann, C. (2012) *Mobilizing on the Extreme Right: Germany, Italy, and the United States*, Oxford: Oxford University Press.

Collins, R. (2004) *Interaction Ritual Chains*, Princeton, NJ: Princeton University Press.

Dalakoglou, D. (2013) '"From the Bottom of the Aegean Sea" to Golden Dawn: Security, Xenophobia, and the Politics of Hate in Greece', *Studies in Ethnicity and Nationalism*, 13 (3): 514–522.

Doxiadis, A. and Matsanganis, M. (2013) *National Populism and Xenophobia in Greece*, London: Counterpoint.

Dufour, P. and Giraud, I. (2007) 'The Continuity of Transnational Solidarities in the World March of Women, 2000 and 2005: A Collective Identity-Building Approach', *Mobilisation*, 12 (3): 307–322.

Ellinas, A. (2013) 'The Rise of Golden Dawn: The New Face of the Far Right in Greece', *Southern European Society and Politics*, 18 (4): 1–23.

France24. (2015) 'French far right rooting for hard-left Syriza in Greek poll', 20 January: www.france24.com/en/20150120-france-far-right-syriza-greece-poll/ (accessed 15 June 2017).

Georgiadou, V. (2013) 'Right-Wing Populism and Extremism: The Rapid Rise of "Golden Dawn" in Crisis-Ridden Greece', in Melzer, R. and Serafin, S. (eds.) *Right-Wing Extremism in Europe: Country Analysis, Counter-Strategies and Labor-Orientated Exit Strategies*, Berlin: Friedrich-Ebert Stiftung: 75–103.

Goodwin, M. (2011) *New British Fascism: Rise of the British National Party*, Abingdon: Routledge: 71–75.

Goodwin, M. (2014) 'Nick Griffin supports the Golden Dawn in Athens as the BNP falls apart', 10 January: http://blogs.spectator.co.uk/coffeehouse/2014/01/nick-griffin-supports-the-golden-dawn-in-athens-as-his-party-collapses/ (accessed 15 June 2017).

Halfman, D. and Young, M. (2010) 'War Pictures: The Grotesque as a Mobilizing Tactic', *Mobilization*, 15 (1): 1–24.

Halikiopoulou, D. and Vasilopoulou, S. (2013) 'Greece: The Rise of Golden Dawn', in Giusto, H., Kitching, D. and Rizzo, S. (eds.) *The Changing Faces of Populism: Systemic Challengers in Europe and the US*, Belgium: Foundation for European Progressive Studies: 117–120.

Ivarsflaten, I. (2006) 'Reputational Shields: Why Most Anti-Immigration Parties Failed in Western Europe, 1980–2005': www.nuffield.ox.ac.uk/politics/papers/2006/ivarsflatenapsa2006.pdf (accessed 15 June 2017).

Jasper, J. M. (1997) *The Art of Moral Protest: Culture, Biography and Creativity in Social Movements*, Chicago, IL: University of Chicago Press.

Kassimeris, G. (2013) *Inside Greek Terrorism*, London: Hurst & Co.

Katsourides, Y. (2013) 'Determinants of Extreme Right Reappearance in Cyprus: The National Popular Front (ELAM), Golden Dawn's Sister Party', *Southern European Society and Politics*, 18 (4): 1–23.

Koronaiou, K. and Sakellariou, A. (2013) 'Reflections on "Golden Dawn", Community Organizing and Nationalist Solidarity: Helping (Only) Greeks', *Community Development Journal*, 48 (2): 332–339.

Koronaiou, K. and Sakellariou, A. (2017) 'Women and Golden Dawn: Reproducing the Nationalist Habitus', *Gender and Education*, 29 (2): 258–275.

Koronaiou, K., Lagos, E., Sakellariou, A., Kymionis, S. and Chiotaki-Poulou, I. (2015) 'Golden Dawn, Austerity and Young People: The Rise of Fascist Extremism Among Young People in Contemporary Greek Society', *The Sociological Review*, 63 (2): 231–249.

Macklin, G. (2013) 'Transnational Activism on the Far Right: The Case of the BNP and the NPD', *West European Politics*, 36 (1): 176–198.

Meyer, M. (2004) 'Organizational Identity, Political Contexts, and SMO Action: Explaining the Tactical Choices Made by Peace Organizations in Israel, Northern Ireland, and South Africa', *Social Movement Studies*, 3 (2): 167–197.

Michalopoulos, S. (2014) 'Marine Le Pen and Golden Dawn "flirting"', 23 May: www.euractiv.com/section/eu-elections-2014/news/marine-le-pen-and-golden-dawn-flirting/ (accessed 15 June 2017).

Olivepress.es (2014) 'Branch of Nazi party Golden Dawn legalised in Spain', 5 November: www.theolivepress.es/spain-news/2014/11/05/branch-of-nazi-party-golden-dawn-legalised-in-spain/ (accessed 15 June 2017).

Pasqua, M. (2012) 'Abla Dorata in Italia, fondata a Trieste costola moviemento filnazista Greco. Al via campagnia di reculatamento sul web', 21 November: www.huffingtonpost.it/2012/11/12/alba-dorata-in-italia-al-via-campagna-adesioni_n_2117058.html (accessed 15 June 2017).

Psarras, D. (2013) *The Rise of the Neo-Nazi Party "Golden Dawn" in Greece*, Brussels: Rosa Luxembourg Stiftung.

Sadurni, S. (2013a) 'Is there a future for England's Golden Dawn?' 2 October: http://news-inchaos.wordpress.com/2013/10/02/is-there-a-future-for-englands-golden-dawn/ (accessed 15 June 2017).

Sadurni, S. (2013b) 'The Golden Dawn have a British Fan Club', *Vice*, 11 November: www.vice.com/en_uk/read/new-dawn-golden-dawn-london-demo (accessed 15 June 2017).

Safi, M. (2014) 'Golden Dawn: Australian branch of far-right Greek party raises cash', *The Guardian*, 29 September: www.theguardian.com/world/2014/sep/29/golden-dawn-australian-branch-of-far-right-greek-party-raises-cash (accessed 15 June 2017).

Savaricas, N. and McDonald-Gibson, C. (2014) 'Just what Greece didn't need: BNP leader Nick Griffin seeks Golden Dawn alliance', *The Independent*, 10 January: www.independent.co.uk/news/world/europe/just-what-greece-didnt-need-bnp-leader-nick-griffin-seeks-golden-dawn-alliance-9052662.html (accessed 15 June 2017).

Shaffer, R. (2014) 'From Outcast to Martyr: The Memory of Rudolf Hess in Skinhead Culture', *JEX: Journal EXIT-Deutschland. Zeitschrift für Deradikalisierung und demokratische Kultur*, 3: 111–124: http://journals.sfu.ca/jed/index.php/jex/article/viewFile/86/115 (accessed 15 June 2017).

Siemens, D. (2013) *The Making of a Nazi Hero: The Murder and Myth of Horst Wessel*, London: I.B.Tauris.

Smith, H. (2013) Greece's neo-Nazi Golden Dawn goes global with political ambitions', *The Guardian*, 1 April: www.theguardian.com/world/2013/apr/01/greece-golden-dawn-global-ambitions (accessed 15 June 2017).

Tipaldou, S. (2015) 'The Dawning of Europe and Eurasia? The Greek Golden Dawn and its Transnational Links' in Laurelle, M. (ed.) *Eurasianism and the European Far Right: Reshaping the Europe–Russia Relationship*, Lanham, MD: Lexington, 193–219.

Uladh, D. (2014) 'Family of murdered Golden Dawn member demand party stop using his image', *EnetEnglish*, 15 October: www.enetenglish.gr/?i=news.en.politics&id=2073 (accessed 15 June 2017).

Van Hauwaert, S. M. and Perrineau, P. (2013) 'Not all roads lead to Rome (or Paris): How channels of diffusion contribute to far right party development and trans-national diffusion patterns between them', Paper prepared for presentation at the annual conference of the Midwest Political Science Association, Chicago, April 11–14.

Vasilopoulou, S. and Halikiopoulou, D. (2015) *The Golden Dawn's "Nationalist Solution"*, London: Palgrave Pivot.

Virchow, F. (2013) 'Creating a European (Neo-Nazi) Movement by Joint Political Action', in Mammone, A., Godin, E. and Jenkins, B. (eds.) *Varieties of Right-Wing Extremism in Europe*, Abingdon: Routledge: 196–213.

Waterfield, B. (2013) 'France's FN to team up with other far Right parties for European elections', *The Telegraph*, 23 October: www.telegraph.co.uk/news/worldnews/europe/france/10400740/Frances-FN-to-team-up-with-other-far-Right-parties-for-European-elections.html (accessed 15 June 2017).

Waterfield, B. and Tzafalias, M. (2014) 'BNP's Nick Griffin defends jailed leader of neo-Nazi party Golden Dawn', *Daily Telegraph*, 10 January: www.telegraph.co.uk/news/worldnews/europe/greece/10565181/BNPs-Nick-Griffin-defends-jailed-leader-of-neo-Nazi-party-Golden-Dawn.html (accessed 15 June 2017).

White, J. A. (2014) 'A conversation with Márton Gyöngyösi on the European Parliament elections – Jobbik to Wilders and Le Pen: Liberalism and Zionism are the enemies, not Islam', 22 February: http://budapesttimes.hu/2014/02/22/jobbik-to-wilders-and-le-pen-liberalism-and-zionism-are-the-enemies-not-islam/ (accessed 15 June 2017).

Willsher, K. (2006) 'France's "racist" soup kitchen's shut down,' *Daily Telegraph*, 19 February: www.telegraph.co.uk/news/worldnews/europe/france/1510908/Frances-racist-soup-kitchens-shut-down.html (accessed 15 June 2017).

11

LOVE WILL TEAR US APART

Emotions, patriotism and the English Defence League

C. M. Quinn

Introduction

Research examining the English Defence League (EDL) has largely focused on its significance as an expression of Britain's 'new' far right and its Islamophobia (Allen 2011; Bartlett & Littler 2011; Garland & Treadwell 2010; Goodwin & Evans 2012; Jackson 2011; Richards 2011). Recent research offers a wider perspective and has tried to break through certain stereotypes. Busher (2016) focuses on grass-roots EDL activism in London and southeast England as a form of anti-Muslim activism rather than 'far-right activism'; Pilkington (2016) examines the relationship between EDL activism and wider political environments and argues that the EDL's aspiration to be non-racist is real. More recently still, Winlow, Hall and Treadwell (2017) shift the focus away from anti-Muslim politics to class politics, and examine the rise of the EDL in terms of the perceived failures of the 'liberal left'.

Taking a sociological approach, my focus is very much on the EDL as a social movement and motivations for participation. My focus is not on anti-Muslim identity, or on class identity, but on *patriotism*. As with any social movement, EDL activity has had its peaks and troughs. Fallouts, factionalism, splinter groups and the departure of its leaders, Tommy Robinson (Stephen Lennon) and Kevin Carroll in 2013, have had a stark impact on its street presence and numbers of committed activists. From having local divisions in most large towns and cities, there are now fewer than fifty divisions. The number of demonstrations have decreased significantly as have the numbers attending. However that is not to say that the EDL or another similar grouping will not become rejuvenated and regain support in the future. By taking a wider approach to the research and analysis of groupings such as the EDL a more holistic understanding of motivations can be achieved.

Since its emergence in 2009 the EDL's public profile has largely been in regard to the violence, community conflict and community tensions that their activities have either instigated or contributed to. Having researched the EDL since 2009, my interest in it has focused on the EDL as a social movement and motivations for participation. Between 2011 and 2013, I interviewed activists from across England's nine regions asking them why they had become activists in the EDL. The activists interviewed included the EDL leadership of the time – Stephen Lennon (also known as Tommy Robinson), Regional Organisers, the EDL Angels and grass-roots activists. Whilst you could be forgiven for assuming that these activists were motivated by anger and hatred what I found was that they were motivated just as much, and possibly more, by love, pride and loyalty, emotions that were rooted in their patriotism and loyalty to England.

Love is often regarded as a positive emotion in that it is seen as a 'good' emotion, one that we should all aspire to experience and share. There are, of course, circumstances where love has been used as a justification for abuse (Secomb 2007) such as domestic violence, with perpetrators rationalising their actions with the mantra: 'I did it because I love you.' Not all expressions of love are positive and raise questions of whether negative expressions of love constitute love at all. Activists' justification for their actions and involvement in the EDL were articulated as stemming from their patriotism, their love, loyalty and pride of England and their need to defend. Can this love be seen as a positive or a negative expression? As the EDL have protested across England, their very public expression of patriotism has often resulted in violent confrontations with opponents and police, damage to property and shops, and rising community tensions. Many local authorities have highlighted the impact of the EDL on local community cohesion and have reviewed their Community Cohesion Strategies to address the negative impact the EDL have had on local cohesion, such as Kirklees (University of Huddersfield 2014) and Luton (Luton Commission on Community Cohesion 2011) which informed their community cohesion strategy. Given the community tensions, violence and fear that escalated due to EDL's street presence, this so-called display of patriotism and love can be seen as a love that is negative in its manifestation and a love that instead of promoting unity and cohesion in communities is in practice tearing communities apart – hence the title of this chapter, taken from the Joy Division classic.

Community divisions did increase in some English towns due to EDL activities, activities that the EDL profess to do in the name of patriotism and their love and defence of England, its people, values and culture. Writing in 2010, Garland and Treadwell were of the view that the EDL was the greatest threat to both community cohesion and public order 'since the heyday of the National Front in the 1970s' (Garland & Treadwell 2010: 19). In contrast, whilst the EDL has had a negative impact on wider community cohesion, as a social movement it stimulated and nurtured unity and cohesion between its activists. This movement cohesion enabled group formation, development and maintenance. Since the emergence of the EDL in 2009, research has identified them as far right (or 'new far right') and a social movement. Yet despite extensive research regarding participation in social movements there still remains a lack of research around social movements that are not seen to be liberation movements, or who are not explicitly leftist in political orientation. To date, social movement theories regarding participation have not been explored in relation to movements such as the EDL in any real depth.

Social movements, grievances and emotions

Collective shared grievances are the most widely accepted explanation for social action (Johnston 1995). These grievances are the catalyst in the arousal of emotions that motivate people into participation (van Stekelenburg & Klandermans 2010; Pinard 2011). Grievances arouse initial emotional responses in individuals, however when grievances are identified as collective grievances, in that they are shared by many, they assist in providing a focus, identity formation and boundaries in movement-making. Collective shared grievances provide movements with justification for action, providing legitimacy for the movement and its actions with the collective grievances used to evidence rationality. Klandermans (1997) has identified three types of grievances: suddenly imposed grievances, illegitimate inequality, and violated principles. Suddenly imposed grievances are unexpected threats to people's rights, status or circumstances. Illegitimate inequality is directly related to deprivation theory and refers to grievances that derived from societal and material inequality. The violated principles grievance is when moral outrage is evoked as a reaction to important principles or moral values being violated. Klandermans' imposed grievances and violated principles, are akin to Jasper's 'moral shock' concept:

> 'Moral shocks', often the first step towards recruitment into social movements, occur when an unexpected event or piece of information raises such a sense of outrage in a person that she becomes inclined toward political action, whether or not she has acquaintances in the movement.
>
> *(Jasper 1998: 409)*

Some or all of these grievances are embodied in all social movements regardless of their political positioning on the right/left spectrum. It is therefore reasonable to assume that if all social movements emerge and persist due to the embodiment of grievances they must also emerge and persist as a result of the emotional responses that are provoked by those grievances, and again this is regardless of their political positioning. Therefore, social movements, regardless of political persuasion, derive from shared grievances and are propelled by the individual and collective emotional responses to those grievances. If the types of grievances that Klandermans has identified are prevalent across movements, though the nature of specific grievances varies, are the emotions that are aroused also the same across movements?

There is a lack of clarity around which emotions are aroused and how and why this happens, 'amazingly little is known about where emotions exactly fit into the context of movement participation' (van Stekelenburg & Klandermans 2010: 171). The role of emotions as motivational in both initial participation and in the maintenance of ongoing participation has continued to be explored by social movement theorists (Jasper 1998; Gould 2009; Groves 1997; Taylor 1995; Wood 2001). Jasper

(1998) argues that emotions are integral to our everyday being, our daily routines, social interactions and social action and therefore are central to the study of protest and social movements. However, the study of emotions has proved both contentious and complex. Much of the contention derives from the psychological legacy of emotions (Erikson 1956; Freud 1922a) where emotions were presumed to be separate from cognition and contrary to rationality, which influenced early study of collective action, and stresses the oppositional nature of cognition and emotions and their function (Barbalet 2001; Freud 1922b). This approach situates emotions as unconscious responses to stimuli and is concerned with how 'negative' emotions can be governed and extinguished (Erikson 1968). Psychological accounts are lacking in that they do not account for the contextual nature of emotions (Kemper 1981; Turner & Stets 2005). Sociological approaches situate emotions as functions and products of interactions and explore the ways that emotions are constructed (Durkheim 1933; Elias 1994). Whilst there is a degree of consensus within psychology and sociology that there is some psychological basis for emotions (Strongman 2003; Turner 1999), there remains contention and complexity around competing typologies of emotions and how those emotions are identified and measured.

Goodwin, Jasper and Polletta (2007) distinguish emotions as being either reactive, which they term 'reflexive emotions', or longer-lasting emotions which are termed 'affective emotions', both of which are relevant to social movement participation. Reflex emotions, which they identify as surprise, anger, disgust, joy, sadness and fear, arise and subside quickly and can stimulate initial participation. Affective emotions, which include love, hate, respect and trust, last over long periods of time and contribute maintenance of participation in movements. They also identify moral emotions as those that include pride, loyalty, shame and guilt which reflect:

> our comprehension of the world around us and sometimes of our place in it. They reflect cultural variations and constructions much more than reflex emotions do. Some of these moral emotions reflect judgements, often implicit, about our own actions.
>
> *(Goodwin et al. 2007: 422)*

EDL activists and emotional responses to grievances

Whilst grievances are widely accepted as a primary motivator (Johnston 1995), it is the fusion of grievances with the emotions that they stimulate that motivates people into participation (Pinard 2011; van Stekelenburg & Klandermans 2010). Jasper (1998) argues that emotions are integral at every stage of protest from recruitment to maintenance of participation through to leaving the movement. The prevalence of emotions as a motivator and maintainer of participation is evident in the EDL. Despite respondents acknowledging that they were concerned about and aware of threats of Islamic extremism prior to the emergence of the EDL, the majority of respondents did not take any action against Islamic extremism. In fact, the majority of respondents (27 out of 32) had never been involved in a protest of any nature prior to the EDL and only three had been involved in a social movement or protest group prior to the EDL. The United British Alliance was one of the first patriotic groups to mobilise around Islamic extremism in response to the 2005 London bombings and only one of the respondents had participated in any of their protests. The majority of respondents, contrary to social network and bloc recruitment theory (Diani 1995, 2007; della Porta 1988; Fernandez & McAdam 1989; Friedman & McAdam 1992; McAdam et al. 1988; Snow et al. 1980) did not enter the movement through friends, acquaintances or existing networks and did not know anyone in the EDL prior to getting involved and attended their first demonstration on their own.

It was events such as the insulting of troops in Luton in 2009, and the burning of the poppies at the Remembrance Day event in London in 2010, which have been cited by all respondents as influencing their decision to become involved in the EDL and which stimulated emotional responses:

> When Luton happened, I remember watching Luton when it was the parade and I nearly kicked my television screen in I was so angry (M26).
>
> Poppy burners, I wanted to do something the day they burned the poppies. To be honest when I first seen that it brought a tear to my eyes. Nothing was done about it really. I was crying when I seen that. That's the ultimate disrespect. I seen it on the TV, I seen it on the internet. I'm just someone who loves my country and I don't like seeing people taking the piss out of it (M11).

These types of unanticipated events or information, I define as ontological shocks rather than moral shocks, whereby people have reflexive emotional responses to events that are seen to challenge or violate dominant ways of living and being. The emotional responses to held grievances that respondents articulated, were anger, outrage, shock, disgust and fear. Whilst shock, anger and outrage were stimulated as reflex emotions to events and do not have a long-term constant prevalence, disgust and fear were evident beyond the initial ontological shocks. Feelings of fear and disgust were voiced consistently by respondents and are dominant as emotional responses to grievances.

Respondents talked of their shock, fear and their anxiety at seeing the confidence and arrogance of the Islamist protestors. Whilst these two events, Luton 2009 and London 2010, were referred to by all the respondents, they also referred to additional events, television and newspaper reports or witnessing 'Muslim street preaching events', as prompting the same emotional response and their call to action. One respondent recounts seeing a street preaching event:

> I was absolutely flabbergasted by what these Muslim guys were saying. There was a guy standing on a plinth, giving a rousing speech to all these Muslim guys, about how we are kuffar, and how we are lower than sheep and cattle, and how Islam is going to dominate and that they should strike out at us. I was getting so angry (M10).

Whereas the insulting of the troops and the burning of the poppies was directly aimed at the British Armed Forces, respondents see these types of events as making attacks on the non-Muslim population and feel personally attacked. As a non-Muslim, this respondent reported to have felt fear, anger and vulnerability by the perceived public denunciation of his status and the threat of being dominated and attacked by Muslims. Whilst these preachers and protestors are not representative of the wider Muslim population, respondents see them as the voices of intent, which the Muslim population needs to denounce, and if they do not, and the respondents feel they do not, they are seen to then be in support. Although disgust, fear, anger and outrage are prevalent emotions voiced in the data, reference to hate in relation to grievances is minimal. When respondents talk of hatred it is in reference to how others feel about them:

> left-wing anti-capitalist types, they hate anything that has to do with us (M06).
> foreigners who have been allowed into our country and hate us with a vengeance and dare to disrespect our soldiers (M01).

Significantly, challenging representations of the EDL as 'fascist', two respondents talked of the hate that they feel, one respondent talked of the hatred he feels for Nazism, National Socialism and Thatcherism, whilst the other proclaimed a hatred of both the National Front and Muslims:

> I hate the National Front. I hate them. I hate them as much as I hate Muslims and I truthfully do. I hate them! (M14)

This was the only reference made to the hatred of Muslims in the entirety of the interview data. So whilst outrage, anger, fear and disgust are the dominant emotional motivators, hate is not a primary motivator for this dataset. Activists themselves acknowledge the pivotal role emotions have played in the EDL's mobilisation. The ontological shocks that respondents cite as motivators stimulated emotional responses but they also tapped into the already held emotions of patriotism.

> We just evolved. We didn't have a strategy, we didn't have a game plan. We just had emotion and passion, that's how we felt (M14).

Patriotism – love, pride and loyalty as motivation

> Yes I'm a patriot we all are and we are defending ourselves. There is no choice. We are not campaigning for this we are defending ourselves against what's coming (M24).

The perceived threat of Islamic extremism or in fact Islam, as these two terms are used interchangeably by respondents, is the overarching grievance held by the respondents. But it is the fusion of the felt emotions stimulated by this grievance, fear, anger, outrage, disgust and the felt emotions of patriotism love, pride and loyalty that relocated respondents from aggrieved citizens to social movement activists. Patriotism can be seen as a portal that not only facilitated activism but justified activism. The EDL has consistently referred to itself as a 'patriot movement' and the respondents refer to themselves as patriots, loyalists and defenders. The name English Defence League situates activists as defenders and any actions that are undertaken are seen as acts of defending, a defence against Islam.

> EDL want to rid the country of Islamic extremism, along with the practice of Sharia Law and Halal slaughter. EDL wishes that Great Britain remains loyal to its own cultures and beliefs before any other. I felt that I was protecting my Christian beliefs and customs. I don't see multiculturalism as a major problem yet, but when the host country's culture is made to feel second best there are bound to be problems in the future (W32).

Defending is integral to patriotism and the mobilisation character of patriotism has been utilised by both the political left and the political right, particularly in relation to harnessing support for war and recruitment to the armed forces. It has been used to defend against change and to defend against enemies in times of war. Respondents are of the view that they are defending against both as is the "expectation" of patriotism. Patriotism is the manifestation of emotions, moral and political positioning, and beliefs that defend and protect the physicality of the country, the people and their morals, values and traditions. Bar-Tal (1993) argues that there are universal fundamental beliefs that are integral to those who see themselves as patriots, which include love, pride, loyalty and care. These beliefs have two purposes:

> These beliefs, on the one hand, serve as antecedents of the motivation and emotion and, on the other hand, function subsequently as its expression, explanation and justification.
>
> *(Bar-Tal 1993: 48)*

Whilst these can be seen as universal fundamentals of patriotism, differing instances of patriotic groups may hold additional specific beliefs in expressing their patriotism, which are specific to the group at particular times and in particular situations and cannot be seen as fundamental. Patriotism gets manipulated and exploited especially in times of war and this has resulted in people feeling that going to war and physically fighting for their country is a patriotic duty however this is not fundamental to patriotism. Patriotism employs symbolism, rhetoric and myth to appeal to those with emotional attachments to the land, country and people. Central to patriotism is its ability to stimulate emotions and bring them to the fore often resulting in action. Respondents became activists though the portal of patriotism. Each of the respondents referred to themselves as patriots, and the EDL as a 'patriotic movement'. Whilst active patriotism is an 'expressive' (Parry et al. 1992: 15) enterprise it is not always about achieving a goal but about expressing grievances, concern and emotions.

Respondents expressed their patriotism in terms of attachment, love, pride, loyalty and concern, those fundamental beliefs that Bar-Tal (1993) identifies.

> Am I patriotic? Yeah. To me it's you care for your community, you care for your country, you love your country. I love England, you know what I mean, and many people do. Many people from lower working-class backgrounds naturally do. I love the queen, I love the royal family, if you ask me why, I don't know (M14).

Respondents discussed how their patriotism has been informed through family, familial values, respect, loyalty, fairness, duty, love of country and making sacrifices that were reinforced at school and through media and government, especially in times of national celebration and times of war. Respondents talked of being from patriotic families and that they have always been patriotic and how 'being patriotic' is an integral part of their culture. All of the activists interviewed had a personal connection to the armed forces – they had served themselves; had family or friends who had or were currently serving; or had applied to join the armed forces (as others in their family had served) but were rejected.

> I'm ex-forces and that's why I joined the EDL ... now its feet on the street. I swore allegiance to Queen and country when I joined the forces and I don't believe it's any different now. They are fighting our soldiers, our soldiers are fighting in Afghanistan and wherever else, it's the same fight that we've got here on our own soil. So while they are there fighting we are going to fight in our own way, the best we can here (M27).

For those who were unsuccessful in their attempts to join the army, the EDL provided them with an alternative.

> I tried joining the army when I was leaving school and they wouldn't have me because I was colour blind, and all my family before me were all in the army and then I couldn't fucking join! I was evil, I was fuming and that's why I became a hooligan, mean like ... I was devastated, all I wanted to do was fight for my country (M01).

This activist took part in a number of interviews and frequently referred to this rejection and his feeling of devastation. This has had a lasting impact on him and he has, by his own analysis, directed his frustration, devastation and anger firstly through 'football hooliganism' for which he has received a number of criminal convictions and prison sentences for violence, and now, in what he views as a more 'constructive and productive' arena through Casuals United and the EDL.

Devastation is again how another young man describes how he felt and still does feel about being rejected in his attempt to join the Army:

> I tried to join the British Army and was rejected … If you get told you can't fight for your country it's the most devastating thing. I don't want to talk about it anymore [starts to get upset, tears in his eyes] (M16).

Patriotism is and has been integral in the recruitment and maintenance of the armed forces in the UK, and throughout the last century 'patriotic duty' was articulated in political and popular discourse to encourage individuals to sign up and fight for their country and for their families to be proud and unquestioning when their family members were killed or injured. When respondents were asked what patriotism felt like, some struggled to find words, others had physical responses such as welling up with tears, smiling, placing their hand symbolically across their chest (heart) whilst they tried to articulate the feelings of patriotism. Biographical narratives surrounding patriotic events and activities from early childhood, with their families, parents, grandparents, friends and neighbours indicate that their patriotism is long-standing and not newly found. There was a reminiscing about 'how things were' by some respondents drawing on stories that they had been told by parents and grandparents of a time there was 'community', 'you knew your neighbours' and 'people respected one another', all of which are presented as a yearning for a (mythical or imagined) English past.

> I am passionate about the cause. We are English we love our country and we love our culture. We want nothing to change, because there is nothing wrong with Great Britain. But at the moment it's full of lefties who just want to destroy our culture and our country and we are bowing down to Islam all the time. You see Muslim extremists, they are traitors and they should've got done for treason actually, for spitting on the soldiers and yet they never got nothing (M21).

The EDL's defence of values and culture is an attempt not only to defend against the perceived domination of Islam but to re-centre Englishness and English values and reclaim the perceived lost past and lost ground. Whilst the focus on Islam and Islamification can be seen as populist in the post 9/11 climate, the need for reclamation of both physical and metaphorical lost ground lies in England's colonial past and loss of empire. Gilroy (2004, 2005) argues that Britain has failed to come to terms with its loss of empire and global standing and whilst respondents recognise the loss of empire, there is a claim of pride in that past status, of imperialist empire builders and a desire for the return of that global status for the nation and themselves as patriots. When respondents talk of their patriotism there is a continual referencing of England's losses.

> We are trying to turn the clock back a bit to how things were, where people were proud of their country, proud of where they lived, proud of their

traditions. I think 13 years of Labour government where they did everything they could to make you not want to feel English, they want everybody to feel European or part of the world rather than proud to actually feel they were part of this country. They made you feel embarrassed about our history, imperialism, colonialism. [Patriotism] it's just a feeling of greatness, a feeling of love for your country and it's everything, you know, your past history. It's a sad thing, we used to run two thirds of the globe, we don't any more but it's nice to harp back to those great days (M10).

Loss of empire, loss of pride and prowess is expressed by respondents and taking to the streets as proud patriots, is seen as a way of not only expressing grievances but expressing patriotism and more importantly making a claim on what they now see as contested space whilst chanting 'Whose streets? Our streets!' Ironically whilst observing a number of EDL protests and counter protests both groups make the same chant staking the same claim 'whose streets our streets', which of course belong to neither one nor the other – those contested spaces are contested on those specific days and times as specific instances, but each group claim a victory in their stake.

> I have considered myself to be firstly a patriot, then a socialist, for as long as I can remember. As a patriotic socialist I stand up against anything that I consider to be a threat to my family, friends and people of this country, whether that be domestic or foreign, such as outside foreign influences, internal government bureaucracy and corrupt police and politicians (W32).

EDL activists see themselves as honourable and heroic 'defenders' and protectors, and regard defence as a key value which is central to their self-identity. The act of defending stems from their belief that their love, loyalty, pride and care for the country and its people, values and culture require them to defend it. The need to defend has been central in catalysing participation and in maintaining participation.

> So the EDL is a patriotic and loyalist organisation that fights for freedom and patriotism in its best sense (M19).
>
> I have always seen loyalty to my Monarch and flag as important and an intrinsic part of my culture. The Queen symbolises Great Britain and what it used to stand for. The Monarch is important as a figurehead separate from transient politicians with agendas and also symbolises the permanence of the state and our way of life. We are the Queen's people, not any governments. Patriotism has become more important obviously, because as working-class people we feel our identity is under attack and patriotism is a key factor in our make-up. Activists refer to each other as 'patriots', but it is a term you earn. To be termed 'a proper patriot' is about as high praise as you can get, our loyalty to each other is something which is vastly underestimated (M02).

The emotions of patriotism

Emotions are the heartbeat of patriotism and passion, love, loyalty, pride, care and attachment are the ingredients of patriotism (Bar-Tal 1993; Primoratz 2007; Rosselli 1994 [1930]; Weil 1952) and it is the prompting or stimulating of these emotions that has propelled these respondents into activism. Vital aspects of patriotism are the moral obligations it is seen to entail. Adherence to values, duties and obligations are demanded in the name of patriotism, for a commitment and readiness to make sacrifices in order to defend and protect (Druckman 1995). Whilst the affective nature of patriotism can be seen to be universal, the obligations are variable. The very concept of patriotism having obligations can be contested if it is accepted that at the root of patriotism is emotion, as emotion has no duty or obligation (Walzer 1970). As discussed earlier the emotions of patriotism have been exploited and utilised for political ends by governments, the political left and the political right, especially in times of war. I suggest that obligations are adjuncts that get attached to patriotism for political ends and that there is no moral obligation or duty embedded within patriotism – the obligations get attached by, and are specific expectations of, those who utilise patriotism for specific ends. Respondents talk about their willingness to make sacrifices in the name of patriotism. Referring to an EDL protest at Tower Hamlets, this respondent talks of her willingness to die for the cause:

> Like Tower Hamlets, my mum said to me, because she'd got told that they were going to plant bombs here there and everywhere, my mum said 'please don't go'. And I said 'no, I'm going and if the worst happened, well I died for the country. I died for the cause.' There aint no bigger thing than that (W05).

The notion of sacrifice has been utilised by successive governments, particularly in times of war, to justify action, policy and ultimately the loss of life. The notion of sacrifice and duty as special obligations are evident in the respondents' beliefs surrounding patriotism. These special obligations have now become synonymous with patriotism and although Miller (1995) and Tamir (1993) are supportive of this notion of citizens having special obligations, and the respondents feeling they have special obligations, I see special obligations as tools of manipulation that are used to advance or achieve political goals, particularly in the case of their use by the state and lack any moral grounding. However, just as patriotism can be and has been exploited for political ends by governments and political parties the EDL is also utilising patriotism for its own ends. The notion of patriotic duty derives from the demands made by those who are exploiting patriotism. Duty implies obligation and there is no obligation to be patriotic, patriotism has not been a part of the social contract in England. It is those combined elements of patriotism that respondents hold and act upon in the face of threat which cements their view of their actions being honourable and patriotism being virtuous (Poole 2007: 129).

Patriots and loyalists

The EDL is not a revolutionary movement and has not participated in protest of a revolutionary nature. There is no desire to overthrow the state and its institutions (as that is what the EDL are defending), although the respondents can be seen to be critical loyalists in their criticism of the government regarding its negligent failure to defend English values and culture. Rather, the EDL's fight against Islamic extremism and its manifestation of defence has gone down a more traditional mainstream protest route of demonstrations, petitions and letter-writing. Activities have focused on online information sharing, national, regional and local protests with rallies at the end of the protest route, flash mobs, petitioning around planning applications for mosques and leafleting about the threat of Islam, Grooming gangs, halal meat and the two-tier justice system, which they argue favours everyone bar the EDL and the working-class English, and attempting to get media coverage to 'spread the word'. There have been some attempts at letter-writing to local and national papers with no publishing success and trying to engage with local councillors and MPs. However, there have been some additional sporadic activities that some respondents participated in, 'defending' their communities during the 2012 London Riots:

> I was in Eltham that night. There was just gangs upon gangs roaming the streets just looking to smash up local shops but we put a stop to that. We stood in the middle of the road and said 'if you want to come and smash this place up you're going to have to come through us first' and they ran for their lives. We chased them out of Eltham, we chased them and I've never seen gangs run so fast in my life (M11).

This activity, although not supported by the EDL leadership, was widely seen as an honourable act of patriotism by defending your community. The mainstream press reported it, not as the acts of honourable patriots but as the acts of vigilantes (Hough et al. 2011).

Many respondents make direct comparison to Ulster loyalists in the north of Ireland in regard to their need to defend. They consider the threats that the Protestant community in the north of Ireland face are the same threats that they face and one reason for taking action now is so that the situation in England does not escalate to the state it has in the north of Ireland. Ulster loyalists see their culture as under attack and that state institutions are not doing enough to protect their culture, identity and status (*BBC Three* 2013). These grievances resonated and are echoed by the respondents and cited as justification to defend just as their fellow patriots, Ulster loyalists, have done. Unlike the some of the loyalist defenders in the north of Ireland, the EDL as yet have not taken paramilitary action.

> We've just been down in Luton and I've been to Belfast and its uncanny, it's just like going to Belfast, you got whole Muslim areas and then you walk around and its all white areas. It's so weird. (M26).

The EDL's support for Ulster loyalism is part of its DNA. As patriots they are loyalists and central to that is loyalty and defence. The football firms' early participation through Casuals United had a significant influence on the boundaries, culture and political affiliations of the movement. Many of the football firms who participated under the Casuals United network had long-standing affiliations and support for Ulster Loyalism, such as Chelsea and Millwall. All the participants voiced support for the Protestant community in the north of Ireland seeing it as a shared cause and drawing on songs and symbolism. The EDL anthem 'Coming Down the Road' is a rewrite of a well-known loyalist song of the same name with UVF being substituted with EDL. Garland and Treadwell (2010) have also highlighted the EDL links with Ulster loyalism.

Conclusion

EDL activists regard patriotism, love of country, as a virtue and as noble and honourable in both identity and action. Patriotism together with emotional responses to grievances has shifted respondents from a passive affective patriotism to an active patriotism whereby respondents started to take action. There has been a lack of focus on the EDL's patriotism and as a consequence this has been largely undervalued in previous research. Although patriotism is recognised, it is seen as an appendage or conflated with nationalism and the positioning of the EDL as far right (Allen 2011; Bartlett & Littler 2011; Copsey 2010; Garland & Treadwell 2010; Goodwin & Evans 2012; Richards 2011). This has meant that when motivations have been examined within this context they have been largely situated within the social breakdown theories of cultural and welfare protectionism and Islamophobia, as opposed to examining the contribution patriotism makes to motivations. The evidence suggests that patriotism plays a central role in motivating participation.

Grievances and the emotional responses to those grievances are the primary motivators for activists. The emotions that are aroused as a result of grievances, anger, outrage, fear and disgust are similar across social movements. Examples of this are Deborah Gould's research focusing on ACT UP activists (Gould 2009) and Jasper and Nelkin's research on the animal rights movement in the US (Jasper & Nelkin 1992). It is these emotions which research participants cite as being the stimulus to initially take action and get involved. These reflex emotions could be seen to be irrational as they emerge without cognitive processing. However, in the case of EDL, as with many activists across social movements, I suggest that they have made activists 'more alert and focused on the problem at hand and therefore more rather than less rational' (Goodwin et al. 2007: 416–417).

The emotional responses to grievances fused with emotions and values of patriotism have propelled EDL activists from aggrieved citizens to social movement activists. Islamic extremism is often cited as the primary grievance and key motivator and is utilised as a validated populist grievance from which an array of additional long-standing grievances around status, identity and societal changes are catapulted into the public domain. The EDL has provided a vehicle for these grievances to be articulated and, although there is a concern about Islamic extremism, respondents are more concerned about their status and identity. Government and media promotion of the supposed threats posed by Islamic extremism are at the roots of the respondent's fears. Islamification, societal changes, fear of change, perceived loss of status and violation of moral values seen through the prism of Islamic extremism, together with the emotions which they have generated, have propelled respondents through the portal of patriotism into activism.

Patriotism is problematic in that it gets presented as noble and virtuous but is used to focus on difference. The manifestation of the EDL's patriotism through its street protests and activities has contributed to community tensions, violence and instilled fear in communities. Patriotic love cannot be used as a justification for abuse, violence and instilling fear in communities. It cannot and should not be used to excuse or justify racism, xenophobia, sectarianism. The EDL's patriotic love has been used as a cohesive force between activists within the movement, whilst outside the movement it has had a negative impact in its escalation of community tensions and the fracturing of communities with the ultimate potential of tearing them apart.

References

Allen, C. (2011) 'Opposing Islamification or Promoting Islamophobia? Understanding the English Defence League', *Patterns of Prejudice*, 45 (4), pp.279–94.

Barbalet, J. (2001) *Emotion, Social Theory and Social Structure: A Macrosociology Approach.* Cambridge: Cambridge University Press.

Bar-Tal, D. (1993) 'Patriotism as Fundamental Beliefs of Group Members', *Politics and the Individual*, 3 (2), pp.45–62.

Bartlett, J. & Littler, M. (2011) *Inside the EDL: Populist Politics in a Digital Age.* London: Demos.

BBC Three, 2013. Petrol Bombs and Peace: Welcome to Belfast, 21:00. 5 August.

Busher, J. (2016) *The Making of Anti-Muslim Protest: Grassroots Activism in the English Defence League.* London: Routledge.

Copsey, N. (2010) *The English Defence League: Challenging our Country and our Values of Social Inclusion, Fairness and Equality.* London: Faith Matters.

della Porta, D. (1988) 'Recruitment Processes in Clandestine Political Organizations: Italian Left-Wing Terrorism', in B. Klandermans, H. Kriesi & S. Tarrow, eds. *From Structure to Action.* Greenwich: JAI Press.

Diani, M. (1995) *Green Networks.* Edinburgh: Edinburgh University Press.

Diani, M. (2007) 'Networks and Participation', in A. Snow, S. Soule & H. Kriesi, eds. *The Blackwell Companion to Social Movements.* Oxford: Blackwell Publishing.

Druckman, D. (1995) 'Social Psychological Aspects of Nationalism', in J. Comaroff & P. Stern, eds. *Perspectives on Nationalism and War.* Oxon: Routledge.

Durkheim, E. (1933) *The Division of Labour in Society.* London: The Free Press.

Elias, N. (1994) *The Civilising Process.* Oxford: Blackwell.

Erikson, E. (1956) 'The Problem of Ego Identity', *The Journal of the American Psychoanalytic Association*, 4 (1), pp.56–121.

Erikson, E. (1968) *Identity: Youth and Crisis.* London: Faber.

Fernandez, R. & McAdam, D. (1989) 'Multiorganizational Fields and Recruitment to Social Movements', *International Social Movement Research*, 2, pp.315–343.

Freud, S. (1922a) 'The Unconscious', *The Journal of Nervous and Mental Disease*, 56 (3), pp.291–294.

Freud, S. (1922b) 'Mourning and Melancholia', *The Journal of Nervous and Mental Disease*, 56 (5), pp.543–545.

Friedman, D. & McAdam, D. (1992) 'Collective Identity and Activism: Networks, Choices, and the Life of a Social Movement', in A. Morris & C. Mueller, eds. *Frontiers in Social Movement Theory*. New Haven: Yale University Press. pp.156–173.

Garland, J. & Treadwell, J. (2010) '"No surrender to the Taliban!" Football Hooliganism, Islamophobia and the Rise of the English Defence League', *Papers from the British Criminology Conference – The British Society of Criminology*, 10, pp.19–35.

Gilroy, P. (2004) *After Empire: Melancholia or Convivial Culture*. Abingdon: Routledge.

Gilroy, P. (2005) *Postcolonial Melancholia*. New York: Colombia University Press.

Goodwin, M. & Evans, J. (2012) *From Voting to Violence? Far Right Extremism in Britain*. London: *Searchlight* Educational Trust.

Goodwin, J., Jasper, J. & Polletta, F. (2007) 'Emotional Dimensions of Social Movements', in D. Snow, S. Soule & H. Kriesi, eds. *The Blackwell Companion to Social Movements*. Oxford: Blackwell Publishing. pp.413–432.

Gould, D. (2009) *Moving Politics: Emotion and ACT UP's Fight Against AIDS*. Chicago: University of Chicago.

Groves, J. (1997) *Hearts and Minds*. Philadelphia: Temple University Press.

Hough, A., Ross, T. & Alleyne, R. (2011) *London riots: vigilantes hurl bottles at police in Eltham*. [Online] Available at: www.telegraph.co.uk/news/uknews/crime/8694472/London-riots-vigilantes-hurl-bottles-at-police-in-Eltham.html (accessed 6 June 2014).

Jackson, P. (2011) *The EDL: Britain's 'New Far Right''s social movement*. Northampton: The University of Northampton.

Jasper, J. (1998) 'The Emotions of Protest: Affective and Reactive Emotions in and Around Social Movements', *Sociological Forum*, 13 (3), pp.397–424.

Jasper, J. & Nelkin, D. (1992) *The Animal Rights Crusade: The Growth of a Moral Protest*. New York: Free Press.

Johnston, H. (1995) 'A Methodology for Frame Analysis: From Discourse to Cognitive Schemata', in H. Johnston & B. Klandermans, eds. *Social Movements and Culture*. Minneapolis, MN: University of Minnesota Press. pp.217–246.

Kemper, T. (1981) 'Social Constructionist and Positivist Approaches to the Sociology of Emotions', *The American Journal of Sociology*, 87 (2), pp.336–362.

Klandermans, B. (1997) *The Social Psychology of Protest*. Oxford: Blackwell Publishing.

Luton Commission on Community Cohesion (2011) *Building Cohesion in Luton*. Luton: Luton Commission on Community Cohesion.

McAdam, D., McCarthy, J. & Zald, M. (1988) 'Social Movements', in N. Smelser, ed. *Handbook of Sociology*. Beverley Hills, CA: Sage. pp.695–737.

Miller, D. (1995) *On Nationality*. Oxford: Clarendon.

Parry, G., Moyser, G. & Day, N. (1992) *Political Participation and Democracy in Britain*. Cambridge: Cambridge University Press.

Pilkington, H. (2016) *Loud and Proud: Passion and Politics in the English Defence League*. Manchester: Manchester University Press.

Pinard, M. (2011) *Motivational Dimensions in Social Movements and Contentious Collective Action*. Montreal: McGill-Queens University Press.

Poole, R. (2007) 'Patriotism and Nationalism', in I. Primoratz & A. Pavkovic, eds. *Patriotism: Philosophical and Political Perspectives*. Aldershot: Ashgate Publishing Ltd. pp.129–146.

Primoratz, I. (2007) 'Patriotism and Morality: Mapping the Terrain', in I. Primoratz & A. Pavkovic, eds. *Patriotism – Philosophical and Political Perspectives*. Aldershot: Ashgate Publishing Limited. pp.17–36.

Richards, J. (2011) 'Reactive Community Mobilization in Europe: The Case of the English Defence League', *Behavioural Sciences of Terrorism and Political Aggression*, pp.1–17.

Rosselli, C. (1994[1930]). *Liberal Socialism [Socialismo Liberale]*. Translated by W. McCraig. Princeton, NJ: Princeton University Press.

Secomb, L. (2007) *Philosophy and Love: From Plato to Popular Culture*. Edinburgh: Edinburgh University Press.

Snow, D., Zurcher Jr, L. & Ekland-Olson, S. (1980) 'Social Networks and Social Movements: A Microstructural Approach to Differential Recruitment', *American Sociological Review*, 45 (5), pp.787–801.

Strongman, K. (2003) *The Psychology of Emotion: From Everyday Life to Theory*. Chichester: John Wiley and Sons Ltd.

Tamir, Y. (1993) *Liberal Nationalism*. Princeton, NJ: Princeton University Press.

Taylor, V. (1995) 'Watching for Vibes: Bringing Emotions in the Study of Feminist Organisations', in M. Ferree & P. Martin, eds. *Feminist Organizations: Harvest of the New Women's Movement*. Philadelphia: Temple University Press. pp.223–233.

Turner, J. (1999) 'The Neurology of Emotion: Implications for Sociological Theories of Interpersonal Behaviour', in D. Franks & T. Smith, eds. *Mind, Brain and Society: Towards a Neurosociology of Emotion*. Greenwich: Stamford JAI Press. pp.81–108.

Turner, J. & Stets, J. (2005) *The Sociology of Emotions*. Cambridge: Cambridge University Press.

University of Huddersfield (2014) *Understanding Concerns about Community Relations in Kirklees*. Huddersfield: University of Huddersfield.

van Stekelenburg, J. & Klandermans, B. (2010) 'Individuals in Movements: A Social Psychology of Contention' in B. Klandermans & C. Roggerband, eds. *Handbook of Social Movements Across Disciplines*. New York: Springer. pp.157–205.

Walzer, M. (1970) *Obligations: Essays on Disobedience, War and Citizenship*. Cambridge, MA: Harvard University Press.

Weil, S. (1952) *The Need for Roots: Prelude to a Declaration of Duties Toward Mankind*. Translated by A. Wills. New York: Harper and Row.

Winlow, S., Hall, S. & Treadwell, J. (2017) *The Rise of the Right: English Nationalism and the Transformation of Working-class Politics*. Bristol: The Policy Press.

Wood, E. (2001) 'The Emotional Benefits of Insurgency in El Salvador', in J. Goodwin, J. Jasper & F. Polletta, eds. *Passionate Politics: Emotions and Social Movements*. Chicago: Chicago University Press. pp.267–281.

12

BRITAIN'S FAR RIGHT SINCE 1967

A bibliographic survey[1]

Craig Fowlie[2]

Introduction

Philip Rees' seminal bibliography *Fascism in Britain* (Rees 1979) featured just *one* book length study of the contemporary[3] post-1967 far-right[4]: *The National Front* by *Guardian* journalist Martin Walker (Walker 1977). Since the beginning of the 1980s however there has been a large number of scholarly monographs, edited collections and articles which have examined the historical and contemporary British far right, including specific parties, movements, subcultures, leaders, activists and intellectuals, as well as more theoretical, comparative and transnational studies.[5]

The British far right has attracted the attention of historians, political scientists, sociologists, psychologists, anthropologists, discourse analysts and cultural studies scholars among others. There have been numerous PhDs on the subject.[6] Think tanks and civil society groups have employed their own researchers and academics to produce reports, briefing papers and policy documents on the far right while several journalists have been inspired to write detailed and well-researched accounts. Activists within the far right as well as their opponents from anti-fascist, civil society and 'watchdog' organisations have also published their own memoirs, biographies and partisan histories.[7]

Discussions of the British far right often focus on its electoral failure (e.g. Cronin 1996; Goodwin 2007; Griffin 1996) especially compared to its European counterparts and there is a strong argument to be made that this is a valid interpretation. The electoral high point for the extreme right was the BNP having two MEPs and over sixty local councillors in 2010, while for the populist radical right, it was UKIP winning the largest number of seats in the European Parliament elections in 2014. But even these successes – which far outstripped the electoral performance of their historical predecessors on the far right – were short-lived, as both the BNP and UKIP have been in considerable organisational turmoil and decline ever since those heady highs.[8] It is important to acknowledge though that far-right activity has never been just about electoral performance or its influence on the policies of the main parties on core concerns like immigration (Carvalho 2014).

The major white power subculture of Nazi skinhead music originated in the UK and is now a worldwide phenomenon (Dyck 2017) and while the BNP and UKIP were floundering electorally, the EDL emerged with a new hybrid ideology as the most significant street-based far-right movement for a generation (Copsey 2010). The EDL was also one of the first far-right social movements to generate significant support and profile through social media (Bartlett and Littler 2011) and inspired the creation of similar organisations abroad (Williams and Lowles 2010). More recently, National Action, an extreme-right *groupuscule* whose violent rhetoric and street posturing was influenced both by traditional Nazi ideology and the stylistic and cultural trappings of European militant nationalists, became the first far-right group ever to be banned by the UK government under anti-terror legislation (Allen 2017).

Structure and scope

In summary then, participation in the far right tends to be in one of three forms[9] – in *political parties*, in *social movements* or in *subcultures* (Mudde 2014: 3).[10] The literature review that follows surveys the research in each of these three areas with a consistent rubric that examines first the scholarly literature on the subject, second accounts by non-academics such as journalists, and third primary source material written by far-right activists and their political opponents. Following a brief discussion of scope below, the structure of the rest of the chapter is in the following sections:

PARTIES

This section first examines general academic histories of the British far right before reviewing the social science literature on parties such as the NF, the BNP and UKIP. Journalistic treatments and primary sources are also discussed. This is, by far, the longest section as far-right parties have dominated the literature.

SOCIAL MOVEMENTS

This section reviews the scholarship, journalistic accounts and primary sources on far-right social movements such as the EDL as well as discussing the historiography of anti-fascist movements.

SUBCULTURES

Various forms of *groupuscular*, cultural, cultic, metapolitical and violent far-right activism are discussed in this section, including the transnational far right, European

New Right, neo-Nazism and fascist occultism, white power music, Holocaust denial, online activism, and racial violence and terrorism.

The chapter concentrates on full-length works on the post-1967 British far right. The focus on books necessitates that this chapter will not cover the vast amount of primary publications and propaganda produced by far-right organisations in the form of flyers, leaflets, posters, blogs, social media posts, videos and other ephemera, nor generally short print publications such as pamphlets, magazines and journals.[11] The same applies to similar material produced by anti-fascists, watchdog and civil society groups opposed to the far right. Some book chapters, journal articles, pamphlets and PhD theses are included when they are particularly significant theoretical or empirical contributions to the scholarship or where they touch on issues that are not covered by the main books on the subject.

Previous bibliographic studies (Rees 1979, 1980, 1984) have examined the pre-1979 literature on fascism in Britain, changing interpretations of British fascism and the European context in the pre-1945 era. But despite several chapters in Thurlow (2000: 1–30) on the historiography and primary sources of British fascism, and an important overview of work on the populist radical right by Mudde (2016a), this will be the first detailed bibliographic survey since Rees of modern scholarship on the contemporary British far right.

1) PARTIES

General histories of the British far right

Historical methodology in researching the British far right has been fairly traditional until recently with the usual emphasis on textual primary and secondary sources – archives, correspondence, private papers, official documents, memoirs, press reports, publications and propaganda etc. – and the scholarship has focused very much on the main far-right parties and their activists and leaders.[12]

While the literature on pre-1945 British fascism and the far right is ever expanding and now remarkably varied, it is beyond the scope of this chapter to do justice to that rich seam of historical scholarship.[13] It is also not possible, given the particularly British focus of this chapter, to examine in any depth the detailed, and occasionally heated, debates[14] on defining generic fascism. (For examples of some of the key positions and debates see Copsey forthcoming; Costa Pinto 2011; Eatwell 1992, 1996a; Gentile 2005; Gregor 2006; Griffin 1993, 1995, 1998; Griffin and Feldman 2004, 2008; Griffin et al. 2006; Hayes 2014; Iordachi 2010; Mann 2004; Mosse 1999; Neocleous 1997; Passmore 2006, 2014; Paxton 2004; Payne 1995; Renton 2000; Sternhell 1986, 1994; Woodley 2010.)

One of the influential legacies of the theoretical discussion on fascism has been the (admittedly still contested) idea of mythic cultural rebirth being central to understanding fascism (Griffin 1993: 26). This has provided a conceptual framework for some historical accounts examining the post-war far right (e.g. Baker 1996; Jackson 2017; Macklin 2007; Thurlow 2000). One other consequence of this has been the 'cultural turn in generic fascist studies' (Copsey and Richardson 2015: 2) which has also impacted on the scholarship on social movements and sub-cultures, discussed later in this chapter. The 'cultural turn' is explored most valuably in the edited collection by Copsey and Richardson (2015). Building on the superb earlier work on culture in interwar British fascism (Gottlieb and Linehan 2004), this examines a broad range of cultural issues within the British far right. These include myths of rebirth, gender, space, fashion, metapolitics and 'cultural Marxism'. The book also explores artistic outputs of the far right including music, neo-Nazi fiction and fashion as well as representations of the far right within mainstream popular culture.

Within the broader historiography of British fascism, there are surprisingly few historical studies covering both the pre-war and post-war far right, even though there are substantial direct continuities between each era and early journalistic accounts often concentrated on this aspect (Cross 1961; Mullally 1946; Thayer 1965). It was a handful of pre-war activists such as A.K. Chesterton, Arnold Leese, Oswald Mosley and Jeffrey Hamm who provided the ideological and organisational impetus to keep the fascist flame alive and then passed it on to subsequent generations of post-war activists (Macklin forthcoming).

Of the main general studies by historians, the three books by Richard Thurlow (1987, 1998, 2000) are still arguably among the best one volume studies of British fascism. Although focused more on the pre-war era, they do include material on the post-war far right including the Union Movement, League of Empire Loyalists, the National Socialist Movement, National Front and (very briefly) the British National Party, and the author makes excellent use of primary source material and official papers released to the National Archives. His longest treatment of the contemporary far right (Thurlow 1998: 203–277) devotes four chapters to the post-war far right and concisely outlines the persistent divisions, and occasional compromises, between the racial populists and national socialists within the NF. Thurlow is surely correct to view the early NF's ideology as a 'witches brew' of Leese's racial nationalism, Mosley's economics and Chesterton's conspiratorial anti-Semitism (Thurlow 1998: 262–263).

These three leading figures are examined in a number of other important studies. While Dorril (2006: 569–647) does provide a useful history of Mosley's activities in the post-war era (see also Lewis 1987), the essential volume for understanding the Mosleyite tradition and its later influence on the contemporary far right is Macklin (2007), which draws on extensive primary and secondary sources to delineate the development of the UM and the evolution of pan-European fascism. The book is particularly strong at revealing Mosley's involvement in currents that would be appropriated by later incarnations of the far right, such as transnationalism, Holocaust denial and 'cultural' racism. The admirable biography by David Baker (1996) of A.K. Chesterton, the first Chairman of the NF, provides a detailed analysis of the development of his conspiratorial anti-Semitism which profoundly impacted on other far-right figures such as John Tyndall, although the book sadly contains little discussion of Chesterton's period in the NF. Macklin's forthcoming

volume looks set to complement these studies with a detailed biographical investigation of six far-right leaders (Leese, Mosley, Chesterton, Jordan, Tyndall, Griffin)
representing the entire British fascist tradition.

Roger Eatwell (1995: 259–275) offers an illuminating potted survey of the evolution of 'neo-fascism' in the UK post-1945, although his study is arguably more
useful for situating developments in Britain in a comparative context with France,
Germany and Italy. Sykes' short monograph (1995) again covers most of the twentieth century fairly briskly and although he devotes a disproportionate amount
of space to the pre-1920s, his coverage of the interwar era is distinguished by an
informed discussion of fascist economics including social credit and distributism
and his later chapters include a rare academic account of how these ideas and others
influenced the ideological peregrinations of the NF in the 1980s. He also briefly
discusses the early 'modernisation' of the BNP and its conflict with Nazi street gang
Combat 18.

A major new contribution to the literature on British fascism is by Richardson
(2017). Building on several earlier valuable works which applied insights from discourse studies and linguistics to the study of the far right (Brindle 2016; Wodak
2015; Wodak, Khosravinik and Mral 2013; Wodak and Richardson 2013), this also
draws on some of the insights from (Billig 1978) to examine fascist history, ideology and practice in the UK. While the book's historical sections on British fascism are very solidly researched and explicated, the close readings of the rhetorical
techniques used by far-right leaders such as Nick Griffin are enormously insightful
and expose the 'back stage' ideology behind the 'front stage' propaganda (Mudde
2000). In many ways these close readings represent a methodological breakthrough
in the study of the British far right and it is to be hoped that other scholars can
apply these techniques to equally powerful effect in future studies. The book also
interrogates ideological and policy areas that are too often under-explored in the
literature on contemporary British fascism, such as the environment, economics
and gender and in so doing exposes the underlying centrality of race and ethnocentrism to the British fascist worldview. Another real strength of the book is that
it tackles the often overlooked issue of the relationship between the far right and
violence, including terrorism, targeted against both political opponents and those
demonised by fascist ideology such as ethnic minorities. This is undoubtedly one
of the most significant books on the British far right to have been published in the
last two decades.

Hayes' (2014) book is a rare attempt to apply theoretical discussion of fascist ideology to the historic specificity of British fascism. Written from an avowedly anti-
fascist perspective – the author is a former member of Red Action and AFA, now a
university lecturer – it eschews traditional academic objectivity and is highly critical
of the liberal historians' 'new consensus' in fascism studies. Despite its polemical
intent, it is well-researched and referenced with a good bibliography (although irri-
tatingly unindexed). While it offers an engaging critical summary of the competing
theories of fascism, the author's own definition of fascist ideology is ultimately a
fairly conventional Marxist take and the book's historical section on British fascism

has little original to say and is slightly over-reliant on secondary sources. But this is still a welcome attempt to provide a radical historically grounded critique of the existing scholarship in comparative fascist studies and it is to be hoped that other scholars can build on this.

There is surprisingly little literature on the relationship between the post-war Conservative right and the far right (although see e.g. Durham 1996; Eatwell and O'Sullivan 1989; Nugent and King 1977; Webb and Bale 2014). Mark Pitchford's (2011) study of the Conservative party and the extreme right is therefore a valuable exception. Drawing heavily on the Conservative party's own archives, the book provides a detailed account of how the Tories reacted to various groupings to their right in the post-war and contemporary era (the book ends in 1975). Sometimes the Conservative hostility resulted in the party actively seeking to counter extremist organisations while on other occasions its strategy was to co-opt far-right ideas and policies into the mainstream right. Despite some weaknesses in its coverage – e.g. nothing on the Economic League (see Hughes 2012) – the book is particularly useful as a history of the non-fascist organisations and pressure groups active on the nether regions of the right as well as opening up new avenues of research in how mainstream parties have historically reacted to the threat from the far right.

Scholarship on parties – NF, BNP, UKIP

In the British case, and in the European context more widely, the main scholarly literature on the far right has overwhelmingly focused on political parties and their voters (Bale 2012; Mudde 2016a) whether this is historians writing about the British Union of Fascists or political scientists analysing electoral support for the NF, BNP and UKIP.

The political science literature on far-right parties has traditionally been divided between 'demand side' and 'supply side' explanations.[15] The 'demand side' approach focuses on the broader social, cultural and economic drivers of far-right electoral support. Such 'externalist factors' (Goodwin 2006) include immigration, anti-establishment feeling, social breakdown (anomie), post-materialism or economic self-interest as the 'losers of globalisation' (Eatwell 2003), 'the left behind' (Ford and Goodwin 2014) or the 'somewheres'[16] (Goodhart 2017).

In contrast, 'supply side' explanations focus more on the far-right *party* itself rather than far-right *voters*. The 'internalist factors' (Goodwin 2006) include the quality of the leadership, the motivations of activists, the retention of party cadres, party organisation and administration, and ideology (Art 2011; Carter 2005; Eatwell 2003; Mudde 2000; Norris 2005).

The studies discussed below contain examples of each of these approaches as well as several examples where both methods are used. There are though still more demand-side studies – especially in the journals literature – and it is hard to argue with Mudde (2016a: 13) that 'more challenging, but even more important, is increased research on the inner life of the parties'.

Scholarship on the NF

Billig's (1978) ground-breaking study of the NF drew on methods from social psychology and was based on empirical research undertaken with a small number of NF members in the West Midlands. The book's most influential finding (see e.g. Eatwell 1996; Feldman and Jackson 2014; Richardson 2017) was that fascist groups have both an esoteric (hidden) and exoteric (public) ideology.[17] In the case of the NF, the esoteric ideology included traditional Nazi-inspired conspiratorial anti-semitism and biological racism while their exoteric propaganda emphasised law and order and ethnocentric nationalism. This fundamental tension between the ideological purity of the 'true believers' and the desire for a more temperate mass base has been a consistent faultline in far-right parties.

Fielding (1981) is a sociological study which contains a brief history and some analysis of the NF's organisational structure and electoral activity but it focuses primarily on the NF's ideology and is based on both interviews and ethnographic observation. Although the book is quite successful in giving some indication of what it was like to be a member of the NF in the 1970s, Fielding's attempt to interpret the NF through the theoretical lens of social deviance theory is largely unsuccessful. A far more coherent and useful analysis, written from a political science perspective is provided by Taylor (1982). There is a strong empirical analysis of the party's membership and its electoral performance, particularly in the 1977 elections. It is also one of the first studies to consider the role of opposing groups in limiting the success of the NF although compelling evidence for this is often intangible.

Husbands' (1983) study provides the most detailed account of the NF's electoral support, especially during its electoral rise and decline from 1974–79 (see also Harrop et al., 1980; Whiteley 1979). In particular Husbands, drawing on literature from urban sociology, developed a more sophisticated account of the geographical specificity of the NF's electoral base, identifying a number of predominantly urban areas of strength – the East End of London, parts of the West Midlands, the East Midlands and West Yorkshire – often adjacent to areas of high immigration. In focusing on the particularities of local history and politics, including recent immigration and social demographics, more concrete evidence is presented of the characteristics of NF sympathisers. They were generally men, under thirty, either self-employed or out of work, and were more likely to attribute the 'decline' in their local area to the presence of black and Asian residents. Identifying the social, cultural and economic determinants of far-right electoral support in the UK would develop more sophisticated models over time (aided by increased quantitative computational power) but much of this literature builds on and enhances Husbands' pioneering work.

The academic literature on the NF's ideological evolution and organisational disintegration in the 1980s is comparatively sparse but the chapter by Husbands (1988) is an indicative survey while Baker (1985) and Eatwell (1996) offer informative analysis of the ideological innovations during this period of considerable upheaval. These are also covered by an unpublished PhD thesis (O'Hara 2000).[18]

There were several minor studies published in the early 1980s including Tomlinson (1981) which looked superficially and briefly at 'extremists' on the left and the right including the NF, BM and League of St George, while Wilkinson (1981) has some useful information on the international connections and violent tendencies of British right-wing extremists. Some later studies examined the NF in comparative context while looking at the rise of the right in Europe in the early 1990s (Ford 1992; Harris 1990; Taylor 1993).

There are some other salient issues related to the NF that are often only covered in passing in the literature above but have better analysis elsewhere – for example, the NF youth wing (Billig and Cochrane 1981; Shaffer 2013, 2017) – while the weighty question of women and gender in relation to the party is discussed most impressively by Martin Durham in a series of studies including a book (Durham 1998) which examines the role of women within the NF as well as gender issues within the fascist party's ideology, discourse and policies (see also Ware 1978). Durham also breaks new ground with a rare academic investigation of the NF and Northern Ireland (Durham 2012). Despite Loyalism (and vehement anti-Republicanism) being a central tenet of the contemporary British far right, this is an under-researched area and is generally only touched upon in passing in the main academic accounts of Loyalist paramilitaries (e.g. Edwards 2017; Wood 2006).

The NF's racism and anti-Semitism is analysed concisely but to great effect in several book chapters, articles and pamphlets (Billig 1988; Eatwell 1989; Edgar 1977; Nugent and King 1979). But the question of NF members – and the far right in general – being involved in violence and racial attacks is again an area that is not well-served in the scholarship (Taylor 1978) although there have been some speculative accounts by anti-fascists (*Searchlight* 1989) as well as some localised studies (Husbands 1982).

Non-academic accounts of the NF

Martin Walker was a *Guardian* journalist and his book (Walker 1977) on the NF is based on the journalist's tools of participation, interviews, cross-referencing and archival research. He was granted interviews by many of the leading figures in the extreme-right party before members were banned from helping him by a directive from the NF Executive Council. His book is frustratingly free of sources and references but still provides impressive historical context on the post-war fascist tradition and key organisational developments on the far right in the 1960s and early 1970s. It is clearly written and strong on the ideological and personality differences which plagued the early years of the NF. It remains one of the best journalistic accounts of the contemporary far right.

Bill Buford's entertaining book (1991) is in the 'gonzo' tradition of American journalism as pioneered by Hunter S. Thompson and others. Its main focus is on football hooliganism and it is an occasionally insightful exploration of what attracts men to the thrills of street-fighting and crowd violence. One section of the book is devoted to his experience of encountering the NF, including a White Noise concert in 1985 hosted by the NF leadership. Unfortunately, the book's success led to a raft of rather less enlightening football hooligan memoirs (e.g. Bushell 2010; Marriner 2015).

Primary sources on the National Front

In 1983 the NF published a collection of essays reflecting its new ideological influences which featured excerpts from the original Nazis and the Strasser brothers as well as chapters by G.K. Chesterton, Robert Blatchford and William Morris (Anon. 1983) and several internal propaganda pamphlets were published during the splits within the party (Anon. 1986). Memoirs by former NF activists include Bean (1999), Collins (2011), Morrison (2003), Owens (2007), Pearce (2013), Portinari (2016), Simms (2016), and Southgate (2010a). Bean was an activist in various Nazi groups in the 1950s and 1960s before joining the NF and later becoming involved with the BNP. He was well acquainted with many of the leaders of the far right and his book provides some insight into the intense internecine disputes among the fascist groups. Another former NF activist with a reputation for disputatiousness, Eddie Morrison's memoirs (Morrison 2003) recall his days as a street fighter in the NF and too many other far-right groups to mention.[19] A similar emphasis on physical violence and criminality is a feature of Joey Owens' memoir (Owens 2007). Owens joined the NF in Liverpool and was involved in street violence against the left before later being imprisoned for sending razor blades through the mail to British Jews. After dropping out of political activity for some time while involved in the criminal underworld, Owens joined Nick Griffin's BNP, ending up as his bodyguard.

Southgate (2010a), a former NF activist, later involved in myriad far-right *groupuscules*, provides a revisionist analysis of the 1980s' NF, drawing on many primary sources that emphasise the 'revolutionary' credentials of its 'radical' wing in which the author himself played a prominent part. Southgate is a prolific writer and has published many volumes of his own writings as well as edited collections on other figures in the right-wing and esoteric traditions (see e.g. Southgate 2010b). He has also been an ideological innovator moving from third positionism through revolutionary English nationalism to 'National Anarchism' (Macklin 2005).

Pearce meanwhile recounts his time as a well-known leader in the NF, who was a working-class activist, particularly influential within the NF's youth wing where he celebrated football hooliganism and was instrumental in connecting the far-right group with the white power music scene. After several spells in prison, he converted to Catholicism, dropped out of extreme-right activism and has since become a much published literary biographer (e.g. Pearce 1996; 2001) with reactionary rather than extreme-right views, although some anti-fascists have questioned the true extent of his ideological shift.

Collins (2011) tells a similar story from a different time period. As a bored young man growing up in working-class South London, he became involved in the NF in the late 1980s but he underwent a change of heart and began working as a mole for

Searchlight. His no-holds-barred account provides insight into the reasons why some young white working-class men are attracted to the macho camaraderie of far-right activism and it contains graphic accounts of the endemic violence as well as exploring the inevitable stress that comes with infiltration. Collins' story takes place against the backdrop of significant changes in the British far right with the demise of the NF, the rise of the BNP and the formation of Nazi street gang Combat 18.

Several 'football hooligan' memoirs recall past experiences in the far right inter-spersed with the usual tales of violence, drinking and criminality (O'Mahoney 2005; Portinari 2016; Simms 2015). O'Mahoney was on the fringes of the NF, BNP and C18 before renouncing racism and helping to expose a British Ku Klux Klan group and fooling nailbomber David Copeland into corresponding with him. Portinari recalls his activism in the NF and involvement with Loyalist paramilitar-ies. But even though he was a leading figure in the British UDA – and eventually imprisoned for gunrunning – it is thin on substantial detail about his political activ-ities and the wider milieu of far-right and loyalist co-operation. Simm's memoir written by a former NF and BNP activist actually has more telling detail on the realities of far-right Loyalist activism and sectarianism although the book is marred by intemperate diatribes.

Scholarship on the BNP

The BNP was the most successful extreme-right party in Britain in electoral terms and so, unsurprisingly, it became the most widely studied party on the British far right since the BUF. There are now three excellent book length studies, which are discussed in more detail below. In addition, there have been some valuable reports on its local campaigning and electoral support by civil society groups (Cruddas et al. 2005; Goodwin and Evans 2012; John et al. 2006; JRRT 2005). There are also a number of articles and book chapters looking in depth at its electoral support (Copsey 1996; Ford 2010; Ford and Goodwin 2010a; Goodwin et al. 2010; John and Margetts 2009), its short-lived breakthrough in 1993 (Husbands 1994), per-formance in local elections (Bowyer 2008; Copsey 1996; Wilks-Heeg 2009, 2010), the 2004 general election (Renton 2005), the 2009 European elections (Cutts et al. 2011) and the 2010 general election (Copsey 2012; Goodwin and Cutts 2012). Its transnational links with European far-right groups have also been studied (Macklin 2013; Peace and Mammone 2012).[20]

Copsey's (2008) monograph is an extremely good overview based on a detailed reading of the party's own publications, local press coverage and the academic lit-erature. Building on his earlier work (2004), it offers a comprehensive narrative history of the BNP's stalled development under the leadership of John Tyndall and then its comparative success under Nick Griffin. The BNP's 'modernisation' during this period is subject to a particularly incisive analysis through an in-depth exami-nation of the party's ideology. The author concludes that the party has retained its core fascist beliefs despite superficial changes which were necessary to broaden its electoral appeal. Several local case studies provide granular evidence to explain the

BNP's successes in council elections in particular areas such as Oldham, Burnley (see also Rhodes 2006) and Stoke. The final section locates the BNP in comparative perspective with electoral rivals in the UK such as UKIP as well as similar parties in mainland Europe such as the French Front National and the Italian MSI.

Drawing on the political science tradition of qualitative and quantitative methodology, Goodwin's monograph (2011) provides vital analysis of the BNP's membership and potential electoral support. The study is based on interviews with a small selection of the party's grass-roots supporters and some of its key activists, including Nick Griffin, as well as an examination of the party's publications – especially *Identity* magazine – and the secondary academic literature. The book is especially strong on what motivates supporters to join the BNP and to remain as activists, as well as offering detailed analysis of the party's electoral performance and the potential support for the far right among the wider electorate.

A broad range of cultural and ideological perspectives on the BNP as well as responses to it from anti-fascists, the media and other extreme-right groups are discussed in the edited collection by Copsey and Macklin (2011). It features a number of very valuable case studies on the BNP in an international context. The BNP's impact on immigration policy is examined in a comparative context by Carvalho (2014) where it is found to have had less of an influence than the Front National in France or the Lega Nord in Italy.

The edited collection by Eatwell and Goodwin (2010) compares the extremism of the BNP with that of radical Islamists and features some of the best interpretations of the BNP's electoral support (Ford 2010; Goodwin et al. 2010). Eatwell's concept of 'cumulative extremism' (Eatwell 2006a) – the way in which one form of extremism can feed off another – is expanded upon here and has proved a fecund, if somewhat contested, analytical tool for subsequent researchers (Bartlett and Birdwell 2013; Busher and Macklin 2015; Carter 2017; Ebner 2017; Feldman 2012; acklin and Busher 2015).[21]

The BNP's party organisation and leadership, ideology, electoral performance and prospects are analysed briefly in a number of the major comparative political science studies of the extreme right (e.g. Carter 2005; Eatwell and Mudde 2004; Hainsworth 1992, 2000, 2008; Harrison and Bruter 2011; Ignazi 2003; Jackson and Feldman 2014; Mammone et al. 2012; Merkl and Weinberg 1997, 2003) and in comparative studies of the populist radical right in Europe (e.g. Art 2011; Burg et al. 2015; Langenbacher and Schellenberg 2011; Liang 2007; Marzouki et al. 2016; Minkenberg 2008; Mudde 2007; Norris 2005; Rydgren 2012; Wodak 2015).

Non-academic accounts of the BNP

The rise (and decline) of the BNP is explored clearly and with much useful empirical material by reporter Daniel Trilling (2012). The author interviewed leading BNP activists including Nick Griffin and Eddy Butler as well as local residents in various areas such as Barking and Dagenham, Bradford and Burnley where the BNP had strong support. The book's most valuable contribution is to provide the wider context of why white working-class voters switched to the BNP. He exposes the now sadly familiar story of how New Labour ignored and took for granted its traditional working-class support in its pitch for socially mobile middle-class voters and how this allowed legitimate resentments about housing, jobs, economic instability and elite indifference to be exploited by the BNP. He is particularly astute in revealing how the responses to the BNP from the mainstream parties was to adopt the populist rhetoric on immigration of the far right rather than attempting to tackle the thornier underlying social and economic challenges.

Primary sources on the BNP

The main book length primary source on the BNP is the interminable political tract by its former leader John Tyndall (1988). Written while he was in prison for race relations offences, it is part autobiography and part definition of his political ideology. Unsurprisingly the book calls for national rebirth and professes vehement anti-liberalism, authoritarianism and racial nationalism as well as conspiratorial anti-Semitism – in short it is clearly a conventional manifesto for a British form of fascism.

Less overtly fascistic in orientation Bowden et al. (1999) is a collection of essays, by BNP activists and 'revolutionary conservatives' from the short-lived Bloomsbury forum, trying to reclaim figures from British history as icons of the extreme right. One of the co-editors, the late Jonathan Bowden, was a one-time BNP member and a prolific public speaker, writer and polemicist involved in the cultural struggle in various fringe far-right *groupuscules* (see e.g. the posthumous collections, Bowden and Johnson 2013, 2014). Other supposedly 'scholarly' contributions from former BNP activists include a conspiratorial antisemitic attack on British Jews (Griffin 1999), a pseudo-history of the white race (Kemp 2006) and an ethno-nationalist anti-feminist tirade on the decline of masculinity in the West (Collett 2017).

Scholarship on UKIP

The first in-depth academic study of UKIP, Britain's very own populist radical-right party (Ford and Goodwin 2014), was published just as UKIP won the majority of seats in elections to the European Parliament in 2014. The book provides an extremely detailed analysis of the party's growth from a small single-issue pressure group to a mass membership political party with national reach. The authors identify the core constituency of 'left behind' white working-class voters that UKIP typically appealed to. These were generally older, economically insecure, less-educated and less-skilled men who were concerned about socio-cultural issues such as immigration, multiculturalism and Islam, and felt marginalised by a political elite that was perceived to be pandering to the middle classes (see also Goodhart 2017). This is essential reading to explain what the historic socio-economic factors were that gave rise first to UKIP and then, in part, to the Brexit vote. UKIP's General Election Campaign of 2015 is the focus of Goodwin and Milazzo (2015). Benefiting from great insider access to many of the key UKIP activists as well as interviews with rival activists from the Labour party, this is a revealingly close up and personal view of the campaign and UKIP's limitations.

There are now many books on Brexit that are beyond the limited focus of this chapter but UKIP's role in the Leave.EU campaign is explored usefully in Clarke, Goodwin and Whiteley (2017) which is the most detailed and rigorous scholarly examination of the specifics of the Brexit vote. The Brexit vote is seen in the wider context of the mainstreaming of the British far right in Stocker's accessible and entertaining history (Stocker 2017) which is more insightful than Faulkner's (2017) underwhelming account. Usherwood (2016) provides a political science perspective on how UKIP's mainstreaming has still not allowed it to exploit the limited opportunity structures available in the British electoral system.

UKIP's party organisation and leadership, ideology, electoral performance and prospects and propaganda are analysed briefly in several comparative volumes on the populist radical right (e.g. Aalberg et al. 2017; Balfour et al. 2016; Kriesi and Pappas 2015; Leplat 2016; Liang 2007; Odmalm and Hepburn 2017; Wodak 2015) while its electoral support is explored in some richly empirical articles (Clarke et al. 2016; John and Margetts 2009; Whitaker and Lynch 2011).

Primary sources on UKIP

The primary source literature on UKIP is somewhat thinner. Farage's autobiography (Farage 2011) is an entertaining read and is impressively candid on his complicated personal life and on the sometimes comical failings of UKIP to attract and retain competent activists and to avoid the fissiparous in-fighting which seems embedded in the party's DNA. His triumphalist follow up volume (Farage 2015) repeats a lot of the earlier material without adding much new or worthwhile. The political case is set out by other leading figures in (Etheridge 2014; Evans 2014) although the activists accounts like Daniel (2005) and Gardner (2006) offer a worthwhile grass-roots perspective on the party's early development. The party's propensity for in-fighting and score-settling is illustrated by Beecher (2017) and Sen (2015). Arron Banks, one of the chief financiers of UKIP and of Leave.EU, offers a frank insider account of the Brexit campaign based on his diary (Banks 2017).

2) SOCIAL MOVEMENTS

According to one of the most authoritative texts in the field, social movements are 'a distinct social process, consisting of the mechanisms through which actors engaged in collective action are involved in conflictual relations with clearly identified opponents, are linked by dense informal networks and share a distinct collective identity' (Della Porta and Diani 2006: 20). This is a description which certainly applies both to the EDL and to anti-fascist groups although only the EDL has been studied using social movement framing and close participation observation.[22] This is a significant development in research into the British far right, especially as social movement studies have previously focused largely on peaceful, progressive, and environmental groups (Pilkington 2016: 8).

The first detailed scholarly accounts of the EDL were reports and policy documents produced for think tanks, civil society groups and academic centres. These examined the movement's history and ideology and also how to categorise it (Copsey 2010; Goodwin 2013; Jackson and Feldman 2011; Lane 2012) and the EDL's place in the wider international 'counter-jihad' movement (Meleagrou-Hitchens and Brun 2013; Mulhall and Lowles 2015).[23] The broad consensus is that the EDL is, as Copsey, states, 'an Islamophobic new social movement' (Copsey 2010: 5).

A number of more specialist articles and theses have since explored issues such as the nature of the EDL's Islamophobia (Allen 2011), its violence (Alessio and Meredith 2014; Meadowcroft and Morrow 2016; Treadwell 2012; Treadwell and Garland 2011), its self-identity and discursive practices (Oaten 2017) and the policy responses to it (Allchorn 2016). The EDL was one of the first British far-right movements to make extensive use of social media so its digital activism has also been the subject of a number of studies (Bartlett 2014: 47–72; Bartlett and Littler 2011; Cleland et al. 2017; Jackson 2011). Britain First, the EDL's rivals in far-right anti-Islam activism, has also started to receive some scholarly attention (Allen 2014) as has PEGIDA UK, the EDL's abortive successor organisation (Bartlett 2017: 47–90).

More recently there have been a number of ethnographic accounts by scholars and journalists which focus more on the EDL supporters, allowing them to explain in their own words what attracted them to the movement and compelled them to remain involved and these are discussed (Busher 2016; Pai 2016; Pilkington 2016; Winlow et al. 2017) along with two significant primary sources, written by EDL activists (Blake 2011; Robinson 2015).

Busher's monograph (2016) is an ethnographic study drawing on 16 months' interaction with a group of EDL activists and supporters based in London and the South East. The author draws on the concept of activism world-making from the literature on social movements to explain why the activists joined the EDL, how they interacted with other members, what intensified their attachment to the EDL and how they reacted to opposing, occasionally hostile, views, especially those accusing them of being racist or far-right. This provides considerable insight into the motivations of grass-roots EDL activists and also does much to expand our understanding of the dynamics of emotional engagement promoted by street-based activism and its self-reinforcing rituals. The book also valuably delineates the personality clashes and ideological faultlines that began to emerge within the EDL and ultimately led to its disintegration following a series of splits.

The ethnographic approach is also used to good effect in Pilkington (2016), once again concentrating on the lived experience and worldview of the EDL activists themselves. Drawing also on the social movement literature, the study focuses on the activism of individual grassroots supporters rather than the EDL as an organisation although it does provide a good potted history of this. The narratives of personal trajectories into the EDL and the descriptions of the emotions and affect prompted by participation in street demonstrations both give useful insights into the motivations of activists. The book's exploration of the EDL's symbolism and iconography as well as its discussion of the role of gender and sexuality in movement also deepens our understanding of the EDL as a far-right social movement.

Winlow et al. (2017) should really be called the 'decline of the left' rather than *The Rise of the Right*. It uses the voices of supporters of the EDL to illustrate how the liberal left has abandoned the white working class and urges the left to give up on identity politics and return to the politics of class. While the book has some important, if hardly original (see e.g. Birchall 2010; Jones 2012) things to say about the failings of the left and the 'liberal elite', it draws on practically none of the existing literature on the radical right, even that which comes from a class perspective (e.g. Flecker 2007; Hayes 2014; Renton 1999; Rydgren 2013) and has no real analysis of the EDL's ideology or its organisational development. There is also no discussion of why left-wing political groups with an explicit class focus, such as the Independent Working Class Association (IWCA), have been largely unsuccessful in the UK.

While all three scholarly books on the EDL discussed here contain some challenging material – with many EDL activists quoted expressing strident anti-Muslim views – there is considerable value in the ethnographic approach and what Pilkington (2016: 1–12) terms 'transgressing the cordon sanitaire', that is, spending extensive research time in the company of far-right extremists. While such an approach has been used very effectively for studies of the American far right (e.g. Blee 2002, forthcoming; Ezekiel 1996; Gardell 2003; Simi and Futrell 2010, 2017) and European far-right activists (e.g. Klandermans and Mayer 2006; Miller-Idriss 2009; Teitelbaum 2017) these are among the first studies of the British far right to do this and it is to be hoped that this research can be built upon by other scholars.[24]

Non-academic sources on the EDL

Pai's book (2016) is a journalistic account of the EDL based on several years' worth of research and the book features interviews with leading activists including Tommy Robinson. Much of its focus is on Luton, Robinson's home town and the birthplace of the EDL, and there is an interesting case study of Darren, an EDL activist (and relation of Robinson) who gradually turns his back on the movement and is now involved in an 'Exit' group helping those who wish to leave the world of far-right extremism. It also features interviews with anti-fascist activists, Muslims and members of the white working class who abhor the EDL. The book is particularly good at detailing the mix of personality and ideological clashes that drove the endlessly sectarian disputes within the EDL. It is rather loosely constructed though and could have done with more reference to the existing academic research on the wider social and political context.

Primary sources on the EDL

There are two primary sources on the EDL. Blake (2011) is an early insider account exploring the EDL's origins in the football hooligan subculture (see also Cardiff and

Marsh 2012) and the initial protests against Islamist extremists in Luton. It glee-fully describes the original marches and street activism and the camaraderie these engendered among participants. The EDL's former leader Stephen Yaxley-Lennon aka Tommy Robinson has been the most high-profile individual anti-Muslim activ-ist in the UK and his autobiography (Robinson 2015) despite being flawed in its interpretation of Islam, contains lots of instructive detail on the materiality of white working-class life in impoverished areas of Britain and does elucidate some of the factors that drive people into street-based anti-Muslim activism. The book covers the main political events of his life – his spell in the BNP, the formation and growth of the EDL, the faction fighting within the EDL and his eventual departure from the movement, facilitated in somewhat dubious circumstances, by the Quilliam Foundation. There is some special pleading on Robinson's behalf about him not being a racist and the various criminal charges he has faced and he is also unpre-pared to think through the effect of the EDL's demonstrations on ordinary Asian and Muslim citizens who could often find themselves being subjected to vicious abuse by his footsoldiers. But even though his views are often inaccurate and offen-sive, he clearly has been the subject of some hands-on policing and the book does raise some challenging questions about the extent of the measures that a democratic state should take to protect itself against extremists (of whatever stripe).

Scholarship on anti-fascism

On anti-fascism, Copsey (2016) is by far the most comprehensive scholarly account covering the subject in detail from its first incarnation in the 1920s to the pre-sent day with meticulous use of primary and secondary source material. One of Copsey's great strengths is that he discusses a broad range of anti-fascist responses rather than just physical opposition from the far left. The second edition is fully updated to cover the opposition to the BNP from both the community-based and the militant wings of the anti-fascist movement. He also examines the street-based responses to the EDL, the appropriateness of opposing UKIP and concludes by positing whether anti-fascism is suffering an identity crisis as the contemporary British far right is so fragmented. The book could perhaps have been enhanced by more interviews with anti-fascist activists (and their opponents) yet it still remains the definitive source on the subject. Copsey's article (2016b) is a rare and construc-tive attempt to explore the transnational aspects of militant anti-fascism.

Copsey's book has been supplemented by some other recent scholarship includ-ing three very good essays on anti-racism and the socialist left (Virdee 2014), Red Action (Hayes 2014) and contemporary anti-fascism (Renton 2014) in an edited collection on the British far left (Smith and Worley 2014) while Smith (forthcom-ing) draws on the party archives to reveal new insights into the British Communist Party's involvement in both broader anti-racist initiatives and the struggle against the NF.

Despite its prominence and large membership in the 1970s and its relaunch in the early 1990s (Bambery 1992), the ANL has not attracted as much literature as the numerically smaller AFA. Renton (2006) provides the most detailed history based on over eighty interviews and archival research. The result is a nuanced and sympathetic account which includes good coverage of important landmark events such as the 'Battle of Lewisham' and the murder of anti-racist Blair Peach in Southall. His second edition (forthcoming) draws on new archival research and sources and updates the original. The cultural politics of the Rock against Racism movement, which was closely aligned to the ANL, are illuminatingly outlined in Goodyer's monograph (2009).

Primary sources on anti-fascism

The other main historical overviews of UK anti-fascism (Hann 2013; Lowles 2007; Testa 2015) are all written by activists. Lowles' edited book focuses on familiar anti-fascist touchstones such as the Battle of Cable Street, the 43 Group, 62 Group and the 1970s ANL as well the Asian Youth Movement and localised anti-racist and anti-fascist committees (AFA is airbrushed from history). The book concludes with a celebration of Hope Not Hate's digitally savvy, liberal, grassroots, community-based anti-fascism.

Hann (2013) and Testa (2015) meanwhile focus almost exclusively on militant physical force anti-fascism – primarily in the UK but with some comparative discussion of interwar European anti-fascist activity (see also Bray 2017). One of the strengths of both books is the number of interviewees adding personal recollections which provide some telling detail. Although both books rely heavily on secondary sources, they are well-researched and readable accounts enhanced by the everyday realities of day to day anti-fascism revealed by activist oral history. Several other personal memoirs have been published by activists which include more detail on the motivations of individual activists and the realities of confrontations with the NF, BM and BNP but most of these would benefit from a discussion of the wider social and political context and the possible limitations of solely physical opposition to the far right (Bullstreet 2001; Hann and Tilzey 2003; Lux 2006; Todd 2012).

Rock against Racism was actually formed before the ANL in 1976 and before the original activist account of RAR (Widgery 1986). The movement is vividly brought to life by two very good recent oral histories (Rachel 2016; Huddle and Saunders 2016) which feature reminiscences from a wide range of activists and artists and provide excellent background on the wider anti-racist struggles at that time. Shelton's photo memoir (2015) is a glossy pictorial memoir.

The radical history of black-led community self-defence in Britain is still underrepresented in the current scholarship so Ramamurthy's (2013) comprehensive history of Britain's Asian Youth Movements, based on numerous interviews and impressive archival work, is a significant and welcome addition to the literature on the UK's anti-racist and anti-fascist struggles.

The most detailed account of AFA is Birchall's comprehensive history (2010). Written by a group of former activists using a *nom de guerre*, it chronicles AFA's activities from the original squads in the late 1970s to its official formation in 1985, relaunch in 1989 and demise in the mid-1990s. AFA was always the most physically effective of the contemporary street-based anti-fascist groups and the book features some graphic descriptions of violent conflicts with the far right. However, despite some macho posturing, this is no hooligan memoir and the book also attempts a political justification for the group's militant 'No Platform' approach that denied the far right space in which to organise and which has been seen as influencing the BNP's decision to abandon street protest for locally focused electoral politics (Hayes and Aylward 2000). One criticism is that the book is very focused on Red Action and the South East so does not do justice to AFA's Northern Network which was dominated more by anarchists and independent anti-fascists (Anon. 2007).

By contrast, Lowles (2014) focuses on the community-based activism organised by Hope Not Hate that generated opposition to the BNP in several northern towns where the far-right organisation had succeeded in council elections in the 1990s. Locally based organising and targeted campaigning successfully managed to overturn the BNP representation on the local council.

3) SUBCULTURES

In an influential article on the contemporary *groupuscular* right Roger Griffin stated that

> the exponential growth in global communications and cultural production since the Second World War, the rise of English as an international lingua franca, and the inexorable spread of the Internet has considerably expanded the potential of groupuscules to develop what will here be called rhizo-mic qualities and thus acquire the properties of a supranational, metapolitical 'super-organism'.
>
> *(Griffin 2003: 28–29 n.5)*

Around the same time as Griffin's article was originally published, the American and Swedish scholars Jeffrey Kaplan and Helene Lööw edited a book that revivified the concept of the 'cultic milieu' which was originally developed by the British sociologist Colin Campbell in the early 1970s to examine fringe religious move-ments (Campbell 1972; Kaplan and Lööw 2002). The cultic milieu was defined as

> a zone in which proscribed and/or forbidden knowledge is the coin of the realm, a place in which ideas, theories and speculations are to be found, exchanged, modified and, eventually, adopted or rejected by adherents of countless, primarily ephemeral groups.
>
> *(Kaplan and Lööw 2002: 3)*

These two quotations provide a framework for the following discussion which examines the transnational, *groupuscular*, metapolitical and cultic milieus of the con-temporary far right. This includes such phenomena as the transnational far right,

European New Right, neo-Nazism and fascist occultism, white power music, Holocaust denial, online activism, and violence and terrorism.

The transnational far right

The study of the transnational far right has emerged as one of the most active research areas in recent years (Albanese and del Hierro 2016; Bale forthcoming; Deland, Minkenberg and Mays 2014; Mammone 2015). These volumes build on earlier works which focused on the diverse anti-communist networks active during the Cold War that often involved both state and non-state actors and elements of the mainstream and extreme right (Dongen et al. 2014; Durham and Power 2010; Ganser 2005; Scott-Smith 2012; Teacher 2015). British far-right activists have been protagonists in a variety of post-war transnational initiatives to create pan-European fascist alliances and trans-Atlantic extreme-right organisations (Camus and Lebourg 2017; Coogan 1999; Jackson 2017; Jackson and Shekhovtsov 2014; Kaplan and Bjørgo 1998; Kaplan and Weinberg 1999; Lee 1997; Macklin 2007; Macklin and Virchow forthcoming; O'Maolain 1987; Shekhovtsov forthcoming).

Coogan's (1999) biography of American extreme-right theorist and activist Francis Parker Yockey explores the myriad hybridity of fascist ideology that has evolved in the post-war era. Yockey is still revered by sections of the 'metapolitical' far right and the book explains his fascinating and mysterious life and influential pro-Soviet, anti-American writings in compelling detail (including his direct impact on British fascist movements). The book is an excellent exploration of the more esoteric ideological positions which continue to influence the *groupuscular* far right in Britain and elsewhere.

Post-war transnational far-right activism between the UK and the US is also the subject of the useful edited collection by Jackson and Shekhovtsov (2014). As well as some much-needed theoretical discussion, the short book includes several case studies of political and cultural exchange and an insightful history of contemporary Anglo-American Nazi networks. Shekhovtsov (forthcoming) is an extraordinarily detailed account of the Russian influence organisationally and ideologically – at party, movement and state level – on the Western far right including the UK. Macklin and Virchow's forthcoming edited collection promises to be the most comprehensive overview of the European and transatlantic extreme-right networks.

Scholarship on the metapolitical European New Right

Since its founding in France in 1968, the European New Right's (ENR) core ideology of anti-liberalism, anti-egalitarianism, ethnopluralism and differential racism and its metapolitical project to influence the hegemonic intellectual and elite culture as a prelude to effecting radical social and political change, have had a profound impact on the discourse and strategies of the European and, increasingly, American far right. Scholarly responses to this include two penetrating book length analyses from Tamir Bar-On (Bar-On 2007, 2013), as well as a number of valuable journal articles which explored the complexities of the ideological repackaging and the relationship of the ENR to generic fascism (e.g. Barnes 1980a, 1980b; Bar-On 2011; Griffin 2000; Taguieff 1993). Other significant studies of influences on the ENR include Sedgwick's valuable monograph on traditionalism, and several works on Italian extremist Julius Evola (Drake 1986, 1989: 114–134; Furlong 2011; Sedgwick 2002; Sheehan 1981).

In Britain, the initial channel for ENR ideas to enter the far right was the magazine *Scorpion* edited by former NF organiser Michael Walker and though this is touched on by some scholars (Eatwell 1996; Goodrick-Clarke 2003), it is explored most fully in Copsey's (2013) article. This is an important piece of research and the most detailed investigation of the ENR's impact on the NF and BNP and the wider British far right. Since 2005, the British New Right *groupuscule*, and its later offshoot, the London Forum, have been the most significant organisations to engage with metapolitical, conspiratorial, esoteric, traditionalist, anti-Semitic and white nationalist ideas (Macklin 2005, 2015).

The ENR has always been a transnational phenomenon and there are now strong links between the British New Right and organisations and activists in Scandinavia (Teitelbaum 2017) and in North America where ENR discourse and ideology have been absorbed and then metastasised into one of the main political currents within the so-called 'alt-right' (Hawley 2017; Lyons 2017; Nagle 2017; Neiwert 2017; Ross 2017). There is also an emerging literature on the European Identitarian movement's influence on British far-right activism (Braouezec 2016).

Primary sources on the ENR

The primary sources from the ENR are extensive but recent significant English language texts include O'Meara (2004); Faye (2011); de Benoist and Champetier (2012); Southgate (2010b); Sunic (2011); Willinger (2013).

Scholarship on neo-Nazism and fascist occultism

The strand of overt neo-Nazism in the UK is explored fully in Jackson (2017), a comprehensive biography of Colin Jordan, who was probably the most important activist to keep alive the tradition of biological racism and vehement anti-Semitism as leader of various neo-Nazi *groupuscules* and later the British Movement. Jordan was also an influential theorist and ideologue with strong international connections, particularly in North America, and his texts are still frequently posted on extreme-right websites worldwide. Jackson's book is a well-researched and pioneering study of transnational 'Universal Nazism'.

The neo-Nazi and occult cultic milieu are explored in great detail in Goodrick-Clarke's excellent monograph (2003). The subject of the occult and fascism often lends itself to sensationalism but this is a sober, meticulously researched and well-referenced account with considerable detail on the British 'Nazi underground' including terror gang Combat 18 and various forms of transnational cultural activity such as fascist black metal music. There are now several other serious academic accounts of fascist occultism (Goodrick-Clarke 1998; Hess-Meining 2012; Kurlander 2017; Versluis 2012). One of the leading figures in Goodrick-Clarke's account is David Myatt, a British neo-Nazi, who has been involved in the far-right, occult and Satanist milieu for decades and also generated controversy after supposedly converting to Islam and becoming a militant Islamist. Unsurprisingly, given his role as a leading ideologue of extremism, he has also received some academic scrutiny (Kaplan and Weinberg 1999; Michael 2006; Monette 2015; Senholt 2012; Sieg 2013).

Primary sources on British neo-Nazism

Myatt has also published several volumes of autobiography which supposedly indicate his rejection of extremism (Myatt 2013a, 2013b). Former British Movement leader, Colin Jordan, was a prolific writer and his long-form publications range from theoretical explications of universal Nazism (Jordan 1981) and a kind of vanguardist Leninism of the right (Jordan 2011) to crudely racist, anti-Semitic and homophobic novels that satirise 'political correctness' (Jordan 1993) and fantasise about a Nazi terrorist group overthrowing the state (Jordan 2004). Jordan's one-time comrade in arms in the National Socialist Movement, Terry Cooper, has written his own occasionally scurrilous but interesting memoir (Cooper 2013) which details his complex relationship with Françoise Dior, Jordan's former wife and their mutual involvement in the UK and European fascist underground in the 1960s and 1970s. The current leader of the BM has also written an unsurprisingly uncritical and laudatory biography of Jordan (Frost 2014) which despite its evident bias is extremely detailed and contains much useful factual information. A different perspective on the BM and Jordan is provided in the short egotistical autobiography by his successor (McLaughlin Walsh 2016) – who is still settling scores from decades earlier – and annoyed others on the right with his criticisms of Jordan.

An important insight into the more violent and extreme wings of the international far right during the 1970s and early 1980s is provided by Hill and Bell (1988). Ray Hill was a racist activist who later recanted on his views and worked as an anti-fascist infiltrator feeding information to *Searchlight* magazine. His actions led to the demise of one *groupuscule*, the British Democratic Party, and also caused considerable dissension in the British Movement in which he was a prominent member. The book is also notable for exposing the transnational organising as UK far-right groups networked with like-minded organisations and individuals in mainland Europe often with the intent of fomenting racist violence and serious social unrest.

White power music

One of the most established transnational far-right movements is the white power music or neo-Nazi skinhead scene (Brown 2004; Corte and Edwards 2008; Cotter 1999; Futrell et al. 2006; Pollard 2016; Schaffer 2013). The edited collection by Silver and Lowles (2008) provides a detailed history of the UK skinhead and white power music scene but also explores the international links, especially with Germany, Scandinavia and the US. Long overdue and much-needed full-length academic accounts of this important and influential far-right subculture are now provided by Shekhovtsov and Jackson (2012) and Dyck (2017). Both feature detailed coverage, based on primary sources, of the UK, Western and Eastern Europe and the United States (and elsewhere) and in-depth analysis of the different international white power music organisations – from Blood and Honour to the Hammerskins. Both books also examine the 'cultural' output – lyrics, a variety of musical styles and symbolism (see also Collins and Gable 2003). More significantly the question of the violence that is promoted and often carried out by members of this subculture is explored in some detail (see also Meleagrou-Hitchens and Standing 2010). More densely theoretical is Love (2016) which, while focused primarily on the US, also examines some of the transnational perspectives and includes material on other 'hate music' forms such as folk and heavy metal. The varieties of far-right musical scenes and their co-option in the wider transnational new right and identitarian cultural struggle are explored from an ethnographic perspective in (Teitelbaum 2017). In the British context, Shaffer (2017) is a welcome addition to the scholarly literature as it attempts to explore the connections between far-right parties such as the NF and BNP and youth and musical subcultures. The book makes use of an impressive range of extensive primary sources and features some telling interviews with leading far-right activists but, despite such rich research material, the analytical insights are comparatively thin. The neo-folk subculture which has featured bands flirting with fascist imagery and ideology has also received some scholarly attention (Shekhovtsov 2009; Webb 2007: 60–109).

Primary sources on white power music and neo-Nazi skinheads

Forbes and Stampton (2015) is a volume focused mainly on the UK but is sympathetic to the white power music scene (one of its authors is a far-right activist). It is a detailed and highly illustrated book concentrating more on the cultural aspects than the politics but despite containing some worthwhile primary source material its utility as a historical record is dubious. Other hagiographies of dead neo-Nazi Ian Stuart Donaldson – the 'godfather' of hate music with his band Skrewdriver – have been written by far-right activists (e.g. London 2002; Pearce 1987). A more balanced history of British skinheads is Marshall (1994) who emphasises the subculture's roots in black culture and affinities with reggae and describes how there were groups of anti-racist skinheads as well as the stereotypical footsoldiers of the right.

Scholarship on Holocaust denial[25]

Attempts by neo-Nazis and other anti-Semites to minimise, relativise or outright deny the Holocaust have always been a transnational phenomenon. The standard scholarly account of the Holocaust denial movement remains Lipstadt (1993), although Seidel (1986), Eatwell (1991), Vidal-Naquet (1992) and Stern (1993) are important overviews with both UK and international context. Lipstadt's book famously prompted Nazi-sympathising 'historian' David Irving to launch a failed libel action against her and her publisher, Penguin Books. Some important responses to the Irving court case include Eaglestone (2001), Evans (2002), Guttenplan (2002), Lipstadt (2005), Pelt (2002) and Taylor (2000), while significant later studies of Holocaust denial include Shermer and Grobman (2009) and Atkins (2009), which is particularly instructive on the transnational dimensions and networks.

Primary sources on Holocaust denial

The primary English language texts written by Holocaust deniers include Hoggan (1969), Butz (1977), Harwood (1987), Leuchter (1988) and Irving (1977) although there are now many other pamphlets, journals and websites which contribute to the dissemination of this distasteful distortion of history. Irving also published an autobiography of his time in prison in Austria (Irving 2008).

The internet and digital activism

Far-right activists in the US were among the first organised groups to use the Internet and the global communication network has understandably been a huge boost to the British far right as well – at one point the BNP was thought to have the most visited political party website in the UK (Gable and Jackson 2011: 21; see also Gibson, Ward and Dixon 2003). There has been a considerable amount of scholarship on the subject, mainly as journal articles, although most of it focuses on North America and the main US white supremacist websites and forums like Stormfront (Brindle 2016; King and Leonard 2014). But some more recent scholarship has moved on from the original literature on building online communities and identities to look in fairly sophisticated ways at the British far right's use of social media such as Twitter, Facebook and YouTube (Conway et al. 2013a, 2013b; O'Callaghan et al. 2015).

An impressive use of social network analysis of over 500 American and European (including UK) extreme-right websites is presented in Caiani and Parenti (2013). The book also draws on the social movement literature to examine both online activity and offline activism including mobilisation strategies for demonstrations and protests. Rich in comparative empirical data, this is essential reading on this topic. For the UK context, Jackson and Gable (2011) is an extremely useful collection of case studies of online activity by the BNP, EDL, far-right music groups and neo-Nazi *groupuscule* Aryan Strike Force. Another important comparative account is the edited collection by Simpson and Druxes (2015) which also explores online radicalisation and briefly discusses Norwegian terrorist Anders Breivik's interactions with the EDL. A detailed criminological study of online and social media anti-Muslim hatred, some of which is instigated by the far right, can be found in Awan (2016). Recent trends such as the development of far-right online trolling, meme generation and 'doxing'[26] are discussed in Bartlett (2014: 47–72) and Nagle (2017).

Violence and terrorism

Despite violence and terror being forever associated with far-right individuals and organisations, the number of dedicated academic books on the subject, especially in a UK context, is surprisingly small although there have been some thought-provoking reports published by civil society groups (Goodwin and Evans 2012; Goodwin et al. 2012). Although there is now a burgeoning criminological literature on racist violence and particularly on hate crime more broadly – see Bean (2017) for a comprehensive overview of the scholarly research – very little of this research touches on the specifics of the far-right as an inspiration for, or a participant in, this violence.

Similarly, although there are several detailed studies of aspects of European right-wing terrorism (e.g. Bale forthcoming; Bjørgo 1995; Cento Bull 2007; Cento Bull and Cooke 2013; Ferraresi 1996; Hemmingby and Bjørgo 2016; Koehler 2016; Wilkinson 1981; Willan 1991), there are few books focusing on right-wing terrorism within the British context and these have tended to be journalistic accounts written by anti-fascists (Gable 1995; Gable and Jackson 2011; Lowles 2001; McLagan and Lowles 2000) rather than scholarly investigations. A rare exception is the valuable edited collection Taylor et al. (2013) which features several chapters on anti-Muslim violence, the transnational counter-Jihad movements and on links between Loyalism in Northern Ireland and the far right.

Several wider academic studies of terrorism do contain some limited references to UK far-right terrorists such as London nailbomber David Copeland (see Spaaij 2012; Gill 2015) while some of the numerous studies of Norwegian far-right terrorist, Anders Breivik, have mentioned his links with British groups such as the EDL (Bangstad 2014; Gardell 2014).

Non-academic sources on violence and terrorism

The C18 story is explored in-depth in Lowles (2001) and in Ryan (2003). Ryan spent six years with far-right activists in the UK, Belgium, Germany and the US while researching his book and his interviewees include notable British activists such as Nick Griffin, Derek Holland, John Tyndall and David Myatt. His account takes place as the BNP made significant gains in council elections in Northern England and while Nazi nailbomber David Copeland was carrying out his short-lived campaign of terror. Copeland's own story is told in rather sensationalist fashion in McLagan and Lowles (2000). The strength of Ryan's book lies in its examination of the spectrum of overlapping far-right activity from the respectable-seeming populist radical right to Holocaust deniers and white supremacist terrorists. But he is weaker on the wider social and political context – some of which is provided by other comparative journalistic accounts such as Fraser (2000) and Roxburgh (2002).

Lowles examines the emergence of this violent neo-Nazi *groupuscule* – initially as a stewarding group for the BNP – and its development from a ragbag street army to an organisation involved in bombing plots. He provides a clear chronological account of the rise to prominence of C18 as well its demise amid a welter of fierce splits and arguments which culminated in the murder of a C18 activist by its leader. Although not sourced, his account is clearly based on interviews with several of the key figures (he also had moles within the organisation) and it also examines the group's literature and propaganda. This is a vivid account of the seedy and vicious *demimonde* of British neo-Nazism.

Conclusion

It is hoped that this chapter does justice to the variegated nature of far-right participation in Britain, which ranges from mainstream political activities like electoral campaigning to the subcultural extremes of esoteric Nazism and terrorism. On the whole, the scholarship has done an excellent job of researching, describing and analysing this multifarious activism.

However, despite the extensive scholarship described in this chapter, it is still possible to identify some areas where future research would be welcome. As mentioned in the parties section, the literature on far-right parties is still dominated by demand-side explanations of electoral support and more research is needed on activists within the parties themselves to deepen our knowledge of internal party dynamics, activist motivation and how these impact on organisational success or failure. There are possibly some insights that could be learned here from the 'internalist' perspectives offered by social movement studies and ethnography. Our understanding of anti-fascist opposition to the far right – which is currently reliant on historians and activists themselves – would also benefit from similar approaches.

One other gap in the party literature stands out. The last book published on the National Front was in 1983 and there is very little scholarly coverage of its trajectory after that turbulent decade. But the NF still exists to this day – 50 years after its founding (as do some of its offshoots) – even if only as a Nazi street gang. But there are lessons in that trajectory of failure and fragmentation which require some academic attention. The creation of the *Searchlight* archive at the University of Northampton should be a boon for researchers as it makes available a vast amount of far-right primary source material.[27]

Another lacuna is the salience and influence of 'charismatic leadership'. While it is normally taken as a given that charismatic leadership helps to grow far-right parties (and social movements and subcultures), our understanding of the real mechanics and effects of this are still rudimentary, especially in the British context. Roger Eatwell has published some suggestive research in this area (Eatwell 2002, 2006b, 2006c; Costa Pinto et al. 2007) but the examples have either been historical or non-British.

As indicated in the section on violence and terrorism, more research is needed on the relationship between the far right and political and racist violence. While the literature on radicalisation (and de-radicalisation) is growing exponentially, it is still focused far more on jihadism than the far right and we need to know more about the drivers of right-wing extremist violence and terrorism (Goodwin, Ramalingam and Briggs 2012). Similarly, the concept of cumulative extremism and its potential policy impact needs further research, especially given that recent terrorist incidents in London (in 2017) can obviously be framed in this way.

Methodologically, whilst recent ethnographic research has deepened our understanding of the motivations of activists, the application of discourse analysis to the study of the far right has produced some stimulating new insights into the articulation of that worldview and more work in this area would be welcome (Brindle 2016; Richardson 2017; Wodak 2015; Wodak and Richardson 2013). Similarly, some of the findings from social network analysis help to deliver more sophisticated models for understanding transnational and decentred far-right activism (Caiani and Parenti 2013; Deland et al. 2014).

Given the protean and syncretic nature of the *groupuscular* far right – look at the ideological hybridity of the factions that made up the US 'alt-right' movement for example (Hawley 2017; Lyons 2017; Neiwert 2017; Ross 2017) – scholars, researchers and civil society will need to also continually develop their own research methods, theoretical models and frameworks for understanding and exposing the far right's ongoing challenge to liberal democracy.

Notes

1   I would like to thank friends and colleagues including Kevin Coogan, Matthew Goodwin, Paul Jackson, Tom Linehan, John Richardson, Spencer Sunshine, David Turner and the volume editors Nigel Copsey and Matthew Worley for helpful feedback and comments on draft versions of this chapter. I must offer particular gratitude to Roger Eatwell and Graham Macklin who offered detailed comments on several drafts. Any errors of fact or interpretation, of course, remain my own.
2   In the interests of full disclosure, I should declare that as an academic publisher at Routledge for over 20 years, I have worked on many of the Routledge volumes discussed here (and also occasionally offered advice and commentary to authors of some of the books produced by other publishers). But I hope that the reader will accept that I have tried to be as objective as possible in my analysis here.
3   Throughout this chapter 'contemporary' should be taken as meaning 'post-1967'.
4   This is not the place to get into the complex debates about terminology used to describe the 'far', 'radical' or 'extreme' right (or 'neo-fascist', 'neo-Nazi' etc.). For the purposes of this chapter, I generally follow Mudde (2007) in using far right as an umbrella term encompassing 1) extreme-right groups that are anti-liberal and anti-democratic 2) radical right organisations that are anti-liberal and anti-pluralism but operate within a democratic framework. In turn the 'populist radical right' describes movements that combine elements of populism, nativism and authoritarianism. I am including UKIP as a populist radical right party but such a characterisation is not shared by all scholars on the subject (see e.g. Mudde 2016b: 37, n.4) even though its post-Brexit trajectory under former leader Paul Nuttall and leadership candidate (at time of writing, July 2017) Anne Marie Waters appears to be increasingly nativist.

5   It is almost *de rigueur* when discussing the extent of scholarship on British fascism to quote Payne (1995: 305 n.22) that 'The volume of literature on the BUF [British Union of Fascists] is inversely proportionate to the group's significance' and/or Thurlow (1998: x) 'rarely can such an apparently insignificant topic have been responsible for such an outpouring of ink'.

6   PhD theses from UK universities can be searched for, downloaded and ordered from the British Library e-theses online website http://ethos.bl.uk/Home.do (accessed 29 April 2017). A fair number of the PhDs on the British far right have later been published as books (examples – this is not a definitive list – include: Baker 1996; Baldoli 2003; Carvalho 2014; Fielding 1981; Goodwin 2011; Linehan 1996; Renton 2000; Tilles 2015).

7   The sudden profusion of activist memoirs and histories has been facilitated by technological advances which have made the self-publishing of print-on-demand books and downloadable e-books far easier. While there have always been a handful of far-right publishers, such as the Britons (Toczek 2016) this technological advance has also increased the number of specialised publishers providing niche content for a far-right market. These publishers fall outside of the scope of the current chapter but are worthy of a brief discussion as they have produced primary source far-right material. Broadly speaking, these publishers include: a) those with a traditional extreme-right agenda re-publishing in print and digital formats original fascist propaganda and pamphlets b) organizations dedicated to a more 'metapolitical' perspective influenced by the European new right who are actively engaged in cultural struggle. In the traditional category, Black House Publishing specialises in reproductions of BUF propaganda from the 1930s, www.blackhousepublishing.com/ (accessed 29 April 2017) and Steven Books (run by the remnants of the Mosleyite League of St George) offers traditional Fascist and National Socialist books and pamphlets www.stevenbooks.co.uk/ (accessed 29 April 2017). Ostara Publications, run by former BNP activist Arthur Kemp, describes itself as a 'Eurocentric' publisher and republishes far-right material as well as original racist publications by Kemp and others http://ostarapublications.com/ (accessed 31 May 2017). In the 'metapolitical' category, see the influential Arktos which focuses on European new right, traditionalist and identitarian content https://arktos.com/ (accessed 29 April 2017] and Wermod and Wermod www.wermodandwermod.com/ (accessed 29 April 2017] run by new right ideologue Alex Kurtagic which has a similar ideological focus to Arktos and shares many of the same authors. Black Front Press run by veteran far-right activist Troy Southgate focuses on traditionalism, the conservative revolution, national anarchism and the European new right http://blackfrontpress.blogspot.co.uk/p/home.html (accessed 29 April 2017). Academic accounts of some of these 'metapolitical' ideological developments and the consequent propaganda outputs include Macklin (2005, 2015). Journalistic accounts include Carter (2012a, 2012b).

8   For UKIP's precipitous decline in local elections in 2017, see www.bbc.co.uk/news/uk-politics-39815444 and for the collapse in its popular vote in the 2017 General Election, see www.bbc.co.uk/news/election/2017/results. The BNP received over 500,000 votes in the 2010 general election http://news.bbc.co.uk/1/shared/election2010/results/ and less than 5,000 in the 2017 general election www.bbc.co.uk/news/election/2017/results (all accessed 23 June 2017).

9   These are porous and occasionally overlapping categories and individual activists are often involved in all three categories (e.g. supporting electoral campaigning by the BNP, joining in on social movement demonstrations organised by the EDL and attending White Power music events). Neither are these categories distinctly sacrosanct from a disciplinary or methodological perspective (historians, political scientists and sociologists have worked on all three categories) but they are useful as a heuristic organising schema when discussing a large amount of literature.

10 It is arguable that a fourth category of far-right participation might be that of 'lone wolves' who are (self-)radicalised through engagement with extreme-right material either in print form or online and then carry out violent or terrorist attacks (Gable and Jackson 2011; Gill 2015; Hamm and Spaaij 2017; Michael 2012; Spaaij 2012).

11 Analysis of such far-right propaganda in the UK includes (Macklin 2014; Richardson 2008, 2015, 2017).

12 See Copsey (forthcoming) for a rich discussion of the historiography of fascism and the contemporary far right.

13 Earlier drafts of this chapter did include an overview of the post-1967 scholarship on the British interwar far right as well as a summary of the recent theoretical debates in defining fascism but both have been excised for reasons of space and consistency.

14 See, for example, the exchange between Roger Griffin and David Renton. Renton, 'Fascism is more than an Ideology', *Searchlight*, 290 (August 1999), 24–25, and Griffin, 'Fascism is more than Reaction', *Searchlight*, 291 (September 1999), 24–26.

15 I do not want to create a false dichotomy here. Many studies of far-right parties examine both demand- and supply-side issues but they tend to be *weighted* to one of the two perspectives. It is arguable though that full-length studies (the main focus of this chapter) are more likely to cover both perspectives while journal articles and book chapters are more likely to concentrate on one of the approaches.

16 In Goodhart (2017: 9) he makes a distinction between the 'Anywheres' who are well-educated, well-travelled and have 'portable "achieved" identities, based on educational and career success' and the 'Somewheres' who are more rooted to a particular location and have 'ascribed identities based on group belonging and particular places'.

17 Billig obviously did not invent this terminology. The distinction between esoteric and exoteric can be traced back to the philosopher Leibniz – see https://plato.stanford.edu/entries/leibniz-exoteric/ and in a socio-political context it was applied by Gabriel Almond (1954) *The Appeals of Communism*. Princeton: Princeton University Press. I am grateful to Tom Linehan for this reference.

18 While Dr O'Hara's PhD thesis is worth reading, his other non-peer-reviewed writings should be treated with caution.

19 An anti-fascist joke about Morrison was that several of the groups he led had more initials than members. Private information.

20 See also Macklin's and Smith's chapters in this volume.

21 See also Carter in this volume.

22 The main scholarly accounts of anti-fascism are all written by historians.

23 For a useful overview of recent scholarly monographs on organised Islamophobia, see Opratko (2017).

24 For an excellent assessment of the benefits and drawbacks of the social movement approach to the far right, see Blee (2017).

25 See also Chapter 1 by Hobbs, this volume.

26 This is revealing personal information discovered through online research or hacking.

27 www.northampton.ac.uk/the-searchlight-archives/

References

Primary sources – books and pamphlets

Anon. (ed.) [Derek Holland] (1983). *Yesterday and Tomorrow: Roots of the National Revolution.* London: Rising Press.

Anon. [Nick Griffin] (1986). *Attempted Murder: The State/Reactionary Plot to Destroy the National Front.* www.aryanunity.com/attempted_murder.html (accessed 15 June 2017).

Anon. (2007). *Anti-Fascist Action – An Anarchist Perspective*. London: Kate Sharpley Library.

Bambery, C. (1992). *Killing the Nazi Menace: How to Stop the Fascists*. London: Socialist Workers Party.

Banks, A. (2017). *The Bad Boys of Brexit: Tales of Mischief, Mayhem and Guerilla Warfare in the EU Referendum*. London: Biteback.

Bean, J. (1999). *Many Shades of Black: Inside Britain's Far Right*. London: Millennium.

Beecher, J. (2017). *Ukip Exposed: An Inside Story of Racism, Corruption and Hypocrisy*. [s.l]: CreateSpace Independent Publishing Platform.

Benoist, A. de and Champetier. C. (2012). *Manifesto for a European Renaissance*. London: Arktos.

Birchall, S. (2010). *Beating the Fascists: The Untold Story of Anti-Fascist Action*. London: Freedom Press.

Blake, B. (2011). *EDL: Coming Down the Road*. Birmingham: VHC Publications.

Bowden, J. and Johnson, G. (ed.) (2013). *Pulp Fascism: Right-Wing Themes in Comics, Graphic Novels, & Popular Literature*. San Francisco, CA: Counter-Currents Publishing.

Bowden, J. and Johnson, G. (ed.) (2014). *Western Civilization Bites Back*. San Francisco, CA: Counter-Currents Publishing.

Bowden, J., Butler, E. and Davies, A. (eds.) (1999). *Standardbearers: British Roots of the New Right*. Beckenham: Bloomsbury Forum.

Bullstreet, K. (2001). *Bash the Fash: Anti-Fascist Recollections 1984–1993*. London: Kate Sharpley Library.

Bushell, G. (2010). *Hoolies: The Stories of Britain's Biggest Street Battles*. London: John Blake Publishing.

Butz, A. R. (1977). *The Hoax of the Twentieth Century*. Brighton: Historical Review Press.

Cardiff, J. and Marsh, S. (2012). *Casuals United*. [s.l.]: Mashed Swede.

Collett, M. (2017). *The Fall of Western Man*. Charleston: [s.n.]: Also available online: www.thefallofwesternman.com/ (accessed 31 May 2017).

Collins, M. (2011). *Hate: My Life in the British Far Right*. London: Biteback.

Collins, M. and Gable, G. (eds.) (2003). *Signs of Hate*. Ilford: *Searchlight* Information Services.

Cooper, T. (2013). *Death by Dior*. London: Dynasty Press.

Daniel, M. (2005). *Cranks and Gadflies: The Story of UKIP*. London: Timewell Press.

Etheridge, B. (2014). *The Rise of UKIP*. London: Bretwalda Books.

Evans, S. (2014). *Why Vote UKIP 2015*. London: Biteback.

Farage, N. (2011). *Flying Free*. London: Biteback.

Farage, N. (2015). *The Purple Revolution: The Year That Changed Everything*. London: Biteback.

Faye, G. (2011). *Why we Fight: Manifesto of the European Resistance*. London: Arktos Media.

Forbes, R. and Stampton, E. (2015). *The White Nationalist Skinhead Movement: UK and USA 1979–1993*. Port Townsend: Feral House.

Frost, S. (2014). *'Twas a Good Fight!' The Life of Colin Jordan*. Heckmondwike: N.S. Press.

Griffin, N. (1999 [1997]). *Who Are the Mindbenders?* 2nd ed. [s.l.]: The Right Image.

Hann, D. (2013). *Physical Resistance: A Hundred Years of Anti-Fascism*. London: Zero Books.

Hann, D. and Tilzey, S. (2003). *No Retreat: The Secret War Between Britain's Anti-Fascists and the Far-Right*. Bury: Milo Books.

Harwood, R. [Richard Verrall pseud.] (1987). [1974] *Did Six Million Really Die?* Brighton: The Historical Review Press.

Hill, R. and Bell, A. (1988). *The Other Face of Terror: Inside Europe's Neo-Nazi Network*. London: Grafton.

Hoggan, D. (1969). *The Myth of the Six Million*. Newport Beach, CA: Noontide Press.

Huddle, R. and Saunders, R. (2016). *Reminiscences of RAR: Rocking against Racism (1976–1982)*. London: Redwords.

Irving, D. (1977). *Hitler's War*. London: Hodder & Stoughton.

Irving, D. (2008). *Banged Up: Survival as a Political Prisoner in 21st Century Europe*. London: Focal Point Publications.

Jordan, C. (1981). *National Socialism: World Creed of the 1980s*. Harrogate: Gothic Ripples.

Jordan, C. (1993). *Merrie England 2,000*. Harrogate: Gothic Ripples.

Jordan, C. (2004). *The Uprising*. Milwaukee: N. S. Press.

Jordan, C. (2011). *The National Vanguard*. Uckfield: Historical Review Press.

Kemp, A. (2006). *March of the Titans: A History of the White Race*. Burlington, IA: Ostara Publications.

Leuchter, F. A. (1988). *The Leuchter Report: The End of a Myth: Auschwitz, Birkenau and Majdanek, Poland by an Execution Equipment Expert*. Toronto: Samisdat Publishers.

London, P. (2002). *Nazi Rock Star – Ian Stuart*. Gothenburg. Midgård.

Lowles, N. (ed.) (2007). *From Cable Street to Oldham: 70 Years of Community Resistance*. London: Searchlight.

Lowles, N. (2014). *HOPE – The Story of the Campaign that Helped Defeat the BNP*. London: Hope not Hate.

Lux, M. (2006). *Anti-Fascist*. London: Phoenix Press.

Marriner, J. (2015). *Kicking The Habit*. Ayr: Fort Publishing Ltd.

McLaughlin Walsh, M. (2016). *Rise of the Sunwheel: Mike Kampf*. [s.l.]: CreateSpace Independent Publishing Platform.

Morrison, E. (2003). *Memoirs of a Street Soldier: A Life in White Nationalism*. London: Imperium Press.

Myatt, D. (2013a). *Myngath: Some Recollections of a Wyrdful and Extremist Life*. [s.l]: CreateSpace Independent Publishing Platform.

Myatt, D. (2013b). *Understanding and Rejecting Extremism: A Very Strange Peregrination*. [s.l]: CreateSpace Independent Publishing Platform.

O'Mahoney, B. (2005). *Hateland*. Edinburgh: Mainstream Publishing.

O'Meara, M. (2004). *New Culture, New Right: Anti-Liberalism in Postmodern Europe*. Bloomington, IN: Bloomington Books.

Owens, J. (2007). *Action! Race War to Door Wars*. Raleigh, NC: LuluBooks.

Pearce, J. (1987). *Skrewdriver: The First Ten Years*. London: Skrewdriver Services.

Pearce, J. (1996). *Wisdom and Innocence: A Life of G.K. Chesterton*. London: Hodder & Stoughton.

Pearce, J. (2001). *Bloomsbury and Beyond: The Friends and Enemies of Roy Campbell*. London: HarperCollins.

Pearce, J. (2013). *Race with the Devil: My Journey from Racial Hatred to Rational Love*. St Benedict Press: North Carolina.

Portinari, F. (2016). *Left-Right-Loyalist*. London: Troubadour Publishing.

Rachel, D. (2016). *Walls Come Tumbling Down: The Music and Politics of Rock Against Racism. 2 Tone and Red Wedge. 1976–1992*. London: Picador.

Robinson, T. (2015). *Tommy Robinson Enemy of the State* [s.l.]: The Press News.

Sen, J. (2015). *How to Get Suspended from UKIP & the BNP in 10 Articles & 2 Tweets*. [s.l.]: London: Paragon Publishing.

Shelton, S. (2015). *Rock Against Racism*. London: Autograph ABP.

Silver, S. and Lowles, N. (eds.) (2008). *White Noise: Inside the International Nazi Skinhead Scene*. London: Searchlight.

Simms, T. (2016). *Match Day: Ulster Loyalism and the British Far Right*. [s.l.]: CreateSpace Independent Publishing Platform.

Southgate, T. (2010a). *Nazis, Fascists, Or Neither?: Ideological Credentials of the British Far Right, 1987–1994*. Shamley Green: Wermod & Wermod.

Southgate, T. (ed.) (2010b). *Tradition & Revolution: Collected Writings of Troy Southgate*. 2nd edn. London: Arktos Media.

Sunic, T. (2011). *Against Democracy and Equality: The European New Right*. London: Arktos Media.

Testa, M. (2015). *Militant Anti-Fascism: A Hundred Years of Resistance*. Edinburgh: AK Press.

Todd, D. (2012). *One Man's Revolution "I Still Hate Thatcher"*. Clacton-on-Sea, Essex: Apex Press.

Tyndall, J. (1988). *The Eleventh Hour: A Call for British Rebirth*. Welling: Albion Press.

Widgery, D. (1986). *Beating Time: Riot 'n' Race 'n' Rock 'n' Roll*. London: Chatto and Windus.

Willinger, M. (2013). *Generation Identity: A Declaration of War Against The '68ers*. London: Arktos.

Secondary sources – books, reports and theses

Aalberg, T., Esser, F., Reinemann, C., Strömbäck, J. and de Vreese, C. H. (eds.) (2017). *Populist Political Communication in Europe*. Abingdon: Routledge.

Allchorn, W. E. C. (2016). *When Anti-Islamic Protest Comes to Town: Political Responses to the English Defence League*. Unpublished PhD thesis, University of Leeds.

Albanese, M. and del Hierro, P. (2016). *Transnational Fascism in the Twentieth Century: Spain, Italy and the Global Neo-Fascist Network*. London: Bloomsbury Academic.

Art, D. (2011). *Inside the Radical Right: The Development of Anti-Immigrant Parties in Western Europe*. Cambridge: Cambridge University Press.

Atkins, S. E. (2009). *Holocaust Denial as an International Movement*. Santa Barbara, CA: Greenwood Publishing Group.

Awan, I. (ed.) (2016). *Islamophobia in Cyberspace: Hate Crimes Go Viral*. Abingdon: Routledge.

Baker, D. (1996). *Ideology of Obsession: A.K. Chesterton and British Fascism*. London: I.B. Tauris.

Baldoli, C. (2003). *Exporting Fascism: Italian Fascists and Britain's Italians in the 1930s*. Oxford: Berg.

Bale, J. M. (forthcoming). *The Darkest Sides of Politics, Volume 1: Postwar Fascism, Covert Operations, and Terrorism*. London: Routledge.

Balfour, R. et al. (2016). *Europe's Troublemakers: The Populist Challenge to Foreign Policy*. Brussels: European Policy Center.

Bangstad, S. (2014). *Anders Breivik and the Rise of Islamophobia*. London: Zed Books.

Bar-On, T. (2007). *Where Have All the Fascists Gone?* Farnham: Ashgate.

Bar-On, T. (2013). *Rethinking the French New Right*. Abingdon: Routledge.

Bartlett, J. (2014). *The Dark Net*. London: William Heinemann.

Bartlett, J. (2017). *Radicals: Outsiders Changing the World*. London: William Heinemann.

Bartlett, J. and Birdwell, J. (2013). *Cumulative Radicalisation Between the Far-Right and Islamist Groups in the UK: A Review of Evidence*. London: Demos.

Bartlett, J. and Littler, M. (2011). *Inside the EDL: Populist Politics in a Digital Age*. London: Demos.

Bean, P. (ed.) (2017). *Hate Crime*. Abingdon: Routledge.

Billig, M. (1978). *Fascists: A Social Psychological View of the National Front*. London: Harcourt Brace Jovanovitch.

Bjørgo, T. (ed.) (1995). *Terror from The Extreme Right*. London: Frank Cass.

Blee, K. (2002). *Inside Organized Racism: Women in the Hate Movement*. Berkeley and Los Angeles, CA: University of California Press.

Blee, K. (forthcoming). *Understanding Racist Activism: Theories and Methods*. Abingdon: Routledge.

Bray, M. (2017). *Antifa: The Anti-Fascist Handbook*. Brooklyn, NY: Melville House.

Brindle, A. (2016). *The Language of Hate: A Corpus Linguistic Analysis of White Supremacist Language*. Abingdon: Routledge.

Buford, B. (1991). *Among The Thugs*. London: Secker and Warburg.

Burg, W.V. D., D'Amato, G., Berkhout, J. and Ruedin, D. (2015). *The Politicisation of Migration.* Abingdon: Routledge.

Busher, J. (2016). *The Making of Anti-Muslim Protest: Grassroots Activism in the English Defence League.* Abingdon: Routledge.

Caiani, M. and Parenti, B. (2013). *European and American Extreme Right Groups and the Internet.* Farnham: Ashgate.

Camus, J.-Y. and Lebourg, N. (2017). *Far-Right Politics in Europe.* Cambridge, MA: The Belknap Press of Harvard University Press.

Carter, E. (2005). *The Extreme Right in Western Europe.* Manchester: Manchester University Press.

Carvalho, J. (2014). *Impact of Extreme Right Parties on Immigration Policy: Comparing Britain. France and Italy.* London: Routledge.

Cento Bull, A. (2007). *Italian Neofascism: The Strategy of Tension and the Politics of Nonreconciliation.* New York: Berghahn.

Cento Bull, A. and Cooke, P. (2013). *Ending Terrorism in Italy.* Abingdon: Routledge.

Clarke, H. D., Goodwin, M. and Whiteley, P. (2017). *Brexit: Why Britain Voted to Leave the European Union.* Cambridge: Cambridge University Press.

Coogan, K. (1999). *Dreamer of the Day: Francis Parker Yockey and the Postwar Fascist International.* New York: Autonomedia.

Copsey, N. (2004). *Contemporary British Fascism: The British National Party and the Quest for Legitimacy.* Basingstoke: Palgrave Macmillan.

Copsey, N. (2008). *Contemporary British Fascism: The British National Party and the Quest for Legitimacy.* 2nd edn. Basingstoke: Palgrave Macmillan.

Copsey, N. (2010). *The English Defence League: Challenging our Country and our Values of Social Inclusion. Fairness and Equality.* London: Faith Matters.

Copsey, N. (2016). *Anti-Fascism in Britain.* 2nd edn. Abingdon: Routledge.

Copsey, N. and Macklin, G. (eds.) (2011). *The British National Party: Contemporary Perspectives.* Abingdon: Routledge.

Copsey, N. and Richardson, J. E. (eds.) (2015). *Cultures of Post-War British Fascism.* Abingdon: Routledge.

Costa Pinto, A., Eatwell, R. and Larsen, S. U. (eds.) (2007). *Charisma and Fascism in Interwar Europe.* London: Routledge.

Cronin, M. (ed.) (1996). *The Failure of British Fascism.* London: Macmillan.

Cross, C. (1961). *The Fascists in Britain.* London: Barrie and Rockliff.

Cruddas, J., John, P., Lowles, N., Margetts, H., Rowland, D., Schutt, D. and Weir, S. (2005). *The Far Right in London: A Challenge for Local Democracy?* York: Joseph Rowntree Reform Trust.

Deland, M., Minkenberg, M. and Mays, C. (2014). *In the Tracks of Breivik: Far Right Networks in Northern and Eastern Europe.* Berlin: Lit Verlag.

Della Porta, D. and Diani, M. (2006). *Social Movements: An Introduction.* 2nd edn. Oxford: Blackwell Publishing.

Dongen, L. Roulin, S. and Scott-Smith, G. (2014). *Transnational Anti-communism and the Cold War: Agents, Activities and Networks.* Basingstoke: Palgrave Macmillan.

Dorril, S. (2006). *Blackshirt: Sir Oswald Mosley and British Fascism.* London: Viking.

Drake, R. (1989). *The Revolutionary Mystique and Terrorism in Contemporary Italy.* Bloomington: University of Indiana Press.

Durham, M. (1998). *Women and Fascism.* London: Routledge.

Durham, M. and Power, D. (eds.) (2010). *New Perspectives on the Transnational Right.* London: Palgrave Macmillan.

Dyck, K. (2017). *Reichsrock: The International Web of White-Power and Neo-Nazi Hate Music.* New Brunswick, NJ: Rutgers University Press.

Eaglestone, R. (2001). *Postmodernism and Holocaust Denial.* Cambridge: Icon Books.

Eatwell, R. (1995). *Fascism: A History.* London: Chatto & Windus.

Eatwell, R. and Goodwin, M. J. (eds.) (2010). *The New Extremism in 21st Century Britain.* Abingdon: Routledge.

Eatwell, R. and Mudde, C. (eds.) (2004). *Western Democracies and the New Extreme Right Challenge.* London: Routledge.

Eatwell, R. and O'Sullivan, N. (eds.) (1989). *The Nature of the Right.* London: Pinter.

Ebner, J. (2017). *The Rage: The Vicious Circle of Islamist and Far-Right Extremism.* London: I.B. Tauris.

Edwards, A. (2017). *UVF: Behind the Mask.* Newbridge, Republic of Ireland: Merrion Press.

Evans, R. (2002). *Telling Lies About Hitler: The Holocaust, History and the David Irving Trial.* London: Faber and Faber.

Ezekiel, R. S. (1996). *The Racist Mind: Portraits of American Neo-Nazis and Klansmen.* New York: Penguin Books.

Faulkner, N. (2017) *Creeping Fascism: Brexit, Trump and the Rise of the Far Right.* [s.l.]: Public Reading Rooms.

Feldman, D. and Jackson, P. (eds.) (2014). *Doublespeak: The Rhetoric of the Far Right Since 1945.* Stuttgart: ibidem-Verlag.

Feldman, M. (2012). *From Radical Right Islamophobia to Cumulative Extremism: A Paper on the Shifting Focus of Hatred.* London: Faith Matters.

Ferraresi, F. (1996). *Threats to Democracy: The Radical Right in Italy after the War.* Princeton, NJ: Princeton University Press.

Fielding, N. (1981). *The National Front.* London: Routledge and Kegan Paul.

Flecker, J. (ed.) (2007). *Changing Working Life and the Appeal of the Extreme Right.* Aldershot: Ashgate.

Ford, G. (1992). *Fascist Europe: The Rise of Racism and Xenophobia.* London: Pluto Press.

Ford, R. and Goodwin, M. (2014). *Revolt on the Right: Explaining Support for the Radical Right in Britain.* Abingdon: Routledge.

Fraser, N. (2000). *The Voice of Modern Hatred: Tracing the Rise of Neo-Fascism in Europe.* London: Picador.

Furlong, P. (2011). *Social and Political Thought of Julius Evola.* Abingdon: Routledge.

Gable, G. and Jackson, P. (eds.) (2011). *Lone Wolves: Myth or Reality?* Ilford: Searchlight.

Ganser, D. (2005). *Nato's Secret Armies: Operation Gladio and Terrorism in Western Europe.* London: Frank Cass.

Gardell, M. (2003). *Gods of the Blood: The Pagan Revival and White Separatism.* Durham, NC: Duke University Press.

Gardner, P. (2014[2006]). *Hard Pounding: The UKIP Story.* London: David Barnby.

Gentile, E. (2005). *Politics as Religion.* Princeton, NJ: Princeton University Press.

Gibson, R. Nixon, P. and Ward, S. (eds.) (2003). *Political Parties and the Internet: Net Gain?* London: Routledge.

Gill, P. (2015). *Lone-Actor Terrorists: A Behavioural Analysis.* Abingdon: Routledge.

Goodhart, D. (2017). *The Road to Somewhere: The Populist Revolt and the Future of Politics.* London: Hurst Publishers.

Goodrick-Clarke, N. (1998). *Hitler's Priestess: Savitri Devi, the Hindu-Aryan Myth, and Neo-Nazism.* New York: New York University Press.

Goodrick-Clarke, N. (2003). *Black Sun: Aryan Cults. Esoteric Nazism and the Politics of Identity.* New York: New York University Press.

Goodwin, M. J. (2011). *New British Fascism: Rise of the British National Party*. Abingdon: Routledge.

Goodwin, M. J. (2013). *The Roots of Extremism: The English Defence League and the Counter-Jihad Challenge*. London: Chatham House.

Goodwin, M. and Evans, J. (2012). *From Voting to Violence? Far Right Extremism in Britain*. London: *Searchlight* Educational Trust.

Goodwin, M. J. and Milazzo, C. (2015). *UKIP: Inside the Campaign to Redraw the Map of British Politics*. Oxford: Oxford University Press.

Goodwin, M., Ramalingam, V. and Briggs, R. (2012). *The New Radical Right: Violent and Non-Violent Movements in Europe*. (Briefing Paper). London: Institute of Strategic Dialogue.

Goodyer, I. (2009). *Crisis Music: The Cultural Politics of Rock Against Racism*. Manchester: Manchester University Press.

Gottlieb, J. and Linehan, T. (eds.) (2004). *The Culture of Fascism. Visions of the Far Right in Britain*. London: I.B. Tauris.

Gregor, A. J. (2006). *The Search for Neofascism: The Use and Abuse of Social Science*. Cambridge: Cambridge University Press.

Griffin, R. (1993). *The Nature of Fascism*. London: Routledge.

Griffin, R. (1995). *Fascism (Oxford Reader)*. Oxford: Oxford University Press.

Griffin, R. (ed.) (1998). *International Fascism: Theories. Causes and the New Consensus*. London: Arnold.

Griffin, R. and Feldman, M. (eds.) (2004). *Fascism: Critical Concepts in Political Science*, 5 Vols. London: Routledge.

Griffin, R. (2008). *A Fascist Century: Essays by Roger Griffin*, Feldman, M. (ed.). Basingstoke: Palgrave.

Griffin, R., Loh, W. and Umland, A. (eds.) (2006). *Fascism Past and Present. East and West: An International Debate on Concepts and Cases in the Comparative Study of the Extreme Right*. Stuttgart: ibidem-Verlag.

Guttenplan, D. D. (2002). *The Holocaust On Trial: History, Justice, and the David Irving Libel Case*. London: Granta.

Hainsworth, P. (ed.) (1992). *The Extreme Right in Europe and the USA*. London: Pinter.

Hainsworth, P. (ed.) (2000). *The Politics of the Extreme Right: From the Margins to the Mainstream*. London: Pinter.

Hainsworth, P. (2008). *The Extreme Right in Western Europe*. Oxon: Routledge.

Hamm, M. S. and Spaaij, R. (2017). *The Age of Lone Wolf Terrorism*. New York: Columbia University Press.

Harris, G. (1990). *The Dark Side of Europe*. Edinburgh: Edinburgh University Press.

Harrison, S. and Bruter, M. (2011). *Mapping Extreme Right Ideology: An Empirical Geography of the European Extreme Right*. Basingstoke: Palgrave Macmillan.

Hawley, G. (2017). *Making Sense of the Alt-Right*. New York: Columbia University Press.

Hayes, M. (2014). *The Ideology of Fascism and the Far-Right in Britain*. Ottawa, Canada: Red Quill Books.

Hemmingby, C. and Bjørgo, T. (2016). *The Dynamics of a Terrorist Targeting Process: Anders B. Breivik and the 22nd July Attacks in Norway*. Basingstoke: Palgrave.

Hughes, M. (2012). *Spies at Work*. [s.l.]: Lulu.com.

Husbands, C. T. (1983). *Racial Exclusionism and the City: The Urban Support for the National Front*. London: George Allen and Unwin.

Ignazi, P. (2003). *Extreme Right Parties in Western Europe*. Oxford: Oxford University Press.

Iordachi, C. (ed.) (2010). *Comparative Fascist Studies: New Perspectives*. London/New York: Routledge.

Jackson, P. (2011). *The EDL: Britain's 'New Far Right' Social Movement.* Northampton: The University of Northampton.

Jackson, P. (2017). *Colin Jordan and Britain's Neo-Nazi Movement: Hitler's Echo.* London: Bloomsbury Academic.

Jackson, P. and Feldman, M. (2011). *The EDL: Britain's 'New Far Right' Social Movement.* Northampton: The University of Northampton.

Jackson, P. and Feldman, M. (eds.) (2014). *Doublespeak: The Rhetoric of the Far-Right since 1945.* Stuttgart: ibidem-Verlag.

Jackson, P. and Gable, G. (eds.) (2011). *Far-Right.Com: Nationalist Extremism on the Internet.* Northampton: *Searchlight* Magazine and the Radicalism and New Media Research Group.

Jackson, P. and Shekhovtsov, A. (eds.) (2014). *The Anglo-American Far Right: A Special Relationship of Hate.* London: Palgrave Pivot.

John, P., Margetts, H., Rowland, D. and Weir, P. (2006). *The BNP: The Roots of its Appeal.* London: Joseph Rowntree Charitable Trust.

Jones, O. (2012). *Chavs: The Demonization of the Working Class.* London: Verso.

JRRT (2005). *The Far Right in London: A Challenge for Local Democracy?* York: Joseph Rowntree Reform Trust.

Kaplan, J. and Bjørgo, T. (eds.) (1998). *Nation and Race: The Developing Euro-American Racist Subculture.* Boston: Northeastern University Press.

Kaplan, J. and Lööw, H. eds. (2002). *The Cultic Milieu: Oppositional Subcultures in an Age of Globalization.* Lanham, MD: Rowman & Littlefield.

Kaplan, J. and Weinberg, L. (1999). *The Emergence of a Euro-American Radical Right.* New Brunswick, NJ: Rutgers University Press.

King, C. R. and Leonard, D. J. (2014). *Beyond Hate: White Power and Popular Culture.* Aldershot: Ashgate.

Klandermans, B. and Mayer, N. (eds.) (2006). *Extreme Right Activists in Europe: Through the Magnifying Glass.* London and New York: Routledge.

Koehler, D. (2016). *Right-Wing Terrorism in the 21st Century. The 'National Socialist Underground' and the History of Terror from the Far-Right in Germany.* Abingdon: Routledge.

Kriesi, H. and Pappas, T. (eds.) (2015). *European Populism in the Shadow of the Great Recession.* Colchester: ECPR Press.

Kurlander, E. (2017). *Hitler's Monsters: A Supernatural History of the Third Reich.* New Haven, CT: Yale University Press.

Lane, H. S. (2012). *A Study of the English Defence League: What draws people of faith to right-wing organisations and what effects does the EDL have on community cohesion and interfaith relations?* London: Faith Matters.

Lee, M. A. (1997). *The Beast Reawakens.* Boston: Little, Brown and Co.

Leplat, F. (ed.) (2016). *The Far Right in Europe.* London: Resistance Books.

Lewis, D. S. (1987). *Illusions of Grandeur. Mosley, Fascism and British Society, 1931–1981.* Manchester: Manchester University Press.

Liang, C. S. (ed.) (2007). *Europe for the Europeans: The Foreign and Security Policy of Populist Radical Right.* London: Routledge.

Linehan, T. (1996). *East London for Mosley: The British Union of Fascists in East London and South-West Essex 1933–40.* London: Frank Cass.

Lipstadt, D. (1993). *Denying the Holocaust: The Growing Assault on Truth and Memory.* London: Penguin.

Lipstadt, D. E. (2005). *History on Trial: My Day in Court with David Irving.* New York: HarperCollins.

Love, N. S. (2016). *Trendy Fascism: White Power Music and the Future of Democracy.* Albany: SUNY Press.

Lowles, N. (2001). *White Riot: The Rise and Fall of Combat 18.* Bury: Milo Press.

Lyons, M. N. (2017). *CTRL-ALT-DELETE: An Antifascist Report on the Alternative Right.* Montreal: Kersplebedeb.

Macklin, G. (2007). *Very Deeply Dyed in Black: Sir Oswald Mosley and the Resurrection of British Fascism after 1945.* London: I.B. Tauris.

Macklin, G. (forthcoming). *White Racial Nationalism in Britain.* Abingdon: Routledge.

Macklin, G. and Virchow, F. (eds.) (forthcoming). *Transnational Extreme Right Networks.* Abingdon: Routledge.

Mammone, A. (2015). *Transnational Neofascism in France and Italy.* Cambridge: Cambridge University Press.

Mammone, A., Godin, E. and Jenkins, B. (eds.) (2012). *Mapping the Extreme Right in Contemporary Europe: From Local to Transnational.* Abingdon: Routledge.

Mann, M. (2004). *Fascists.* Cambridge: Cambridge University Press.

Marshall, G. (1994). *Spirit of '69: A Skinhead Bible,* 2nd edn. Dunoon: ST Publishing.

Marzouki, N., McDonnell, D. and Roy, O. (eds.) (2016). *Saving the People: How Populists Hijack Religion.* London: Hurst.

McLagan, G. and Lowles, N. (2000). *Mr. Evil: The Secret Life of Pub Bomber and Killer David Copeland.* London: Blake.

Meleagrou-Hitchens, A. and Brun, H. (2013). *A Neo-Nationalist Network: The English Defence League and Europe's Counter-Jihad Movement.* Kings College. London: The International Centre for the Study of Radicalisation and Political Violence. Hyperlink: http://icsr. info/wp-content/uploads/2013/03/ICSR-ECJM-Report_Online.pdf (accessed 1 May 2017).

Meleagrou-Hitchens, A. and Standing, E. (2010). *Blood and Honour: Britain's Far Right Militants.* London: Centre for Social Cohesion. Available online: http://henryjacksonsociety.org/wp-content/uploads/2013/01/BLOOD-AND-HNOUR.pdf (accessed 6 June 2017).

Merkl, P. and Weinberg, L. (eds.) (1993). *Encounters with the Contemporary Radical Right.* Boulder: Westview.

Merkl, P. and Weinberg, L. (1997). *The Revival of Right-Wing Extremism in the Nineties.* London: Frank Cass.

Merkl, P. and Weinberg, L. (eds.) (2003). *Right-Wing Extremism in the Twenty-First Century.* Abingdon: Routledge.

Michael, G. (2006). *The Enemy of my Enemy: The Alarming Convergence of Militant Islam and the Extreme Right.* Kansas: University Press of Kansas.

Michael, G. (2012). *Lone Wolf Terror and the Rise of Leaderless Resistance.* Nashville: Vanderbilt University Press.

Miller-Idriss, C. (2009). *Blood and Culture: Youth, Right-wing Extremism. and National Belonging in Contemporary Germany.* Durham, NC: Duke University Press.

Minkenberg, M. (2008). *The Radical Right in Europe: An Overview.* Gütersloh: Verlag Bertelsmann Stiftung.

Monette, C. R. (2015). *Mysticism in the 21st Century,* 2nd edn. Wilsonville, OR: Sirius Academic Publications.

Mosse, G. L. (1999). *The Fascist Revolution: Toward A General Theory of Fascism.* New York: Howard Fertig.

Mudde, C. (2000). *Ideology of the Extreme Right.* Manchester: Manchester University Press.

Mudde, C. (2007). *Populist Radical Right Parties in Europe.* Cambridge: Cambridge University Press.

Mudde, C. (ed.) (2014). *Youth and the Extreme Right.* New York: International Debate Education Association.

Mudde, C. (2016b). *On Extremism and Democracy in Europe.* Abingdon: Routledge.

Mulhall, J. and Lowles, N. (2015). *The Counter-Jihad Movement: Anti-Muslim Hatred from the Margins to the Mainstream*. London: Hope not Hate Publications.

Mullally, F. (1946). *Fascism Inside England*. London: Claud Morris Books.

Nagle, A. (2017). *Kill All Normies: The Online Culture Wars from Tumblr and 4chan to the Alt-Right and Trump*. London: Zero Books.

Neiwert, D. (2017). *Alt-America: The Rise of the Radical Right in the Age of Trump*. Brooklyn, NY: Verso.

Neocleous, M. (1997). *Fascism*. Buckingham: Open University Press.

Norris, P. (2005). *Radical Right: Voters and Parties in the Electoral Market*. Cambridge: Cambridge University Press.

Nugent, N. and King, R. (eds.) (1977). *The British Right. Conservative and Right Wing Politics in Britain*. Farnborough: Saxon House.

Oaten, A. (2017). *Understanding a Populist Discourse: An Ethnographic Account of the English Defence League's Collective Identity*, Unpublished PhD thesis, University of Birmingham.

Odmalm, P. and Hepburn, E. (eds.) (2017). *The European Mainstream and the Populist Radical Right*. London: Routledge.

O'Hara, L. M. (2000). *Creating Political Soldiers? The National Front 1986–1990*, Unpublished PhD thesis, University of Birkbeck, London.

O'Maolain, C. (1987). *The Radical Right: A World Directory*. Santa Barbara, CA: ABC-Clio.

Pai, H.-H. (2016). *Angry White People: Coming Face-to-Face with the British Far Right*. London: Zed Books.

Passmore, K. (2014). *Fascism: A Very Short Introduction*. 2nd edn. Oxford: Oxford University Press.

Paxton, R. O. (2004). *The Anatomy of Fascism*. London: Allen Lane.

Payne, S. G. (1995). *A History of Fascism 1914*–45. London: UCL Press Ltd.

Pelt, R. J. V. (2002). *The Case for Auschwitz: Evidence from the Irving Trial*. Bloomington, IN: Indiana University Press.

Pilkington, H. (2016). *Loud and Proud: Passion and Politics in the English Defence League*. Manchester: Manchester University Press.

Pitchford, M. (2011). *The Conservative Party and the Extreme Right 1945–1975*. Manchester: Manchester University Press.

Ramamurthy, A. (2013). *Black Star: Britain's Asian Youth Movements*. London: Pluto Press.

Rees, P. (1979). *Fascism in Britain: An Annotated Bibliography*. Hassocks, Sussex: The Harvester Press.

Rees, P. (1984). *Fascism and Pre-Fascism in Europe, 1890–1945: A Bibliography of the Extreme Right*. Brighton: Harvester Press.

Renton, D. (1999). *Fascism: Theory and Practice*. London: Pluto Press.

Renton, D. (2000). *Fascism, Anti-Fascism and Britain in the 1940s*. Basingstoke: Macmillan.

Renton, D. (2006). *When We Touched the Sky: The Anti-Nazi League 1977–1981*. London: New Clarion Press.

Renton, D. (forthcoming). *The Anti-Nazi League 1977–1981*, 2nd edn. Abingdon: Routledge.

Rhodes, J. (2006). *Far Right Breakthrough: Support for the BNP in Burnley*. Unpublished PhD thesis, University of Manchester.

Richardson, J. E. (2017). *British Fascism: A Discourse-Historical Analysis*. Stuttgart: ibidem-Verlag.

Ross, A. R. (2017). *Against the Fascist Creep*. Chico, CA : AK Press.

Roxburgh, A. (2002). *Preachers of Hate: The Rise of the Far Right*. London: Gibson Square.

Ryan, N. (2003). *Homeland: Into a World of Hate*. Edinburgh: Mainstream.

Rydgren, J. (ed.) (2012). *Class Politics and the Radical Right*. Abingdon: Routledge.

Scott-Smith, G. (2012). *Western Anti-Communism and the Interdoc Network: Cold War Internationale*. Basingstoke: Palgrave Macmillan.

Sedgwick, M. (2002). *Against the Modern World: Traditionalism and the Secret Intellectual History of the Twentieth Century*. New York: Oxford University Press.

Seidel, G. (1986). *Holocaust Denial: Antisemitism, Racism and the New Right*. Leeds: Beyond the Pale Publications.

Shaffer, R. (2017). *Music, Youth and International Links in Post-War British Fascism: The Transformation of Extremism*. London: Palgrave Macmillan.

Shekhovtsov, A. (forthcoming). *Russia and the Western Far Right: Tango Noir*. Abingdon: Routledge.

Shekhovtsov, A. and Jackson, P. (eds.) (2012). *White Power Music: Scenes of Extreme-Right Cultural Resistance*. London: *Searchlight* Publications.

Shermer, M. and Grobman, A. (2009). *Denying History: Who Says the Holocaust Never Happened and Why Do They Say It?* 2nd edn. Berkeley, CA: University of California Press.

Simi, P. and Futrell, R. (2010). *American Swastika: Inside the White Power Movement's Hidden Spaces of Hate*. Lanham, MD: Rowman & Littlefield.

Simi, P. and Futrell, R. (2017). *American Swastika: Inside the White Power Movement's Hidden Spaces of Hate*, 2nd edn. Lanham, MD: Rowman & Littlefield.

Simpson, P. A. and Druxes, H. (eds.) (2015). *Digital Media Strategies of the Far Right in Europe and the United States*. Lanham, MD: Lexington Books.

Smith, E. (forthcoming). *British Communism and the Politics of Race*. Leiden: Brill.

Smith, E. and Worley, M. (eds.) (2014). *Against the Grain: The British Far Left from 1956*. Manchester: Manchester University Press.

Spaaij, R. (2012). *Understanding Lone Wolf Terrorism: Global patterns. Motivations and Prevention*. Dordrecht: Springer.

Stern, K. S. (1993). *Holocaust Denial*. New York: American Jewish Committee.

Sternhell, Z. (1986). *Neither Right nor Left: Fascist Ideology in France*. Berkeley, CA: University of California Press.

Sternhell, Z. (1994). *The Birth of Fascist Ideology: From Cultural Rebellion to Political Revolution*. Princeton, NJ: Princeton University Press.

Stocker, P. (2017). *English Uprising: Brexit and the Mainstreaming of the Far-Right*. London: Melville House.

Sykes, A. (1995). *The Radical Right in Britain: Social Imperialism to the BNP*. Basingstoke: Palgrave Macmillan.

Taylor, K. (2000). *Holocaust Denial: The Irving Trial and International Revisionism*. London: *Searchlight* Educational Trust.

Taylor, M., Currie, P. M. and Holbrook, D. (eds.) (2013). *Extreme Right Wing Political Violence and Terrorism*. London: Bloomsbury.

Taylor, S. (1982). *The National Front in English Politics*. London: Macmillan.

Teacher, D. (2015). *Rogue Agents: The Cercle and the 6I in the Private Cold War 1951–1991*. 4th edn. Available at http://powerbase.info/index.php/Rogue_Agents (accessed 31 May 2017).

Teitelbaum, B. (2017). *Lions of the North: Sounds of the New Nordic Radical Nationalism*. New York: Oxford University Press.

Thayer, G. (1965). *The British Political Fringe: A Profile*. London: Anthony Blond.

Thurlow, R. (1987). *Fascism in Britain: A History 1918–1985*. Oxford: Basil Blackwell.

Thurlow, R. (1998). *Fascism in Britain: From Oswald Mosley's Blackshirts to the National Front*, 2nd edn. London: I.B. Tauris.

Thurlow, R. (2000). *Fascism in Modern Britain*. Stroud: Sutton.

Tilles, D. (2015). *British Fascist Anti-Semitism and Jewish Responses 1932–40*. London: Bloomsbury Academic.

Toczek, N. (2016). *Haters, Baiters and Would-be Dictators: Anti-Semitism and the UK Far Right*. Abingdon: Routledge.

Tomlinson, J. (1981). *Left, Right: The March of Political Extremism in Britain*. London: John Calder.

Trilling, D. (2012). *Bloody Nasty People: The Rise of Britain's Far Right*. London: Verso.

Vidal-Naquet, P. (1992). *Assassins of Memory: Essays on the Denial of the Holocaust*. New York: Columbia University Press.

Walker, M. (1977). *The National Front*. Glasgow: Fontana/Collins.

Webb, P. (2007). *Exploring the Networked Worlds of Popular Music: Milieu Cultures*. Abingdon: Routledge.

Wilkinson, P. (1981). *The New Fascists*. London: Pan Books.

Willan, P. (1991). *Puppetmasters: The Political Use of Terrorism in Italy*. London: Constable.

Williams, D. and Lowles, N. (2012). *The 'Counter-Jihad' Movement: The Global Trend Feeding Anti-Muslim Hatred*. London: Hope Not Hate.

Winlow, S., Hall, S. and Treadwell, J. (2017). *The Rise of the Right: English Nationalism and the Transformation of Working-class Politics*. Bristol: The Policy Press.

Wodak, R. (2015). *The Politics of Fear*. London: Sage.

Wodak, R. and Richardson, J. E. (eds.) (2013). *Analysing Fascist Discourse: European Fascism in Talk and Text*. Abingdon: Routledge.

Wodak, R., Khosravinik, M. and Mral, B. (eds.) (2013). *Rightwing Populism Across Europe: Discourse and Politics*. London: Bloomsbury.

Wood, I. S. (2006). *Crimes of Loyalty: A History of the UDA*. Edinburgh: Edinburgh University Press.

Woodley, D. (2010). *Fascism and Political Theory: Critical Perspectives on Fascist Ideology*. Abingdon: Routledge.

Secondary sources – book chapters, articles and pamphlets

Alessio, D. and Meredith, K. (2014). Blackshirts for the Twenty-first Century? Fascism and the English Defence League, *Social Identities*, 20 (1), pp. 104–118.

Allen, C. (2011). Opposing Islamification or Promoting Islamophobia? Understanding the English Defence League, *Patterns of Prejudice*, 45 (4), pp. 279–294.

Allen, C. (2014). Britain First: The 'Frontline Resistance' to the Islamification of Britain, *Political Quarterly*, 85 (3), July–September, pp. 345–361.

Allen, C. (2017). Proscribing National Action: Considering the Impact of Banning the British Far-Right Group. *The Political Quarterly*. doi:10.1111/1467-923X.12368.

Baker, D. (1985). A.K. Chesterton, the Strasser Brothers and the Politics of the National Front, *Patterns of Prejudice*, 19, pp. 23–33.

Bale, T. (2012). Supplying the Insatiable Demand: Europe's Populist Radical Right, *Government and Opposition*, 47 (2), pp. 256–274.

Barnes, I. R. (1980a). The Pedigree of GRECE – I, *Patterns of Prejudice*, 14 (3), pp. 14–24, DOI: 10.1080/0031322X.1980.9969575.

Barnes, I. R. (1980b). The Pedigree of GRECE – II, *Patterns of Prejudice*, 14 (4), pp. 29–39, DOI: 10.1080/0031322X.1980.9969590.

Bar-On, T. (2011). Transnationalism and the French *Nouvelle Droite*, *Patterns of Prejudice*, 45 (3), pp. 199–223, DOI: 10.1080/0031322X.2011.585013.

Billig, M. (1988). Rhetoric of the Conspiracy Theory: Arguments in National Front Propaganda, *Patterns of Prejudice*, 22 (2), pp. 22–34.

Billig, M. and Cochrane, R. (1981). The National Front and Youth, *Patterns of Prejudice*, 15 (4), pp. 3–15, DOI: 10.1080/0031322X.1981.9969634.

Blee, K. M. (2017). How the Study of White Supremacism is Helped and Hindered by Social Movement Research, *Mobilization: An International Quarterly*, 22 (1), March, pp. 1–15.

Bowyer, B. (2008). Local Context and Extreme Right Support in England: The British National Party in the 2002 and 2003 Local Elections, *Electoral Studies*, 27, pp. 611–620.

Braouezec, K. (2016). Identifying Common Patterns of Discourse and Strategy among the New Extremist Movements in Europe: The Case of the English Defence League and the Bloc Identitaire, *Journal of Intercultural Studies*, 37 (6), pp. 637–648.

Brown, T. S. (2004). Subcultures, Pop Music and Politics: Skinheads and 'Nazi Rock' in England and Germany, *Journal of Social History*, 38, pp. 157–178.

Busher, J. and Macklin, G. (2015). Interpreting 'Cumulative Extremism': Six Proposals for Enhancing Conceptual Clarity, *Terrorism and Political Violence*, 27 (5), pp. 884–905, doi:10.1080/09546553.2013.870556.

Campbell, C. (1972). The Cult, the Cultic Milieu and Secularization, in Hill, M. (ed.) *A Sociological Yearbook of Religion in Britain 5*. London: SCM Press, pp. 119–136.

Carter, A. (2012a). Packaging Hate – The New Right Publishing Networks, *Searchlight*, February – March, pp. 8–11, available online at www.searchlightmagazine.com/wp-content/uploads/2017/05/Far-right-publishers-FebMar2012.pdf (accessed 31 May 2017).

Carter, A. (2012b). Dreaming of a Parallel Culture, *Searchlight*, April, pp. 5–8, available online at www.searchlightmagazine.com/wp-content/uploads/2017/05/Alex-Kurtagic-April-2012.pdf (accessed 31 May 2017).

Carter, A. J. (2017). Cumulative Extremism: Escalation of Movement–Countermovement Dynamics in Northern Ireland between 1967 and 1972, *Behavioral Sciences of Terrorism and Political Aggression*, 9 (1), pp. 37–51, DOI: 10.1080/19434472.2016.1236830.

Clarke, H., Whiteley, P., Borges, W., Sanders, D. and Stewart, M. (2016). Modelling the Dynamics of Support for a Right-wing Populist Party: The Case of UKIP, *Journal of Elections, Public Opinion and Parties*, 26 (2), pp. 135–154, DOI:10.1080/17457289.2016.1146286.

Cleland, J., Anderson, C. and Aldridge-Deacon, J. (2017). Islamophobia, War and Non-Muslims as Victims: An Analysis of Online Discourse on an English Defence League Message Board, *Ethnic and Racial Studies*, DOI: 10.1080/01419870.2017.1287927.

Conway, M., Carthy, J., Cunningham, P., Greene, D. and O'Callaghan, D. (2013a). *The Extreme Right Filter Bubble*. CoRR, abs/1308.6149.

Conway, M., Carthy, J., Cunningham, P., Greene, D. and O'Callaghan, D. (2013b). Uncovering the Wider Structure of Extreme Right Communities Spanning Popular Online Networks. Proceedings of the 5th Annual ACM Web Science Conference, Paris, France, pp. 276–285.

Copsey, N. (1996). Contemporary Fascism in the Local Arena: The British National Party and the 'Rights for Whites', in Cronin, M. (ed.) *The Failure of British Fascism*. London: Macmillan, pp. 118–140.

Copsey, N. (2012). Sustaining a Mortal Blow? The British National Party and the 2010 General and Local Elections, *Patterns of Prejudice*, 46 (1), pp. 16–39, DOI: 10.1080/0031322X.2012.655597.

Copsey, N. (2013). Au Revoir to 'Sacred Cows'? Assessing the Impact of the Nouvelle Droite in Britain, *Democracy and Security*, 9 (3), pp. 287–303, DOI: 10.1080/17419166.2013.792249.

Copsey, N. (2016b). Crossing Borders: Anti-Fascist Action (UK) and Transnational Anti-Fascist Militancy in the 1990s, *Contemporary European History*, 25 (4), pp. 707–727. DOI: 10.1017/S0960777316000369.

Copsey, N. (forthcoming). Historians and the Contemporary Far Right: To Bring (or Not to Bring) the Past into the Present? in Ashe, S., Busher, J., Macklin, G. and Winter, A. (eds.) *Researching the Far Right: Theory, Method and Practice*. Abingdon: Routledge.

Corte, U. and Edwards, B. (2008). White Power Music and the Mobilization of Racist Social Movements, *Music and Arts in Action* (online journal), 1 (1), pp. 4–20.

Cotter, J. M. (1999). Sounds of Hate: White Power Rock and Roll and the Neo-Nazi Skinhead Subculture, *Terrorism and Political Violence*, 11 (2), pp. 111–140, DOI:10.1080/09546559908427509.

Cutts, D., Ford, R. and Goodwin, M. J. (2011). Anti-immigrant, Politically Disaffected or Still Racist After All? Examining the Attitudinal Drivers of Extreme Right Support in Britain in the 2009 European Elections, *European Journal of Political Research*, 50 (3), pp. 418–440.

Drake, R. (1986). Julius Evola and the Ideological Origins of the Radical Right in Contemporary Italy, in Merkl, P. H. (ed.) *Political Violence and Terror: Motifs and Motivations*. Berkeley, CA: University of California Press, pp. 61–89.

Durham, M. (1996). The Conservative Party, the British Extreme Right and the Problem of Political Space, 1967–83, in Cronin, M. (ed.) *The Failure of British Fascism*. London: Macmillan, pp. 81–98.

Durham, M. (2012). The British Extreme Right and Northern Ireland, *Contemporary British History*, 26, (2), pp. 195–211.

Eatwell, R. (1989). Fascism and Political Racism in Post-War Britain, in Kushner, T. and Lunn, K. (eds.) *Traditions of Intolerance: Historical Perspectives on Fascism and Race Discourse in Britain*. Manchester: Manchester University Press, pp. 218–238.

Eatwell, R. (1991). The Holocaust Denial: A Study in Propaganda Technique, in Cheles, L., Ferguson, R. and Vaughan, M. (eds.) *Neo-fascism in Europe*, London: Longman, pp. 120–146.

Eatwell, R. (1992). Towards a New Model of Generic Fascism, *Journal of Theoretical Politics*, 4 (2), pp. 161–194.

Eatwell, R. (1996). On Defining the 'Fascist Minimum': The Centrality of Ideology, *Journal of Political Ideologies*, 1 (3), pp. 303–319. DOI: 10.1080/13569319608420743.

Eatwell, R. (2002). The Rebirth of Right-Wing Charisma? The Cases of Jean-Marie Le Pen and Vladimir Zhirinovsky, *Totalitarian Movements and Political Religions*, 3 (3), pp. 1–23, DOI: 10.1080/714005489.

Eatwell, R. (2003). Ten Theories of the Extreme Right, in Merkl, P. and Weinberg, L. (eds.) *Right-Wing Extremism in the Twenty-First Century*. Abingdon: Routledge, pp. 45–70.

Eatwell, R. (2006a). Community Cohesion and Cumulative Extremism in Contemporary Britain, *The Political Quarterly*, 77 (2), pp. 204–216.

Eatwell, R. (2006b). The Concept and Theory of Charismatic Leadership, *Totalitarian Movements and Political Religions*, 7 (2), pp. 141–156, DOI: 10.1080/14690760600642156.

Eatwell, R. (2006c). Explaining Fascism and Ethnic Cleansing: The Three Dimensions of Charisma and the Four Dark Sides of Nationalism, *Political Studies Review*, 4, pp. 2263–2278.

Edgar, D. (1977). *Racism, Fascism and the Politics of the National Front*. (Pamphlet). London: Institute of Race Relations.

Ford, R. (2010). Who Might Vote for the BNP? Survey Evidence on the Electoral Potential of the Extreme Right in Britain, in Eatwell, R. and Goodwin, M. J. (eds.) *The New Extremism in 21st Century Britain*. Abingdon: Routledge, pp. 145–168.

Futrell, R., Simi, P. and Gottschalk, S. (2006). Understanding Music in Movements: The White Power Music Scene, *Sociological Quarterly*, 47 (2), pp. 275–304.

Gable, G. (1995). Britain's Nazi Underground' in Cheles, L., Ferguson, R. and Vaughan, M. (eds.) *The Far Right in Western and Eastern Europe*. Harlow: Longman, pp. 245–263.

Gardell, M. (2014). Crusader Dreams: Oslo 22/7, Islamophobia, and the Quest for a Monocultural Europe, *Terrorism and Political Violence*, 26 (1), pp. 129–155.

Goodwin, M. J. (2006). The Rise and Faults of the Internalist Perspective in Extreme Right Studies, *Representation*, 42 (4), pp. 347–364, DOI:10.1080/00344890600951924.

Goodwin, M. J. (2007). The Extreme Right in Britain: Still an 'Ugly Duckling' but for How Long? *The Political Quarterly*, 78 (2), pp. 241–250. (DOI:https://doi.org/10.1111/j.1467-923X.2007.00851.x).

Goodwin, M. J. and Cutts, D. (2012). Mobilising the Workers? Extreme Right Party Support and Campaign Effects at the 2010 General Election, in Rydgren, J. (ed.) *Class Politics and the Radical Right*. Abingdon: Routledge, pp. 190–205.

Goodwin, M. J., Ford, R., Duffy, B. and Robey, R. (2010). Who Votes Extreme Right in 21st Century Britain? The Social Bases of Support for the National Front and British National Party in the New Extremism in 21st Century Britain, in Eatwell, R. and Goodwin, M. (eds.). London: Routledge, pp. 191–210.

Griffin, R. (1996). British Fascism: The Ugly Duckling, in Cronin, M. (ed.) *The Failure of British Fascism*. London: Palgrave Macmillan, pp. 141–165.

Griffin, R. (2000). Between Metapolitics and *Apoliteia*: The *Nouvelle Droite's* Strategy for Conserving the Fascist Vision in the 'Interregnum', *Modern & Contemporary France*, 8 (1), pp. 35–53, DOI: 10.1080/096394800113349.

Griffin, R. (2003). From Slime Mould to Rhizome: An Introduction to the Groupuscular Right, *Patterns of Prejudice*, 37 (1), pp. 27–50, DOI: 10.1080/0031322022000054321.

Harrop, M., England, J. and Husbands, C. T. (1980). The Bases of National Front Support, *Political Studies*, 28, pp. 271–283. https://doi.org/10.1111/j.1467–9248.1980.tb01250.x.

Hayes, M. (2014). Red Action – Left Wing Political Pariah, in Smith, E. and Worley, M. (eds.) *Against the Grain: The British Far Left from 1956*. Manchester: Manchester University Press, pp. 229–246.

Hayes, M. and Aylward, P. (2000). Anti-Fascist Action: Radical Resistance or Rent-A-Mob? *Soundings*, (14), Spring, pp. 53–62.

Hess-Meining, U. (2012). Right-Wing Esotericism in Europe, in Backes, U. and Moreau, P. (eds.) *The Extreme Right in Europe: Current Trends and Perspectives*. Göttingen: Vandenhoeck & Ruprecht, pp. 383–408. https://doi.org/10.17813/1086-671X-22-1-1.

Husbands, C. (1988). Extreme Right-Wing Politics in Great Britain: The Recent Marginalisation of the National Front, in Von Beyme, K. (ed.) *Right-wing Extremism in Europe*. London: Frank Cass, pp. 65–79.

Husbands, C. T. (1982). East End Racism 1900–1980: Geographical Continuities in Vigilantist and Extreme Right-wing Political Behaviour, *The London Journal*, 8 (1), pp. 3–26, DOI: https://doi.org/10.1179/ldn.1982.8.1.3.

Husbands, C. T. (1994). Following the 'Continental Model'? Implications of the Recent Electoral Performance of the British National Party, *Journal of Ethnic and Migration Studies*, 20 (4), pp. 563–579, DOI: 10.1080/1369183X.1994.9976454.

Jackson, P. (2011). The English Defence League: Anti-Muslim Politics Online, in Jackson, P. and Gable, G. (eds.) *Far-Right.Com: Nationalist Extremism on the Internet*. Northampton: Searchlight Magazine and the Radicalism and New Media Research Group, pp. 7–20.

John, P. and Margetts, H. (2009). The Latent Support for the Extreme Right in British Politics, *West European Politics*, 32 (3), pp. 496–513. DOI: 10.1080/01402380902779063.

Lööw, H. (1998). White Power Rock 'n' Roll: A Growing Industry, in Kaplan, J. and Bjørgo T. (eds.) *Nation and Race: The Developing Euro-American Racist Subculture*. Boston, MA: Northeastern University Press, pp. 126–147.

Macklin, G. (2005). Co-opting the Counter Culture: Troy Southgate and the National Revolutionary Faction, *Patterns of Prejudice*, 39 (3), pp. 301–326. http://dx.doi.org/10.1080/00313220500198292

Macklin, G. (2013). Transnational Networking on the Far Right: The Case of Britain and Germany, *West European Politics*, 36 (1), pp. 176–198, DOI: 10.1080/01402382.2013.742756.

Macklin, G. (2014). Teaching the Truth to the Hardcore: The Public and Private Presentation of BNP Ideology, in Feldman, M. and Jackson, P. (eds.) *Doublespeak: The Rhetoric of the Far Right since 1945*. Stuttgart: ibidem-Verlag, pp. 123–146.

Macklin, G. D. (2015). The 'Cultic Milieu' of Britain's 'New Right': Meta-political 'Fascism' in Contemporary Britain, in Copsey, N. and Richardson, J. E. (eds.) *Cultures of Post-War British Fascism*. Abingdon: Routledge, pp. 178–201.

Macklin, G. and Busher, J. (2015). The Missing Spirals of Violence: Four Waves of Movement–Countermovement Contest in Post-war Britain, *Behavioral Sciences of Terrorism and Political Aggression*, 7 (1), pp. 53–68. doi:10.1080/19434472.2014.977329.

Meadowcroft, J. and Morrow, E. (2016). Violence, Self-Worth, Solidarity and Stigma: How a Dissident, Far-Right Group Solves the Collective Action Problem, *Political Studies*, 65 (2), pp. 373–390.

Mudde, C. (2016a). *The Study of Populist Radical Right Parties: Towards a Fourth Wave*. Oslo: C-REX Working Papers 1. www.sv.uio.no/c-rex/english/publications/c-rex-working-paper-series/Cas%20Mudde:%20The%20Study%20of%20Populist%20Radical%20Right%20Parties.pdf (accessed 31 May 2017).

Nugent, N. and King, R. (1979). Ethnic Minorities, Scapegoating and the Extreme Right, in Miles, R. and Phizacklea, A. (eds.) *Racism and Political Action in Britain*. London: Routledge and Kegan Paul, pp. 28–49.

O'Callaghan, D., Greene, D., Conway, M., Carthy, J. and Cunningham, P. (2015). Down the (White) Rabbit Hole: The Extreme Right and Online Recommender Systems, *Social Science Computer Review*, 33 (4), pp. 459–478.

Opratko, B. (2017). Islamophobia: The Bigger Picture, *Historical Materialism*, 25 (1), pp. 63–89. DOI: 10.1163/1569206X-12341512.

Passmore, K. (2006). Generic Fascism and the Historians, in Griffin, R., Loh, W. and Umland, A. (eds.) *Fascism Past and Present, West and East*. Stuttgart: ibidem-Verlag, pp. 168–274.

Peace, T. and Mammone, A. (2012). Cross-national Ideology in Local Elections: The Case of Azione Sociale and the British National Party, in Mammone, A., Godin, E. and Jenkins, B. (ed.) *Mapping the Extreme Right in Contemporary Europe: From Local to Transnational*. Abingdon: Routledge, pp. 288–302.

Pilkington, H. (2016). *Loud and Proud: Passion and Politics in the English Defence League*. Manchester: Manchester University Press.

Pollard, J. (2016). Skinhead Culture: The Ideologies, Mythologies, Religions and Conspiracy Theories of Racist Skinheads, *Patterns of Prejudice*, 50 (4–5), pp. 398–419, DOI: 10.1080/0031322X.2016.1243349.

Rees, P. (1980). Changing Interpretations of British Fascism: A Bibliographical Survey, in Lunn, K. and Thurlow, R. (eds.) *British Fascism: Essays on the Radical Right in Inter-war Britain*. London: Croom Helm, pp. 187–204.

Renton, D. (2005). 'A Day to Make History'? The 2004 Elections and the British National Party, *Patterns of Prejudice*, 39 (1), pp. 25–45, DOI: 10.1080/00313220500045170.

Renton, D. (2014). Anti-Fascism in Britain, 1997–2012, in Smith, E. and Worley, M. (eds.) *Against the Grain: The British Far Left from 1956*. Manchester: Manchester University Press, pp. 247–263.

Richardson, J. E. (2008). 'Our England': discourses of 'race' and class in party election leaflets, *Social Semiotics*, 18 (3), pp. 321–335, DOI: 10.1080/10350330802217105.

Richardson, J. E. (2015). 'Cultural Marxism' and the British National Party: A Transnational Discourse, in Copsey, N. and Richardson, J. E. (eds.) *Cultures of Post-War British Fascism*. Abingdon: Routledge, pp. 202–226.

Searchlight (1989). *From Ballots to Bombs: The Inside Story of the National Front's Political Soldiers*. London: *Searchlight*.

Senholt, J. (2012). Secret Identities in the Sinister Tradition: Political Esotericism and the Convergence of Radical Islam, Satanism and National Socialism in the Order of Nine Angles, in Faxneld, P. and Petersen, J. (eds.) *The Devil's Party: Satanism in Modernity*. New York: Oxford University Press, pp. 250–274.

Shaffer, R. (2013). The Soundtrack of Neo-Fascism: Youth and Music in the National Front, *Patterns of Prejudice*, 47 (4–5), pp. 458–482, DOI: 10.1080/0031322X.2013.842289.

Sheehan, T. (1981). Myth and Violence: The Fascism of Julius Evola and Alain de Benoist, in *Social Research*, 48, pp. 45–73.

Shekhovtsov, A. (2009). Apoliteic Music: Neo-Folk, Martial Industrial and 'Metapolitical Fascism', *Patterns of Prejudice*, 43 (5), pp. 431–457, DOI: 10.1080/00313220903338990.

Sieg, G. (2013). Angular Momentum: From Traditional to Progressive Satanism in the Order of Nine Angles, *International Journal for the Study of New Religions*, 4 (2).

Taguieff, P.-A. (1993). From Race to Culture: The New Right's View of European Identity, *Telos*, 98–99, pp. 99–125.

Taylor, S. (1978). Race, Extremism and Violence in Contemporary British Politics, *New Community*, 7 (1), pp. 56–66.

Taylor, S. (1993). The Radical Right in Britain, in Merkl, P. H. and Weinberg, L. (eds.) *Encounters with the Contemporary Radical Right*. Boulder, CO: Westview, pp. 165–184.

Treadwell, J. (2012). White Riot: The English Defence League and the 2011 English Riots, *Criminal Justice Matters*, 87 (1), pp. 36–37, DOI: 10.1080/09627251.2012.671016.

Treadwell, J. and Garland, J. (2011). Masculinity, Marginalisation and Violence: A Case Study of the English Defence League, *British Journal of Criminology*, 51 (4), pp. 621–634.

Usherwood, S. (2016). The UK Independence Party: The Dimensions of Mainstreaming, in Akkerman, T., Rooduijn, M. and de Lange, S. (eds.) *Radical Right-Wing Populist Parties in Western Europe: Into the Mainstream?* Abingdon: Routledge, pp. 247–267.

Versluis, A. (2012). Savitri Devi, Miguel Serrano and the Global Phenomenon of Esoteric Hitlerism. In *Occultism in a Global Perspective*. London: Acumen Publishing Limited, pp. 121–134.

Virdee, S. (2014). Challenging the Empire, *Ethnic and Racial Studies*, 37 (10), 1823–1829. ISSN0141-9870.

Ware, V. (1978). *Women and the National Front*. (Pamphlet) Birmingham: A. F & R Publications.

Webb, P. and Bale, T. (2014). Why Do Tories Defect to UKIP? Conservative Party Members and the Temptations of the Populist Radical Right. *Political Studies*, 62, pp. 961–970. doi:10.1111/1467–9248.12130.

Whitaker, R. and Lynch, P. (2011). Explaining Support for the UK Independence Party at the 2009 European Parliament Elections, *Journal of Elections, Public Opinion and Parties*, 21 (3), pp. 359–379, DOI: 10.1080/17457289.2011.588439.

Whiteley, P. (1979). The National Front Vote in the 1977 GLC Elections: An Aggregate Data Analysis, *British Journal of Political Science*, 9 (3), pp. 370–380.

Wilks-Heeg, S. (2009). The Canary in the Coalmine? Explaining the Emergence of the British National Party in English Local Politics, *Parliamentary Affairs*, 62 (3), pp. 377–398.

Wilks-Heeg, S. (2010). A Slow and Painful Death? Political Parties and Local Democracy in Two Northern Towns, *Local Government Studies*, 36 (3), 381–399, DOI: 10.1080/03003931003738181.

INDEX

activism 36, 38, 41, 43, 179–181, 190–192, 218, 221, 233, 237; community-based 193, 241; digital 7, 237, 246; far-right 27, 44, 169, 185, 208, 225, 232–233, 242; online 226, 242; in support for GD 190, 200; transnational 29, 199

activists 39–40, 42–43, 100–101, 185–195, 209, 213–15, 220–221, 236–238, 240, 248–249; anti-fascist 7, 156, 238–239; anti-Muslim 239; Bernadette Devlin 93; Blair Peach 107; and the English Defence League 214; far-right 69–70, 74, 84, 169, 225, 245–247; former NF 232; Francis Parker Yockey 242; motivations of 6, 229, 238, 248–249; murdered 189, 191; neo-Nazi 30; post-war 227; pre-war 227; Roberto Fiore 196, 200; seasoned political 118; social movement 214, 220; working-class 232; young 119, 126–127

The Age 69, 77–78, 80

AIDS 153–154, 159–164; crisis 6, 154–155, 160–162, 164

Albanese, Matteo 29, 242

All Lewisham Campaign Against Racism and Fascism 99

ALoR 70, 73–74; *see also* Australian League of Rights

American Nazi Party 33, 35, 44

Angolan civil war 79

ANL (Anti-Nazi League) 85, 102–103, 106–107, 113, 122, 239–240

anti-fascism 103, 239–240; community-based 240; contemporary 239; militant 239; physical force 240

Anti-Fascist Action 124

Anti-Fascist Network 174

anti-fascists 5, 32–33, 76–77, 90–96, 98–102, 106–108, 124, 135–138, 224–226, 238–241; campaigns 133; committees 240; counter-demonstrations 85; determined 100; far-left 108; and fascists 5, 90–91, 96, 101, 106, 108, 110; groups 14, 17, 27, 99, 107, 236, 241; independent 241; infiltrators 33, 244; leftist 108; militant 94, 99–100; mobilisations 92–93; monitoring 32; movement 5, 17, 71, 76, 92–93, 95, 106, 225, 239; protestors 77, 83, 117; reprisals 124; responses 239; targets 93; violent 107; young 96

anti-homosexuality party 153

anti-racism 114, 117, 239

anti-Semitic 21, 60, 62, 243–244; conspiracy theory 9, 17–19, 60, 66, 74; content of distributism 65; prejudices 195; terminology abbreviated to its acronym 'ZOG' 195

anti-Semitism 12, 17–18, 51, 61, 74, 195, 198, 231

arrests 97, 99, 187, 189; of gay men 155; and imprisonment for denial in European courts 19; of Michaloliakos 195

Asian Youth Movement 96–98, 100, 107, 240

ASIO (Australian Security Intelligence Organisation) 69, 73, 80–81, 83–84

Australian League of Rights 70, 73–74

The Australian Nationalist 78–80

Australian Nationalist Movement 70

Australian politics 71–72
AYMs (Asian Youth Movements) 96–98, 100, 107, 240

Baker, David 51–52, 226–227, 230
Bale, Jeffrey 28, 229, 242, 247
bands 1, 103, 113, 120–124, 126, 132–134, 137–140, 143–144, 187; all-white 118; black metal 187; neo-fascist 5, 132–133, 137, 140–142, 145–146; punk 113, 120, 138; skinhead 124; socialist 136
Bar-Tal, D. 214–215, 218
Barisione, M. 170–171
Bartlett, J. 175, 225, 234, 237, 247
BBC 19, 42–43, 101, 150, 178, 189, 219
Bean, John 56, 75, 120, 150, 232, 247
Belloc, Hilaire 60–63
Bild 175
Birtley, Alan 81–82, 106
Blee, K. 169, 175–177, 179–181, 238
Blood & Honour (music based political movement) 114, 125–127, 143, 145
BM (British Movement) 17, 30–33, 42, 44, 96–97, 113, 115–116, 119–121, 133, 243–244
BNP (British National Party) 1–4, 6–7, 17–20, 150–165, 177–178, 189–195, 197–201, 224–225, 232–235, 245–248; activists 192–194, 233–235; the anti-homosexuality party 153; candidates 192; homohysteria 162, 165; opposition to gay men 6; party organisation 234; publications 6, 154, 159–161, 163; support for their Greek counterparts 191–192; and UKIP 224–225, 229
Bolton, Kerry 77, 82
Bows, Hannah 6, 169–181
Britain First 172–173, 176–177, 237
British Communist Party 239
British far-right ideology 12, 24
British fascism 48, 54, 59, 71, 75, 114–116, 151, 155, 165, 226–228; changing interpretations of 226; contemporary 228; early 151, 155; gender history of 165; and imperial ties 71; *see also* fascism
British Fascism, contemporary 228
British Fascisti 71
British Fascists 34, 48, 53, 66, 155
The British Worker 58–59, 64
British workers 57–59, 64
British youth culture 113, 116, 127; and far-right organisations 5; politicised nature of 114; and punk 113
Brons, Andrew 7, 17, 60–61, 64

BUF (British Union of Fascists) 2, 11, 49–50, 71–73, 75, 78, 151–152, 155, 229, 233
Bulldog (Young National Front magazine) 109
Butler, Eddy 74, 234
by-elections, parliamentary 7, 92, 96, 117

campaigns and conflicts 38, 91–92, 95–96, 98–99, 101, 104–106, 174, 236
Campbell, Colin 29, 58, 71–72, 241
The Canberra Times 77
capitalism 10, 49–54, 56–57, 59–66; advanced 64; and communism 52–4, 62, 64; democratic 52; global 62; international 48, 53, 59; liberal 108; productive 56; rehabilitated 5, 50; and socialism 54, 57, 60
Carroll, Kevin 208
Carter, Alex 5, 90–110, 170, 176, 229, 234
Centre Party 72–73
Chesterton, Cecil 2, 11, 13, 18, 20, 49, 53, 59, 62, 74; and Enoch Powell's 'Rivers of Blood' speech 75; and his conspiratorial anti-Semitism 60, 227; resignation as chairman of the National Front 75; speech urges a more acceptable face for post-war British far-right ideology 12
Chesterton, A.K. 82, 227–228
Chesterton, G.K. 60, 232
Chryssi Avgi (Golden Dawn newspaper) 197
civil society groups 224, 226, 233, 237, 247
civil war 79
Clapton, Eric 103, 118
class politics 208, 238
class war 49, 94, 138
CNF (Commonwealth National Front) 5, 70–71, 79–82, 84
collective identities 188–190
Commerer, B. 152–154
communities 98–99, 107, 109, 145, 191, 193, 209, 215–216, 219, 221; black 102; country's émigré 193; deprived white working-class 173; ethnic minority 99; Europe and settler colonial 84; Greek diaspora 186; immigrant 102; large African-Caribbean 77; LGBT 176; minority 95–96, 101, 103, 105, 108–109; neo-fascist skinhead 136; non-white 95, 98, 109; small farming and craft 60; tensions in 96, 208–209, 221; violence and instilling fear in 221
Conservative Monday Club 115
Conservative Party 14, 42–43, 77, 229
Copeland, David 156, 159, 247

Copsey, Nigel 1–7, 92, 106–107, 114–127, 150–152, 157–158, 225–227, 233–234, 237, 239
council elections 104, 234, 241, 247
counter-demonstrations, anti-fascist 85
Crane, Nicky 119, 124, 142
Crawford, David 70, 77, 82

demonstrations 70, 97–98, 172, 174, 188–90, 208, 219, 246; and mobilisation strategies 246; political 101; and protests 246; street 237
Devlin, Bernadette 93
digital activism 7, 237, 246
Durham, Martin 14, 17, 29, 151–152, 170, 174, 177, 179–180, 229, 231

East London 91, 93, 104–105, 124, 192–193
Eatwell, Roger 5, 28, 76, 90, 226, 228–231, 234, 243, 246, 248
economic ideology 5, 50–51
economy 5, 48, 51–53, 55–56, 72; capitalistic 144; decentralised 60; global free market 52; honest working 51; national 49, 51–52, 57–59; permanent war 52; state-directed private ownership 52; third way 50
EDL (English Defence League) 3, 6–7, 85, 172–178, 180, 208–215, 217–221, 225, 236–239, 246–247; activities 208–209; ideology 238; leadership 209, 219; patriotism 220–221; protests 217–218; as a social movement 208; supporters 4, 237
EDL activists 6, 217, 220, 237–238; and emotional responses to grievances 211–217; and the wider political environment 208, 220, 237
education 12, 17, 23–24, 117, 170–172, 176; attainment 176; authorities 160; and the increasing awareness of the Holocaust 18; levels of 170, 172; and remembrance 23; systems 160
elections 12, 17, 20, 22, 92–93, 95, 185–186, 194, 199, 230; council 104, 234, 241, 247; democratic 50; federal 82; general 2–3, 50, 53, 55, 76, 82, 107, 185, 192, 233; local 2, 36–37, 92, 99, 104, 159, 192, 233; popular 50; presidential 3
emotions 4, 189, 208–211, 213–215, 218, 220–221, 237; affective 211; arousal of 210; and beliefs 189; moral 211; of patriotism 213, 218; reflex 211–212, 220; and values of patriotism 220

ENR 242–243; see also European New Right An Essay on The Restoration of Property 60
essays 60, 132, 139, 144, 232, 235, 239
European National Front (succeeded by the Alliance for Peace and Freedom in 2015) 199
extreme-right organisations 29, 44, 242

far-right activism 27, 44, 169, 185, 208, 225, 232–233, 242
far-right activists 69–70, 74, 84, 169, 225, 245–247
far-right groups 2, 6, 71, 79, 81, 83, 169, 171–176, 180–181, 232; British 12; contemporary 177; European 233; first to be banned by the UK government under anti-terror legislation 225; League of Empire Loyalists 74; supporting of 173; women's involvement in 169
far-right movements 85, 169, 172–175, 177, 180–181, 244; and the anti-immigration parties 175; in Australia 70–71, 83; in Britain and Europe 6, 84, 107, 169, 242; and dedicated activists 85, 245, 249; and neo-Nazi history 20
fascism 28–29, 48–49, 51–52, 71–72, 94–96, 98–99, 114–116, 151, 165, 226–228; British 48, 54, 59, 71, 75, 114–116, 151, 155, 165, 226–228; 'classical' 74; exporting across the Commonwealth 69–85; ideological 151; as an ideology aiming to regenerate a modern society though an anti-liberal and revolutionary agenda 28; pan-European 227; and racism 91–92, 95–96, 98–99, 106; 'transnational' 84; and women 179
fascist groups 29, 162, 170, 230, 232
Fascist Italy 51–52, 72
fascist occultism 226, 242–244
fascist politics 114, 121, 126
fascists 48–49, 51–54, 60–61, 65–66, 72–73, 92–96, 99–100, 102, 108–110, 151; and anti-fascists 5, 90–91, 96, 101, 106, 110; contemporary 152; racial 52; young 120–121, 124
fear 72, 79, 90, 108, 154, 157, 162, 209, 211–213, 220–221; instilling of 221; nascent 152
Federation of Bangladesh Youth Organisations (FBYO) 104
feminism 151, 177, 179–181
feminists 179–180
finance capitalism 49, 57–58, 60
Fiore, Roberto 196, 200

First World War 1
Fountaine, Andrew 75, 96, 157–158
Fowlie, Craig 6, 224–249

Gable, G. 132, 134, 245–247
Garland, Carol 160, 171–173, 178–179, 209, 220, 237
GD (Golden Dawn Party, Greece) 6, 185–201; activists 185, 187, 194, 197, 199–200; activities 192–193; and the English language website 192, 199; leadership 187, 189, 195; transnational impact 186
gender gap 169–173, 175, 177, 179, 181
general elections 2–3, 50, 53, 55, 76, 82, 107, 185, 192, 233
genocide 14–16, 18–19, 22–24; and atrocities 23; denial 9; and ethnic cleansing 22; of European Jewry 4, 23; white 21–22, 24, 191
Gifford, S. 31, 35, 38–39
gigs 113–114, 117, 120–124, 126–127, 137, 141
GK Weekly 60
Goodwin, Matthew J. 151–152, 154, 171–174, 176, 211, 220, 229, 233–237, 247, 249
gothic lettering and Nazi symbolism 138–139, 142–143
Gottlieb, Julie V. 151, 170, 227
Greason, David 74, 81
Greater Britain Movement 2, 13, 75, 115
Greece 6, 185–187, 191–195, 199–200
Greek government 6, 185–188, 195, 197
Greek neo-Nazi group Chrysi Avgi 185
Greek politics 185–186
grievances 57, 95, 189–190, 192, 197, 210–213, 219–221
Griffin, Nick 2, 17–20, 22, 62, 159, 191, 193–201, 226, 228, 233–234
groups 4–5, 27–33, 35–37, 39–40, 42, 69–71, 91–99, 107–110, 172–173, 189–191; anti-fascist 14, 17, 27, 99, 107, 236, 241; civil society 224, 226, 233, 237, 247; disparate 75, 191; extreme 170, 199; extreme-right 32, 39, 43, 201, 234; far-right 2, 6, 71, 79, 81, 83, 169, 171–176, 180–181, 232; fascist 29, 162, 170, 230, 232; fledgling 44, 85; neo-Nazi 4, 28–30, 42; new 31, 42, 176; political 133, 238; rival 28, 39, 82; third-party 95
groupuscular right 27–29, 44, 225, 241–242, 249
groupuscules (small groups) 4, 6, 27–29, 36–38, 41, 43–44, 241, 243–244, 246, 248

Heartfield, John 140, 246
Hess, Rudolf 144–145, 188
heterosexual men 154, 156, 161, 164, 173
Hill, Ray 17, 42, 82, 116, 244
historians 15–16, 18–19, 28, 133, 143, 155, 161, 224, 227, 229; of British fascism 29, 155; growing school of 15; liberal 228; professional 19
Hitchcock, Gary 119, 121, 124, 127
Hitler, Adolf 10–11, 14, 19–20, 31, 35, 42, 51–52, 55, 61, 155
HIV/AIDS 153–154, 159–164
Hobbs, Mark 1, 4, 7, 9–24
Holland, Derek 61–62, 117, 247
Holocaust denial 4, 7, 9–24, 41, 155, 178, 196, 226–227, 242, 245–247; academic cloak of respectability to 14; and anti-Semitic conspiracy thinking 9; arguments of 15; in Britain 24; and conspiracy 24; and far-right ideologies 10, 20; international 14; and the Jewish conspiracy theory 16; literature 13–14; movement 245; and Nazism 16; perspectives of 4; policy of 18; studies of 246; themes 41; trajectory of 16
Holocaust News 17
homohysteria 6, 150, 153–156, 158–165
homophobia 150, 152–155, 159, 161–162, 164–165, 176; and homohysteria 150, 153, 155, 159, 161, 164
homosexuality 4, 6, 150–162, 161–162, 164–165; British fascism and the interaction with 153; debate 157; endemic 157; and its place within late twentieth-century British fascism 152; legalised 152; opposition to 150, 158, 165; outlawing of 159–161; paedophilic 163; perceived 156; proscribing 159

ideology 9–12, 20, 22, 24, 28, 60, 172, 186, 228–230, 236–237; anti-multiculturalist 176; anti-Muslim 173; British far-right 12, 24; economic 5, 50–51; esoteric 230; failed 10; fascist imagery and 245; nationalist 61; Nazi 27, 31, 225; political 23, 235; political-economic 48; traditional 181
IMG (International Marxist Group) 92, 94, 98
immigration 38, 73, 75, 115–116, 151–152, 174, 176–177, 225, 229–230, 235; black 76; group's 73; issues 91; non-European 190; non-white 91, 115; policies 14, 234
internationalism 49, 51, 53, 57, 59–60; cosmopolitan 48; perfidious 52; and usury 60

Islam 173–174, 178, 212, 214, 216, 219, 235, 239, 244
Islamic extremism 211, 213–214, 219–221

Jackson, Paul 21–22, 27–44, 155, 160, 226, 230, 234, 237, 242–243, 245–247
Jasper, J. M. 189, 210–211, 220
Jewish conspiracy 10, 13–14, 16, 20–21, 23–24, 195
Jews 10–11, 13–14, 16–19, 21–22, 52–55, 58, 60–62, 65, 162, 192–193
Jones, Daniel 4, 27–44, 238
Jordan, Colin 12, 20, 31, 35–36, 44, 75, 116, 120, 243–244
Joyce, William 52–53, 58
'JuJitsu Politics' 109

Kingsley-Read, John 76, 115
Koehl, Matt 32–33, 35

labour movement 92, 94–95, 102
Labour Party 55, 91, 98, 236
leadership 2, 13, 15, 17, 30–31, 73, 75–76, 176–177, 233–234, 236; charismatic 248; communal 97; of the EDL 209, 219; of the GD 187, 189, 195; national 106; new radical 61; of the NF 2, 13–14, 91, 105, 115, 157–158, 232; of the NFA 81; of Nick Griffin 62; by Tyndall and Webster 18, 76
League of Empire Loyalists 2, 74
League of St George 42
Leese, Arnold 11–12, 14–15, 20, 34, 75, 227–228
Lennon, Stephen 208–209
Lewandowski, Michal 190, 194
The Liberal Party 2
Ling, Peter 39–40, 42
local elections 2, 36–37, 92, 99, 104, 159, 192, 233
Lööw, Helene 29, 241
Lowles, Nick 114, 125, 132, 156–157, 225, 237, 240–241, 245, 247–248
Lux, Martin 93, 96, 100, 102, 240
Lynch, Leslie 38, 236

Macklin, Graham 6, 29, 74, 82, 101, 185–201, 226–227, 232–234, 242–243
Mammone, Andrea 29, 151, 233–234, 242
marches 1, 77, 85, 92–100, 116, 120, 174, 188, 192, 239; annual Remembrance Day 91; NF 93, 99; processional 117
martyrdom 141, 143, 185, 187, 190
McAdam, Doug 95, 212
Miller, Linda 54, 161–163, 218

minorities 79, 106, 134, 151, 163, 193; ethnic 228; mobilized 151, 153, 155, 157, 159, 161, 163–165; sexual 153–154, 165
Monday Club 76
money power 53, 55, 58, 60, 63–64
Moore, Andrew 70, 72, 74, 81, 83
Morrison, Eddy 118–120, 122–123, 156, 158–159, 232
Mosley, Sir Oswald 49, 51, 55, 71–74, 82, 115, 117, 151, 155, 227–228
Mosse, George 28, 226
motivations of activists 6, 229, 238, 248–249
Mudie, Donald 35–43
Mudie, Pearl 36, 38
Myatt, David 156, 244, 247

National Action Party 70, 81–83, 156, 225
National Front 11–17, 53–66, 69–71, 74–78, 80–82, 91–100, 102–107, 115–118, 155–158, 227–233; and John Tyndall 42, 69, 76, 85, 106; and the Monday Club 76; and nationalist economics 49–66
National Socialist White People's Party (formally called The American Nazi Party) 35
National Socialists 12, 14, 21, 30–31, 35, 38, 56, 73, 115, 187
National Vanguard 81
nationalism 57, 59, 61–62, 64–65, 73, 116, 123, 162, 194, 200; ethnocentric 230; exclusionary 60; in Greece 194; pro-British Commonwealth 79; racial 60, 84, 227, 235; threatening British 163
nationalists 48–49, 65, 119, 124, 126–127, 133, 162, 188, 191, 195; economics 48–66; movement 78–79, 164, 191
Nationalist Workers' Party 82
Nazi Germany 5, 16, 50, 52, 72, 134, 137, 146, 155; and Nazi groups 35, 232, 244; and Nazi ideologues 27, 31, 51, 225; and the Nazi regime 10, 16, 28, 31
Nazis 12, 16, 23, 51–52, 95, 102, 124, 127, 134–136, 142
NBU (New British Union) 189–191
NDFM (National Democratic Freedom Movement) 156
NDP (National Democratic Party) 75
neo-fascism 135, 138, 140, 145–146, 228; global 135
neo-fascist bands 5, 132–133, 137, 140–142, 145–146
neo-fascist skinhead culture 133, 136, 138, 142
neo-fascists 1, 75, 133–136, 138, 142, 144–145, 198

neo-Nazi groups 4, 28–30, 42
neo-Nazi magazines 42–43
Neocleous, M. 51, 66, 226
New British Fascism 152
New Guard 71–72
New Labour 235
New National Front 17, 82, 116, 156, 158
New Zealand 5, 70–71, 80–82, 84
New Zealand Democratic Nationalist
    Party 77
newsletters 79, 153, 172; *The Australian
    Nationalist* 78–80; *Spearhead* 13, 42, 48,
    53, 75, 77–78, 96, 107, 153, 157–163;
    *The Thunderer: The Newsletter of the British
    National Party Christian Fellowship* 153
newspapers 50, 58–59, 69, 77, 132, 175,
    197; *The Age* 69, 77–78, 80; *Bild* 175; *The
    British Worker* 58–59, 64; *The Canberra
    Times* 77; Chryssi Avgi (Golden Dawn)
    197; *National Vanguard* 81
NF 1–2, 11–17, 60–66, 74–78, 80–82,
    91–100, 102–107, 115–118, 155–158,
    227–233; and ANL supporters 122;
    and anti-fascist protestors in Britain 83;
    and BM supporters 114, 134; British 5,
    70–71, 74, 77, 79–80, 82–85; leadership
    2, 13–14, 91, 105, 115, 157–158, 232;
    marches 93, 99; policies 135; youth wing
    231; *see also* National Front
NF members 75, 77, 81, 93, 96, 98–100,
    105–106, 121, 230–231; groups of 98;
    and Loyalists 93; rank-and-file 75; and
    Walter Barton 93; young 121
NFA (National Front of Australia) 5, 69–71,
    77–85; leadership 81
NFNZ (National Front of New Zealand)
    77, 81–82
NIP (National Independence Party) 76
NP (National Party (split from the NF in
    1976)) 58–59, 74, 76, 95, 115
NSG (National Socialist Group) 4, 27–44
NSPA (National Socialist Party of
    Australia) 81, 83

O'Brien, John 75–76, 122
online activism 226, 242
organisations 27–28, 30–31, 33, 39–40,
    43–44, 73, 91, 180–181, 188–189,
    247–248; animal rights 137; anti-fascist
    92, 102; anti-imperialist 92; British
    Asian 106; clandestine 4; criminal 187;
    cultural 31; extreme-right 29, 44, 242;
    extremist 5; far-right 5, 171, 174, 177,
    226, 241; independent 145; international
    white power music 245; National Front

80; non-fascist 229; paramilitary 71–72;
    political 30, 84, 158–159, 196;
    proto-fascist 6; social movement 95, 103,
    108; umbrella 198
The Outline of Sanity 60
Owens, Joey 1, 232

Palmer, George 38, 41
pamphlets, *Holocaust News* 17
parliamentary by-elections 7, 92, 96, 117
party magazines 50
Peach, Blair 107, 240
Pearce, A. 14, 16, 21, 60, 65, 109, 115,
    117–120, 122–123, 232
Pearce, Joe 109, 113, 139
police 77, 82, 85, 92–94, 96–102, 104–105,
    107, 137, 188, 195; and anti-fascist
    counter-demonstrations 85; and
    anti-fascists 188; and demonstrators 107;
    and media 98; riot 101, 107
police stations 97, 100–101, 174
policies 11–12, 58–59, 64–65, 70, 73, 151,
    153, 164–165, 229, 231; anti-national
    51; autarkic 52, 57; contemporary 53;
    distributist 65–66; economic 48–50, 56,
    62; extremist 12; far-right 9, 12, 18;
    pan-European 141; racial 73; social 49
political action 74, 82, 210; and Golden
    Dawn activists in Greece 192; joint
    188, 191
political-economic theory 50, 55, 60
political economies 4–5, 48, 50–51, 56, 58,
    60, 62, 66
political groups 133, 238
political parties 2, 12, 29, 69, 72, 80, 218,
    225, 229, 235; American Nazi Party 33,
    35, 44; Australian League of Rights 70,
    73–74; Australian Nationalist Movement
    70; British Communist Party 239; British
    Fascisti 71; British Fascists 34, 48, 53,
    66, 155; British National Party 1–4, 6–7,
    17–20, 150–165, 177–178, 189–195,
    197–201, 224–225, 232–235, 245–248;
    Centre Party 72–73; Commonwealth
    National Front 5, 70–71, 79–82, 84;
    Constitutional Movement 116; English
    Defence League 3, 6–7, 85, 172–178,
    180, 208–215, 217–221, 225, 236–239,
    246–247; European New Right 242;
    League of St George 42; The Liberal
    Party 2; National Action Party 70, 81–83,
    156, 225; National Front 11–17, 53–66,
    69–71, 74–78, 80–82, 91–100, 102–107,
    115–118, 155–158, 227–233; National
    Front of Australia 5, 69–71, 77–85; The

National Front of New Zealand 77, 81–82; National Socialist White People's Party (formally called The American Nazi Party) 35; Nationalist Workers Party 82; New British Union 189–191; New Guard 71–72; New Labour 235; New National Front 17, 82, 116, 156, 158; New Zealand Democratic Nationalist Party 77; World Union of National Socialists 30, 32–33, 39–40, 44

political violence 84, 90, 97

post-war fascist movement 74

post-war period 12, 14, 48, 70–71, 73, 152, 155, 226–227, 229

Potter, Tim 99, 102, 109

Powell, Enoch 75–76, 91, 110, 118

production 17, 51–52, 60, 62, 82; capitalist commodity 66; capitalist mode of 57, 63–66; cultural 241; socio-economic 119

profits 50–51, 57–59, 64–66, 137; funneling towards the NF 137; private 64

punk bands 113, 120, 138

punk gigs 120–124

'queers' 153, 158, 163

Quinn, C.M. 6, 208–21

Raabe, John 114

RAC (Rock Against Communism) 113–114, 119, 122–127, 133, 139, 141, 144

racism 3, 6, 13, 15, 48, 52, 97–98, 103, 105, 108; accusations of 200; biological 230, 243; cultural 227; and cultural spaces associated with punk used to propagate 114; denouncing of 123; differential 242; and fascism 91–92, 95–96, 98–99, 106; institutional 101; rational arguments for conspiracy and 13

racist attacks 98, 104

racists 15, 21, 23, 84–85, 109–110, 118, 120, 176, 178, 237

Ramamurthy, Anandi 97, 104–105, 108–110, 240

Raposo, Ana 6, 125, 132–146

RAR (Rock Against Racism) 103, 113, 118, 120, 122, 126, 133, 139, 240; see also Rock Against Racism

Red Action (later Anti-Fascist Action) 124, 133, 138, 162, 228, 239, 241

Rees, Philip 48, 224, 226

refugees 80, 94, 96

Renton, Dave 74, 102–103, 117, 226, 233, 238–240

Rhodesia 70–71, 78, 84

Rhodesian civil war 79

Richardson, John E. 4–5, 48–66, 227–228, 230, 249

right-wing groups 19, 169, 179–180, 187–188, 190, 198

Robinson, Tommy 208–209, 237–239

RUC (Royal Ulster Constabulary) 101

Sabin, Roger 6, 119, 125, 132–46

Saleam, Jim 81, 83

Sargent, Charlie 119, 127

Searchlight (anti-facist magazine) 2, 17, 19, 32–33, 36, 41–43, 231, 233, 244, 248

Second World War 4, 12, 16–17, 21, 34, 41, 72, 74, 137, 146

The Servile State 60

Severs, George J. 6, 150–165

Shaffer, R. 114, 132, 155, 188, 231, 245

Shekhovtsov, Anton 29, 84, 242, 245

Sisson, Rosemary 69, 77–82, 85

skinheads 83, 113, 119, 121, 123, 138–139, 142, 144

Skrewdriver (punk band) 113, 121, 123–125, 132, 138–142, 144–145

Smith, Bradley 5, 14, 98, 186, 239

Smith, Evan 5–6, 69–85

social movements 4, 6, 85, 90–91, 94–95, 208–212, 220, 225, 227, 236–237

solidarity 5, 79, 84, 187–191, 195, 197, 199; and the British Commonwealth 79; and the common struggle 197; expressive demonstrations of 191; futile gestures of 188; symbolic act of 190; white supremacist 70, 78

Spearhead 13, 42, 48, 53, 75, 77–78, 96, 107, 153, 157–163

Spoonley, Paul 77, 82

Stocker, Paul 71, 236

swastikas 37, 119–120, 125, 132, 134–135, 138, 140, 145

SWP (Socialist Workers' Party) 98–100, 102–103, 107–109, 113, 122

Taylor, Stan 4, 76, 94–96, 98, 104–107, 210, 230–231, 246–247

Thatcher, Margaret 14, 83, 116

Thompson, Hunter S. 77, 150, 231

The Thunderer: The Newsletter of the British National Party Christian Fellowship 153

Thurlow, Richard 13, 55, 75–76, 226–227

transnational activism 29, 199

Turner, A.W. 22, 211

Tyndall, John 1–2, 12–17, 55–58, 69–70, 75–77, 80, 82, 115, 118, 157–158; and Cecil Chesterton 13; and the Greater Britain Movement 2, 75; leadership by

18, 76; and Martin Webster 75, 110; and the National Front 42, 69, 76, 85, 106; and Nick Griffin 22; political histories of 92; resignation of 76; and the speech to the National Front of Australia 69–70, 80, 108

UKIP 3, 7, 127, 224–225, 229, 234–236, 239

Verrall, Richard 13–15, 17–18, 114
Virchow, Fabian 28, 188, 191, 242
voters 3, 10, 175, 179, 194, 229; BNP 3; Conservative 76; disaffected Labour 77; educated 176; mobile middle-class 235; NF 3; white working-class 235
votes 2–3, 7, 20, 22–23, 115, 170–171, 175–176, 185–186, 192, 194; female 175; male 175; radical-right 171; working-class 115

Walker, Martin 12, 58, 75, 91–94, 98, 108, 115, 121, 224, 231
Wallace, George 35, 37
war 11–12, 14, 53, 106, 109–110, 119, 121, 135, 214–215, 218; civil 79; class 49, 94, 138
Webster, Martin 39, 44, 49–50, 75–76, 91–92, 96, 98, 108, 110, 157
'White Power' 123, 125, 136, 139
white youths 104–105, 109, 113, 115, 117, 119–121, 123, 125, 127
Whitford, Troy 70, 83

Wilkinson, P. 231, 247
Williams, Tony 114, 225
Wilson, David 77–78, 80
women 4, 6, 33, 99, 113, 151–152, 162, 169–181, 186, 231; and attitudes to anti-immigration and Islamophobia 173; and the difficulty in reconciling the key principles of feminism with their involvement in patriarchal frameworks 181; in far-right political and activist groups 6, 169, 173, 179–181; and fascism 179; and fascism in Britain 179; instances of advocating violence against Muslims 178; looking at the far right as an anti-modernist option 176; right-wing 179; role of 177, 179, 231
Woodbridge, S. 120, 172
workers 51, 56, 63–66, 94, 140
World War Two 13
Worley, Matthew 1–7, 114–127, 132, 239
WUNS (Word Union of National Socialists) 30, 32–33, 39–40, 44

YNF (Young National Front) 109, 113, 117, 133, 140
Yockey, Francis Parker 242
young people 96, 114, 117–118, 120, 159, 162
youth culture 4, 118–119, 126–127, 136
youths 5, 97, 117–119, 121, 123, 126–127, 245

Zündel, Ernst 14, 196

Taylor & Francis eBooks

Helping you to choose the right eBooks for your Library

Add Routledge titles to your library's digital collection today. Taylor and Francis ebooks contains over 50,000 titles in the Humanities, Social Sciences, Behavioural Sciences, Built Environment and Law.

Choose from a range of subject packages or create your own!

Benefits for you

- » Free MARC records
- » COUNTER-compliant usage statistics
- » Flexible purchase and pricing options
- » All titles DRM-free.

Benefits for your user

- » Off-site, anytime access via Athens or referring URL
- » Print or copy pages or chapters
- » Full content search
- » Bookmark, highlight and annotate text
- » Access to thousands of pages of quality research at the click of a button.

eCollections – Choose from over 30 subject eCollections, including:

Archaeology	Language Learning
Architecture	Law
Asian Studies	Literature
Business & Management	Media & Communication
Classical Studies	Middle East Studies
Construction	Music
Creative & Media Arts	Philosophy
Criminology & Criminal Justice	Planning
Economics	Politics
Education	Psychology & Mental Health
Energy	Religion
Engineering	Security
English Language & Linguistics	Social Work
Environment & Sustainability	Sociology
Geography	Sport
Health Studies	Theatre & Performance
History	Tourism, Hospitality & Events

For more information, pricing enquiries or to order a free trial, please contact your local sales team:
www.tandfebooks.com/page/sales

 Routledge
Taylor & Francis Group

The home of
Routledge books

www.tandfebooks.com